ILLUSTRATED DICTIONARY OF
TROUT FLIES

COLLINS

ILLUSTRATED DICTIONARY

OF

TROUT FLIES

JOHN ROBERTS

CASTLE BOOKS

To Ibbie
with love and thanks

Originally published in English by HarperCollins Publishers, Ltd.
under the title:
COLLINS ILLUSTRATED DICTIONARY OF TROUT FLIES
©John Roberts, 1995.
The author asserts his moral right to be identified
as the author of this work.

This edition published by arrangement and agreement with
HarperCollins Publishers, Ltd. of Pulham Palace Road,
Hammersmith, London W6 8JB and PO Box Glasgow G4 0NB.

Copyright © 1998 by CASTLE BOOKS,
a division of Book Sales, Inc.

Published by CASTLE BOOKS
A Division of Book Sales, Inc.
114 Northfield Avenue, Edison, New Jersey 08837

Colour plate photographs by Terry Griffiths
Colour origination by Colourscan

ISBN 0-7858-0892-2

Manufactured in the United States of America.

Contents

Introduction

Even in the relatively short time since I prepared the first edition of this book there has been considerable progress in trout fly development. There are new synthetic materials which are finer, softer, more reflective, more translucent, hairier, smoother, more colourful, lighter, more durable, or quite simply more lifelike than those previously available. Many trout flies are now entirely synthetic, without recourse to fur or feather. As well as taking into account these materials in modern patterns I also include the new techniques used with some of the traditional materials, as well as discussing flies using 'new' natural materials such as cul de canard.

In this second edition I have included some trout and grayling flies from Continental Europe and North America. There a few from even farther afield that are finding their way into broad international use. Such has been the trend in the last decade or more to look more widely for new materials and more effective pattern designs and fishing techniques. The modern fly box is truly cosmopolitan and I would imagine that the majority of anglers worldwide carry many patterns devised for lakes and rivers on other continents. Omitted from this second edition are the stillwater lures that proved to be of transitory popularity and a few of the more obscure river and lake patterns. I have drawn much more widely on expert anglers and fly tyers in Europe

and North America for the very best of their patterns that are found in use internationally. Some patterns have been in use for a century or more; they have survived that most critical of tests, time, and have proved reliable takers of trout.

My aim, as with the first edition, is to produce a modern reference work that is more comprehensive than any other, and to include flies for both stillwater and river fishermen, covering the widest possible range – natural flies and their imitations, general, traditional and fancy patterns, and lures.

In all my books I have included, where possible, illustrations of artificials tied by their creators, so giving an accurate picture of what the tyer's intentions were in devising each pattern. Almost all of the flies illustrated have been tied by their creators, or, in the case of traditional patterns, tied by expert tyers. Not only are these examples an invaluable guide to the tying of each dressing, but they are a unique collection of modern patterns from some of our most inventive and thoughtful fly tyers.

I have credited the reader with a certain amount of fly-tying knowledge, but if you are a beginner you should learn the basics from a more specialised book, although I do detail in the glossary the materials and styles used. The methods are straightforward and only in particular circumstances do I elaborate on them. I recommend the following books for their clear and precise tying instructions: *The Handbook of Fly Tying* by Peter Gathercole, Peter Deane's *Guide to Fly Tying* and for more advanced tying Oliver Edwards' *Flytyers' Masterclass*.

No one angler will need all the patterns described, and the cynics will say just that. Indeed, no hospital patient needs all the drugs in the pharmacy, nor does the concert violinist have to perform all the classics, but they are there to be drawn on if need be.

Our trout flies are works of art, craft and science, the culmination of centuries of angling theory and practice, and an inheritance to be used, enjoyed and developed further.

John Roberts
February 1995

Acknowledgements

Just as fly dressers draw upon all that has gone before, so, inevitably, do angling writers. Izaak Walton was not the first to do this, nor shall I be the last. I owe a great debt to all those fly fishers, past and present, whose patterns I have included within these pages. The authors and publications referred to are listed in the bibliography.

However, I have not simply compiled a list of previously published flies selected for their present relevance, but I have carefully drawn upon the help of a number of contemporary fly creators and fly dressers for their comments on their own well-known and widely used patterns. Others are experts in a style of fly fishing; some I have approached because of their knowledge of flies from a region. I am indebited to all those listed below who have provided examples of their flies for the illustrations. Some responded beyond all expectation and offered advice on the best method of fishing the pattern, or gave background information as to how and why a fly was developed. I am pleased to acknowledge the help of:

Simon Ashworth
Theo Bakelaar (Hol.)
Bob Barden
Al Beatty (USA)
Geoffrey Bucknall
Nick Bradley
Dennis Burmester (Den)
Charles Burns
Paul Canning
Bob Carnill
Bob Church
Brian Clarke
Peter Cockwill
Alice Conba (Ire)
Tom Cross
Howard Croston
Arthur Culley
Peter Deane
Larry Duckwall (USA)
Oliver Edwards
Mogens Espersen (Den)
Marjan Fratnik (Slov.)
Roger Fogg
Gordon Fraser
John Goddard

Terry Griffiths
Franz Grimley (Scot.)
John Gross
Stephen Gross
Vince Gwilym (Wales)
Brian Harris
René Harrop (USA)
Stan Headley (Scot..)
Tony Hern
Alan Hudson
P. T. Jacobsen (Den.)
Ian James (Can.)
Charles Jardine
Adrian Jones (Wales)
Shane Jones (Wales)
Chris Kendall
Hans van Klinken (Hol.)
Sid Knight
Gary LaFontaine (USA)
Peter Lapsley
Michael Leighton
Wayne Luallen (USA)
Carl Lynch
Peter Mackenzie-Philps
Gordon Mackie

Paul Marriner (Can.)
A. J. Mearns (Scot.)
Tony Millardship
Marcelo Morales (Arg.)
Roman Moser (Aus.)
Robin Mulholland
Iain Murray-Thomson (Scot.)
Colin Nice
Lars-Åke Olsson (Swe.)
Peter O'Reilly (Ire.).
Donald Overfield
Steve Parton
Neil Patterson
Alan Pearson
Tony Pepper
Taff Price
Freddie Rice
Reg Righyni
R. B. Roy
Terry Ruane
Pat Russell
Tom Saville
David Scriven
John Seed (Ire.)

Dave Shipman
Adam Sikora (Pol.)
Robert Sloane (Aust.)
Jennifer Smith (USA)
Robert Spiller
Brian Steventon
Dave Tait
David Train
Juha Vainio (Fin.)
Conrad Voss Bark
Tony Waites
Les Walker
Richard Walker
Simon Ward
Ian Warrilow
Mike Weaver
Hans Weilenmann (Hol.)
Barrie Welham
David Westwood
Philip White
Harry Whitmore
Dave Whitlock (USA)
Davy Wotton (Wales)
Lee Wulff (USA)
Ruth Zinck (Can.)

I am particularly indebted to Simon Ashworth, Alice Conba, Peter O'Reilly and John Seed for advice and patterns from Ireland; John and Stephen Gross of Lureflash Products for advice and examples of some of the modern synthetic materials; Colin Nice for information about his father's patterns and for tying in his father's style; David Westwood for tying some of the North Country spiders.

Reader's Note

The natural and artificial flies listed in this book have been arranged for the most part in alphabetical sequence. The exception to this rule is when there is an over-riding logic in listing flies of a particular species, family or series together rather than in disparate, unrelated positions throughout the book. In such instances flies have been listed in the order of nymph, dun and spinner. If you have any difficulty in finding a particular fly, you should refer to the index on page 229.

The flies in the colour sections have been photographed on a background of a selection of Japanese art papers.

Collins
Illustrated Dictionary
of Trout Flies

Aberdeen Angus
Plate 9

Stan Headley recommends this fly as a very good utility loch-style pattern for the Scottish lochs and reservoirs. It was devised by Angus Woolhouse. Stan comments that on a new water he would certainly consider putting one on a cast as a first line of attack.

Hook: 10–12
Thread: Brown
Tail: Bunch of medium red-brown hackle fibres
Body: Rear half, Invicta yellow seal's fur; front half, bright red seal's fur
Rib: Narrow flat gold
Hackle: Longish medium red-brown hen

Ace of Spades
Plate 3

This matuka-style lure was devised by Dave Collyer. It is an excellent pattern that has received much praise. It is best fished deep during the early part of the season and retrieved slowly with pauses. The brown version is known as the BROWN BOMBER.

Hook: Long shank 6–10
Thread: Black
Body: Black chenille
Rib: Oval silver tinsel
Beard hackle: Guinea-fowl fibres
Wing: Two hackles dyed black and tied back to back with the rounded tip extending beyond the hook. The underside fibres are stripped so that the feather quill rests on the body. The rib is taken through the wing fibres. For fuller details of the winging style, see in the section headed MATUKAS
Overwing: Dark bronze mallard or goat hair dyed ginger

Adams
Plate 24

This North American standard utility dry fly and dun imitation has found its way into fly boxes the world over. It is, quite possibly, the most popular dry fly pattern in the world. It is one of the most useful general patterns. Also see Stillborn Foam Adams under EMERGERS.

Hook: 14–16
Thread: Grey
Tail: Grizzle hackle fibres
Body: Blue-grey dubbed wool or fur
Wings: Two grizzle hackles tied upright
Hackle: Red and grizzle cock wound together

Parachute Adams
Plate 24

This variation is extremely popular. Its white upright wing offers high visibility for the angler and will catch fish on freestone rivers all season. The fly illustrated was provided by Bozeman guide, Jennifer Smith.

Hook: 12–20
Thread: Grey
Tail: Light or medium blue-dun cock fibres
Body: Dubbed grey muskrat fur
Wing: White polypropylene yarn or calf tail, tied upright
Hackle: A grizzle and natural red cock wound together round the wing base

Adams Trude   *Plate 25*

This is a hybrid with the Trude and is an excellent attractor or search pattern recommended by Mike Weaver.

Hook: 12–14
Tail: Dark moose hair fibres
Body: Dubbed grey fur
Wing: White calf tail or poly yarn 45 degrees over the back
Hackle: A grizzle and red cock, one wound through the other

ALDER
(Sialis lutaria, S. fuliginosa)

These are two common species which can be considered together. The adults are commonest during May and June on rivers and stillwaters. The head and legs are nearly black, and the wings are hard, shiny and roof-shaped, like those of a sedge. The wings lack the hairs of the sedge; otherwise the two species are at first glance similar.

The eggs are laid on overhanging plants and the newly-hatched larvae fall into the water to live in the mud for some months before pupation. The larvae are about 25 mm (1 inch) long and are dark brown. They are carnivorous and move about the lake or river-bed in search of smaller fauna, even caddis larvae, to eat. Brian Clarke aptly called the alder larva the Ghengis Khan of the aquarium world, so be warned if you intend to keep a few at home for observation. The larvae crawl ashore and burrow in the damp margins to pupate, and the adults emerge after a few days.

The imitation is best fished as a sub-surface pattern on lakes, but on rivers both the sunken and floating imitations are effective. The expert entomologist fly-fisher, David Jacques, was at pains to point out in his book, *The Development of Modern Stillwater Fishing*, that 'during the alder season – and only then – it is one of the fly-fisher's best flies'. See also OMBUDS-MAN, MR NASTY.

Alder Larva *(Bob Carnill)*   *Plate 8*

Bob Carnill comments: 'I have been fishing this pattern since the late 1960s or early 1970s. It's a good all-purpose "bottom-crawler" pattern, but it really comes into its own during late April. It is usually fished from the bank on a floating line and a long leader. The retrieve should be either figure-of-eight or short, slow draws. The marginal areas are the most productive'.

Hook: Extra long shank 10
Thread: Waxed brown Gossamer
Tail: Bunch of medium-brown cock hackle fibres or one biot quill dyed light brown
Underbody: Lead wire
Body and thorax: Dark chestnut seal's fur
Gills and legs: A small pale ginger hackle tied in by its tip at the tail end of the abdomen, laid over the back, and secured by its stem at the head end of the abdomen before the thorax is formed.
Rib: Oval gold tinsel

Alder Lava

Hook: Standard or long shank 10
Thread: Brown
Body: Copper-wire underbody with dubbed mixed brown and ginger seal's fur over
Hackle: Palmered cream cock hackle with the fibres trimmed on the top and undersides to about 3 mm
Head: Hare's fur

Herefordshire Alder

This is a popular Welsh Border fly which has proved itself on waters further afield.

Hook: 10–14
Thread: Yellow
Body: Cock pheasant centre tail feather fibres
Hackle: Medium blue-dun cock

Alevin   PLATE 5

Taff Price seems to specialise in producing a fly for every possible occasion and this is one such pattern utilising entirely synthetic materials.

Hook: Long shank 8–14
Thread: White
Tail: Pearl Crystal Hair
Underbody: Fluorescent red floss
Body: Pearly PVC sheet folded and cut to shape
Egg sac: Fluorescent orange yarn
Eyes: Doll's safety eyes glued to the PVC

Alexandra   Plate 7

This is a fry-imitating fly fished on both rivers and stillwaters which, according to Courtney Williams, has been around since about 1860. So successful a pattern was it that it is reputed to have been banned on some waters. It is best fished in the manner of a small fish, in what has been described as dance-time, i.e. slow, slow, quick, quick, slow. It can also be fished as a tandem lure with a tail on the rear hook only and a hackle and wing on the front hook only. In the dressing known as the Jungle Alexandra swan fibres dyed red are replaced in the wings with jungle-cock feathers or a substitute.

Hook: 10–12
Tail: Red ibis or swan fibres dyed red as a substitute
Body: Flat silver tinsel
Rib: Oval silver tinsel
Hackle: Black hen
Wing: Peacock sword herls, flanked either side with swan fibres dyed red

Allrounder

John Ketley devised this pattern as a general sub-surface fly, and he claims success for it when it is used on a top dropper as a hatching-sedge imitation, or as a small fry imitator. The dressing can be varied by substituting a hen-pheasant wing when the lighter sedges are about or by using a silver body, which seems to do well on cloudy days. I have used this as a late-evening fly with satisfactory results, fishing it slowly just below the surface.

Hook: 10
Thread: Black
Tail: Four honey hackle fibres
Body: Flat gold Mylar with five turns of honey cock hackle
Wing: Rolled heavily-barred teal
Hackle: Honey cock

Amber Nymph

This is one of the patterns devised by Dr H. A. Bell, a nymph-fisher on the Bristol reservoirs during the 1920s and 30s. Bell is very much the father-figure of stillwater nymph fishing. In an era when winged lures were the norm for lake fishing, he devised a series of flies based upon items he found in trouts' stomachs. He set about copying many of the natural food sources in a lifelike fashion. Most of his patterns were entirely new.

Although this pattern is called a nymph, it is in reality probably a sedge-pupa imitation, and certainly it can be fished as one. It has come to be highly regarded over the past sixty years, and, in spite of more accurate and complex sedge imitations being available, it continues to have a popular following.

Hook: 10–12
Body: Amber floss silk
Rib: Black tying thread
Wing: Dark red hackle fibres tied fine and close to the body
Thorax (optional): Dark brown/black wool

A variation of this pattern is given below. Whether this was a variant developed by

Bell or whether it evolved much later, I am unable to say.

Thread: Yellow
Body: Rear half, amber floss or seal's fur; front half, brown or hot-orange seal's fur
Back: Woodcock wing or speckled-brown turkey feather
Legs: Honey-coloured hackle fibres

The larger sizes are used in the early part of the season. The smaller sizes are tied with the orange thorax and are used mid-season onwards.

Amber Spinner

An excellent river pattern that can be fished both as a dry fly and below the surface. It is a fair blue-winged olive copy and an imitation of any of the amber-bodied spinners. I have found it a useful grayling fly. As a wet fly it should be fished upstream, because the spent wings are unsuitable for fishing downstream.

Amber Spinner *(Thomas Clegg)*

Hook: 14
Thread: White
Body: Orange DFM floss
Rib: Brown Naples silk
Wing: Six lengths of grey DFM floss, equally divided and tied spent
Hackle: Two cock hackles dyed light blue-grey with the upper and lower fibres trimmed off so that the remaining fibres give the impression of spent wings

Anna *Plate 3*

The Golden Anna and Silver Anna are two streamer lures from Taff Price. They should be fished fast.

Silver Anna

Hook: Long shank 6-8
Tail: Swan dyed red
Body: Embossed silver tinsel
Wings: Two lemon hackles tied back to back with a cree hackle either side

Cheeks: Jungle cock eyes
Beard hackle: Scarlet cock

Annabelle *Plate 9*

Charles Jardine came up with this highly attractive stillwater pattern. It has become well established on some of the Midlands reservoirs as a top or middle dropper fly when fishing in the loch style. It works under a range of conditions but best in a medium to big wave.

Hook: Kamasan B175, size 10–14
Thread: Primrose
Tail: Hot orange or fluorescent yellow Glo-Brite floss
Body: Gold Lurex
Rib: Fine gold wire
Body hackle: Palmered light ginger cock
Head hackle: Grizzle cock

Anorexic Nymphs *Plate 8*

Very recently there has been a highly successful trend towards tying and fishing very slim, short nymph dressings on stillwater. The style was created by Bob Barden originally for the Kent reservoirs. Some misleading information about them has been published so I am grateful to Bob and Paul Canning for putting the record straight. Paul describes them as 'the stillwater corollary to the Yorkshire Spiders. They are impressionistic and slim, but heavy.' The key to the flies is to half tie them along a heavy wire hook. It is completely wrong to use light hooks, tying to the bend, making them too hairy or including tags or tails. The material should be very sparse. Sometimes a red head is included. The flies drop through the water quickly and are fished as droppers with a heavier pattern on the point. The usual retrieve is a very slow figure-of-eight, or allow them to drift in the wind. An Anorexic Hare's Ear and an Anorexic Buzzer are illustrated.

ANTS (Hymenoptera)

Ants are terrestrial, but some develop wings at mating time in July and August and appear over water in large numbers. Wingless ants may fall on to the water if a nest is near a river-bank. When on the water their weight and spread legs ensure that they rest in the film, neither floating on the surface nor sinking. Their detection may be difficult.

The ant body is generally black or brown or more rarely, red, but on the two occasions on which I have experienced the phenomenon of flying ants over a river I have seen only the black variety. I have not had the need to use an imitation on stillwater, but I have found the black patterns useful in mid-summer on rivers.

McMurray Ant   Plate 22

A highly effective unsinkable pattern of US origin utilising a pre-made body available from Orvis.

Hook: 14–22
Thread: Black
Body: Two small cylinders of balsa wood affixed to a strand of mono, varnished black or brown
Hackle: Black or red cock wound in the middle of the body and trimmed top and bottom

Black Ant

Hook: 14
Thread: Black
Body: Black tying thread built up to form an abdomen and a thorax with a waist in the middle, and then varnished
Wings: Blue-dun or white cock hackle tips tied spent
Hackle: Black cock wound at either the waist or the shoulder

Superant

An American pattern of Randy Swanberg's.

Hook: 12–20
Thread: Black
Thorax and abdomen: Black Plastazote foam SuperAnt body or other cylindrical Plastazote
Legs: Black polypropylene mono, heat-kinked to bend

APHIS

These tiny green terrestrial flies are sometimes blown on to a lake or river surface during June and July. If they become available to the trout in large numbers, they are often eagerly devoured. Even when they are not in evidence, I often find, when river fishing in mid-summer, that a small green dry fly will catch fish. The same pattern can do well in October for grayling, but then it could hardly be taken for an aphis. Roger Fogg tells me that a green version of his latex pupa (see under SEDGES) kills well when fish are preoccupied with aphis.

The fly below was devised by Derek Bradbury as an imitation of a floating bunch of aphis. For other suitable imitations see GREEN INSECT and GREEN MIDGE.

Hook: 14–16
Thread: Olive
Body: Signal-green DRF floss
Wings: White DRF floss, two strands per wing, two or three pairs tied spent along the body
Hackle: Tiny light-olive hackles tied at each set of wings, with all the fibres trimmed from the underside of the body

Appetiser   Plate 1

Bob Church devised this popular lure in 1972. He says it was the first British lure to use marabou in the dressing. Bob claims that it is, as well as being a general attractor, the best-ever fry lure when fished near the surface. I wouldn't argue with a man of Bob's experience of lure fishing. Any fly that has caught a limit totalling thirty-one pounds has to be worth having in the box. This one is a real fish-catcher.

Hook: Long shank 6
Thread: Black
Tail: Mixed dark-green and orange cock hackle fibres and silver mallard breast feathers
Body: White chenille
Rib: Fine oval silver tinsel
Beard hackle: A mixture of dark-green and orange hackle fibres with silver mallard breast feathers
Wing: A generous spray of white marabou herl overlaid with a bunch of natural grey squirrel hair. Gluing the wing roots increases the life of the fly
Head: Black tying thread

AUTUMN DUN or AUGUST DUN (Ecdyonurus dispar)

See EPHEMEROPTERA
This species of upwinged dun is found mostly on rivers in South Wales, the West Country and parts of northern England. It prefers rivers with stony beds, but is on occasion found in the margins of big, stony lakes. The nymphy is a large, flat, stone-clinging type. The duns are large and appear from June to October, being most prolific in July and August.

The duns and spinners are similar to those of the late March brown, the former being so similar that only close examination of the veins of the wings enables certain identification.

The male dun has grey wings with black veins. The abdomen is yellow-olive on the upper side, with dark brown bands on the sides. The legs are long and are dark brown-olive, and the two tails are dark grey. The female dun has light fawn wings with black veins. The abdomen is yellow-olive or pale olive-brown on the upper side. The legs and tail are as in the male.

The female spinner (also known as the great red spinner) has transparent wings with dark brown veins. The abdomen is reddish-brown with a darker underside. The two long tails are dark brown and the legs are olive-brown. The male spinner is of little interest.

The dun can be imitated with a MARCH BROWN, and the spinner with a RED SPINNER or GREAT RED SPINNER.

August Dun Nymph
(Thomas Clegg)

Hook: 12–14
Thread: Light green
Tail: Yellow guinea-fowl fibres
Abdomen: Signal-green DRF floss
Rib: Copper wire
Thorax: Blue-dun/yellow-olive grass monkey fur
Wing-case: Squirrel-tail hair
Legs: Thorax fur picked out

August Dun   *(Roger Woolley)*

Hook: 12–14
Tail: Brown ginger cock hackle fibres
Body: Brown floss silk or brown quill
Rib: Yellow floss
Wing: Pale mottled hen pheasant wing
Hackle: Brown ginger cock

August Dun Spinner
(G. E. M. Skues)

Hook: 16
Thread: Hot-orange
Tail: Honey-dun hackle fibres
Body: Orange seal's fur
Hackle: Red cock

Aylott's Orange

A useful sedge-pupa imitation devised in the late 1960s by Richard Aylott. It works best when fished in a sink-and-draw style on a floating line. An alternative version has a signal-green fluorescent wool body and is a suitable imitation of the green-bodied sedge pupa.

Hook: 12
Body: Arc-chrome DRF wool

Hackle: Natural red cock
Head: Peacock herl tied in front of the hackle

Baby Doll
Plate 5

An excellent lure, devised in 1971 by Brian Kench. It has become one of the most successful stillwater fly patterns ever created. Bob Church, who did much to publicise the fly, says that the fluorescent white wool is a 'key reason why this lure kills an undue share of trout'. He discards each white pattern after a day's use because it collects dirt and loses some of its fluorescent qualities.

John Goddard believes that the white Baby Doll may be taken for the pupa of one of the larger species of sedge.

Hook: Long shank 6–10
Thread: Black
Body, back and tail: White nylon Sirdar baby wool
Head: Black tying thread

The white body has been successfully matched with a back and tail of yellow, orange, red, black, green and brown. Other body colours have been used of fluorescent or ordinary baby wool - lime-green, pink, orange and non-fluorescent black. The black variant is known as the Undertaker. Other versions have suitable beard hackles added, hot-orange in the case of the white Baby Doll. Perhaps the most successful variant is the Peach Doll devised by England Team Captain Geoff Clarkson. It is made entirely from peach-coloured wool and has no hackle.

Richard Walker described a Baby Doll variant called Nell Gwynne after a certain 'doll' who became involved with oranges. The dressing is as for the standard white Baby Doll, but includes a back and tail of orange wool and an orange collar hackle.

More modern materials are sometimes used to improve on the original baby wool. These are two exmples.

Fluorescent Lime Doll
(Stephen Gross) *Plate 1*

Hook: Long shank 8–10
Thread: Black
Tail and back: Fluorescent lime Antron Lureflash Bodywool
Body: Wound Bodywool as above
Head: Varnished black

Pearly Weighted Baby Doll
(Sid Knight) *Plate 5*

Hook: Kamasan B830 Long shank size 8–10
Thread: Black
Underbody: Fifteen touching turns of fine lead wire
Body: Pearly Mother of Pearl Mobile
Rib: Silver wire
Back: White Twinkle and Pearly Mother of Pearl mixed together

Badger Series

These are principally grayling flies which can be fished wet or dry. They have served me well on the northern streams on which I do most of my grayling fishing. I have found them most successful as floating flies rather than wet. All have the badger hackle in common.

Double Badger *(Roger Woolley)*

A floating pattern which I have found to be one of the best of the series.

Hook: 14–18
Body: Peacock herl
Hackles: Badger cock at either end of the body. The rear hackle should be slightly smaller than the front hackle

Red Badger

Hook: 14–18
Body: Red floss tipped with silver tinsel
Rib: Silver wire through the hackle
Hackle: Palmered badger cock or hen

The Green Badger is as above except that it has a green floss body. The Blue Badger has a blue floss body.

Badger Red Tag *(Roger Woolley)*

This is a variant of the Red Tag.

Hook: 14–18
Tag: Red wool or floss
Tip: Silver tinsel
Body: Bronze peacock herl
Hackle: Badger wound at the shoulder, not palmered

Silver Badger

Hook: 14–18
Tag: Red wool
Body: Flat silver tinsel
Rib: Oval silver tinsel
Hackle: Palmered badger cock or hen
Head: Red wool tag

The Gold Badger has a gold tinsel body and rib

Banded Squirrel Bucktail

(Taff Price)

Hook: Long shank 8–10
Thread: Black
Tail: White squirrel tail with a black band, tied in at the black section
Body: Pale mauve wool or white wool tied fairly bulky
Rib: Flat narrow silver tinsel
Wing: Barred squirrel tail (white tip, black bar, brown root)
Throat hackle: Red and white hackle fibres or white bucktail the length of the body with red bucktail tied as a shorter throat

Barney Google

Richard Walker created this phantom midge larva imitation. It is highly spoken of by many lake-fishers.

Hook: 12–14 silvered hook
Body: Stretched clear polythene in narrow strips, tied thin
Hackle: A wisp of speckled grey mallard fibres
Eyes: Two small red beads bound in with figure-of-eight turns of tying silk

Barret's Bane   *Plate 25*

This is a reverse-hackle dry fly of Welsh Border origins. The hackle at the bend succeeds in hiding the bend of the hook.

Hook: 14–16
Thread: Brown
Body: Wound cock pheasant tail fibres
Rib (optional): Fine gold wire
Hackle: Blue dun cock

Barrie Welham Nymph   *Plate 16*

This is a forerunner of some of the modern patterns specially developed for small clear lakes where fish stalking is the principal style of fishing. Barrie Welham says of his pattern:

'In the early 1960s I was visiting a lot of small, clear, stillwater fisheries where one could visually select the quarry and so avoid undersized fish. A nymph that would fall quickly was sometimes required, but a nymph that would sink slowly, to intercept fish feeding just below the surface, was often more useful.

'Around that time Lieut-Col. (Rags) Locke, of tiger-hunting fame, was one of the most successful rods at the famous Two Lakes water, and although he was not 'selecting' fish in the way I tried to do, he still wanted a slow-sinking nymph. To get this performance, Rags used a plain, brown-wool-bodied nymph that he called the BW, Brown Woolly.

'As the tying was developed, the white wing tuft, which soon got dirty, was changed to a white feather hackle and a tail of DFM floss was added. At first the tail was quite long, but this resulted in a lot of false takes and a high proportion of fish hooked outside the mouth. When the

DFM material was reduced and shielded, this no longer occurred.'

As well as proving a successful fly on stillwater, the BW Nymph has also brought good results on rivers for both trout and grayling. It has also taken at least one salmon.

Hook: 10–12
Thread: Black
Tail: Short red and yellow DFM floss
Body: Brown wool
Rib: Fine oval gold tinsel
Breathers: A short tuft of white hackle fibres tied back over the body

Barton Bug

This is a good pattern to represent hatching medium olives. It is fished with the rear half submerged and the front half of the fly floating, in the way that some of W. H. Lawrie's emerging patterns are fished. It was devised by Roy Darlington for some very selective trout taking emerging duns on the Itchen.

Hook: 12–14
Thread: Primrose
Tail: Long fur fibres from a rabbit's neck
Body: Hare's ear fur dressed thinly with a slight thorax
Rib: Fine gold wire round the abdomen only
Hackle: High-quality short-fibred blue-dun cock

Barret's Bane

This is a Welsh Border fly of some repute for trout and grayling, and one which I have used to good effect on its home waters. The dressing came from Cosmo Barret, a tackle-dealer in Presteigne, who tied it with a reverse hackle.

Hook: 12–16
Body: Cock pheasant centre tail fibres
Hackle: Blue-dun cock

Beacon Beige   *Plate 27*

Peter Deane amended and renamed a pattern originally called the Beige, a West Country olive dun imitation. The original pattern was tied by a member of the Wills family during a period of leave from the Somme in the First World War. Peter Deane regards it as the best-ever olive dun imitation. It is certainly a great general-purpose dun imitation.

Hook: 12–18
Thread: Yellow
Tail: Plymouth Rock (grizzle) cock hackle fibres
Body: Well-marked stripped peacock eye quill
Hackle: Plymouth Rock (grizzle) cock with a red Indian game-cock wound through

Bees

Although bee imitations seemed popular with bygone fly fishers, it is rarely so today. In high summer there may be an occasional opportunity to use a floating pattern. The imitation is more popular on the Continent, and it is highly rated for chub.

Hook: 12
Thread: Black
Body: Banded yellow, brown or black seal's fur, mohair or silk
Wing: Hen pheasant or partridge flat across the back
Hackle: Furnace cock

BEETLES (Coleoptera)

In addition to the range of water beetles (see WATER CRICKET and WATER TIGER), there are scores of species of terrestrial beetles, some of which sometimes fall on the surface of rivers and lakes. The permutations of size, colour and shape of these are almost endless, but some of the commoner species can be represented by the patterns below. For centuries the imitation has been fished as a dropper on a wet fly cast; the Coch-y-bondhu is one of the better-known patterns.

Now, in addition to being fished on a team of flies, a suitable imitation is often fished in the nymph style upstream to individual fish or into likely lies. I know of no better pattern for this style of fishing than Eric's Beetle. On a number of occasions a black beetle pattern has turned a potentially blank period of the day into a fruitful one. On many rivers the mid-afternoon period of a bright sunny summer's day is hardly worth fishing. But under just these conditions a small caterpillar or beetle cast under high banks or overhanging bushes has often caught fish for me when they have moved to nothing else. See also under COCK-CHAFER, COCH-Y-BONDHU, CHOMP-ER, and PALMERS.

Eric's Beetle   *Plate 22*

A pattern devised by Eric Horsfall Turner, a gentleman who could wield both rod and pen with great skill. This fly is a fantastic killer of trout, particularly on hot summer afternoons when nothing is moving. It is fished on a greased leader and allowed to sink just a few inches below the surface.

Hook: 8–12
Thread: Black
Body: An underbody of yellow wool with bronze peacock herl tied fat wound over. The yellow wool is exposed as a butt at the rear
Hackle: Two turns of black cock or hen

Red-Eyed Derbyshire Beetle

Plate 22

Courtney Williams suggested that this should be fished as a floating pattern, but I understand that it is usually fished wet. In the summer of 1980 I fished as a guest on a club water on the Nidd in North Yorkshire. During a frustrating period when I caught nothing, another rod

fished his way upstream casting this fly under trees and in the river margins. He caught four trout when all other flies were being refused. I was using Eric's Beetle, which I usually rate as second-to-none for just these circumstances. It seemed the red beads made all the difference.

Hook: 12
Body: Bronze peacock herl
Hackle: Long-fibred black cock or hen
Head: Two tiny red beads

Sailor Beetle

This natural beetle appears from June to August and has a reddish body and dull-blue wings. This is Taff Price's pattern:

Hook: 12
Thread: Black
Body: Brown floss
Wing-case: Dark blue Raffene
Hackle: Black

Soldier Beetle

This is similar to the Sailor Beetle, but has a dull yellow body, orange-red wings with bluish tips, and is about 24 mm (1 inch) long. This is G. E. M. Skues' pattern.

Hook: 14
Thread: Hot-orange
Body: Bright red-orange seal's fur
Back: Cock pheasant breast fibres
Hackle: Red cock sparsely tied

Bob's Black Beetle   *Plate 22*

This is a pattern from Bob Carnill. It is significant in that it is one of the few beetles developed for stillwater. It floats in the film with its back just touching the surface. It should be fished static and works well in heat wave conditions. Do not over-stretch the foam.

Hook: Drennan midge hook (short shank):12
Thread: Black
Antennae: 2 black-dyed cock pheasant tail fibres, thick ends, trimmed to about 3 mm

Back and head: Strip of fine Plastazote, approx. 4 mm x 3 mm, trimmed to shape
Abdomen: Dubbed fine black fur
Legs: Short black hen hackle, 2 or 3 turns with upper fibres trimmed away

Deer Hair Beetle

(Mike Weaver) *Plate 22*

The deer hair clump is tied to the hook shank extending at the front and rear; the rear portion is brought to the front to form a back, and then flared with tight turns of thread; three hairs are left on each side to create legs and the remainder clipped loosely to form a neat head. Black is the most useful, but green or natural brown may be tried.

Hook: 16
Body: Bronze peacock herl (optional)
Back, head and legs: Deer hair dyed black

Bibby

Plate 2

This unusual lure was devised by Basil Squires of Owdy Lane Fishery. It has a buoyant head and utilises the attraction of Lureflash's Fritz chenille. Colours should be as for other proven lure combinations.

Hook: Long shank 8–12
Thread: Black
Tail: Marabou
Body: Lureflash Fritz; rear third one colour, front two-thirds another colour, and clipped short after winding
Head: Half a Booby foam cylinder pushed over the shank and glued

Bibio

Plate 8

An excellent early-season lake fly. It is most effective as a top dropper dibbled through the surface when fished from a boat during a dark midge hatch. The hackles should be bushy enough to create a little wake on the water and should not be so soft as to collapse against the body when the fly is being retrieved. The original dressing had an orange middle section.

Hook: 10–14
Thread: Black
Body: Black seal's fur with a middle section of red seal's fur
Rib: Silver wire through the hackle
Hackle: Palmered black with two turns at the shoulder

Bibio variants have sprung up and John Seed has suggested these three (Plate 10). The body and hackle colour are changed to dark olive, light olive or yellow, with the red seal's fur middle section remaining. One very successful variant is the Pearly Bibio and the dressing given below comes from Sid Knight (Plate 8).

Hook: Kamasan B170 size 12
Thread: Black
Body: Pearly Mobile Mother of Pearl with a centre body of fluorescent red wool
Hackle: Palmered black cock
Rib: Silver wire

Big Grey

Plate 25

This Scottish pattern was devised by Franz Grimley and works particularly well during April and May when the large dark olives and March browns are expected, and in high summer when fished on faster water. The lower hackle fibres should be trimmed flat with the body.

Hook: Featherweight hook size 12
Thread: Primrose yellow Cobweb
Body: Dark hare's ear fur, black or olive fine poly dubbing
Hackle: Well marked grizzle showing more black than white (if possible a smoky grey and black) and lightly palmered and with the lower fibres trimmed flat

Big Monster

Plate 12

Few people have done as much to publicise the use of gold bead heads as Dutchman Theo 'Mr Goldbead' Bakelaar. He demonstrates their tying techniques all over Europe and North America. Lefty Kreh wrote to Theo that on a recent trip to the North West Territories the Big Monster was 'the best fly for lake trout 80 feet down.' It is a great taker of fish in deep waters. It is to be tied in a black or brown version.

Hook: Mustad 5263 long shank 4-6
Thread: Black or brown
Tail: Two goose biots, brown or black
Body: Twisted peacock herls with a few turns in front of the legs
Legs: Black or brown hackle clipped to length after winding
Head: 5 mm gold bead

Bi-Visibles   *Plate 25*

A series of highly visible floating flies devised for fast water or for use in failing light. They originated in the USA from the vice of E. R. Hewitt in 1898. Hewitt was later to become a notable angling author with three good books to his credit. In theory, any floating pattern can be made into a Bi-visible by the addition of a white cock hackle in front of the usual hackle. Some of the patterns tied on considerably larger hooks are used for dapping.

Black Bi-Visible

Hook: 10–12
Tail: Two small black hackle tips
Body: Palmered black cock
Hackle: White cock at the shoulder

The tail and body can be tied with blue, brown, badger or grizzle hackles to prod - uce appropriately named alternatives

Black-and-Orange Marabou

Plate 1

This stillwater lure, devised by Taff Price, is highly recommended, particularly for the first three months of the season. It is best fished in a steady retrieve close to the bottom.

Hook: Long shank 8–10
Tail: Orange hackle fibres
Body: Flat gold tinsel
Rib: Oval gold tinsel
Wing: Black marabou

Throat hackle: Orange
Cheeks: Jungle cock

Black and Peacock Spider

One of the greatest influences on stillwater fly fishing in the 1950s and 1960s was Tom Ivens, author of *Still Water Fly Fishing* of 1952. This is evident in part from the thousands of reservoir and lake fishers who regularly use Ivens' B&P, which has become one of the best stillwater flies of modern times. It is an excellent general fly, catching fish no matter at what depth it is fished.

Ivens wrote that it was deadly fished slowly just a few inches below the surface when trout are head-and-tailing during the evening rise. It is probably taken for a beetle, or a snail when fished near the surface when snails are about. It is, despite its simplicity, or perhaps because of it, a truly great fly and worthy of a place on any stillwater leader. Few patterns have caught trout so consistently. Perhaps the best catch I have heard of with the Black and Peacock Spider was one by Bob Church and Peter Dobbs who when fishing at Packington in 1976 managed 27 fish between them weighing 44 lb and all for a morning's work with this one fly.

Hook: 8–12
Body: Bronze peacock herl tied fat and tapering to the rear
Hackle: Long-fibred black hen sparsely tied

Black and Silver Bucktail

A bucktail lure of Taff Price's devising.

Hook: Long shank 4–8
Tail: Swan fibres dyed scarlet
Body: Flat silver tinsel
Rib: Oval silver tinsel
Wing: Black bucktail
Head: Black with a painted white eye and black pupil

The Black and White Bucktail is as for the above dressing except that it uses a wing of black bucktail over white bucktail.

Black Bear's Hair Lure

John Goddard has described this pattern, devised by Cliff Henry, as 'an exceptional lure'. The soft bear hair makes a very mobile wing and enables the fly to be fished slowly with pauses to give life to the wing. In the early season it should be fished deep; in the summer it does well fished fairly fast just below the surface.

Hook: Long shank 8–12
Thread: Black
Body: Black seal's fur
Overbody: A 3 mm (⅛-inch) strip of black bear hair with the skin extending slightly beyond the shank. This is ribbed with oval silver tinsel through the hair so that the hair fibres appear in matuka style

Black and Red   *Plate 26*

The original pattern goes back many years and is a popular fly for the Clyde and its tributaries. The well-known Scottish angler Franz Grimley has amended the dressing by beefing up the body to produce a denser silhouette. Franz describes it as a good Bi-visible for difficult days and that one should be wary of overhackling. By varying the ratio of grizzle to red a number of variants are produced. Franz ties his flies backwards, finishing off at the rear.

Hook: 14–16
Thread: Primrose yellow cobweb
Body: Hare's ear fur or black fine poly dubbing
Hackle: One grizzle palmered (approx. five turns), then one natural red wound through with three turns. The red hackle has black fibres at the base and red above
Tip: Tying thread

Black Chenille

Many stillwater lures have black chenille bodies. This one was created by Bob Church in 1970.

Hook: Long shank 6–8
Thread: Black

Tail: Black hackle fibres or hackle tip
Body: Black chenille
Rib: Medium silver tinsel
Beard hackle: Black hackle fibres
Wings: Four black hackles of equal length extending beyond the hook

BLACK GNAT
(Bibio johannis)

The term black gnat is given to a number of species belonging to the flat-winged *Diptera Order*, but *Bibio johannis* is probably the commonest. The differences between the species are so minimal that they need not bother the angler seeking to imitate them with an artificial fly. The naturals are found on the water only as a result of being blown there or after falling after mating. The mating pattern is useful if swarms of paired gnats are in evidence. The larger sizes of the Knotted Midge are then useful. The female has a dark brownish-olive body and brownish legs, and the male has a slimmer body and is nearly black. They appear throughout the trout season, from April until September. They can be a major feature in the trout diet. My fishing colleague Roy Shaw found an amazing eighteen hundred in just one trout. See also FOG BLACK.

Black Gnat (Mike Weaver)   *Plate 22*

Mike Weaver's design is exactly the same as my own – there is only so much you can do to imitate the natural. It is simple but highly effective and one of my top six dry flies.

Hook: 18–20
Thread: Black
Body: Dubbed fine black fur
Wing: White poly yarn tied low over the back (Mike Weaver uses Lureflash Antron Body Wool)
Hackle: Black cock

Black Gnat *(John Goddard)*   *Plate 22*

John Goddard has devised this pattern in which one of the key features is the wing of rainbow Krystal Flash which imitates the translucent wing of the natural which seems to sparkle and reflect the rainbow colours. Its creator describes its success as 'phenomenal'.

Hook: 16–18
Thread: Black
Body: Black or dark grey sparkle wool
Wing: A dozen strands of rainbow Krystal Flash sloping over the body
Hackle: Short-fibred black cock

Black Gnat *(C. F. Walker)*

This is based on earlier pattern by J. W. Dunne.

Hook: 16
Body: Dark turkey tail fibres with a bronze sheen
Wing: Hackle fibres dyed bottle-green and wine-red (in a ratio of 2:1). The fibres should be thoroughly mixed and tied flat with the points clipped in a V-shape
Hackle: Black cock

Black Gnat Variant

(Philip White)   *Plate 22*

Hook: 16–22
Body: Rear half, black thread; front half, Black Superfine Dubbing wound to form a distinct thorax
Wing: White turkey biot tied flat behind the thorax (convex side uppermost) and trimmed slightly longer than the shank
Hackle: Dark dun, natural black or grizzle palmered over the thorax with the upper and lower fibres cut away

Black Jack

An excellent grayling dry fly that is effective when the fish are smutting. It was devised by York fly fisherman Bob Spink, but as far as I know he never had a name for it and he did not tie it particularly for grayling. I gave the pattern a name when I referred to it in *The Grayling Angler*. I know of few better flies for difficult grayling feeding off small surface flies and refusing all artificials.

Hook: 14–18
Body: Brown seal's fur
Wings: Two small wings of dyed hackle fibres, one bright red, the other yellow or light green. They should be set slanting rearwards at about 45 degrees and should be smaller than the hackle
Hackle: Black cock

Black Joe

Scottish loch patterns abound. This one is well recommended as a general nondescript fly usually fished on the top dropper. The fluorescent material greatly improves its attraction in a slightly coloured water or on a dull day.

Hook: 14–16
Body: Rear half, bright red or DRF red floss; front half, black floss or black ostrich herl
Hackle: Long-fibred black hen tied sparsely

BLACK LURES

Dozens of black lures must have been devised over the years. Black Marabous are currently popular and a suitable dressing is given in the section headed Marabou. Other black lures can be found under ACE OF SPADES, BLACK BEAR HAIR LURE, BLACK CHENILLE, PULSATORS and BLACK MAGICIAN. Most are early-season patterns, when they are most effective fished deep.

Black Lure *(John Veniard)*

A streamer-style lure sometimes known as the Black Leech and an appropriate pattern to represent the natural leeches.

Hook: Long shank 4–8 or two or three standard hooks in tandem

Body: Black seal's fur, wool or floss
Rib: Flat or oval silver tinsel
Wings: Two black cock hackles or hen hackles. Hen hackles give a broad wing, the cock hackles a slim one. Jungle-cock cheeks are a useful addition

Black Lure

A tandem hairwing pattern.

Front hook
Body: Black floss
Rib: Silver tinsel
Wing: Black squirrel-hair extending to the tail of the rear hook
Hackle: Black

Rear hook
Tail: Fluorescent blue floss
Body: Black floss
Rib: Silver tinsel

Black Magic

The name of this Wharfe fly was coined by Frederick Mold but it is likely that the dressing was passed on to him by a local angler. Malcolm Greenhalgh writes favourably of a very similar pattern of the same name which fishes closer to the surface than Mold's, which was intended to fish slightly deeper. I am indebted to Professsor Tom Cross who wrote to me of the fly's history. It is a general black terrestrial imitation to be fished wet as a river pattern although Tom Cross uses it successfully on stillwater. Malcolm Greenhalgh's dressing is below.

Hook: 14–16
Abdomen: Pearsall's black Gossamer silk
Thorax: Bronze peacock herl
Hackle: Two or three turns of black hen

Frederick Mold's dressing is:

Hook: 16
Body: Black silk, from a point opposite the barb to a point two-thirds along the shank.
Thorax: Fine copper wire covered with two twisted strands of copper-coloured peacock herl and ribbed with silk
Hackle: A tiny black hen, two turns

Black Magician

Angling writer Brian Harris rarely uses lures, but this is one pattern which he says is good for late dusk when all else has failed. It is fished slowly, with long pulls, almost as a nymph. The leaded version should be fished deep and slow, but may also be twitched at speed, the lead keeping it just sub-surface and avoiding wake.

Hook: Long shank 10–12
Thread: Black
Tail: Doubled fire-orange DRF floss silk clipped to about 3 mm (⅛ inch)
Body: Optional underbody of lead wire (0.037 mm gauge) varnished after winding over a varnished shank. The overbody is fine black chenille.
Rib: Fine oval gold tinsel
Throat hackle: Hot-orange cock extending about half-way along the body
Wing: Black marabou turkey fibres about twice the length of the body
Head: Red Cellire varnish

Black Nymphs

There must be dozens of black nymphs, most varying from each other in detail only. None, so far as I am aware, was tied to represent an imitation of a specific nymph or other food item, but all are generally suggestive of food, and trout find them acceptable. They are of most use as stillwater patterns. See also Black Pheasant Tail Nymph under PHEASANT TAIL NYMPH.

Black Nymph

Hook: 10–16
Thread: Black
Tail: Black hackle fibres
Body: Black floss tapering to the rear
Rib: Silver wire
Thorax: Black seal's fur
Hackle: Short-fibred black cock

Black Booby Nymph   *Plate 12*

This is a highly buoyant pattern for fishing just below the surface. Gordon Fraser devised the Booby series and he also tied olive and brown versions.

Hook: Long shank 10–12
Thread: Black
Tail: Black hackle fibres
Body: Black seal's fur with a pronounced thorax
Rib: Silver wire
Eyes: Two foam-bead eyes trapped in a stocking mesh either side of the shank just behind the eye. They are tied in with figure-of-eight turns of tying thread with a light dubbing of black seal's fur between the eyes

Black Fuzzy Nymph

Hook: 10–14
Thread: Black
Tail: Grey squirrel body fibres
Body: Black angora wool well picked out
Rib: Fine silver wire
Hackle: Sparsely tied grey squirrel body fibres

Black Spiders

Black spider patterns have always been fished in the rough, faster streams of the hilly areas. Every region has its slight variation on the main theme, so I have selected two well-proven dressings which will take trout internationally. They are so nondescript that they represent many different terrestrial and aquatic creatures and are a good general imitation of the midge pupa. One essential feature is the sparsely dressed soft hackle which gives a lifelike impression when worked in the current. They are well worth a try at any time.

Black Spider *(Lars Olsson)*   *Plate 20*

Hook: 16–22
Thread: Black
Shoulder: A small knob of black or dark brown fur or peacock herl behind the hackle
Hackle: Black-green metallic neck or shoulder feather from a starling, or a black hen as a second choice

Parry's Black Spider

This is a Welsh pattern.

Hook: 12–16
Tip: Flat silver tinsel
Body: Black stripped quill
Hackle: Dark starling

Blae and Black   *Plate 20*

Small winged wet flies are popular for fishing in traditional loch style. This is one of the older patterns still in use. No one has been able to pinpoint the date of its creation, but it seems to be a fly which has evolved from obscure Scottish origins. It is best fished in the early season on the top dropper, and it is likely that in such a position it is taken for a hatching midge pupa. The Blae and Gold and the Blae and Silver are in the same series. They differ only in their flat gold or silver tinsel bodies.

Hook: 12–16
Tail: Golden pheasant tippet fibres
Body: Black tying thread or black seal's fur
Rib: Oval silver tinsel
Wing: Grey duck or small starling feather
Hackle: Black hen

Blagdon Buzzer

Dr H. A. Bell created this midge-pupa pattern for Blagdon, where he was one of the first stillwater anglers to practise nymph fishing. This was probably the first stillwater midge-pupa imitation. Hundreds of others have followed.

Hook: 10–12
Body: Black wool tapering slightly
Rib: Flat gold
Breathing filaments: A bunch of white floss silk on top of the hook behind the eye

Bloas

All these patterns are sparsely hackled wet spider-type flies of North Country origin for the rough, faster streams of the area. Many have their origins more than 200 years ago when, in a simple fashion, the northern angler sought to imitate the nymphs, emerging and crippled duns and drowning spinners in his rivers. Simple these patterns may be, but they are no less effective than the complex constructions we sometimes use today.

These flies are as deadly for trout and grayling as when they were first devised, and they are extensively used throughout the North. Bloa is an old name meaning bluish or slate-grey colour. On all North Country spiders the body is tied short, typically ending in line with a point midway between the point and barb and sometimes as short as in line with point.

Dark Bloa

Hook: 14–16
Body: Red-brown or dark claret silk
Tail (optional rarity): Two black cock hackle fibres
Hackle: Dark feather from a moorhen wing

Dark Bloa

Roger Fogg's book, *The Art of the Wet Fly*, is a modern classic. The author has followed in the steps of Jackson, Pritt and Edmonds and Lee, and has knowledgeably updated many of the old patterns by using more readily obtainable materials. He correctly points out that the Dark Bloa and Broughton's Point are one and the same fly, both being part of local North Country oral fly-tying tradition until the mid-

nineteenth century, when the dressings were first recorded. It seems likely that the latter was originally a lake pattern to imitate the claret dun, but now both patterns are used as early-season river flies for March and April. The dressing below is Roger Fogg's hackled version.

Hook: 14–16
Tying silk: Claret or brown
Body: Dark claret seal's fur lightly dubbed
Hackle: Dark grey feather from a jackdaw's throat, or black hen

Dark Olive Bloa

This is a pattern from John Jackson's *The Practical Fly-Fisher* of 1854. It has not been improved upon in 130 years.

Hook: 14–16
Body: Lead-coloured silk
Wing: Inside of a waterhen's wing
Hackle: Dark olive or black hen

Olive Bloa   *Plate 32*

This is one from T. E. Pritt's list. He favoured it for cold, windy March, April and May days, and it was probably intended to represent the large dark olive but it will work for all olives. It is still a very good fly.

Hook: 14–16
Body: Yellow silk
Hackle: Lapwing's back feather or substitute (see pattern below)
Head: Orange tying silk

Olive Bloa *(Roger Fogg)*

A modern counterpart of Pritt's dressing. Colouring French partridge hackles with Pantone pens enables a wide range of hackles to be produced for a variety of hackled spider patterns.

Hook: 14–16
Body: Superfine olive Cobweb thread, pre-waxed
Hackle: A small dull grey hackle from the marginal coverts of a French partridge

wing, coloured a dull green-olive with a Pantone pen, shade 104F

Poult Bloa   *Plate 32*

Also called the Light Bloa, this is an excellent trout and grayling fly most frequently used to imitate the pale watery and spurwings. Some writers have described it as excelling on cold, dull days. It has done well for me whatever the weather. Like all bloas, it is an old fly, and its dressing can be traced back to 1807. Poult means a young bird or pullet.

Hook: 14–16
Body: Yellow or primrose tying silk with an optional very sparse dubbing of natural red fur
Hackle: Slate-blue feather from a young grouse underwing

Roger Woolley's dressing uses dubbed ginger hare's fur on the body.

Snipe Bloa

A useful early- and late-season pattern.

Hook: 14–16
Body: Straw-coloured silk or yellow silk sparsely dubbed with mole's fur
Hackle: Feather from the inside of a snipe's wing

Starling Bloa

Probably a pale watery and medium olive imitation. The dressing given is Pritt's, and it is recommended by him as being suitable for 'cold days in May, and late evenings in June and July'.

Hook: 16–18
Body: Straw-coloured or white silk
Hackle: Lightest feather from a young starling's wing

Waterhen Bloa   *Plate 32*

An all-time great North Country fly which, like most of the others in the series, is as effective now as it was a hundred years ago. No northern angler would wish to be without a copy in his fly box. It is best used as an early-season fly and again at the end of the season, in September and beyond, for grayling. It is a suitable iron blue or dark olive imitation. The fly illustrated was tied by Oliver Edwards.

Hook: 14–16
Body: Yellow tying silk (Pearsall's Gossamer No. 4) sparsely dubbed with grey water-rat's fur or mole's fur
Hackle: The inside of a moorhen's wing (originally known as a waterhen), the smoky-grey feather from the under coverts (the darker side of the feather towards the eye)
Head: Yellow silk

Yellow-Legged Bloa

A useful May and June pattern. Roger Fogg believes this is a North Country version of the Greenwell Spider.

Hook: 14–16
Body: Well-waxed primrose silk
Hackle: Ginger hen

Blood Fly

This lake wet fly was devised by Roger Fogg and named after its bright red hackle. Its creator says: 'It had been in my fly-box simply because it looked "interesting", until one warm and breezy summer evening when I knotted it on to the cast in desperation. Fish had been rising on the reservoir quite consistently, yet nothing had managed to tempt them until the Blood Fly came into action. It drew "first blood". Under similar conditions it has always produced fish (particularly rainbow trout), and it is always a useful fly to try when little else works. Although it does well on the point, it is excellent as a top dropper on a team of three. It makes no pretence at imitation and attracts merely because of its brightness.'

Hook: 12–14
Tip: Small flat oval gold tinsel
Body: Rear half, light olive; front half, dark olive seal's fur
Rib: Narrow gold tinsel
Hackle: Blood-red hen

BLUEBOTTLE

This terrestrial fly rarely finds its way on to the water, but one or two fly creators have found the need to have an imitation. See also HOUSEFLY.

Bluebottle *(Taff Price)*

Hook: 12–14
Thread: Black
Body: Blue Lurex wrapped with black ostrich herl
Wing: Two blue-dun hackle points tied flat
Hackle: Black cock

Blue Dun *Plate 27*

The name blue dun is used to describe almost any olive species but the term is dying out as more specific names and imitations are used. I like this modern dressing which serves for many duns when tied in the appropriate sizes.

Hook: 12–16
Thread: Pale blue-dun fibres
Body: Dubbed blue rabbit's fur
Rib: Yellow thread
Hackle: Mixed grizzle and blue-dun cocks

Blue Upright *Plate 26*

A dressing by R. S. Austin which has West Country origins. It can be fished wet or dry (usually the latter) as an imitation of the dark olive or iron blue. G. E. M. Skues suggested replacing the hackle and tail-fibres with a pale honey-dun hackle to make a useful imitation of the lighter olives.

Hook: 10–14
Tail: Medium blue-dun hackle fibres

Body: Well-marked peacock eye quill
Hackle: Medium blue-dun cock or hen

BLUE-WINGED OLIVE *(Ephemerella ignita)*

See EPHEMEROPTERA
Probably the commonest of the upwinged flies. It is found on all types of running water and on some larger lakes. The adults usually appear in mid-June, although in some parts of the country they may be as early as May. Hatches continue into October and November. Hatches usually occur in the evening, but on some rivers afternoon hatches are also seen, and then the imitation is well worth using. The duns frequently emerge immediately below stretches of broken water. C. F. Walker records that the adults sometimes experience difficulty breaking free of the nymphal skin, so becoming easy prey for trout.

The blue-winged olive is a medium-to-large-sized fly with a body of about 9 mm and large wings that slope back slightly over the body. The male's body is orangy or olive-brown. The female's body darkens from olive-green to rusty-brown at the end of its season. The blue-winged olive is the only olive with three tails. J. R. Harris observes that in neutral or acidic waters the colour of the duns is subdued and they are often smaller. The nymph is a moss-creeping type and is fairly inactive, living on moss-covered stones and obstructions on the river-bed.

Others have commented on how easy it is to recognise the natural, but how difficult it is to imitate it. Many fly tyers have offered variations on the theme, but I have detailed only those patterns that have been recommended to me or I have found to work well. G. E. M. Skues was the first to realise the value of the Orange Quill as an excellent late-evening imitation of the blue-winged olive, and this has long been used on rivers all over the country.

The male dun has dark blue-grey wings and an orange-brown or olive-brown abdomen of which the last segment is yellow. The legs are brown-olive and the three tails are dark grey with brownish rings. The female dun also has dark blue-grey wings and a greenish-olive body changing to rusty-brown later. The legs are dark olive and the three tails are light grey-brown with dark brown rings.

The male spinner is one of the few that are of interest to trout and grayling. The wings are transparent with light brown veins and the abdomen is dark or rich brown. The legs are pale brown and the three tails are fawn with black rings. The female spinner is distinctive with its little green ball-like egg-sac carried at the rear of the abdomen. The wings are transparent with pale brown veins and the abdomen varies from olive-brown to sherry-red. The legs are pale brown and the tails are olive-grey with light brown rings. The female spinner is commonly referred to as the sherry spinner. My own experience is that it is extremely difficult to imitate successfully.

In addition to the patterns below, suitable imitations may be found under ORANGE QUILL , PHEASANT TAIL, POULT BLOA, ORANGE SPINNER, RED QUILL, USD PARADUNS, HARE'S LUG AND PLOVER, GREENWELL'S GLORY, NO-HACKLE FLY.

B-W.O. Nymph
(Preben Torp Jacobsen)   *Plate 17*

Hook: 14
Thread: Hot-orange
Tail: Three or four brown speckled partridge hackle fibres
Abdomen: A small amount of otter's fur spun on the tying thread
Thorax: Soft red cow's hair
Hackle: Small dark-blue hen hackle

B-W.O. Nymph
(Oliver Edwards)   *Plate 17*

After the wire underbody is applied cover with Dave's Flexament or Floo Gloo before covering with tying thread.

Hook: 18–20 medium or fine wire 2X long or curved shank, Partridge L3A, K14ST or E1A
Thread: Danville's Spiderweb
Underbody: Very fine copper wire at the thorax
Tail: Four fibres from a speckled partridge tail in two bunches of two
Abdomen and thorax: Medium brown or dark brown both with a reddish tinge of two plys of knitting yarn, either 100 per cent synthetic or natural-synthetic blend, preferably with the addition of reflective sparkle fibres. The two plys are twisted into a tight rope and wound up the body
Legs: Dark partridge tail quill fibres
Wing buds: Black quill feather section, natural or dyed, either side of the upper thorax so that a space is clear over the back of the thorax
Head (optional): One or two ruddy barbs from a cock pheasant

B-W.O. Flymph

See under FLYMPHS for a full description of the method of dressing.

Hook: Long shank 14 or 16
Thread: Primrose or green
Tail: Blue-dun hackle fibres
Body: Dubbed green wool or seal's fur
Hackle: Medium blue-dun

B-W.O. Dun *(Jim Nice)*   *Plate 26*

A pattern of which its creator wrote: 'A simple pattern, but effective, especially in the early mornings'. Colin Nice writes that his father used this when all else failed.

Hook: 14–16
Thread: Yellow
Tail: Blue-dun or olive cock hackle-fibres
Body: Front half, blue DFM floss; then the whole body, including the front half, covered with lime-green DFM floss
Hackle: Blue dun or olive cock

B-W.O. Dun

This pattern was devised by Reg Righyni, who was dissatisfied with available dressings. He said it worked better than all the others he had tried.

Hook: 14–16
Thread: Yellow
Tail: Blue-dun hackle fibres
Body: Tying thread moderately dubbed with pinkish-beige opossum fur
Hackle: Blue-dun followed by a red game-cock hackle

Sherry Spinner (William Lunn)

The late Dave Collyer said that he found this as useful on stillwater as on the southern chalk-streams for which it was originally tied. It is a very effective spinner imitation.

Hook: 14–16
Thread: Pale orange
Tail: Light-ginger cock fibres
Body: Deep-orange floss or hackle-stalk dyed orange
Rib: Gold wire on the floss-bodied version only
Wing: Pale blue-dun hackle-points tied spent
Hackle: Rhode Island Red cock

Sherry Spinner (Freddie Rice)

Hook: 14
Thread: Light yellow
Tail: Natural buff-barred cree fibres or the same dyed light-olive
Tip: Light-yellow rayon floss
Body: One dark and one light moosemane hair, the lighter dyed olive-brown or shades of sherry through to pinkish-red, wound together to give the impression of a segmented body
Wing: Pale ginger cock hackle fibres wound on and bunched in the spent position
Hackle: Natural light -red game-cock

Sherry Spinner (James Nice)

James Nice liked the use of mixed hackles, particularly in light-and-dark combinations to give the impression of wings and legs.

Hook: 14–18
Thread: Pale brown or orange
Tail: Light red or ginger cock fibres
Body: Front half fluorescent scarlet floss, then the whole body is covered with fluorescent orange
Hackle: Mixed blue dun and natural red cocks; blue dun only on the smaller sizes

Bob's Bits

A modern general stillwater dry fly, most effective in a midge hatch, devised by Bob Worts for Grafham. Colours can be varied to match the natural.

Hook: Fine wire 10–14
Body: Seal's fur
Wing: White goose or swan wing
Hackle: Furnace cock

Bolton Wanderer   Plate 1

The significant feature about this lure is the dual-coloured head. Often trout are attracted to one colour more than another and this pattern hedges its bets by using two fluorescent colours as target points for rainbow trout. It was devised by Charles Burns and Guy Bolton of York. It is an extremely successful lure.

Hook: Long shank 8–10
Thread: Black
Body: Flat silver ribbed with silver wire
Wing: Black marabou
Head: Fluorescent red chenille followed by fluorescent green chenille

Boobies   Plates 1 and 12

These are variations in the dressing of traditional stillwater nymphs, wet flies and lures. The variation is the addition of two large foam beads trapped in a stocking mesh and tied in behind the eye of the hook with figure-of-eight turns of the tying thread. Almost any stillwater fly can be so adapted. The foam makes the flies buoyant and unweighted patterns can be fished just below the surface film.

Booby-adapted nymphs and lures can be fished in an attractive way on a sinking line. When the line is retrieved, the flies sink, and when there is a pause, they rise in the water to dive again when further retrieved. Some lures may be improved by the painting of eyes on the large beads. The Boobies were named and made popular by Gordon Fraser, a professional fly tyer from Leicester.

For examples, see under NOBBLER and BLACK NYMPHS. See also under SUSPENDER MAYFLY NYMPH.

Borderer

This is a Welsh Border dry fly devised by W. M. Gallichan, a prolific writer. Among other titles, he wrote nine books on angling between 1903 and 1926. This is probably the best known of his patterns. Courtney Williams described it as 'deadly'; a description still used by Border anglers today.

Hook: 14
Tail: Rusty-dun cock fibres
Body: Blue rabbit's fur with a tip of red tying silk
Hackle: Rusty-dun cock

Bottom Scratcher   Plate 12

This is Charles Jardine pattern devised after a trip to the Austrian River Traun. It is a general river pattern for fishing deep, imitating a wide range of food items.

Hook: Long shank 10–14
Thread: 6/0 primrose
Tail: Black marabou
Body: Hare's mask fur ribbed with copper wire
Thorax: Dubbed deer hair
Head: Gold bead

Bousfield's Fancy   Plate 8

I have found no record of a published dressing of this name but Tony Millardship who kindly sent me the fly tells me that it has been used with great success by three generations of his family for almost eighty years. It was used by Tony's father on Coniston Water for over sixty years and has been successful for Tony on rivers as well as lakes in Herefordshire. It works best on warm summer evenings just under the surface and is probably a sedge imitation.

Hook: Fine wire 12
Tail: Cock pheasant tail fibres
Body: Orange thread dubbed with orange seal's fur ribbed with fine gold wire
Hackle: Dark partridge, rather long-fibred

Bow-Tie Buzzer

Frank Sawyer was a river keeper on the Wiltshire Avon where he spent much of his life keenly observing trout and grayling and the fly life of his river. He was an expert nymph fisher, an informative writer and an original creator of artificial flies. All his patterns show that he was aware that trout could be duped by general imitations, caricatures of the real nymphs, but he was doubly aware of how those patterns ought to behave beneath the surface to emulate their natural counterparts.

This pattern is a buzzer (midge pupa) and gnat larva imitation. The fly is not tied to the leader, but the tip of the leader is passed through the down-eye of the hook and a tuft of white nylon wool is tied on and pulled up to the eye. The knot and the wool ensure that it is not pulled through the eye. On being retrieved, the fly spins in the water, imitating the larger species of midge pupae as they struggle in the surface film.

Hook: 12
Thread: None
Tail: Pheasant tail fibres
Body: An underbody of gold-coloured

copper wire is wound on to give also a slight thorax and is then overlaid with flat silver tinsel. Copper wire is used to tie in the materials. The overbody of four or five cock pheasant tail fibres is wound on so that the silver tinsel is visible through it
Bow-tie: A small tuft of white nylon wool

Bradshaw's Fancy

An excellent grayling fly devised for northern rivers about a century ago. It is now used throughout the country. Reg Righyni includes it on the point of his favourite three-fly cast.

Hook: 14–16
Thread: Purple
Tag: Crimson wool or floss
Body: Copper peacock herl
Hackle: Norwegian or hooded crow (pale blue-dun)
Head: Two turns of crimson wool or floss, or a small tag similar to that at the rear but slanting forward at 45 degrees

Brassie   Plate 17

This is a North American pattern, mainly passing as a midge larva or pupa imitation for lake or river fishing. On rivers it is fished upstream in the usual nymph manner. It works on both slower spring creeks and the riffles of the freestone streams.

Hook: 14–20
Thread: Black
Body: Fine copper wire in a single layer
Thorax: A small head of fine black dubbing or light-coloured muskrat

Breathaliser

A stickleback imitation and general stillwater lure devised by Alec Iles and based on an earlier Canadian lure.

Hook: Long shank 8
Tail: Black hen hackle fibres
Body: Flat silver tinsel

Wing: Two hot-orange hackles with two Green Highlander hackles on the outside tied in streamer style
Eyes (optional): Jungle cock tied in close to the head
Collar hackle: Badger
Head: Black varnish

Broughton's Point   Plate 32

Tradition has it that Broughton was a Penrith cobbler who fished Coniston Water and Ullswater in the mid-19th century. Although Broughton's name is associated with this dressing, it seems likely that the pattern had been around for some time, as an almost identical fly (except for the addition of a tail) is given in John Jackson's *Practical Fly-Fisher* of 1854. Jackson called it the Dark Bloa. It is likely that Broughton's Point was a lake fly to imitate the nymph of the claret dun, which is fairly common in the relatively acid waters of the Lake District. The dressing remains an excellent lake fly for this purpose. It is also a useful trout and grayling fly.

Hook: 12–14
Body: Dark-claret or ruddy-purple silk
Wing: Medium-blae starling wing feather
Hackle: Black hen

Courtney Williams includes a smaller secondary red hackle, but this is not as the original dressing or as quoted by Jackson, T. E. Pritt or Edmonds and Lee.

Brown Bomber

Dave Collyer created this first cousin to his Ace of Spades. Both are excellent matuka-style lures.

Hook: Long shank 4–10
Thread: Brown
Body: Brown chenille
Rib: Heavy copper wire
Wing: Brown hen hackle tied in matuka style with a bronze mallard overwing the length of the hook
Hackle: Two bunches of cock pheasant centre tail fibres tied one on either side

Brown Nymphs

There are a number of general brown nymph imitations, some of which go under other names. See COLLYER NYMPHS, IVENS BROWN NYMPH, and PHEASANT-TAIL NYMPH. The pattern below is an olive nymph imitation useful on river and stillwater. It was devised by the expert Devon fly dresser, Jim Nice. His son, Colin, comments that his father would sometimes include an underbody of fluorescent orange, red or yellow floss to create an opaque appearance as well as a range of olive/dun colours (Plate 20).

Hook: 14
Tail: Three brown-olive cock hackle fibres
Body: Opaque PVC dyed brown, each turn just overlapping
Thorax: Brown seal's fur or brown herls
Wing-case: Brown feather fibres
Hackle: Brown-olive hen

Brown and Yellow Nymph

Bob Church recommends this pattern in his book *Reservoir Trout Fishing*. It was devised by John Wilshaw. It is recommended when sedges are hatching or are expected.

Hook: Long shank 8
Tail: Pheasant tail fibres
Body: Rear two-thirds, brown seal's fur; front one-third, yellow seal's fur
Rib: Narrow gold tinsel
Hackle: Short-fibred yellow cock

Brown Owl　　　　　　*Plate 32*

This old North Country pattern is still a useful spider-type of wet fly. It is effective when the willow flies are about, but can be profitably employed throughout the season as suggestive of stoneflies and sedges.

Hook: 14
Body: Orange tying silk

Hackle: A reddish feather from the outside of a brown owl's wing, sparsely wound
Head: Peacock herl

Brown Trout Streamer　　　*Plate 3*

This imitation, created by Taff Price, will prove useful on stillwaters where small brown trout are stocked or breed naturally.

Hook: Long shank 4–8
Tail: A tuft of olive-green hackle fibres
Body: Thin, tapering green floss
Rib: Flat gold tinsel or Lurex
Wings: Six cock hackles – two fiery-brown tied back to back, two dark-olive either side, and two badger on the outside
Beard hackle: Dark green-olive with a few long strands of white hackle fibres tied under the olive to body length
Cheeks: Jungle cock or substitute

Bucktails

The generic name for lures or fry-imitating lures with wings of animal hair. Bucktail (deer) was originally the commonest material, but now squirrel, stoat, bear, monkey, calf and almost any other animal hair is used. These lures were developed in the USA and became popular on our reservoirs. Marabou wings have, to some degree, superseded bucktail.

The conventional wing has a bunch of hair flat over the back, extending beyond the hook-bend. A single colour may be used or a combination of two or three, one over the other or mixed. Double-winged versions have a shorter front wing, with a second wing half-way down the body, the front wing overlapping the second. The life of the fly is greatly increased if the wing roots are soaked in varnish or quick-drying glue and allowed to become tacky before being bound to the shank. All patterns have a varnished head which is sometimes improved with a painted eye.

For examples see BANDED SQUIRREL BUCKTAIL, YELLOW

BUCKTAIL, BLACK-AND-SILVER BUCK-TAIL, ORANGE BUCKTAIL and SWEENEY TODD.

Buff Bug

On lakes and reservoirs aquatic beetles of various sorts often figure in the trout's diet. They mainly inhabit the shallower areas, and imitations should be fished near the bottom or near weed-beds. This pattern is an imitation of the striped-back aquatic beetle.

Hook: 12
Thread: Brown
Body: Light-brown wool or ostrich herl
Back: Oak turkey
Paddles: Two strands of oak turkey swept back and tied in at the shoulder or half-way along the body

Buff Buzzer

This pattern was devised by Steve Parton, who comments: 'This is a good mid-summer middle dropper nymphing pattern. Do not use it before the start of June. It is best fished in a figure-of-eight style until the light has really faded. Then it can be most effective thrown in front of rising fish and retrieved in twitches. The reason for its effectiveness is probably that it is an excellent imitation of the pupal form of a green-bodied sedge that appears around that time of year'.

Hook: 10–24 sproat bend
Body: Swan herl dyed palest beige
Rib: Gold wire
Thorax: Seal's fur dyed beige (ginger/pink)
Wing-case: Body herl butts

Bullhead

The small fish known as the bullhead is found in many lakes and rivers. The excellent imitation given below is by Taff Price. It needs to be fished on a sinking line and a short leader. Also see SCULPINS and Sculpin Muddler under MUDDLERS.

Hook: Up-eyed salmon hook 8
Underbody: Copper wire
Body: Mixed hare's fur and green seal's fur
Rib: Wide oval gold tinsel
Wing: Brown squirrel flanked by dyed olive-brown hackles
Cheeks: Dark game-bird feathers, one tied flat on top of the fly, and one on each side of the wing
Head: Spun deer hair, large and clipped to shape

Bumbles

There are two series of flies known as Bumbles. The first are probably of Derbyshire origin. The palmer-style hackles suggest an ancestry earlier than the fifteenth century. Bumbles were no doubt originally fished wet, but they are now also fished as floaters. F. M. Halford, recalling the pattern's use on the Test, describes it as 'the priceless Bumble'. As well as being a trout fly, it is an excellent grayling pattern.

Claret Bumble

Hook: 12–14
Body: Claret thread
Rib: A strand of peacock sword herl
Hackle: Palmered furnace cock or hen

The Furnace Bumble is as above except that it has an orange floss body.
    The Red Bumble is as above except that it uses a red floss body.
    The Ruby Bumble is as for the Claret Bumble except that it uses a palmered pale blue-dun hackle.

Honey-Dun Bumble

Hook: 14–16
Body: Salmon-pink floss
Rib: A strand of peacock sword herl
Hackle: Palmered honey-dun cock or hen

Orange Bumble
Plate 20

This and the Pearly Bumble are very good autumn grayling flies originating on the waters of the upper Severn.

Hook: 14–16
Body: Orange floss with a palmered honey dun hen (wet) over the front half of the body; palmered honey dun cock over the length of the body (dry); both with a peacock sword feather ribbing
Rib: Gold wire or fine gold tinsel
Collar hackle: As for the body hackle but slightly longer

Pearly Bumble
(Adrian Jones)
Plate 20

Hook: 12–14
Thread: Brown or olive
Tail: Olive hackle fibres
Body: Pearl Lurex ribbed with olive-dyed grizzle
Rib: Silver wire
Collar hackle: As for the body hackle but slightly longer

Purple Bumble

A grayling fly recommended by Reg Righyni for use when iron blues are on the water.

Body: Purple silk
Hackle: Palmered blue-dun

Steely-Blue Bumble

An excellent grayling fly.

Hook: 14
Body: Alternate bands of orange, light-orange and cherry-coloured floss silk
Rib: A strand of peacock sword herl
Hackle: Steely-blue hen or cock

Yellow Bumble

Body: Primrose floss silk
Rib: A strand of peacock herl
Hackle: Palmered blue-dun hen or cock

Bumbles
Plate 10

This is second series devised originally by T. C. Kingsmill Moore, the author of that beautiful book, *A Man May Fish*. He held the Claret Bumble lake pattern in high esteem. It has experienced a revival in popularity. John Seed has also suggested a very useful variant which has a very dark claret body and hackles and a pink floss butt.

Hook: 10–12
Tail: Golden pheasant tippets
Body: Claret seal's fur with a palmered black cock and claret cock wound together
Rib: Oval gold tinsel
Head hackle: Blue jay, slightly longer-fibred than the body hackle

Claret Bumble Muddler
Plate 9

Stan Headley has produced this excellent-looking variant. Although it is exceptionally difficult to tie correctly, it is well worth the effort, as it is a proven fish-taker during dark midge hatches, especially in its smaller sizes. In such cases Stan dispenses with the claret cock palmering hackle and relies on the teased out body fibres to compensate. Occasionally he substitutes the tippet tail with GloBrite Nos 11 and 12 when midge hatches distract daphnia feeders. He regards the fly as totally indispensable.

Hook: Slightly long shank 12–16 Partridge SH2
Thread: Black or red
Butt: Two turns of fine flat silver
Tail: Golden pheasant tippets dyed-hot orange or see text
Body: Claret seal's fur, palmered with a matched pair of claret and black cock hackles, over-ribbed with fine oval silver
Hackle: Blue jay
Head: Fine roe deer, clipped to a bullet shape, retaining some fine tips as a hackle

Boghill Bumble
Plate 10

John Seed thoroughly recommends this bushy pattern as a bob fly whenever olives, crane-flies or sedges are about. It is a good, reliable all-rounder.

Hook: 10–14
Thread: Claret or blood-red
Tail: Golden pheasant tippets
Body: Mixed dark red and olive seal's fur with two palmered hackles, one blood-red, the other olive
Rib: Fine oval gold
Head hackle: Partridge

Golden Olive Bumble
Plate 10

Hook: 10–14
Thread: Orange
Tail: Golden pheasant topping
Body: Yellow seal's fur mixed with Lite-Brite ribbed with golden olive-dyed red game
Rib: Oval gold
Head hackle: Partridge hackle dyed blue

See also CONNEMARA BLACK BUMBLE.

Burleigh

Loch Leven used to be one of the best three or four stillwater fisheries on the UK mainland. Sadly it is no longer as prolific a trout water as it once was, but a number of flies developed there have survived and are still killing Scottish loch trout. This is one of them. Tom Stewart, a knowledgeable Scottish fly-fisher, suggested that it fished well either on the point or as a dropper and that it was at its best from early June onwards.

Hook: 10–14
Tail: Ginger hackle fibres
Body: Well-waxed yellow silk
Rib: Silver wire
Wing: Starling wing feather tied low over the body
Hackle: Ginger hen

Butchers
Plate 7

A series of attractor flies for both stillwater and river. They have been catching trout for more than 150 years. The Butcher was originally known as Moon's Fly, but the name was changed about 1838 to the name of the trade of one of its co-inventors, Moon and Jewhurst. It is generally accepted as being a small fry imitation, although John Goddard believes that fished slowly under the surface film it could be taken for an orange-and-silver midge-pupa. It is without doubt an effective general attractor pattern on river, loch or reservoir. A number of variants have been developed.

Hook: 10–14
Thread: Black
Tail: Red ibis or swan dyed red
Body: Flat silver tinsel or Mylar
Rib: Oval silver tinsel or silver wire
Wing: Blue mallard, crow wing or magpie tail feather
Hackle: Black

The Teal-Winged Butcher has a wing from a barred teal feather.

The Bloody Butcher (Plate 7) has the black hackle replaced with a scarlet one.

The Gold Butcher is as the standard dressing except that it has a gold tinsel body and gold rib

Kingfisher Butcher

Hook: 10–12
Body: Flat gold tinsel
Rib: Oval gold tinsel
Tail: Kingfisher wing feather-fibres or substitute
Wing: Black hen or as for the standard dressing
Hackle: Orange cock

This pattern tied with a whitish-grey squirrel-tail hairwing is known as Morning Glory.

CADDIS

See SEDGES

CAENIS or BROADWING

See EPHEMEROPTERA.

The six species within this family are known as the angler's curse because of the difficulty in tempting fish feeding upon them into taking an artificial. Three species are confined to rivers. Of the remaining species, one is extremely small, fairly uncommon and appears only at dawn, while the other two are similar and found on stillwater.

The family is common throughout Britain on slow-moving rivers and lakes, but it is principally on stillwater that the prolific hatches appear. The nymphs inhabit the bottom mud or silt. The adults are the smallest of the *Ephemeroptera*. They are easily recognised by their cream bodies, broad whitish wings and three tails. They usually hatch in the early mornings or evenings between May and September. Trout seem to prefer the spinners, which are considerably whiter than the duns. The males have much longer tails than the female.

The difficulty of catching trout on the artificial cannot be understated. Not only does the fly have to be very small, but frequently so many spinners are on the water that it must be by sheer chance that a trout selects the artificial. A further difficulty is that duns and spinners appear over the water at the same time, as the adult life lasts only about ninety minutes. Fishing a hatch or fall of spinners can be frustrating. Sometimes artificials 'work', and at other times they fail completely.

Some fly-tyers tie imitations on hooks as small as size 24 or 26 and claim success with them. I can claim moderate success when dropping down to these sizes. The difficulty then becomes not rising the fish, but hooking and playing them.

For further imitations see GODDARD'S LAST HOPE, ENIGMA, GREY DUSTER and POLYSTICKLE.

Caenis Nymph   (Bob Carnill) Plate 16

Bob Carnill comments on his dressing: 'This nymph stems from the middle to late 1960s. It was first used with success on Eye Brook Reservoir. I usually fish with a team of three when I anticipate a caenis hatch. However, the pattern often continues to catch even after the trout have turned their attention to the hatching duns. I usually tie the nymph slightly larger than the natural, and for a better hook-hold and surface penetration, short-dress it on a size 14 hook. The caenis nymph is fished just sub-surface on a floating line and a light leader. The retrieve should be a slow figure-of-eight.'

Hook: 14–16
Thread: Brown
Tail: Three brown partridge hackle fibres or tail fibres
Body: Drab-brown swan, goose or heron herl
Rib: Stripped peacock quill
Thorax: Hare's ear fur
Wing-case and thorax cover: Biot quills from the narrow side of a heron primary feather, tied with the broad ends facing rear over the body and tied in at the head and rear of the thorax. Trimmed and shaped (rounded) so that they extend half-way down the body
Legs: Partridge fibres

Caenis Nymph

(Paul Canning)   Plate 16

Hook: 14
Thread: Black
Tail: Grizzle or badger cock fibres
Abdomen: White ostrich herl
Rib: Fine oval silver
Thorax: Brown/golden olive ostrich herl

Caenis Nymph   Plate 16

Hook: 14–16 Partridge L2A
Thread: White
Tail: Three brown partridge fibres
Body: White or cream seal's fur or poly dubbing

Rib: Fine oval silver tinsel
Hackle: Sparse grey partridge

Caenis Dun (Frank Sawyer)

Hook: 18-20
Thread: Midge thread
Tail: Short cream cock fibres
Body: Mole's fur
Thorax: Stripped black ostrich herl, shiny side uppermost
Hackle: Three turns of a very small dark-blue hackle

Caenis Spinner

(Terry Ruane)   Plate 21

Hook: 12–18 Partridge E6A
Thread: White
Tails and antennae: Widely spaced Microfibetts
Abdomen: Tying thread or fine dubbing
Thorax: Brown Furry Foam wound over the wing roots
Wing: Spent bunches of Magic Spinner wing fibres

Caenis Spinner

(Stuart Canham)   Plate 21

Hook: 18
Thread: Fine special midge thread
Tail: Three white cock hackle fibres
Body: White polythene
Thorax: A single turn of brown condor or turkey herl
Wings: White hen hackles cut out with a wing-cutter and tied spent
Hackle: White cock trimmed along the bottom edge

Caenis Spinner

(Charles Jardine)   Plate 21

Hook: 16–18
Thread: White midge
Tail: Three widely spaced Microfibetts or white nylon paintbrush fibres
Abdomen: Cream-dyed rabbit's fur or Antron/hare mix

Thorax: Brown or black rabbit's fur or Antron/hare mix
Hackle: One or two pale blue-dun or white cock wound through the thorax with four or five turns with a V cut out top and bottom

Caenis Muddler

(Stan Headley)   Plate 9

A major problem with catching caenis-feeding trout on wet flies is that the fish are feeding so high in the water that the imitation fishes below them. The surface distrupting and low relative weight of muddler heads makes then at least visible to trout. Stan Headley noticed that mini-muddlers worked well in this situation, as did gold-bodied patterns with white wings, so the merger became successful.

Hook: Slightly long shank 12–16 Partridge SH2
Thread: Irrelevant, normally black
Body: Brassy flat gold, ribbed with gold wire or very fine oval
Wing: Tuft of white marabou
Head: Fine roe deer, clipped to a bullet shape, retaining some fine tips as a hackle

Cahill

The Cahill, Light Cahill and Dark Cahill are North American dry flies developed in the 1880s by Daniel Cahill, a New York railroad worker. They are extensively used throughout their home country and they have successfully carved a niche for themselves on some of our rivers.

Hook: 10–14
Tail: Brown cock hackle fibres
Body: Peacock eye quill
Wing: Speckled mandarin flank fibres tied in a single upright bunch-wing, or in a split V-shape
Hackle: Brown cock

Dark Cahill

A fair imitation of the large summer dun.

Hook: 10–12
Tail: Mandarin duck breast fibres
Body: Muskrat fur or any fine brown fur
Tip: Gold tinsel
Wing: Mandarin duck fibres tied upright or in a split V-shape
Hackle: Brown cock

Light Cahill

Hook: 10–12
Tail: Mandarin duck breast fibres or fibres of the hackle used
Body: Creamy fox fur or pale cream-grey wool
Wing: Mandarin duck breast or flank fibres tied upright or in a split V-shape
Hackle: Brownish-grey or buff cock

Campbell's Fancy

One of a few North American fancy lake flies which have been introduced into Great Britain. It is recommended for fishing in a wave on a bright sunny day and as a summer evening pattern.

Hook: 8–14
Tail: Golden pheasant crest feather
Body: Flat gold tinsel
Rib: Gold wire on the larger sizes only
Wing: Barred teal feather
Hackle: Coch-y-bondhu

CATERPILLARS

It is a common sight in summer to see small caterpillars descending from trees on slender gossamer threads. The slightest breeze breaks the thread and they may be blown on to any nearby water. Larger caterpillars are more likely to fall in the water from plants and grass on the bankside, and the artificial is best fished near overhanging trees and bushes. Often in mid-summer, there is a mid-afternoon period of inactivity. Two patterns work better than most to change a trout's apathy into avarice. One is Eric's Beetle, the other is a small caterpillar. Both sometimes seem too tempting for a fish to pass them by.

See also CHENILLE GRUB and PALMERS.

Caterpillar *(John Roberts)*

Hook: Long shank 12–14 with a slight downward bend imparted to give the impression of the caterpillar wriggling
Body: A layer of floss silk covered with matching heron herl or ostrich herl (white, green or brown)
Head: Peacock herl

Floating Caterpillar
(Richard Walker)

Hook: Long shank 10
Underbody: Varnished polythene foam
Overbody: Dyed ostrich herl over the wet varnish. Suitable colours are brown, black, white and green
Rib: Crimson or buff silk soaked in diluted Durofix adhesive and allowed to dry

Catgut Nymph   *Plate 30*

This is not really a nymph but a free-swimming caddis larva imitation from Adam Sikora. He and his Polish colleagues in their national fly-fishing team are experts at fishing patterns like this one on a very short line in fast rivers. Adam comments that the catgut is essential. It is a natural material which swells when wet, becomes soft and slightly transparent and imitates the segments on the natural very effectively. The catgut should be dampened before winding on.

Hook: Tiemco 2457, 2X short, 2X heavy, 2X wide, size 8–12
Thread: Black
Underbody: Lead wire
Abdomen: Green-dyed catgut
Thorax: Black wool with legs fibres picked out
Wing-case: Black plastic in three segments

Cat's Whisker

Plate 1

David Train devised this very successful lure in the mid-1980s. The original had a few cat's whiskers supporting the tail. It may be fished in a wide range of retrieves and at different depths. It is also very popular as a mini-lure on size 10 and 12 standard hooks. As both standard and mini-lure and in a wide range of colour combinations or in a single colour the fly has had considerable success. The original is below. Other versions also include leadhead and painted eyes instead of the bead chain, or gold bead chain eyes, or a single gold bead, or without eyes.

Hook: Long shank 6–10
Thread: Black
Tail: White marabou
Body: Fluorescent yellow chenille ribbed with fine oval silver or gold
Wing: White marabou
Eyes: Silver bead chain

Chatsworth Bug

Plate 18

Robert Spiller devised this general bug imitation for fishing on the Derbyshire Derwent. It is good for trout and grayling. It is fairly typical of a number of goldbead nondescript river bugs that are proving very successful for fishing close to the river-bed.

Hook: 10–14 standard or long shank
Thread: Brown 6/0
Tail: Six short strands of pearl Krystalflash
Body: Pine squirrel body fur ribbed with gold wire
Collar (optional): Green or orange fluorescent dubbing

Chenille Grub

This is Roger Fogg's caterpillar or general grub imitation. A weighted version lands with a 'plop' that often draws attention to itself as a natural caterpillar might falling on to the water. In *The Art of the Wet Fly*, Roger Fogg writes of a small wooded bay on a reservoir he fishes, where trout regularly feed on caterpillars blown on to the water. The difficulty was casting to trout that were well protected by overhanging branches. Roger finally managed to get his brown Chenille Grub into the water beneath the branches and a 3 ¼ lb trout was the result. He also took three brown trout the next evening from a river on the same pattern.

Terrestrial insects and grubs often figure in the diet of trout. Their imitation should not be overlooked, particularly if fish are feeding but the usual nymphs or dry flies are being refused.

Hook: 12–14
Thread: Black
Body: White, green, yellow or brown chenille, attached to the shank behind the eye only with the remainder left free to move in the water.
Head: Black tying thread

Chew and Blagdon Lure

A three-hook tandem lure devised by Tom Saville.

Rear hook
Tail: Swan fibres dyed red
Body: Flat silver tinsel

Middle hook
Body: Flat silver tinsel

Front hook
Body: Flat silver tinsel
Wings: Badger hackles tied back to back the length of the three hooks
Hackle: Brown

Chew Nymph

Thomas Clegg, author of an interesting little book, THE TRUTH ABOUT FLUORESCENTS, 1967, devised this general stillwater nymph pattern incorporating some fluorescent materials.

Hook: 8–10
Thread: Red
Tail: Three short neon-magenta DRF floss fibres

Body: Mole's fur tied fairly fat
Rib: Neon-magenta DRF floss
Back: Mottled turkey feather fibres
Legs: Brown hen hackle.

Chief Needabeh

A streamer lure of North American origin.

Hook: Long shank 6–10
Tag: Silver tinsel
Body: Scarlet floss
Rib: Oval silver tinsel
Wing: Two yellow cock hackles tied back to back with two orange hackles outside with jungle cock at the shoulder (optional)
Collar hackle: Mixed yellow and scarlet cock
Head: Black varnish

Chompers

An excellent range of impressionist patterns devised by Richard Walker to represent a number of food sources. The variations and their natural counterparts are listed below. Each should be fished in a manner to imitate the intended natural. The white version has been my most useful pattern, usually fished on a greased leader fairly close to the surface. The series is the antithesis of all that exact imitation represents. There could hardly be a simpler pattern, nor a more broadly imitative one.

Hook: 10–14
Body: Herls as below, or wool of the appropriate colour. Optional underbody of lead-foil strips
Back: Coloured Raffene tied in at the head and tail

The following patterns can be used to represent various natural fauna.

Back	Body material	Thread	Imitation
Clear	Golden yellow ostrich	Black	General imitation
Brown	Olive ostrich	Olive	General imitation
Brown or white	White ostrich	White	General imitation

Back	Body material	Thread	Imitation
Pale buff	Buff ostrich	Brown	Shrimp
Pea green	White ostrich	Olive	Small corixa
Black	Peacock herl	Black	Beetle
Speckled turkey	Golden yellow ostrich	Black	General imitation

Christmas Tree

A popular lure on the big Midlands reservoirs, where the tandem versions are much used by boat fishers. The original single-hook was lure devised by Les Lewis for Rutland.

Hook: Long shank 6–10
Thread: Black
Tail: Fluorescent green wool or floss
Body: Black chenille
Rib: Oval silver tinsel
Wing: Black marabou
Cheeks: Red fluorescent wool or floss

The white tandem variant was evolved by Steve Parton on Rutland Water where, after a fairly unspectacular start, it took three large brown trout in about nine casts in blazing sunshine and near-flat-calm conditions. For the next three seasons it was rarely absent from Steve's leader when he was boat fishing, and it accounted for more than 800 trout to his rod alone. It should work on big waters throughout the country.

The dressing for both hooks of the tandem is the same.

Hook: Long shank 6–10
Thread: Black
Tail: Arc-chrome fluorescent floss
Body: White chenille
Rib: Oval silver tinsel
Wing: White marabou
Cheeks: Green fluorescent wool tied above the wing

In the black tandem version the tails are replaced by neon-magenta wool. It has a black body and wing.

Church Fry

This fry-imitating pattern was devised by and named after its inventor, Bob Church. It was first fished in 1963 at Ravensthorpe when trout were feeding on perch fry. It is an excellent pattern for use throughout the season, even when no perch fry are in evidence.

Hook: Long shank 4–10
Thread: Black
Tail: White hackle fibres
Body: Orange floss or chenille
Rib: Flat gold tinsel
Wing: Natural white-tipped grey squirrel-tail hair extending just beyond the bend of the hook
Beard hackle: Orange or crimson hackle

Cinnamon and Gold   Plate 7

This winged wet fly is used mainly on stillwaters as an imitation of the cinnamon sedge pupa as well as being a useful general pattern for a three-fly leader. An alternative dressing has a yellow wool body ribbed with oval gold tinsel.

Hook: 10–12
Thread: Black
Tail: Golden pheasant tippets
Body: Flat gold tinsel
Rib: Oval gold tinsel
Wing: Cinnamon-dyed or natural hen wing quills
Hackle: Cinnamon hen

Cinnamon Quill

This old-established dry fly is fished as a general spinner imitation, suggestive of the female spinners of the MARCH BROWN, IRON BLUE, BLUE-WINGED OLIVE, PALE WATERY and OLIVES.

Hook: 14–16
Thread: Sherry spinner
Tail: Ginger cock hackle fibres
Body: Pale cinnamon quill
Hackle: Ginger cock

Clan Chief   Plate 6

A modern traditional-style fly from Orcadian John Kennedy which was originally devised for and has success with migratory fish. It has some notoriety on the Scottish mainland for brown trout. It has combined Bibio and Claret Bumble elements. The smaller sizes are difficult to tie unless the palmering hackles are stripped of fibres down one side. Do not wind the palmering too close together, as this destroys the translucency of the pattern and spoils its action.

Hook: 8–12
Butt: One turn medium flat silver
Tag: Tuft of red wool over yellow (Stan Headley recommends FloBrite floss for trout)
Body: Black seal's fur palmered with one crimson and one black cock hackle, over-ribbed with medium oval silver
Hackle: Longish black hen

CLARET DUN
(Leptophlebia vespertina)

See also EPHEMEROPTERA

The claret dun is fairly common on some stillwaters. It prefers acidic water and is rarely found on rivers. The reddish-brown nymph is slow-moving and lives among stones and moss on the bottom, usually in shallow water. The adults appear in May and June, often around midday. The female spinners are usually encountered in the early evening. The species is similar to the slightly larger sepia dun, which has the same habitat but appears later in the season. The size of the adults seems to vary across the country. J. R. Harris describes them as being as large as the large dark olive, John Goddard records them as medium to large, and C. F. Walker as being medium to small.

The male dun has dark-grey wings with pale hindwings. The abdomen is dark black-brown with a grey-black underneath, the last three segments having a claret tinge. The legs are dark black-brown and the three tails are dark grey-brown. The female dun has dark-grey wings with pale-buff hindwings. The abdomen is dark brown with a claret tinge. The three tails are dark brown, as are the legs.

The female spinner has transparent wings with pale-brown veins. The abdomen is brown tinged with claret. The legs are pale to medium brown and the three tails are pale brown with light black rings. The male spinner is of no interest as it dies over land without returning to water.

The nymph can be imitated with a PHEASANT-TAIL NYMPH or BROUGHTON'S POINT and the dun with an IRON BLUE DUN, or with those patterns below. Small versions of the GROUSE AND CLARET or MALLARD AND CLARET also take fish when the duns are hatching.

Claret Nymph (*John Henderson*)

Hook: 14
Thread: Dark claret
Tail and body: Cock pheasant tail fibres dyed dark claret
Rib: Gold wire
Thorax: Dark claret seal's fur
Hackle: Two turns of dark dun hen

Claret Dun (*John Henderson*)

Hook: 14
Thread: Claret
Tail: Very dark rusty-dun cock hackle fibres
Body: Very dark claret seal's fur
Rib: Fine gold wire
Hackle: Very dark rusty-dun cock

Claret Spinner

Hook: 14
Thread: Black
Tail: A bunch of honey-dun or badger hackle fibres
Body: Dark claret floss or seal's fur
Rib: Fine gold wire
Wings: Light honey-dun or badger cock

hackle wound full and bound in bunched spent wings, or wound full with the upper and lower hackles cut away
Hackle: None

Clear Wing Spinner   *Plate 21*

Gary LaFontaine devised this using the Antron fibres he has done so much to publicise. Rarely are the natural spinner's wings smooth and flat; they are invariably pleated. The Antron collects little air bubbles in the manner of the natural pleated wings.

Hook: 14–20
Thread: To match the body
Tail: Two widely spaced Microfibetts or cock fibres
Abdomen and thorax: Natural fur or fine poly dubbing to match the natural
Wing: Bunched clear Antron fibres

Clyde Sandfly

This is a Scottish imitation of the gravel bed. In some areas sandfly is the name given to a species of sedge, but this is not a sedge imitation.

Hook: 12–14
Body: Black silk
Wing: Hen pheasant centre tail, without the black bars, laid flat across the back
Hackle: Long-fibred black cock

Coachman

The Coachman and its many variants make it probably the most widely used trout fly. It is known in one of its various guises to fly fishers throughout the world. The original was devised in the first half of the nineteenth century, and was probably named after the occupation of its inventor. Thomas Salter's *The Angler's Guide* of 1814 says: 'There is a fly very much used at Watford, in Herts, called Harding's Fly, or the Coachman's; the merits of such flies experience will teach how to appreciate'.

Its merits are still evident today. It is an

excellent general fly for both river and lake, and, in its larger sizes, for sea trout. It can be fished wet or dry. Wet it is a passable hatching sedge copy; dry it can be fished as a moth imitation. Some of the more extreme variations have taken place across the Atlantic, where Coachman variants are held in high esteem. The Royal Coachman Bucktail (below) is one example.

Coachman

Hook: 8–16 (the larger sizes for sea trout)
Thread: Black or brown
Body: Bronze peacock herl
Wing: White duck or swan fibres
Hackle: Natural light-red cock or hen. A wingless version has a white cock hackle with a shorter natural red cock in front or wound together

The Leadwing Coachman is as above, but with a wing of grey duck or starling wing.
The Grayling Coachman, which is always fished dry, has an additional red wool tag and often the wing is of white hackle fibres slanting over the body or set upright.

Clipped Coachman

A Taff Price recommended fly as a searching pattern on first approaching a river.

Hook: 12–14
Thread: Black
Body: Peacock herl wound over an optional underbody of copper wire
Wing: Short tuft of white feather fibres
Hackle: Sparse brown hen

Hackle Point Coachman

(Dave Collyer) *Plate 26*

A floating pattern which Dave Collyer said had probably accounted for more fish for him than any other.

Hook: 10–14
Thread: Red spinner

Body: Bronze or green peacock herl wound over wet varnish for durability
Wing: White cock hackle points tied semi-spent
Hackle: Ginger or natural red cock with the underside trimmed flat in line with the hook-point

Royal Coachman

The 1878 variation by the American John Haily changes the pattern into a fancy one. Dozens of variations have followed. The Royal Trude Coachman has a calf-tail wing over the body extending to the middle of the tail.

Hook: 8–16
Thread: Black
Tail: Golden pheasant tippets
Body: In three parts – peacock herl, red floss, peacock herl as for pattern below
Wing: White duck or swan
Hackle: Light red game

Royal Coachman Bucktail

Hook: Long shank 8–10
Thread: Golden pheasant tippets
Body: Peacock herl at either end of the body for a short length only; red floss in the middle
Wing: White bucktail
Cheek: Jungle cock
Throat hackle: Brown

Coch-y-Bondhu
Plate 20

This terrestrial beetle has been imitated by fly fishers for centuries. Its Welsh origin is betrayed by its name, meaning 'red with black trunk'. The natural is sometimes blown on to the water in June, but the fly can be fished successfully throughout the season. Courtney Williams devoted five pages of his book to the fly. It is an effective beetle imitation and general river wet fly. The dressing is so generally nondescript that it passes as a variety of beetle species.

Hook: 12–14
Thread: Black

Tag: Gold tinsel
Body: Bronze peacock herl
Rib (optional): Red floss silk
Hackle: Coch-y-bondhu (red game hackle with a black centre and black tips)

A West Country pattern is detailed below. It is reputed to be a good grayling fly.

Hook: 14
Body: Bronze peacock herl
Wing-case: Long strands of golden pheasant tippets tied so that the black rib of the tippets is on top of the body
Hackle: Coch-y-bondhu

Cockchafer

This is a terrestrial beetle sometimes found on the water. It is similar to the Coch-y-bondhu, but is larger, being about 25 mm (1 inch) long, and has a barred black and grey underbody. It appears in May and June. The pattern below is from John Henderson.

Hook: 8
Thread: Brown
Tail: Two light-dun cock hackle-points about 16 mm (⅝ inch) long
Body: Oval-shaped cork with a flat underside. A groove is cut in the cork, the shank is glued and the cork pushed over the shank. This is painted dark grey
Wing-cases: Two cock-pheasant breast feathers (brownish-red) which are heart-shaped with black edges, tied on top of each other over the back of the body
Hackle: Large natural red cock

Cockwill's Red Brown   *Plate 16*

Peter Cockwill needs no introduction as an expert in small stillwaters. This is his adaptation of the Ivens Brown and Green and is intended to imitate the small sticklebacks early in the year. It is also a good general-purpose nymph or small fish imitation.

Hook: Partridge Stronghold 10
Tail, back and head: Peacock herl

Body: Copper/gold fingering or similar ribbed with brown ostrich herl
Thorax collar: Neon magenta chenille
Throat hackle: Greenwell hen

Coleman Lake Special   *Plate 8*

Peter Deane thoroughly recommends this wet fly. He has tried it on every possible hook size for trout and salmon. It excels on the Irish loughs but Peter has used it with success on South of England stillwaters. The original dressing calls for tails of unbarred mandarin but a cheaper alternative is grey mallard flank dyed brown-olive.

Hook: 10–14 wide-gape for trout
Thread: Yellow Gossamer
Tail: Grey mallard flank dyed brown-olive
Body: Dubbed Russian grey squirrel or muskrat
Wing: White calf tail over a varnish base
Hackle: Fox-red cock wound as a collar after the wing
Head: Black

Collyer Nymphs

A series of general stillwater nymphs devised by Dave Collyer. They are extremely effective as general imitations and I have successfully used the brown and green versions on both rain-fed rivers and chalk-streams. On stillwaters they are best fished slowly near weedbeds on which one expects to find natural nymphs.

Hook: 10–12
Tail: The tip of the body feather fibres
Thorax: Ostrich herl dyed as for the body
Wing-case: Body fibres taken over the thorax and tied in at the head
Body: Swan herl dyed olive and ribbed oval gold tinsel for the Green Nymph. Cock pheasant centre tail fibres ribbed oval gold tinsel for the Brown Nymph. Natural heron herl ribbed oval silver tinsel for the Grey Nymph. Turkey herl dyed black and ribbed fine silver Lurex for the Black Nymph

Colonel Downman's Fancy

As its name suggests, this is wholly a fancy lake fly. It is used mainly on Scottish lochs.

Hook: 12–14
Thread: Black
Tail: Teal fibres
Body: Black floss
Rib: Silver tinsel
Wing: Blue jay wing with a small jungle-cock eye on each side
Hackle: Black cock

Colonel's Gamepie Nymph

Plate 17

I first came across this pattern in Michael Leighton's excellent little book *Trout Flies of Shropshire and the Welsh Borderlands.* He attributes it to Colonel George Ellis, a keen shooter who makes the most use of the plumage of his birds by tying this very successful general impressionist nymph. It works very well on both rivers and stillwaters. My friend Nick Bradley, who swears by the fly insists that in keeping with the fly's materials it should be leaded only with the foil from a bottle of claret. The original has a beard hackle although Nick ties his Defoe-style flat across the top of the thorax before the wing-cases are pulled over.

Hook: 12
Thread: Brown
Tail: Bronze mallard fibres
Body: Dark hare's ear fur ribbed with gold wire
Thorax: Rabbit fur, underfur and guard hairs well mixed over an optional lead underthorax
Wing-case: Cock pheasant tail fibres
Legs: Brown partridge fibres

Comparadun

Americans Al Caucci and Bob Nastasi named and popularised this style of tying a dun imitation. The main feature is the 180-degree wing of flared deer's face hair, which they believe offers a distinct wing silhouette. The wing breadth represents the flapping natural's wings prior to take-off. The body rests on or in the film more in the manner of an emerger than a fully adult dun. Suitably coloured materials may be used for different naturals. Wing material is tied in by the butts. Pull gently but firmly on the thread so that the fibres flare, and bind in a semi-circle.

Hook: 12–18
Thread: Olive
Tail: Widely spaced cock fibres or Microfibetts
Body: Fine natural or synthetic dubbing
Wing: Deer's face hair

Concrete Bowl

Plate 2

This marabou-tail lure is one of a number of similar patterns popular on stillwaters. It was devised for Toft Newton, hence the fly's name. The most successful colour combinations are black and fluorescent yellow, white and fluorescent green, orange and fluorescent yellow.

Hook: Long shank 6–10
Tail: Marabou
Body: Wound marabou ribbed with oval silver (or gold on the orange body)
Head: Chenille

Connemara Black

Plate 10

Like Guinness, the Connemara Black is a black Irish export that has been well received on this side of the Irish Sea. It is a lake and river fly that is also used, in its larger sizes, for sea trout and salmon and as a dapping fly. It is an excellent general stillwater pattern which is probably best fished in its smaller sizes just below the surface on the top dropper. Like many traditional flies new variants have been tied with synthetic materials, particularly those with highly reflective qualities. A successful variant to the dressing below has a Lureflash Twinkle tail (Plate 6). When a slimmer version is required omit the palmered body hackle and wind just a couple of turns at the throat before tying in the blue jay.

Hook: 6–14
Thread: Black
Tail: Golden pheasant topping
Butt: Lemon floss silk
Body: Black wool, seal's fur or ostrich herl
Rib: Oval silver tinsel
Wing: Bronze mallard shoulder feather
Hackles: Black cock or hen palmered with a throat hackle of barred blue jay feather

Connemara Black Bumble

Plate 10

Irish angler John D. Seed, now resident in England, has advised me on some of the Irish patterns. This is his very successful variation.

Hook: 12–14
Thread: Black
Tail: Golden pheasant topping
Body: Black seal's fur palmered with a black cock
Rib: Fine silver oval
Hackle: Partridge dyed blue

Copper Hopper

Muddler variations abound on both sides of the Atlantic. This British fly was devised by Terry Griffiths and is based upon the American Hopper patterns. It is heavily leaded to overcome the buoyancy of the deerhair head. It is fished deep on a sinking line and retrieved slowly. It is not unusual for takes to come in the form of a couple of shy knocks followed by a more confident 'thud' on the fly line. It could well be taken for a small fish grubbing about on the lake-bed.

Hook: Extra long shank 8
Thread: Brown
Tail: A loop of the body material
Body: Copper glitter yarn ribbed with a red game-cock hackle
Wing: Brown-barred squirrel overlaid with mottled peacock wing tied flat
Head: Dome-shaped natural deerhair in

Muddler style on the front one-third of the shank with a few underside fibres trailing to the rear

Copper Squirrel

Plate 18

I hope I may be permitted an indulgence by including one of my own patttterns. Three days after tying it it accounted for my largest tally of river brown trout in a single session. Fifty-nine brown trout, most of which were wild, and thirteen grayling fell to this one late September day on a Yorkshire stream. A week later it also caught thirty-four grayling in just two hours fishing on the Wylye. Like all such bugs it should be cast upstream and the leader closely monitored for takes. The pattern evolved from a Hare's Ear Gold Head which also has caught me very many fish. I prefer the colour and the 'bugginess' of the squirrel and the copper bead which is more muted in its flashiness than a gold version. The soft hackle also gives it additional mobility.

Hook: 12–14
Thread: Brown or orange
Body: Grey squirrel fur ribbed with very fine gold tinsel or wire
Hackle: Brown partridge tied behind the bead
Head: Copper bead 2 mm

CORIXAE

The best-known member of this family is the lesser water boatman. Corixae are found predominantly on stillwaters and are widely distributed throughout the country. Their imitation though should not be confined to stillwaters as many patterns work well on rivers. They vary in size, but some reach 12 mm (0.5 inch) in length and all have shiny backs and two long hind-legs which resemble oars. The coloration of the backs varies depending upon the species, but brown is the dominant colour, with shades of yellow, grey and dark brown blended in. The underbody is invariably white.

Corixae have a preference for shallow

water as they have to return to the surface to take in air, held in a bubble under the wings. Artificials incorporating a flash of silver in the dressing to represent the bubble are often more successful than those without this refinement. Corixae prefer to be near weed-beds, where they can find food and protection, but they are found in open water. Although some 30 species are known, their value was largely overlooked until the last 20 years. Imitations are useful throughout the season, but their greatest effectiveness is during the August and September period.

Some of the patterns listed are buoyant and the best way to fish them is on a sinking line or sink-tip. The artificial can be made to dive towards the bottom as it is retrieved. During pauses between retrieves the buoyant fly heads towards the surface – all very lifelike.

Theo's Corixa
Plate 16

Dutch fly fisherman Theo Bakelaar has produced these unusual corixa patterns which work extremely well on his home waters. They look very realistic. They use oval plastic beads and a straight-eyed hook is required for the beads to fit. Theo ties two dressings, as below and the second with a back of black Flexibody and legs of two black goose biots.

Hook: Partridge K14ST or TMC 101 size 12–16
Thread: Black or brown
Tail: A few rabbit hairs
Bead: Oval silver plastic
Back: Pheasant tail fibres
Legs: Brown or olive goose biots

Corixa (Roger Fogg)

Hook: 10–14
Thread: Brown
Tag: Silver tinsel or Mylar
Body: An underbody of lead foil covered with a dubbing of dirty-white or pale-lemon angora wool
Rib: Fine silver wire

Back: Pale-orange raffia stretched over the back and stroked with a brown Pantone pen to give a mottled finish
Hackle: Two bunches of brown hen fibres at either side of the body

Large Brown Corixa
(Richard Walker)

Hook: 10
Body: White floss silk tied fat
Rib: Flat silver tinsel
Tip: Silver tinsel
Back and paddles: Brown speckled turkey feather fibres

The Small Green Corixa can be copied with a size 14 hook to include a back and paddles of pale olive-green swan herl. The Yellow Corixa is tied with a primrose floss silk body and olive-green feather fibres for the back and paddles.

Woven Corixa
(Davy Wotton)
Plate 16

It may come as a suprise for some fly dressers lately 'discovering' this process that Davy Wotton has been weaving fly bodies since the 1970s. Since then his corixa imitation has taken hundreds of trout for him. The weaving technique: Take approximately 20 cm of oval silver and micro-chenille and tie in on top of the shank at the bend, the silver on the far side, the chenille at the near. Tie in 15 cm of Lurex and wind it up the body and tie in and trim. Whip finish the tying thread which will be in the way and cut off. Turn the vice towards the tyer, eye facing. Take hold of the oval silver and chenille, bringing them forward in front of the eye, and tie a simple overhand knot, ensuring that the tinsel goes over the chenille first. Having made a loose knot, place the loop of the knot over the eye so that the chenille is above and the tinsel below, and take the loop to the bend. In position, gently pull it closed with equal tension from either side. This process is repeated until the back is completed about 3 mm from the eye. Tie in the thread again and add the paddles and head.

Hook: 10
Thread: Brown or black
Underbody: Three or four strands of fine lead wire twisted together to form a rope, and secured along each side of the shank and covered with tying thread
Body: Flat silver Lurex
Weaving materials: Back, brown microchenille; belly, oval silver tinsel (strong enough to withstand weaving)
Paddles: Two biot quills from a mallard flight feather
Head: Tying thread

Plastazote Corixa (Dave Collyer)

A buoyant pattern.

Hook: 12–14
Body: A rectangular piece of plastazote slotted on to the shank, glued and shaped with a sharp knife
Back and oars: Pheasant tail fibres, with the oars extending well beyond the bend

Cove Nymph   *Plate 16*

This nymph pattern was devised by Midlands stillwater nymph expert, Arthur Cove. In *Stillwater Flies*, Vol. III, Taff Price describes Arthur Cove as 'a human heron, so still he stands, very slowly retrieving his flies in a figure-of-eight retrieve and allowing the natural drift of the water to work his flies. He is the most patient of anglers'. There are lessons to be learned from such an attitude and technique.

The Cove Nymph is an impressionist nymph, probably being taken for a midge pupa, sedge pupa, small fry and possibly other sub-surface food items. In addition to the pattern below, it can be tied with dyed seal's fur of the following colours as alternatives for the thorax: black, grey, olive, claret, orange, red, yellow, amber or brown. The original pattern is best and most popular for general use, but for water green with algae the orange or green thorax version works better. The

pattern was originally intended to be fished on the end of a long leader and inched slowly across the bottom, but it takes fish higher in the water, too.

Hook: Standard shank 6–12
Body: Ruddy pheasant tail fibres extending round the bend
Rib: Fine copper wire wound in the normal manner or criss-crossed along the body
Thorax: A round ball of rabbit's underbody fur
Wing-case: Pheasant tail fibres

Cow-Dung Fly (Scatophaga stercoraria)

A flat-winged terrestrial species, a member of the *Diptera*. The flies are yellow and hairy and their principal habitat and breeding ground, cow dung, hardly makes them appealing. Nevertheless, there are occasions when trout seem to find them attractive. The imitation given was devised by Taff Price. It should be fished wet just below the surface.

Hook: 12
Thread: Yellow
Body: Mixed yellow and olive seal's fur
Wing: Cinnamon hen wing
Hackle: Light ginger, tied on the underside only

CRANE-FLY (Tipulidae)

Nearly 300 species of crane-fly or daddy-long-legs are known. Many of them are found in the vicinity of water, as some species are semi-aquatic. They are poor fliers and from June to September crane-flies are often found struggling on the water surface. The artificial is of particular value as a stillwater pattern when fished in a wave. During hot, flat days of mid-summer, this large mouthful often seems a stimulus to lethargic, cruising fish.

If trout are rising to the artificial, but are not being hooked, it is worth while not to react to the first splashing rise, but to wait until the second sub-surface swirl as the trout turns to take the drowned fly. This is fine if your nerves can stand it. An alternative is to fish a wet pattern such as the Stan Headley version given below, which I can thoroughly recommend.

Some of the patterns below have specific leg appendages. The natural insect has six legs, but where the legs are not very durable it is better to tie in more than this on the artificial as invariably they break off when a fish is being played. I doubt if trout can count up to six, and additional legs make the fly last longer.

Crane-Fly *(Richard Walker)*   *Plate 11*

Hook: Long shank 8–10
Body: Pale cinnamon turkey fibres
Wings: Two badger cock hackle points tied slanting over the body and well divided
Legs: Eight cock pheasant tail fibres knotted in two places and trailing to the rear
Hackle: Pale ginger grizzle

Daddy Long-Legs
(Geoffrey Bucknall)   *Plate 11*

Hook: Long shank 10
Body: Brown floss
Legs: Strong knotted black or grey nylon monofilament
Hackle: Ginger cock
Wing: Ginger cock hackle tips tied spent

Demented Daddy   *Plate 11*

Robert Spiller ties this killing pattern as a marabou-tailed variant of his Gold Head Daddy (Plate 11) which has a highly fluorescent Antron or Multi-Yarn tail. A lot of big fish have fallen for both patterns, including one of over 21 lb pounds to this dressing. Be aware that takes come on the drop as well as on a slow retrieve.

Hook: 10
Thread: 6/0 wine-coloured
Head: 4 mm gold, silver or copper bead
Tail: Coloured marabou, tied long

Body: Cock pheasant centre tail ribbed with copper or gold wire
Legs: Six cock pheasant centre tail fibres, double knotted, three each side
Hackle: Soft red game
Head: Brown Scintilla or SLF Finesse

Drowning Daddy   *Plate 11*

This Oliver Edwards pattern is especially good for dropping in the path of cruising fish, and also a good dapping fly. The wings, hackle and abdomen should be treated to float, the legs treated to sink. The legs are heat-kinked with tweezers – this is much quicker than knotting.

Hook: Curved grub hook Partridge K4A, size 8–12
Thread: Brown or tan 6/0 Uni-Thread
Extended abdomen and thorax: Natural grey-brown deer hair, pre-fashioned on a needle, ribbed with tying thread spirally or circumferentially (see Darrel Martin's book *Fly-Tying Methods*)
Wings: Cock hackle tips, grizzle dyed light brown, or cree, tied spent
Hackle: Longish cock grizzle dyed light brown, or cree, wound as a full collar then trimmed flush on the underside
Legs: 6–8 lb BS brown nylon mono, heat-kinked with tweezers, 2–3 times the body length, arranged to dangle down and slightly backwards

Wet Daddy *(Stan Headley)*   *Plate 11*

Stan Headley comments: 'For anyone who has spent a frustrating day trying desperately to keep an artificial "Daddy" floating on the surface, this pattern is a gift from Heaven. It is fished in standard wet-fly style and will kill fish whether it is retrieved fast or slow. It is an absolute must from August through to September or whenever trout expect the occasional daddy to appear. I've had fish to it in June, during a very patchy trickle of naturals. It works very well indeed, and usually a lot better than any floating artificial. I've experimented with added refinements such as knotted pheasant-tail fibres as legs, tied in at the tail, and hackle-tips for wings, but none made any appreciable improvement to an already excellent fly.' It will work on all stillwaters and is a popular Midlands pattern. Stan says that the Welsh have kidnapped the pattern, given it a yellow palmered hackle and called it the Welsh Daddy. Stan has amended the original dressing to include a body hackle to help support the main hackle.

Hook: Long shank 10–12
Thread: Black
Body: Natural raffia with a palmered red/brown cock over the front half of the body
Rib: Fine gold wire
Hackle: Large brown partridge hackle and golden pheasant tippet feather, mixed

CRAYFISH

The freshwater crayfish is a notable delicacy for big chub and trout. I've not yet experimented with a 'fly' imitation of one but Oliver Edwards and Taff Price offer these suggestions. The naturals vary in colour from almost black to various shades of olive. The only time they are not a drab colour is during the moults, which they do two or three times a year. The freshly moulted crayfish is quite pale.

Immature Fleeing Crayfish

Plate 11

Oliver Edwards ties this with a fanned tail to act as a vane to produce something like the darting action of the natural. The flared hair is cemented in a flat configuration using Flexament or Floo Gloo, then trimmed to shape. Slots should be cut in the tail to allow water to pass through; a solid vane can produce spin. The pattern illustrated is a dark olive and all the materials should be the same colour. Drab cream, pale buff, watery olive or sandy tan can be tied.

Hook: Partridge K6ST Swimming Nymph hook 8–12
Thread: Kevlar or Kevlar blend Pantoned to match the general colour
Underbody: Strips of wine bottle lead foil
Rib: 4-6 lb BS clear or pale-coloured nylon mono
Tail: Deer or elk hair appropriately dyed or coloured, well flared
Abdomen and thorax: Fine chenille – micro, ultra, suede, venille, etc.
Dorsal abdomen and carapace cover: Clear polythene or clear Flexibody
Legs: Two small dyed grizzle marabou plumes, one stacked above the other, tied in semi-Defoe style (i.e. pulled over and tied down)
Pincers: Two small dyed grizzle marabou plumes, one on either side, tied in whole by the stalk end and set well spread to give maximum action. Tethered to create joints, once or twice
Eyes (optional): Heat-balled thick nylon mono
Antennae: Two stripped hackle quills, three-quarters the body length

Crayfish (Taff Price)

Hook: Mustad salmon 800500 BL or Partidge CS10/1 size 8–1/0
Thread: Brown or black
Body: Brown/olive dubbing
Tail, back, claws: Brown leather or leatherette cut to shape
Rib: Clear nylon mono
Eyes: Two mapping pins
Feelers: Moose mane or brown bucktail
Legs: Cock pheasant brown body feather

Cree Duster
Plate 26

This dry fly was devised by Roger Fogg, who uses it on stillwaters, where it has caught a number of large rainbow trout. It floats well and is highly visible. Roger tells me that it fishes well in May and June. I have used it on only two rivers, but on both occasions two brown trout and an out-of-season grayling were duped by it. I have yet to try it on stillwater, but Roger Fogg speaks highly of it.

Hook: 14
Thread: Brown
Tail: Cree hackle fibres
Body: Pale blue rabbit's underfur and hare's ear equally mixed. The body should be fairly short
Hackle: Two cree cock hackles tied back to back so that the duller sides face each other. Three turns of each produces a generous hackle

Cul de Canard

The feathers from a duck's preen gland have risen to worldwide popularity over the last decade. They had been used by a small number of anglers in the Swiss Jura region for about a century. Marjan Fratnik popularised them in the 1980s with his seminal F Fly from which a hundred others have evolved. The feathers are naturally coated with oil from the duck's preen gland; this makes the feather quite water-repellent. Each feather also has a very high number of barbules to aid buoyancy. In the air the feather is extremely mobile and will flutter to simulate life in the slightest breeze. For this reason alone it makes a good wing imitation.

Some of the patterns using CDC feathers are listed elsewhere in the book but many more have been devised. In reality these others, dun imitations for the most part, are but a single tying style with just a body colour or dubbing variation on the theme of the original F Fly. A body dubbing and a few feathers as a wing are all that most of these comprise. They are very effective, especially in their smaller sizes. Spinner imitations can be tied using natural or appropriately dyed CDC feathers in the spent position.

The North American fly tyer René Harrop has devised a series of emergers and duns utilising the CDC feathers. One of the emergers can be found under that heading. Here is his imitation of the fully emerged winged adult dun. It should be colour- and size-matched with the naturals.

Culard
Plate 30

Hans van Klinken devised this emerger for rivers and stillwaters. It is fished as a dry fly or in the film or just below the surface with a very slow retrieve. The cul de canard feather wing is the stiffer central quill and not the usual fibres. It is a useful midge, smut or terrestrial imitation.

Hook: 4X fine long shank 16–18
Thread: Black
Body: Herl fibres from a black wing feather of a peacock (for grayling) or dark grey or dark blue-dun synthetic dubbing (for trout)
Rib: Extra-fine gold wire or yellow Pearsall's silk
Wing: Four cul de canard feathers pulled together and cut half-way along the body length
Hackle: Two turns of a very small dark blue-dun cock (dry) or a starling body feather (for the emerger)

CDC Tailwater Dun
Plate 24

Hook: TMC 100 wide gape
Thread: 6/0
Tail: Six to ten stiff cock hackle fibres divided equally on each side of a small dubbing ball
Body: Harrop fine dubbing (or fine natural substitute)
Wing: Two cul de canard feathers arranged to flare away from each other and mounted in the normal wing position
Legs: Butts of the CDC wings tied back along the sides and clipped even with the rear of the abdomen

Dabblers
Plate 10

A series of Irish lough flies, I believe originally devised as bob flies. Also fished fast on Hi D lines and in a team of three assorted Dabblers. Their body and hackle colours vary black body and hackle with a green or red butt, yellow body and natural red hackle with orange butt, or olive body and hackle with red butt. A pearl-bodied Dabbler is also effective.

Hook: 8–10
Tail: Cock pheasant tail fibres tied twice the shank length
Butt: Seal's fur
Body: Seal's fur ribbed with fine oval gold
Body hackle: Natural red game
Wing: Bronze mallard

Dambuster

The Wormfly is an old reservoir pattern, and Richard Walker tied this version of it. He suggested that it should be fished from a boat on to the waves coming off a dam wall. The stiff hackles help to prevent the hook catching on the dam wall, and they cause the fly to bounce in a lively way off the stones. Richard Walker claimed that fishing it the length of the dam in a good wave usually brings several good fish.
Hook: Long shank 8–12
Tag: Yellow or arc-chrome fluorescent wool
Bodies: Peacock herl
Hackles: Two, one at the shoulder and the other in the middle of the shank between the divided body, both natural red cock

DAMSELFLY
(Odonata zygoptera)

Imitations of damsel nymphs are extremely important on all stillwaters, especially on many smaller lakes. The adults appear from May to August, at the same period as the dragonfly. They are distinguished from the latter by the way the wings are closed when at rest. They are poor fliers and rarely venture far from water. The adults are occasionally of interest to trout, but the nymphs are more eagerly taken.

The nymphs are slim and browny-green and live among weeds, where they are well camouflaged from predators. It is likely that their colour darkens as the season progresses. They swim with a distinctive wiggle towards the shore before crawling up vegetation and splitting their skins to emerge as adults, usually blue or green.

It is when the naturals are making this bankward journey that the sunken artificial is best employed. During the early season the nymphs are quite small, 12–14 mm long. Before emerging they may be as long as 40 mm, and it is these that the nymph fisher usually imitates. Green-bodied lures or green traditional patterns such as the Woodcock and Green seem likely to be taken for the larger nymphs. See also WIGGLE NYMPH and ESKIMO NELL.

Damsel Nymph
(Peter Lapsley)   Plate 13

This is a mid-to-late-season imitation which Peter Lapsley says is one of his two most frequently used flies for small lakes. The other is the Gold-ribbed Hare's Ear. He fishes it on a slow-sinking line or leaded on a long leader and a floating line. Peter advocates a careful watch on the line as most takes come on the drop.

Hook: Long shank 8–10
Thread: Green
Tail: Three medium-olive cock hackle points about 6 mm (0.75 inch) long
Abdomen: Olive, green or brown seal's fur
Rib: Fine oval gold tinsel
Thorax: As for the abdomen, but tied fatter
Wing-case: Cock pheasant centre tail fibres with the rear fibres clipped short (3–6 mm long) and sticking out to the rear and slightly to each side
Legs: The points of eight hen pheasant tail fibres divided four each side
Head: Varnished tying thread

Damsel Nymph
(Chris Kendall) *Plate 13*

Hook: Long shank 8
Thread: Green
Tail: Three olive cock hackle points, widely spaced
Abdomen: Seal's fur or any fine dubbing, 10 parts olive, 1 dark olive, 1 golden olive, 1 white
Rib: Fine gold wire
Thorax: As for the abdomen without the rib, dubbed in front of the rear pair of legs and both sides of the front legs and round the eyes
Back: Olive-dyed duck or similar over the thorax
Legs: Olive-dyed partridge flank or neck feather fibres, in four bunches, two each side at the rear and half-way along the thorax
Eyes: Brown mono nylon with melted ends in a dumb-bell shape

Damsel Nymph
(Peter Cockwill) *Plate 13*

Hook: Partridge Stronghold 10
Tail: Olive cock fibres
Underbody: 0.33 mm lead wire
Body: Mixed seal's fur dub (Equal parts light olive, medium olive, brown, hot orange, amber) tied slim
Rib: Fluorescent yellow floss
Hackle: One turn of olive dyed partridge

Damsel Nymph
(Terry Griffiths) *Plate 13*

Terry Griffiths based this imitation after advice on mixed dubbings from Richard Walker. Terry comments that the tail seems to be incongrous but it has been on the pattern since its inception in 1972 and will remain so while it continues to take countless trout each season. Terry fishes the fly solo on an 15–18 ft leader with a slow-to-medium figure-of-eight retrieve.

Hook: Long shank 8–10 Mustad 9762
Thread: Yellow
Underbody: Lead foil or wire
Tail: Fluorescent green wool teased out
Body: Rear half yellow seal spectrumised dubbing; front half, medium olive seal spectrumised dubbing
Rib: Medium oval gold tinsel
Hackle: Grey partridge dyed bright green

Distressed Damsel
Plate 13

Charles Jardine comments that his nymph imitation works particularly well when trout become fussy about areas of realism. This colour and other colour variants, golden-olive, very soft peach, medium brown have all proved devastating in the UK and in Montana.

Hook: 1X or 2X long shank nymph hook size 10
Thread: Olive 8/0
Tail: 2–4-inch marabou plume, medium to dark olive
Body and thorax: Dubbed mixed seal's fur: 50 per cent med olive, 30 percent golden-olive, 10 percent light blue, 10 percent fluorescent orange
Wing-pad: Olive raffia clipped to shape
Hackle: Grey partridge dyed golden-olive. Tie in on top of the thorax by the tip, concave side uppermost, then secure down before the wing-pad
Eyes: Pearl or red beads secured by a strand of Powergum, singed to create pupils and to seal the ends

Sparkle Damsel Nymph *Plate 13*

This is a pattern from David Scriven which is typical of a number using reflective synthetics to enhance a fly's attraction. It accounted for forty-five trout in three visits to Llandrinio's West Lake.

Hook: 8–14 standard shank
Thread: Black
Tail: Olive marabou with a few strands of Crystal Hair
Body: Olive seal's fur ribbed with Lure-flash Twinkle, light green

Legs: Lureflash Twinkle, light green
Thorax cover: Lureflash Pearl Bodyfilm
Eyes: 2 mm bead chain

Cooper's Yellow Damsel *Plate 13*

A Montana Nymph variant devised by Peter Cooper but popularised by Peter Cockwill. It is very effective in summer on all stillwaters and particularly on the drop.

Hook: Long shank 8–12
Tail: Red game cock fibres
Abdomen: Pale or Naples yellow chenille
Thorax: Arc chrome chenille with a red game cock hackle wound through
Wing-case: Arc chrome chenille

Gold Head Damsel

(Robert Spiller)   *Plate 13*

This is one of a number of gold-headed damsels to appear in the last few years. Robert Spiller's was possibly the first in 1990 and for all its simplicity I doubt if it has been bettered. Its main use is in small stillwaters and it works all year round.

Hook: Long shank 8–12
Thread: 6/0 primrose or olive
Tail: Olive marabou
Body: Seal's fur damsel mixture ribbed with gold wire
Hackle: Grey partridge dyed yellow
Head: Gold bead

Adult Damselfly

Professional fly tyer Dave Tait devised the following pattern which incorporates an unusual detached body. He comments: 'It was during the 1979–80 season that the Flyline Damsel was evolved after two fellow Gloucestershire fly-fishers had prompted me to develop a damsel-fly imitation which would take the damsel-feeding trout in Wiltshire's Lower Moor Fishery, particularly during those hot sunny days when trout could be seen trying to catch the blue male damsels in the air.

'The Flyline Damsel is best cast to margin-feeding trout which are patrolling a particular beat. Watch out for any floating plant or weed where damsels are seen to alight. Study of such plants may show that the trout visit them solely to try to pick off the damsels, which may well be only a matter of inches above the surface.

'A few fishermen each season take numbers of fish on this damsel pattern during trying days when trout are not really on the feed due to hot sunshine. It is usually during these hot days that sedges, buzzers and other fly-life are not in evidence because of the heat. During such days, the natural damsels are abundant, and this is when this pattern scores. Time after time, I have caught trout during heatwave conditions by leaving this damsel pattern afloat near or on top of a small weed patch which has been visited regularly by patrolling fish.'

Blue Male Flyline Damsel

Hook: 10
Thread: Black
Body: A detached body made from an old No. 7 or No. 8 floating line, dyed blue and ribbed with black tying silk with a small butt of silk at the end
Wings: Four black cock hackle points in two groups of two in a V-shape
Hackle: Black or grizzle cock
Eyes: Ethafoam balls covered in stocking mesh and tied in with figure-of-eight turns to secure and separate them

DAPHNIA

So small are these tiny creatures that individually they are impossible to imitate, but they are important and do form a large source of food on some of the bigger stillwaters. In *Reservoir Trout Fishing*, Bob Church goes so far as to suggest that at Grafham daphnia are the most important food available to trout.

The problem of being unable to imitate them has been overcome largely by the considerate attitude of trout, which seem to find orange lures and nymphs attractive when gorging themselves on daphnia. During the summer billions of light-sensitive daphnia move up and down at various depths depending upon the brightness of the sun. On a typical sunny day the daphnia will be nearest the surface during the late evening, throughout the night and in early morning. When the sun rises they will sink deeper. If the weather is dull but warm then it could well be that the upper layers will hold vast quantities of daphnia throughout the day. Find the daphnia and you'll probably find trout.

For suitable patterns to fish when daphnia are in evidence, see under ORANGE LURES and ORANGE NYMPHS, and ORANGE MUDDLERS under MUDDLERS.

DARK OLIVE
(Baetis atrebatinus)

See EPHEMEROPTERA.

This is a species of upwinged dun with a preference for alkaline streams. It is found on the rivers of southern England and on some northern rivers, but it is rare in the rest of the country. The nymph is an agile-darting type and the medium-sized adults appear during the first two months of the season and again in September and November. They are similar to, but smaller than, the large dark olive.

The male dun has grey wings and a dark olive-brown abdomen, with the last segment of the underside yellowish. The legs are pale olive and the two tails are dark grey-olive.

The female is similar to the male except that the tails are greyer. The female spinner has transparent wings. The upper abdomen is dark reddish-brown with paler rings and the lower abdomen is light olive. The legs are brown-olive and the two tails grey-olive with faint red rings. The male spinner is of little interest.

KITE'S IMPERIAL is a suitable imitation, as are some of the general olive imitations under OLIVES and the medium-sized patterns of the LARGE DARK OLIVE.

Dark Moor Game   *Plate 32*

This is one of T. E. Pritt's dressings, a good early season North Country fly.

Hook: 14–16
Thread: Orange waxed with cobbler's wax to a dark shade
Body: Tying thread
Hackle: A black and orange feather from a grouse, preferably a hen
Head: Orange thread or peacock herl

Dawson's Olive   *Plate 2*

To judge by the correspondence I received when I omitted this pattern from the first edition this is a very popular and successful lure. It was originally tied by the late Brian Dawson, formerly the fishery manager at Witton Castle in County Durham, from where it has spread to a national following. No north-eastern angler travels without one. It is essentially a damsel nymph imitation and may be fished statically or twitched back on a floating line. I have received many variants like jungle cock cheeks or an over-wing of two green or pearl Crystal Hairs.

Hook: Long shank 8–14 or standard 12–14 for the mini-lure version
Thread: Brown or olive
Tail: Golden yellow or amber marabou. Three GloBrite No. 11 artificial hairs can be added to withstand wear
Body: Olive chenille ribbed with silver or gold wire
Wing: Olive marabou
Throat hackle: Blue dyed or natural gallina
Head: Varnished black

Diawl Bach

This stillwater general nymph or midge pattern is a first choice for many reservoir anglers. It is highly recommended by

Chris Ogborne and John Horsey, who recommends fishing a team of three with a size 14 on the bob, size 12 on the dropper and a size 10 on the point. Cast a floating line across the wind and let the team swing round without retrieving. The larger sizes are used as a deep point fly.

Hook: 8–14
Tail: Red game cock fibres
Body: Three strands of bronze peacock herl twisted together
Rib: Medium oval gold or copper wire
Throat hackle: Red game cock fibres

DIPTERA

These flat-winged flies are the largest Order of flies of interest to the fly fisherman, but only a relative handful concern both fish and fisherman. Some of the Order never venture near water, but those that do, or are aquatic, are the CRANE-FLY, REED SMUT, BLACK GNAT, MIDGE, COW-DUNG FLY, HOUSEFLY, HAWTHORN FLY, HEATHER FLY, and PHANTOM MIDGE.

All members of the Order have two transparent wings that lie flat across their backs. Each is considered separately under its own heading.

Dog Nobbler

See NOBBLERS.

Dogsbody   Plate 26

In 1924, Harry Powell, a famous Welsh fly dresser, created this general river dry fly. It is a reliable pattern. The fly was named after the body material was obtained from a family pet from one of the customers in Powell's barber's shop. Create your own variant by combing your own dog, cat, gerbil or chimpanzee!

Hook: 12–14
Tail: Pheasant tail fibres
Body: Camel-coloured dog's hair spun on brown tying silk

Rib (optional): Oval gold tinsel
Hackle: Plymouth Rock followed by a second natural red cock, or wound together

Doobry   Plate 6

A useful pattern for those reservoir fishermen who like to take their fish in traditional style. The mixed head hackle produces that extra sparkle which can prove the undoing of wary fish. Stan Headley, who devised the fly, suggests that in small sizes it can be fished anywhere on the leader, on any density of line, but in its bigger sizes and for truly wild fish it does better on the bob on floating lines. It is effective for brown trout and sea trout in stillwaters and excels in coloured water on bright days, and in gin-clear water on dull days. It has become a standard Scottish rainbow fly and has become a first line of attack on Loch Leven and other premiere Scottish waters in its smaller sizes.

Hook: 8–16
Thread: Black
Tail: Fluorescent fire-orange/red wool
Body: Brassy flat gold palmered with a black cock hackle, ribbed with gold wire or fine oval gold
Hackle: Two, hot-orange first, with two turns of black hen in front

Dotterel Series

A series of old North Country wet flies. The silk body colour is varied to imitate the nymphs of various upwinged duns and stoneflies. Golden plover is a suitable substitute for the dotterel, which is a migratory bird rarely seen today. The soft hackle feather can be tied at the shoulder only or semi-palmered a third of the way along the shank. Tied in the latter manner, the flies are profitably fished upstream just below the surface where they give a good impression of an emerging dun or drowned adult.

Hook: 14–16
Body: Silk or thread of one of the follow-

ing colours: orange, red, yellow, purple, claret, brown, slate, green, olive

Hackle: Golden plover; small wing feather, pale brown or dark ash with yellow tips

It has been suggested that the orange body is possibly a stonefly imitation, the yellow a pale watery, and the green a sedge.

Double Legs   *Plate 18*

The double hackle on Theo Bakelaar's bug gives it considerable mobility. Even when fished in a dead drift the current enlivens the hackles of this nondescript utility pattern.

Hook: Tiemco TMC 3761 size 10
Thread: Brown
Head: 4 mm gold bead
Butt: Fluorescent Kreinik metallic braid
Legs: Two or three turns of grey partridge
Body: Brown squirrel or rabbit fur
Hackle: Several turns of grey partridge

Double Wing   *Plate 25*

This is an attractor series devised by Gary LaFontaine. Their creator comments that the body hackle gives some stability on the surface and the impression of legs. The trout viewing it from below sees through the hackle fibres to the translucent body and beyond, through the deer or elk hair and white overwing in a blurring blend of colour. This is the Golden Double Wing.

Hook: 10–14
Thread: Orange
Body: Mixed golden Sparkle Yarn (Antron) and brown fur
Body hackle: Dyed red cock, clipped top and bottom
Underwing: Pale yellowy-orange deer or elk hair
Overwing: White calf tail, slightly longer than the underwing

Dove Bug

This bug of my own was originally tied to catch deep-lying grayling, but it has also caught a good many trout. It was named after the small North Yorkshire stream on which it was first tried. I have caught scores of chalk-stream grayling on it, a few over 2 lb, and trout to 4 lb. I caught my biggest UK grayling, 2 lb 6 oz, on it from the Driffield Beck. It came during a short period in which I made five casts and had three memorable grayling for a total of 6 lb 1 oz.

My original dressing had a small red tag as I thought this would prove more attractive to grayling. However, I seem to catch far more rainbow trout on the tagged version. Grayling seem to prefer the tagless version. Its sinking rate and attraction have been improved by the inclusion of a copper bead head.

Hook: 10–12
Thread: Brown
Body: An underbody of copper or lead wire. Rear half, a mixture of orange and pink seal's fur; front half, orange and brown seal's fur
Rib: Fine gold tinsel or copper wire

DRAGONFLY
(Odonata anisoptera)

The nymphs are large, growing to almost 50 mm (2 inches) long, and live among mud and stones on the lake- or river-bed. They are carnivorous, feeding even on small fish. They normally move slowly, but they have the ability to dart forward rapidly to attack prey. Their coloration is dull and blends with the lake-bed.

The adults appear from May to the end of August. They are attractive, but are rarely taken by trout. The nymphs are more usefully imitated. The adult is distinguished from the damselfly by its wings, which are held open at rest. The damselfly closes its wings. They are stronger fliers than the damselflies and are often found some miles from the nearest water. See also GREEN PALMER and WONDERBUG. A more buoyant pattern can be tied to keep the fly off the bottom or weed by tying in the booby style. See BOOBIES. Also see ESKIMO NELL.

Dragonfly Nymph

A simple pattern to dress is this version of Richard Walker's Chomper.

Hook: 10
Thread: Green
Body: Green ostrich herl
Tail: Green marabou fibres
Back: Green Raffene on the front half of the body only

Dragonfly Nymph (Taff Price)

This pattern may be weighted if desired and small amounts of fluorescent material included in the body dubbing.

Hook: Long shank 8–10
Thread: Black
Tail: Two spiky goose quill fibres dyed olive
Body: Dubbed brown and olive wool mixed equally
Rib: Yellow silk
Hackle: Brown partridge
Head: Peacock herl

Driffield Dun

The Driffield Beck is a delightful chalk-stream tucked away in east Yorkshire. This fairly old dry fly is named after it. No one knows for sure what it is intended to represent. Some sources have suggested it is a spider-type of fly or a Whirling Blue Dun, but Driffield-born angling historian, Donald Overfield, discounts these. He has been unable to trace its origins, but tells me that on the Driffield Beck the fly is of most use when the pale wateries are about.

Hook: 14–16
Tail: Ginger hackle fibres
Body: Mole's fur
Rib: Yellow silk

Wing: Pale starling wing
Hackle: Ginger cock

DRONE-FLY

This member of the Diptera Order is sometimes of sufficient interest to trout to warrant fishing an imitation. The larval and pupal stages of some species are at least part aquatic. The adults are bee- or wasp-like in appearance. The larvae of the commoner stillwater species are known as rat-tailed maggots and they inhabit the muddy bottom of the shallows. Their grey bodies are about 12–20 mm long and have a long breathing tube which extends to the water surface. The female adult returns to the surface to deposit her eggs.

Drone-Fly (Richard Walker)

To be fished just below the surface.

Hook: 12
Abdomen: Yellow wool or fluorescent wool tied fat
Rib: Broad black wool
Thorax: Black wool tied smaller than the abdomen
Wing: Blue-dun cock hackle points tied slanting over the back
Hackle: Dyed yellow cock sparsely tied
Head: Crimson thread with a single bright red ostrich herl round it

Duck's Dun   Plate 25

This is Charles Jardine's incorporation of the cul de canard feather into a very versatile and highly successful dun imitation. It is his first choice pattern style when duns are on the surface. It can match the natural in different sizes and colours. Charles comments that if he had to be restricted to a single dun imitation this would be it. High praise indeed.

Hook: 14–20 Partridge E1A or TMC 921
Thread: Primrose micro
Tail: Three, four or five fibres of grizzle hen or jungle cock spade feather

Body: Light yellow-olive Haretron or soft Antron
Wing: Two cul de canard feathers, tied back to back and upright
Hackle: Dark blue dun cock wound through the thorax and clipped in a V underneath

Dunkeld *Plate 7*

Originally a salmon fly. Its smaller sizes are used for sea trout and lake trout. Its origins are obscure, but a similar fly was mentioned by Francis Francis in *A Book on Angling* in 1867. It has survived so long because it is a good attractor pattern on both lowland reservoirs and Highland lochs. It works well on difficult, bright days.

Standard pattern
Hook: 10–12
Tail: Small golden pheasant crest
Body: Flat gold tinsel
Rib: Oval gold tinsel
Hackle: Palmered orange cock
Wing: Brown mallard shoulder feather with jungle cock on either side

Dunkeld Muddler

(Stan Headley) *Plate 9*

Stan Headley comments that on Loch Leven he would rather go afloat without his rod than be without this pattern! It is good when fish are feeding on daphnia, in which case the fluorescent tail is preferred to the golden pheasant used for general work.

Hook: Slightly long shank 12–16 Partridge SH2
Thread: Irrelevant, normally black
Tail: Mixture of GloBrite No. 11 and 12 or golden pheasant crest feather
Body: Flat gold, palmered with a hot-orange hackle, over-ribbed with gold wire
Wing: Paired slips of hen pheasant secondary
Head: Fine roe deer, clipped to a bullet shape, retaining some fine tips as a hackle

Dun Spider

A renowned Scottish wet pattern of W. C. Stewart, one of his successful trio of spider patterns that killed thousands of brown trout. I don't think the dressing is commercially available now, but there is no reason why it should not still catch trout. What it was taken for did not interest Stewart; he was content to know that it was sufficiently generally imitative to suggest a variety of nymphs and emerging duns.

Hook: 12–16
Body: Well-waxed yellow tying silk
Hackle: Soft dun, or ash-coloured feather palmered part way down the body. Originally a dotterel wing feather was used, but the inside of a starling wing is a suitable substitute

Dun Terrestrial *Plate 22*

The highly experienced Derbyshire angler Philip White uses this general terrestrial imitation for a wide range of flies from a Hawthorn imitation on size 12 hooks, down to size 22 for tiny flies and beetles. It is fished very naturally, low in the film.

Hook: 12–22
Body: Rear half, black tying thread; front half, two strands of peacock herl
Hackle: Dark dun, natural black or grizzle palmered over the front half of the body and clipped top and bottom leaving only the side fibres

DUSKY YELLOWSTREAK (*Heptagenia lateralis*)

See EPHEMEROPTERA
This upwinged fly has a localised distribution on upland lakes and smaller rivers in Devon, Wales, the north of England and Scotland. The nymphs are stone-clingers and are usually found fairly close in to the water's edge. The medium-sized dun has dark grey wings, a dark grey-brown body and two tails. A distinguishing

feature is the yellow streak on each side of the front of the thorax. The spinner has an olive-brown body with the same yellow streak. The flies appear from May to September.

No artificials are tied specifically to represent the species. However, in his book *Trout Flies of Stillwater,* John Goddard suggests a DARK WATCHET to represent the emerging dun, an IRON BLUE QUILL for the dun, and a PHEASANT-TAIL SPINNER for the female spinner, all on size 14 hooks.

Dutch Panama
Plate 26

This semi-palmered floater is a variation on the original French pattern. It is a good riffle fly.

Hook: 12–14
Thread: Grey
Tail: Golden pheasant tippets
Body: Green peacock herl at the rear, fluorescent green wool or dubbing at the thorax
Hackle: Semi-palmered natural red or brown over the thorax

EARLY BROWN
(Protonemoura meyeri, Nemoura variegata)

See STONEFLIES
These stoneflies have a preference for faster water and they are most prolific and of the greatest importance in the north of England. The nymphs are about 9 mm (1/3 inch) long and live on moss-covered stones. The adults, which appear from February to May, have small reddish-brown bodies with brown-grey wings. The head has a distinctive pale bar across the top. The wet fly given below is Roger Fogg's dressing. He also has a dressing for the floating imitation in which the hackle below is replaced with a dun-coloured cock hackle.

Hook: 14
Thread: Red spinner
Body: Reddish-brown seal's fur tied slim

Hackle: Slate-coloured coot, palmered half-way down the body

Early Olives

The early olive is a popular name for the large dark olive. See LARGE DARK OLIVE. Most imitations are known by the latter name, but the following two dressings are known thus.

Early Olive Nymph
(Geoffrey Bucknall)

Hook: 12–14
Thread: Dark grey
Tail: Dark-olive cock fibres
Abdomen: Water-rat or mole fur
Rib: Fine gold wire
Thorax: Dark-olive seal's fur
Wing-case: Waterhen feather fibres
Legs: The ends of the wing-cases divided either side of the thorax

Early Olive Dun *(Roger Woolley)*

Hook: 14
Tail: Fibres of the hackle used
Body: Blue rabbit, water-rat or mole fur
Rib: Gold wire
Hackle: Medium or dark blue-dun cock

Emerged Dun
Plate 25

Expert fly dressing demonstrator Davy Wotton has devised this, his favourite generic pattern for adult dun imitations. Davy regards a representation of the wing as essential. A body in the film is seen by fish from a wider area and probably noticed by fish at a greater depth than one supported wholly above the surface. To copy different species alter the body colour and make slight changes to the wing colour as necessary. The pattern below is a blue-winged olive.

Hook: 16–22 (depending on species) Partridge L3A, L4A, K14ST, E1A
Thread: Danvilles Spider Web or Uni 8/0

Tails: Microfibetts or Cock de Leon tied very long
Body: SLF (Synthetic Living Fibre) dubbing, Oliver Edwards Masterclass No.8
Wings: Davy Wotton FC Softwing dyed BWO shade

EMERGERS

In the last twenty years there has been a proliferation of patterns to represent the hatching nymph or emerging dun. There is no doubt that trout often concentrate on the struggling insect hanging below the surface or in the film or the trapped adults with semi-erect wings. They represent an easy source of food. It is not suprising that fly tyers have turned their attentions to this important stage in the lifecycle. In years gone by I have no doubt that some wet flies and spider patterns were fished just below the surface as emergers, just as many dry flies with their tails below the surface and bodies on the surface are also good imitations of the dun trying to free itself of its nymphal shuck. Many parachute flies hold the body in the film in the manner of a transitional nymph or dun. They all work well enough but the following patterns have been specifically devised for the emerging insect.

Also see under FLYMPHS, SPARKLE DUN EMERGER, HATCHING NYMPH. Also see under SEDGES, MIDGES and MAYFLY for their respective patterns.

A.D. Buoyant
Plate 17

This is a floating agile-darting nymph from Charles Jardine.

Hook: Partridge GRS17MMB size 16–20
Thread: Hot orange or olive
Tail: Three ostrich or emu herl tips dyed mid-olive
Body: Mid-olive Haretron
Thorax: Dark olive dyed grey squirrel body fur

Wing pad: Black ethafoam or plastazote strip
Hackle: Thorax fibres picked out

Balloon Emerger
Plate 29

Roman Moser produced this imitation of the emerger for the moment when it 'blows up its thorax to almost a ball shape. The upper side of the thorax back splits and the wings appear…some fish really concentrate on just this shape and stage of the emerger.' The fly described is a small olive.

Hook: 14–18
Thread: Orange 8/0
Exoskeleton: Point of a cul de canard feather tied rear-facing in the middle of the shank
Abdomen: Two layers of tying thread secured with superglue
Thorax: Thinly dubbed fine olive poly
Blown-up thorax: Five to ten strands of olive, light grey or light brown marabou fibres, tied in by the tips and brought forward over the thorax
Legs: These are created by the rest of the CDC feather after the tip has been used for the exoskeleton. This is laid flat, rear-facing, so that the single herls are sideways. They are pressed close to the fly, tied down and sealed with a small head of thorax dubbing

Cling-Film Emerger
(Shane Jones) *Plate 29*

This was devised for stillwater but I suggest it will work equally well on rivers. Its creator recommends it for the flat calms and cast accurately to fish sipping from the film and fishes it on a long 3 or 4 lb double-strength leader.

Hook: Partridge Emerger K14ST size 20
Body: White silk at the rear, tapering round the bend; olive silk at the front, both with a cling film overbody
Rib: One strand of Danville's white silk
Wing stub: Orange Antron body wool

Hackle: Stiff grizzle in parachute style round the wing-stub base
Thorax: Black seal's fur

Cul De Canard Transitional Dun
Plate 29

René Harrop ties this imitation of the dun with upright wings but still attached to the nymphal shuck. Trout know that here is a helpless insect.

Hook: 12–16
Thread: 6/0 waxed
Tail: Tuft of coarse dubbing to match the nymph colour, tied over three or four turkey hackle fibres
Abdomen: Harrop fine natural dubbing or similar to match the natural
Wing: Two cul de canard feathers
Legs: Butts of the wings tied back along the sides of the fly and clipped even with the back of the abdomen

Davy Wotton Emerger
Plate 28

Davy ties this for the larger upwing species, the Mayfly and particularly the March browns on his native Usk. The design ensures that there is an illusion of bulk at the thoracic region, just like the confused blur of the struggling emerging insect and shuck. The method of tying the body dubbing is given under the S.F. EMERGER in the Sedge section.

Hook: Partridge GRS12ST
Thread: Danville's 6/0
Trail: Small bunch of grizzled marabou, from the tip of the feather
Body: A patch of SLF (Synthetic Living Fibre) about 1½ inches x ½ inch
Rib (optional): Nylon
Wing case: Raffene over the wing, thorax and hackle fibres
Wing: Light shades of long hair from the cheek of a hare's mask, or fine deer hair from the inside leg
Thorax: A darker shade of SLF
Hackle: Grizzle marabou about one inch long (25 mm), coloured to match the natural, bound in at the tip end. Divided

into two equal bunches by the wing-case, the fibres should be secured in a horizontal plane in line with the wings

Delta Wing Emerger
Plate 29

This is an imitation of the struggling dun with its wings spread out as it battles to erect the wings and lift them from the surface. It is Roman Moser's pattern and he fishes it a quarter downstream and imparts slight movement to the fly to imitate the natural's struggle to emerge fully. It is to be fished just under the surface.

Hook: 12–14
Thread: Light brown 6/0
Tail: Tip of a cul de canard feather, tied in flat to imitate the empty shuck
Abdomen: Light brown hare's ear mixed with white Antron or SLF fibres
Wing: Dun-coloured cock hackles in a rear-facing horizontal V
Thorax: As for the abdomen
Wing-case: Pearl Lurex strip (Krystal Hair or Flashabou Pearl) with a rear-facing and slightly upward-pointing 2 mm stub at the back of the thorax

Floating Nymph

There are times when trout definitely express a preference for a nymph in the film or on the surface rather than for just half an inch below the surface. They need to see a clear nymphal shape on the surface. Often a parachute 'dun' will work because it provides a clear body in the film. Sometimes a normal nymph pattern greased to float will work but the following pattern has been specifically devised.

Jardine's Floating Nymph
Plate 28

Hook: 14
Tail: Wood-duck fibres
Body: Dark olive Antron/Hare mix tapering to the rear
Rib: Translucent white yarn

Thorax: A dubbed ball of fine grey poly dubbing
Hackle: Golden-olive cock wound in parachute style round the base of the thorax

Foam Post Emerger — *Plate 28*

This is a highly visible and almost unsinkable emerger from Canadian Paul Marriner. The commercially available foam post is split with scissors and resulting legs tied in fore and aft on top of the shank. Paul ties the hackle by winding it round the post last of all and then, taking a needle, pushes it through the base of the post and inserts the tip of the hackle in the eye of the needle and pulls it through the post. Clip the waste hackle and secure with a little cement or glue in the hole. Other patterns can be adapted by the foam post addition.

Hook: 12–18 slightly long shank Partridge CS28
Tail, abdomen and thorax: To suit the natural
Foam post: Flycraft foam cylinder
Hackle: Cock hackle wound round the base of the post

Halo Emerger — *Plate 28*

Gary LaFontaine devised this after studying the emerging nymph/dun from below the surface. He found that the edges of the splitting nymphal skin glow with an aura of diffused light which he imitates with the use of closed -cell foam. Colour to match the insect.

Hook: 12–16
Thread: Black
Tag: Clear Antron wrapped round the bend
Tail: Marabou fibres
Body: Thinly dubbed seal's fur, thicker at the thorax
Halo: Large closed-cell foam in two short clumps either side of the thorax
Wing: Fluorescent orange dyed deer hair tied sparse, extending over the eye

Hatching Elk

Mogens Espersen's pattern floats in the film and is a caricature of a wide range of hatching duns.

Hook: Mustad 94833 size 12–14
Thread: Brown
Tail: Four or five elk hairs, fairly long
Body: Two grey heron herls, tied in together
Thorax: Mixed furs from a hare's forehead spun in a dubbing loop
Wing: Downy fibres from a partridge body feather

Moser Emerger — *Plate 28*

This blur of materials is both a caddis and an ephemerid emerger, depending upon its colouring and size and which natural flies are on the water. Fish see in it what they want to. The sample shown is tied by Charles Jardine.

Hook: Lightweight dry fly size 12–18 Partridge E6A
Tail: Spade hackle fibres from a jungle cock cape or grizzle hen
Body: Mixed deer hair dubbed, colours to match the natural
Wing: Smoky blue-dun/grey Antron
Hackle: Cul de canard, one and a half turns, clipped short if necessary

Shuck Emerger — *Plate 29*

Shropshire angler Brian Steventon ties this pattern that appears to feature almost all the characteristics of the natural which fish may be keying into: nymphal shuck, abdomen, accentuated thorax, semi-erect wings and legs. It should be colour-matched to the naturals. The tails should well wetted before casting so that the fly sits in the film.

Hook: 14–16
Thread: To match
Shuck: Coloured cul de canard fibres, about 25–30
Abdomen: SLF (Synthetic Living Fibre) ribbed with fine gold wire

Wings and legs: White, coloured or mixed poly yarn to create two stubby slightly rear-tilting wings (create one wing and divide in two). The end fibres are finished off as spread legs after the thorax is dubbed
Thorax: SLF

Soft-Hackle Emerger

This is an American name for the North Country wingless spider which when fished awash in the film is a fair copy of an emerging dun or drowned dun. The Soft-Hackle Emergers are fished dry. Carl Richards wrote that ithis is the deadliest pattern he knows when trout are taking emergers.

Hook: Fine wire 14–16
Thread: To match the body dubbing
Tail: Widely spaced cock hackle fibres
Body: Fine natural or synthetic fur
Hackle: Soft game bird feather or hen hackle

Stillborn Foam Adams   *Plate 28*

Argentinian angler Marcelo Morales has produced this stillborn pattern with a detached abdomen to copy the nymphal shuck. Standard dry fly patterns can be amended in this way. The detached body is tied by tying the tail end of a piece of Furry Foam over a needle, on to which the three tail fibres are tied. The needle is withdrawn and the fibres secured with superglue.

Hook: 12–20
Thread: 8/0 to colour-match the pattern
Tails: Three long and widely spaced Cock de Leon fibres
Shuck: Grey or light brown Furry Foam
Body: Dubbed blue-grey fur
Wing: Grizzle hackle tips in an upright V
Hackle: Natural red and grizzle cocks wound together

Swisher and Richards' Wet Emerger   *Plate 29*

Doug Swisher and Carl Richards devised this versatile emerger for fishing either very wet to imitate those rarer species which eclode below the surface, or in the film as a traditional emerger. Fine wire hooks should be used for the floater, heavier hooks for the wet pattern.

Hook: 14–16
Thread: Olive
Tail: Barred wood duck fibres
Body: Dubbed fur or poly dubbing to match the natural
Wings: Dark-grey hen hackle tips, wide and webby
Legs (optional): Dyed partridge hackle or wood duck fibres to match the natural

Endrick Spider   *Plate 9*

Simple patterns so often turn out to be the best, and the Endrick Spider gives weight to that premise. It is a general pattern devised by John Harwood for salmon and sea trout but it also excels as a general stillwater trout fly. I can vouch for its trout-taking qualities after using it for almost a decade. It is one of those patterns that represent nothing at all, yet it is a fair impression of something aquatic and edible.

Hook: 8–12
Tail: Cock pheasant tail fibre tips
Body: Lead or copper wire underbody covered with cock pheasant tail fibres tapering to the rear
Rib: Copper wire
Hackle: Brown partridge hackle

Enigma

This is an excellent pale watery dun imitation devised by Pat Russell. It is a good riser of trout and grayling. In Pat Russell's own words: 'It is a very good "bringer-upper" for fish which can be seen lying doggo. Sometimes an apparently non-feeding fish can be brought on to the feed after it has been covered five or six times. It is tied palmer-fashion and floats rather well.'

The Enigma is a useful caenis copy, and a slight variation on a pattern being used to represent the caenis is to include a few turns of tying thread on each side of the hackle to represent the thorax.

Hook: 14–18
Thread: Brown
Tail: Pale-cream cock fibres
Body: Cream cock hackle stalk
Hackle: Top-quality glassy pale-cream cock

EPHEMEROPTERA

Unlike most other Orders of flies of interest to fishermen, this group has no common collective name. The term Mayfly is sometimes applied to all the members of the Order, but this leads to confusion with the two species *E. danica* and *E. vulgata*, which are more particularly known as Mayfly. They are sometimes called upwinged duns because of the way the adults carry their wings perpendicularly when at rest. They are of the greatest importance to the fly fisher. Stillwater trout feed to a lesser extent on the nymphs, duns and spinners of the Order, but river trout and grayling consume these species in considerable quantities. Their value to the fly fisherman has never been underestimated, and most of the natural flies the dry-fly fisher attempts to imitate belong to the Order.

All members of the Order, from the caenis, the smallest, to the Mayfly, the largest, have physical characteristics and aspects of their life-cycle in common. The eggs are laid on the surface of the water and immediately sink to the river- or lake-bed, where they stick to stones or weed. The female spinners of the Baetis species, which include the iron blue, medium and dark olives, lay their eggs directly on underwater objects by crawling down reeds and stakes, etc. Depending upon the species, and the water temperature,

the eggs hatch after an incubation period of between a few days and many weeks.

The length of time spent at the nymph stage varies greatly between species. Some remain nymphs for only two to three months, while the Mayfly nymph, *E. danica*, takes up to two years to mature according to some authorities. The time taken is greatly affected by water temperature. Nymphs of the same species hatching from eggs in October may take nine months to mature over a cold winter, but nymphs hatched in the early summer may take only two to five months.

The nymphs generally live on or close to the river-bed. Some, like the Mayfly nymph, burrow in mud, while others, such as the blue-winged olive, crawl along the bottom among weeds and stones. Yet others cling to vegetation. Most nymphs are extremely agile. Some swim in a jerky stop-start motion, others in a steadier, slower movement. Their growth is by a series of moults or a shedding of the outer skin. One species passes through twenty-seven different nymphal stages, but most go through far fewer. Finally the mature nymph is ready to leave its watery habitat to take to the wings which have been forming beneath its skin.

The mature nymph rises to the surface where, temporarily trapped in the surface film, it emerges into its winged state, the dun. (See EMERGERS.) It pauses on the surface while its wings dry. Generally speaking, the warmer the air temperature, the quicker the dun dries and leaves the surface. On cooler, damp days the dun lingers on the surface for some minutes, and in early spring and in autumn the duns often remain on the water for quite a while. Most duns spend between twenty-four and thirty-six hours as sub-imagos, but the caenis has a total adult lifetime of about ninety minutes.

Characteristic features of the adults of the Order are that they carry their wings upright when at rest, and that they have six legs, two or three tails, and a segmented body. They are thus distinguished from any other fly on the water. The dun is, as its name suggests, a rather sombre colour.

Spring or autumn hatches are frequently darker-coloured than the mid-summer hatches of the same species. Additionally, the air temperature on the day of the hatch may affect the colour of the duns; the cooler the air, the darker the colour of fly.

The dun moults and the metamorphosis from sub-imago to imago, from dun to spinner is complete. The legs and tails become longer, the body brighter, and the wings shiny and transparent. The colour of the spinners of a species may vary. The reasons are unclear, but most spinners darken with age, and the females darken after mating, which they do in flight.

The males of most species die over land and are of little interest to the fly fisher, but the females return to the water, on which they lay their eggs. They then die on the surface, and the spent spinners, their wings trapped horizontally in the water, drift downstream to be devoured eagerly by the trout. Spent spinners of the Baetis species are likely to be found below the surface, because the females lay their eggs under water. Such is the sad end to a life-cycle that has been a battle for survival through four different stages.

The species of greater or lesser interest to trout and grayling are listed on pages 214–17. They are examined in more detail elsewhere under their common names. The differences between some species is minimal and evident only on close examination. No trout could determine some of these differences or tell apart the sexes of some species, but I have detailed them to aid identification.

Eskimo Nell   *Plate 13*

Iain Murray-Thomson, creator of the excellent Scottish lure the Honey Bear, also devised this pattern to answer the problem of trout splashing at adult blue damsel lies. Not only is this a good pattern for these circumstances, it also excels as a sea-trout fly on the Spey, Deveron, Dee and Earn and has caught salmon. As a trout fly it is tied on a single hook, for migratory fish on a double or a Waddington with squirrel all round.

Hook: 10–12
Thread: Black 6/0
Tail: Golden pheasant tippet or topping
Body: Electric blue Lurex
Rib: Oval silver or wire on the small sizes
Hackle: Guinea fowl as a beard hackle or badger on the small sizes
Wing: Grey squirrel to show the white tip
Head: Black

Everton Mint   *Plate 9*

This is a Shane Jones stillwater pattern for fishing in Booby style on a sinking line or to be pulled briskly through the waves. It is a pattern that works in difficult circumstances.

Hook: Partridge Stronghold SHI size 10
Tail: Fluorescent white Antron body wool
Tip: Oval silver tinsel
Body: Black and white deer hair in 3 bands
Hackle: Grizzle saddle wound through the body
Head: Black thread, tied small

Faisan et Orange   *Plate 20*

Robert Spiller amended the original Orange et Faisan devised by Frenchman Raymond Rocher. The amended version was tested on the Derbyshire Wye during a Grayling Society day and was hailed as a great success for trout and grayling.

Hook: 12
Thread: Black
Underbody: Fine copper or lead wire
Tail and back: Cock pheasant tail fibres
Body: Orange suede chenille ribbed with gold wire

Feather Duster

This marabou-winged lure probably uses more marabou than other lure, which gives it an unusual action in the water. The bulk of the wing enables the lure to hang in the water, hardly sinking at all. The slowest of retrieves is sufficient to enliven the marabou. The lure can be fished deep and slow, either as an early-season pattern or on those terrible hot, still summer days when fish are hard to come by.

Hook: Long shank 6–8
Thread: To match the wing colour, or red for the white version
Tail and wing: Black, white, orange or yellow marabou. Ten or twelve plumes each with their butt ends spun between wetted finger and thumb into a shuttlecock. The first is tied in just slightly round the bend as the tail. The remainder are tied in over a layer of silk along the back and finished with a varnished head of tying silk

FEBRUARY RED
(Taeniopteryx nebulosa, Brachyptera risi)

See STONEFLIES
For some obscure reason these members of the stonefly Order are also known as Old Joan. The first species is common in parts of the north of England, Scotland, Wales and in the west of England. It is the only stonefly that does not live up to its name, as it prefers to inhabit the vegetation of slower-moving waters. The nymph varies in size between 8 mm and 12 mm.

The adults are between 7 mm and 11 mm and appear from February to April. The female is larger than the male with longer red-brown wings with two dark bands. The last three segments are also red-brown. The second species is similar and common and does inhabit stony-bedded rivers. The adults begin to appear in March and continue into July.

February Red (John Veniard)

A wet pattern.

Hook: 14
Body: Reddish-claret mohair at the tail; remainder lightish-brown mohair.

Wing: Speckled hen wing
Hackle: Dark grizzle-dun cock

February Red (Roger Fogg)

This pattern has its roots in one of Alfred Ronalds' dressings which Roger Fogg has updated. He tells me that it succeeds as an imitation of any of the small brown stoneflies, and that as an early-season pattern it has caught for him larger fish than the more popular patterns, such as the Partridge and Orange. It is recommended as top dropper of a three-fly cast fished upstream.

Hook: 12–14
Thread: Dark orange
Body: Claret and brown seal's fur, dressed slim
Rib: Brown tying thread
Hackle: Woodcock hackle over a third of the body on the wet fly. Reddish-brown cock hackle on the dry fly

February Red

A floating pattern.

Hook: 14
Body: Peacock quill dyed claret
Hackle: Rusty blue-dun cock

F Fly   Plate 25

Marjan Fratnik is largely responsible for the revival of the use of cul de canard feathers now proving popular in trout flies across the world. He has been using this very water-repellent material since the early 1980s. The F Fly series are very simple flies indeed but they are very effective as midge, dun or emerger imitations. The original was tied without any body material at all and the only amendment has been to add a very sparsely dubbed grey body. Other body colours may be used though Marjan Fratnik does not believe it necessary. One feather is used for hooks 18–20, two feathers for size 14–16, and three for size 12.

Hook: 12–20
Thread: Black or grey 8/0 or to match the body colour
Body: Tying thread or very fine dubbing
Hackle and wing: The hackle and wing are combined – cul de canard feathers (see text) trimmed to shape

F Sedge
Plate 31

This is Marjan Fratnik's extension to the cul de canard series to represent various sedges. A remarkable number of similar patterns have been produced since Marjan's original in 1985.

Hook: 12–14 standard or slightly long shank
Thread: Brown
Body: Very fine beige dubbing tied slim
Hackle: Palmered natural red cock
Wing: Two cul de canard feathers, tied slightly longer than the shank

Fiery Brown
Plate 8

With more than 500 years of angling literature on which to look back, it is not surprising that we can trace some of the flies in present use back to their origins centuries ago. Although the Fiery Brown is generally accepted as an Irish lake fly, it is likely that its real origins are English. Courtney Williams suggested that Charles Cotton's seventeenth-century pattern, Bright Brown, might be its ancestor.

In recent years the dressing has been so widely adapted that there is no 'correct' formula. Courtney Williams' pattern has a body of reddish-brown seal's fur. Other sources also give the one body colour, but include a tag of orange floss. A variant has a body with hot-orange seal's fur for the rear third.

It is generally accepted as a sedge imitation but Simon Ashworth suggests that the smaller sizes are excellent in a buzzer hatch with a corresponding body colour. See also Fiery Brown under SEDGES.

Hook: 8–14
Thread: Brown
Tail: Golden pheasant tippets
Body: Fiery brown seal's fur or
Rib: Gold wire or oval gold tinsel
Wing: Bronze mallard
Hackle: Fiery brown

Fishfinder
Plate 4

Theo Bakelaar ties this searching lure. He admits that it is simply a hook, a gold bead and some marabou feathers, but it produces life and movement through the water. The colours and sizes can be varied for the prevailing conditions and species. It also catches salmon and sea trout.
Hook: Mustad long shank 5263 size 2–8
Thread: Black
Tail: Marabou fibres with a few optional strands of Flashabou or similar
Legs/wings: Marabou fibres in two colours wound as a hackle, one in front of the other
Head: 5 mm gold bead

FISH FRY

In the latter half of the season on many stillwaters trout search the margins for shoals of fry, minnows and other small fish. It is not uncommon to see a commotion in the water, with small fish jumping out and the wake of trout chasing them. Another tell-tale sign that a shoal of fry is about might be seagulls swooping over the area of the shoal and feeding on the fry. The larger brown trout of many fisheries often fall to a suitable imitation at the end of the season. Trout feed on small fish throughout the year and an imitation has always a chance of success. Suggested artificials include ALEVIN, MUDDLERS, CHURCH FRY, PERCH FRY, APPETISER, MINNOW STREAMER, POLYSTICKLE and WHITLOCK MATUKA SCULPIN.

Floating Fritz Fry
Plate 5

This Lureflash fry imitation was responsible for the downfall of the record wild rainbow trout of 29 lbs 12 oz, caught by Andrew MacIntyre from Loch Tay. The Lureflash Fritz is available in a wide range of colours.

Hook: Long shank 10
Thread: Black
Tail: As for the body
Back: White 5 mm Ethafoam or Plastazote cut to shape with a V in the tail
Body: Mother of Pearl Lureflash Fritz
Head: Black

Pearly Pin Fry

This is a useful pattern to imitate the tiniest of fry although it can also be tied on larger hooks. It is best cast into the areas where trout are seen to be hitting the fry. Try letting the fly rest without retrieval; alternatively it can be stripped back quickly.

Hook: 8–12
Thread: White
Tail: Two green cock hackle tips
Body: Pearly Mylar
Wing: Green cock hackle fibres extending just past the hook bend
Head: White thread with black eyes

Plushille Fry   *Plate 5*

This unusual material has been developed by Roman Moser and produces excellent, realistic small fish imitations. Full instructions for using the material come with each packet.

Hook: Long shank 2–8
Thread: White
Eyes: Krystal glass eyes 5–7 mm
Tail and body: Plushille trimmed to shape and brushed with Velcro
Colouring: Pantone pens

Flashabou Pretty Dog

A lure devised by professional fly tyer Dave Tait, of Gloucestershire. It has attained widespread popularity among reservoir fishers. Flashabou and similar materials are now being incorporated into other lures.

Dave Tait says of his lure: 'The Flashabou Pretty Dog is an improved version of a lure called the Pretty Dog which I developed during 1981. The original pattern had a marabou tail with a chenille body and bead-chain eyes. During 1983, I obtained a new material called Flashabou from America. It is in fact a fine, limp tinsel and it was incorporated in the Pretty Dog. Flashabou comes in many colours, and it was obvious that it had a great deal to offer.

'Pretty Dog lures were the first UK lures to incorporate Flashabou, and during the first trials some very good catches were made from South Cerney's Rainbow Lake. During the long, hot summer of 1983 Flashabou took a number of trout at times when other lures were catching nothing. Fish of 9 lb 13 oz, 8 lb 12 oz and 6 ½ lb were taken during a four-day spell at South Cerney.

'During 1984, a fuller appreciation of the lure's potential was gained. For instance, a seven-fish bag was taken at Chew Valley lake, the best of which was 7 lb-plus. Trout and salmon fell to the Flashabou Pretty Dog. A 9 lb-plus brown trout was taken at Rutland on it only a matter of weeks after the fly was introduced nationally. I also took three 8 lb rainbows during one busy day at a small fishery called Brook Farm in Gloucestershire.

'Yellow Pretty Dogs were the original flies of that name, and this is my favourite lure colour.

'I always fish the Pretty Dog on a sinking line, because I can then fish all the water layers. Floating lines do produce fish, but I think that correct depth and possibly better presentation is gained by using a sinking line. The lure should be fished slowly, because stripping tends to destroy its action. Slow-retrieving gives that undulating flashing of the Flashabou tail that trout find so irresistible.

'I would suggest that a mix of colours is advisable in the tail. Two or three colours of Flashabou combined with the marabou tail give a nice flashing colour spectrum.'

Hook: 6–8
Thread: To match the body colour
Tail: Marabou plus strands of Flashabou, the colour of your choice
Body: Coloured chenille
Rib: Oval silver tinsel
Eyes: Bead-chain from a sink-plug chain

Tinsel strips can be used effectively as an alternative to Flashabou. These are not as soft and as mobile as Flashabou, but they do provide a workable and cheaper alternative.

Fledermaus Nymph

This was originally an American lake trout pattern devised by Jack Schneider. It has become more widely used, also on rivers. It does not resemble a standard nymph type for rivers but it can work very well. It should be fished in a straight drift.

Hook: Long shank 12–16
Thread: Brown
Body: Muskrat body fur of mixed-length fibres tied to look very shaggy
Wing: Grey squirrel tail about the same length as the shank

Flue Brush   Plate 9

This is an interesting fly devised by Lynn Francis. It is easy to see how the name originated, but what the trout take it to be I'm at a loss to say. It fishes well in August and September as an ungreased point fly in a wave.

Hook: 8–12
Thread: Brown
Body: Palmered white, green and red hackles
Rib: Fine copper wire

Flymphs

Between the sub-surface mature nymph and the adult dun on the surface is an intermediate stage when, in the surface film, the wingless nymph changes in a matter of seconds into the winged dun. At this critical and vulnerable moment, the nymphs/duns become attractive targets for feeding fish. Various patterns have been devised to represent this important stage. This series of aptly named flies was devised by an American, V. S. Hidy, to imitate the struggling insect emerging through the surface film. All his patterns are wingless and use soft-to-medium hen hackles, unless they are intended for use on turbulent water, when a stiffer hackle is needed. All the hackles are tied rear-slanting. The fly bodies are tapered from body fur spun between two strands of tying silk. For the detailed patterns see under IRON BLUE, TUP'S INDISPENS-ABLE, BLUE-WINGED OLIVE.

Partridge Flymph   Plate 29

Danish angler Mogens Espersen devised this combining the best of the Gold-Ribbed Hare's Ear and the Flymph design. It is fished upstream to bulging fish. The hackle may be wound with the tip tied in first, with the good side facing the eye, and then wound backwards towards the body. The thread can be secured behind the hackle to ensure it has a 'kick' or wound through to the eye. The hackle may also be wound Stewart-style semi-palmered down the front of the body.

Hook: 14–16 Partridge GRS2A (for a heavier fly) or L2A (for a lighter fly)
Thread: Light orange
Tail: Summer duck or substitute
Body: Mixed hairs from the base of a hare's ear or lighter from a hare's mask, spun in a dubbing loop
Rib: Finest oval gold
Hackle: Soft, well marked partridge

Fog Black   Plate 32

This was one of T. E. Pritt's patterns which, without the wing, was known as the Little Black. In addition to being a fair trout fly and black gnat copy, it is also an excellent grayling fly. Indeed, Pritt considered this to be his favourite top dropper for the species. Some fly fishers may scorn the use of so old a pattern, but a number of grayling fishers of my acquaintance, some with more than forty years' experience on nothern streams, rate this fly highly. Fog is the name given in upper Wharfedale to the short lush grass which grows after haymaking, and the small black member of the Diptera Order which inhabits the grass often finds its way on to the water.

Hook: 12–14
Body: Dark purple silk or thread
Rib: Magpie or ostrich herl
Wing: Starling wing quill as a substitute for the bullfinch originally specified
Hackle: Starling neck feather

Footballer

This midge-pupa imitation devised by Geoffrey Bucknall was probably the first of the more modern style of buzzer dressing. It was originally tied for Blagdon reservoir in the 1960s. The original pattern used black horsehair, but red, green, orange, brown, olive and claret have followed and the materials have been revised. No breathing filaments were tied on the original, but they have been added since. The name developed from the original black-and-white striped pattern, which looked like a football strip. Perhaps the ideal fly to fish in a team! Geoffrey Bucknall's revised dressing is as follows:

Hook: 8–16 standard or caddis hook
Tail: White fluorescent floss
Body: Stripped black and white hackle stalks wound side by side from about half-way round the bend. They should be wound from the tips, so that the body thickens towards the thorax
Thorax: Grey seal's fur
Head: Two turns of bronze peacock herl
Breathing tubes: A tuft of white fluorescent floss forward over the eye

Footprint Dun   *Plate 25*

The six legs of the natural adult dun on the water when viewed from below the surface create six dimples of light in the film. Sometimes it is simply the sight of this light pattern that is the trigger to the rise. After the fish's interest has been stimulated by the light pattern it may require a clear view of the wings or body, or both, to be persuaded to feed. Oliver Edwards has created the Footprint Dun to provide a realistic light pattern by the spread legs. A clear view of the wing and body is also offered. Use an appropriate colour and size to match the naturals.

Hook: 12–20 Partridge E1A or E4A
Thread: Danville's Spiderweb Pantoned to match the dressing
Tails: Microfibetts, one, two or three on either side. One for size 20's, two for size 16–18, three for size 12–14, colour to match the tail or legs of the natural
Wings: Ultrazine multifibred poly yarn, tied in loop fashion, three-quarters to once body length, colour to match the natural
Legs: Butt ends of the Microfibetts fixed at right angles to the body, a third to half the body length
Abdomen and thorax: Fine synthetic dubbing

Fore-and-Aft

This is not a pattern of fly so much as a style of dressing a dry fly developed on the Piscatorial Society's waters on the Kennet by Horace Brown earlier this century. In addition to the head hackle, a slightly smaller hackle, often of a different colour, is wound in at the rear of the body. This causes the fly to float with its body well clear of the surface, resting only on the hackle tips and imitating the natural upwinged fly, of which only the legs would be on the water. Also see JANUS and RENEGADE.

Fraser Nymphs   *Plate 16*

Professional fly dresser Gordon Fraser, more famous for his Booby series, also devised these two highly regarded stillwater nymphs. The first, simply known as the Fraser Nymph is a very good pattern for when any pale insects are hatching. The Olive version works when pond and lake olives and olive buzzers are about. Note how extremely slim they are tied, just like the agile-darting natural nymphs and slim midge pupae. The Olive Fraser Nymph is as below except for a rib of olive green thread and a thorax of fine olive fur-dyed olive moleskin is recommended.

Hook: Long shank 10–12 or nymph hook size 10–14
Thread: Fawn
Tail: Centre or side fibres from a hen pheasant tail
Body: Hen pheasant tail ribbed with fawn thread
Thorax: Fine beige fur
Wing-case and legs: Hen pheasant tail fibres. The legs are formed by bending back the tips of the wing-case fibres

Freeman's Fancy

Courtney Williams records the inventor of this lake fly as Captain W. Freeman, who first tied it about 1900. Williams rated it highly: 'No other fly can approach it' when a brightly-coloured pattern is required. Stillwater fishing has developed dramatically since Williams wrote that, but winged wet flies in the traditional style are still popular and catch thousands of trout each season.

Hook: 8–12
Tail: Orange toucan or substitute
Body: Flat gold tinsel
Wing: Brown mallard with jungle cock cheeks
Hackle: Magenta cock or hen

Frog Nobblers

See NOBBLERS

FROGS

This unlikely food source has been imitated by the following pattern from Taff Price. It should be fished close to the surface. Although I have read reports of big trout taking frogs, I have never seen one do so, despite fishing frequently at two lakes which, during spring, seem to have more frogs than trout. Perhaps the Frog would succeed as a pike fly.

Hook: Long shank 4–6
Body: Clipped deer hair tied fairly bulky and coloured with indelible felt-pens, green on top and yellow underneath
Legs: Two sets of legs widely divided at the front and rear of the body. Green bucktail for the front, and yellow for the rear; or a mixture of both for both sets of legs

Funnelduns   Plate 25

Neil Patterson's Funnelduns were evolved from the thinking behind John Goddard's and Brian Clarke's USD Paraduns, in that he realised the basic idea of the bend of a dry-fly hook facing downwards was second best to having a fly that would float with the hook upside down, point in the air and beyond a trout's view. Neil modestly says that the dexterity needed for the USD Paraduns was beyond him and he set about devising an easier alternative. He wrote in *Trout Fisherman* magazine:

'In the beginning, the Funneldun set out to put to rights three basic design faults I believed afflicted the traditional dry-fly tying method. First, that dry flies require the sort of quality cock hackle that I couldn't find. And when I did, couldn't afford. Second, that the traditional mounting of the hackle at right-angles to the shank ingeniously helped the fly to sink. In this 90-degree position, the full weight of the hook and fly bears down on the needle-sharp hackle-point piercing the surface skin. Third, that in the trout's window, the natural's thorax in outline – clearly visible from an underwater tank vantage – is absent on the traditional dry-fly pattern.

It was while experimenting with how to mount the hackle so that the fly is supported on a broader base that the idea of 'funnelling'' the hackles over the eye – therefore offering up the flattened edge of the hackle flues to the surface – first came about.

'Tying-in a standard small dry-fly hackle at the eye and pulling it forward made the fly too long in profile. And winding the silk over the roots of the flues to hold them in position shortened the hackle, leaving me with prickly stubs.

'To overcome this problem, I experimented by winding in the hackle a third of the way down the hook-shank, not at the head, using larger hackles than those you'd use to dress a dry fly Halford fashion. By using these longer hackles, I found I was no longer dependent on capes that sported a luxurious spread of tiny hackles. Instead, I was plucking feathers from an area on a cape rarely used by dry-fly dressers - the zone you'd reach if (God forbid) you were to tie your olives on size 8s or 10s. Even a ten bob Indian cock cape has a super-abundance of these. And I had a stack of these in a bottom drawer.

'The drawback about these hackles is that, although the points and stems of each individual flue are as sharp and as bright as a top-grade Metz, at the foot of the flue, where it meets the stalk, they seem to wear woolly socks. They have fuzzy, flimsy bases. This, I discovered, softens when the fly gets wet or a fish crunches it, causing the hackle to lose its spring and shape and collapse pathetically along the body.

'However by "funnelling" them forward, and winding turns of silk over the roots to hold them sloping over the eye, you cover the woolly bases up, leaving the crisp, sharp stems to support the fly, flues that won't fold up under stress. To keep these "funnelled" hackles at 45 degrees over the eye, like an umbrella part blown out by the wind, I dubbed on a lump of fur in front of the hackle, in the vacant third between the hackle and the eye.

One thing led to another, logically and naturally. I was now tying grade A dry flies from streamer capes. I had broadened the base of the fly where hackle meets surface, taking the weight off the pin-prick hackle-points. I had added a thorax which, as well as giving the fly a more realistic outline, also served an important function. And I had added it in exactly the place it is on the natural, in front of the wings at the head. Since the Funneldun is a system, a method of tying a dry fly – and not a pattern – you can tie any fly you like, even patterns of your own making.

'Because the hackles protrude slightly in front of the Funneldun, making it a little longer than if it were tied by the conventional method, if I want a size 14 fly, I tie it on a 16. For a 16, I tie on an 18, and so on. This is a bonus. It means the hook is smaller and lighter in proportion to the fly-size. With less iron to carry, the Funnelduns float like balsa wood. And I don't add ribbing as extra ballast aboard.

'Don't be terrified of whip-finishing at the tail. It's easier than at the head. There's no wing or hackle to get in the way. When you tie in the the tail, tie it a little way round the bend, but not too much, otherwise the fly will rest on the body, rather than on the tail tips. After your first effort, you'll get to judge this distance according to the hooks you use.

'While the fly is still in the vice, cut out a small "V", by clipping off a few small hackle flues at the base, from the top-side of the hackle. This will be the underside of the fly when you chuck it on the table and it flips monotonously upside down.'

If you insist on adding wings, Neil suggests that feather-fibre wings are the best and recommends the breast feathers of teal, widgeon or mallard.

'Take the breast feather and peel off the flues, leaving the tip. Secure this lightly on the underside of the hook after you've tied in the dubbed thorax. Pulling the stem through the loose turns of silk, judge the height of the wings. Then figure-of-eight round the base to hold the wing upright. I like to let it slope slightly forward towards the eye. Clip the butt and continue the Funneldun as prescribed.

'The Funneldun allows me to fish upside-down flies without turning me inside out at the vice. It allows me to fish upside-down flies all the time to every fish.'

Furnace
Plate 26

This is an old southern chalk-stream dry fly which F. M. Halford described as 'a very favourite hot-weather pattern'. Despite this, I doubt whether I would have included it here had I not read that Dave Collyer found it to be an 'excellent winter grayling fly'.

Hook: 14–16
Thread: Light brown
Tail (optional): Furnace cock fibres
Body: Orange floss
Rib: Peacock sword feather herl
Hackle: Furnace cock

G.E. Nymph
Plate 17

A slim, agile-darting nymph imitation from Charles Jardine. It represents all such nymph types and is a very useful river patterns as well as being a useful imitation of the pond and lake olive nymphs. The G.E. Hatching Nymph differs with the addition of two black goose biots tied in behind the thorax pointing towards the bend. These are then clipped into paddle shapes, representing the embryonic wings.

Hook: TMC 921 size 12–18
Thread: Olive micro
Underbody: Weight at the thorax
Tail: Three summer duck or fibres dyed olive
Body: Olive goose cosset or dyed pheasant tail
Rib: Extra fine silver wire
Thorax: Dubbed squirrel fur dyed olive
Throat hackle: Summer duck or dyed olive or gold
Shellback: Summer duck dyed black or any dark feather fibre

The Gerroff
Plate 19

John Goddard created this pattern for small, clear stillwaters and clear, slow-moving rivers. Its first outing accounted for two limit bags of twelve trout totalling 49 lb for two rods. The fly was so named because unwanted smaller fish took the slow-sinking fly time and again before larger fish took it. The fly was christened by the angler shouting 'Gerroff'. John Goddard suggests that its success is due to the small body on a large hook which allows the fly to sink slowly, which trout seem to find irresistible.

Hook: 10–14 slightly longer shank than standard
Body: Mixed olive-brown and pink seal's fur (three parts to one) tied on the front half of the shank
Back: A strip of olive-dyed PVC over the top of the body

Ghosts

A series of streamer lures from the USA which, suprisingly, are still fairly popular in the UK.

Badger Ghost

Hook: Long shank 6–8
Tail: Yellow or orange hackle fibres
Body: Black floss
Rib: Embossed silver tinsel
Throat hackle: Yellow or orange hackle fibres
Wing: Four dark badger hackles

Black Ghost
Plate 3

Tail: Golden pheasant crest fibres
Body: Black wool
Rib: Silver tinsel
Throat hackle: Golden pheasant crest fibres or yellow hackle
Wing: Four white hackles with jungle cock cheeks

Gimriver Duns
Plate 25

These are two duns (same design, different colours) from Lars Olsson. Their success in copying newly emerged duns, especially Baetis and Ephemerella species, has been proved in Scandinavia, Britain and North America. They are based on the Catskill design which Lars has improved on by placing the wing and hackle more naturally closer to the middle of the shank. It is tied in olive or grey shades.

Hook: Tiemco TMC 13–19
Thread: Olive or grey
Tail: Four Microfibetts, in two 45-degree groups
Body: Olive-green dyed or grey natural fur, with a couple of turns in front of the hackle
Wing: A single bunch of male mallard mottled breast fibres
Hackle: Blue-dun cock wound over the thorax and with a V clipped from the underside

Ginger Quill

For more than a hundred years a fly of this name has been representing the pale watery and lighter olive duns. Some of the earlier patterns had upright wings, but more recent dressings omit these in favour of an optional blue-dun hackle at the head, in front of the ginger.

Hook: 14
Thread: Brown
Tail: Ginger cock hackle fibres
Body: Natural or lightly dyed well marked peacock quill
Hackle: Ginger cock

Ginger Spinner

The Ginger Spinner is a general spinner imitation suitable for representing a variety of natural upwinged spinners on rivers. This particular dressing was devised by G. E. M. Skues.

Hook: 14–16
Tail: Pale sandy-dun cock fibres
Body: Pale-orange seal's fur on hot-orange tying thread
Rib: Gold wire
Hackle: Pale sandy-dun cock

Girdle Bug

Also known as Rubber Legs. This American nymph (?) bug (?) lure (?) has found its way on to some English reservoirs. Who knows what it is taken for but I'm told they sometimes work. When they first arrived in the UK I tried one out on Leighton reservoir where the largest trout that I've seen in my life followed it and turned away. A few days later a 17 lb trout was caught from the same spot. Had that fish taken my fly I might be more inclined towards them.

Hook: Long shank 8–14
Legs, tail and antennae: Black, grey or white rubber legs
Body: Coloured chenille (often black or grey) sometimes with a fluorescent butt

Glowstickle

This is a Richard Walker variant of his own Polystickle. The luminescence is activated by shining a torch over the fly. The fly is particularly good when fished at dusk.

Hook: Long shank 6–8
Body: Luminous plastic strip, wound to produce a carrot-shaped body
Tail: White cock hackle fibres
Hackle: Sparsely tied white cock
Head: Black tying silk

Goddard's Last Hope   Plate 26

This is John Goddard's imitation of the pale watery dun. It is also effective when other small flies are on the surface, including the caenis.

Hook: Fine wire 16–18
Tail: At least six of the hackle fibres
Body: Pale-yellow tying thread overlaid with buff condor herl or Norwegian goose breast feather fibres. Light-coloured herls are used for the early season and dark grey from mid-June onwards
Hackle: Short-fibred dark honey-dun cock

Goddard's Red or Green Larva

Few angling writers have influenced fly fishers over the last thirty years as much as John Goddard, and it is fitting that this book includes a number of his more widely used patterns. This is his imitation of the large midge larvae found in the muddy lake or reservoir bottom. He suggests that it is best fished by allowing it to rest on the bottom and giving the line an occasional slight twitch.

Hook: Long shank 8–12
Thread: Brown
Tail: Red ibis quill or substitute about 12 mm (½ inch) long from the curly section, or the curved tip, of a cock hackle dyed red or green
Body: Crimson or olive condor herl covered with fluorescent floss of the same colour
Rib: Narrow silver Lurex
Thorax: Buff condor herl

Goat's Toe   Plate 6

This Irish pattern has become more widespread in its use, also as a salmon and sea-trout fly on the West Coast lochs of Scotland. The original dressing had a red floss body ribbed with peacock herl but John Kennedy of the South Uist Estates improved and strengthened it by ribbing a herl body with red wool. Stan Headley includes a fluorescent floss ribbing and tail with a bottle green peacock hackle as opposed to the metallic blue of the original. His variant has succeeded in such diverse venues as Rutland, Blythfield, Leven and many Highland and Orkney lochs.

Hook: 10–12 or long shank 12 for salmon and sea trout
Thread: Black
Butt: One turn medium flat gold
Tag: Fluorescent red wool
Body: Two strands of bronze peacock herl, one wound up the shank, one down, ribbed with four strands of GloBrite No. 5, twisted

Hackle: Bottle green peacock neck feather (one and a half times the body length). A bolstering black hen hackle may be optionally tied to support the peacock hackle.

Golden Olive

A number of Irish lough patterns have become established lake flies in the UK, and the Golden Olive is one of the better known. It is a useful general pattern, particularly when lake olives are about. Michael Rogan, son of the original tyer of the fly, suggests that the body colour is improved by using a mixed dubbing of 3:1 yellow and orange seal's fur.

Hook: 8–12
Tail: Golden pheasant crest feather
Body: Golden-olive seal's fur
Rib: Oval gold tinsel
Wing: Brown mallard flank feather
Hackle: Golden-olive cock or Rhode Island Red cock

Goldheads   Plate 18

In central Europe just after the turn of the century fly fishers were using glass or metal beads on their flies. In isolated pockets the practice continued while the rest of the fly-fishing world remained in ignorance and with our fish count much lower. A decade ago Austrian Roman Moser and others, notably Theo 'Mr Goldbead' Bakelaar from Holland, gave these a great deal of publicity. Now it seems that a gold or silver bead has been adapted to every subsurface fly that is known. I have even seen gold bead versions of North Country spider patterns. The prefix Goldhead or Gold Bead to a named pattern means that the original dressing has been amended by the addition of the bead. The two most important advantages of the gold bead are that it provides weight, and underwater the gold or silver bead looks like an air bubble, ideal for imitating a sedge pupa. Two lesser aspects are that because the weight is at the front of the fly it will sink head first and can be jigged. The bright colour often is an attraction. Goldheads enable nymphs to be fished on faster, deeper rivers where previously anglers would have great difficulty in reaching the bottom feeding zones.

In addition to the usual gold or silver beads, copper beads are also available. I have taken to using these on some of my patterns after Charles Jardine related how on the clear waters of the River Traun the grayling shoals would sometimes part to let a Goldhead pattern through but that a copper bead version was eagerly taken. In clear water or bright sunlight I now opt for copper bead patterns like the COPPER SQUIRREL.

Goldie

This bucktail lure was created by Bob Church in 1976. It was originally tied for the brown trout of Rutland. Bob comments: 'They love it.' He recommends a tandem version for use on a lead-core line from a boat.

Hook: Long shank 6–10
Tail: Yellow hackle fibres
Body: Gold tinsel
Rib: Gold wire
Wing: Yellow goat or skunk hair with black goat or skunk hair over
Throat hackle: Yellow hackle fibres
Head: Black varnish

Gold-Ribbed Hare's Ear

A fly with origins way back beyond the last century. Whether fished as a nymph or a floater, it is an excellent medium olive or dark olive copy, and as a general impressionist nymph and dun it probably has no peer. It is a killer wherever olives hatch, whether on river or stillwater.

It was originally tied without a hackle, with merely the body fibres picked out for legs. The wings were a-late-nineteenth century addition. No matter how one chooses to fish the fly, and with which dressing, it is one of the few really dependable patterns. It is taken also for a

sedge pupa when fished just in or below the surface. Although Halford later discarded the fly, probably because it was just too nondescript for his liking, he believed it to be the most killing pattern used on southern chalk-streams in his time. Many writers over the years have described the wingless version as one of the best-ever nymph-suggesting imitations.

A Hare's Ear or Hare's Lug is known throughout the country with minor variations in the dressing. A Gold-Ribbed Hare's Ear with a gold bead head has become a very successful river trout and grayling pattern. Also see RED TAG HARE'S EAR.

Gold-Ribbed Hare's Ear
Plate 29

Hook: 12–18
Tail (optional): Three long body strands
Body: Dark fur from the base of a hare's ear spun on yellow tying thread
Rib: Flat gold tinsel
Legs: Long body fibres picked out
A hackled version can be tied with a rusty blue-dun cock or hen.

Gold-Ribbed Hare's Ear Palmer
Plate 9

This pattern of Dave Shipman's works well from May onwards when the green buzzers are hatching. It is usually fished as a middle dropper and rarely requires Ginking as the palmer hackle keeps it afloat. Its creator comments that it is an ideal point fly with other dries on the droppers. The hare's mask tail represents the trailing shuck.

Hook: Kamasan B100 gold-coloured
Tail: White hare's mask
Body: Hare's ear fur with a palmered badger hackle
Rib: Fine gold wire
Thorax: Orange seal's fur with a few loose fibres trailing into the hackle
Thorax cover: Dark brown feather fibre

Gold Bead Hare's Ear Shaggy

Plate 18

Like all gold bead variants they fish deep with the bead giving a suggestion of an air bubble within a pupal skin. The weight at the front of the hook makes it possible to jig the fly with movement. This is one of Theo Bakelaar's patterns. Its materials are mobile and impart some life to the fly.

Hook: 10–12 Tiemco 3761
Thread: Brown
Bead: 4 mm for size 10; 3 mm for size 12
Tail: Bunch of rabbit/fox fur
Body: Hare's ear fur, also wound between the hackle and the bead
Rib: Fine gold tinsel
Hackle: Mottled hen

American Gold-Ribbed Hare's Ear

Only the Americans could tie this nymph pattern without actually using any hare's ear fur. Peter Lapsley tells me that he uses this as an imitation of the lake olive nymph and comments that it is 'one of the most deadly patterns I know.'

Hook: 12–14
Thread: Black or brown
Tail: Hare's body hair
Body: Hare's body hair
Rib: Oval gold tinsel
Thorax: Hare's body hair with some strands picked out for legs
Wing-case: Dyed black turkey-tail fibres

Orange Gold-Ribbed Hare's Ear

Plate 8

Since Tom Saville devised this it has become his first choice point fly for reservoir fishing from boat or bank. When the fish are really 'on it' he adds a smaller unweighted version on the middle dropper. Normally it is fished with a slow figure-of-eight retrieve off the bank but it also catches when loch-style pulling. The tail colours can be altered to suit conditions; see Fluorescence in the Glossary.

Hook: Kamasan B830 size 10–14
Thread: Orange monocord
Tail: Tuft of Glo-Brite floss, shade 3, 4, 5, 7, 12 or 16
Rib: Fine oval gold
Body: Dubbed with a blend of two-thirds hare's body fur and one -hird orange Antron fibres

Gordon

The Gordon and Quill Gordon are both North American flies named after their creator, Theodore Gordon, the father-figure of American fly fishing. Few dry-fly fishers across the breadth of North America fail to give space in the fly box for these patterns. Both are excellent general flies taken for a variety of naturals. Over the last seventy years these have become the most famed of all American trout flies. Various dressings have appeared in print, largely because Gordon varied the dressings to match the different species hatching. I believe the dressings given are close to the original.

Hook: 12–14
Tail: Speckled mandarin flank fibres (brown mallard as a substitute)
Body: Gold floss silk
Rib: Gold tinsel
Wing: Bunched speckled mandarin flank fibres
Hackle: Badger cock
A wet version is sometimes tied with a hen hackle and a flat gold tinsel tip.

Quill Gordon

Plate 24

Hook: 12–14
Tail: Three summer duck feather fibres (brown mandarin)
Body: Dark stripped bi-coloured peacock quill (for spring use); lighter-coloured quill for summer use
Wing: Summer-duck feather-fibres set upright
Hackle: Smoke-grey cock, or dark-blue

dun (spring use); or pale honey-dun (summer)

Mallard fibres with a brownish-olive tinge make a good substitute for summer duck.

Grafham Grey Lure

A three-hook tandem lure devised by Tom Saville.

Rear hook
Tail: Golden pheasant crest
Body: Grey fur or wool
Rib: Silver wire

Middle hook
Body and rib: As for the rear hook

Front hook
Body and rib: As for the rear hook
Wing: Two badger cock hackles tied back to back
Cheek: Jungle cock
Hackle: Badger

GRASSHOPPER

The Americans have produced some lifelike imitations of the natural grasshopper. Laying one in my hand, I almost expect it to leap into the air with a click of its heels. I doubt if quite so realistic an imitation is needed, and I think the two patterns given will be sufficient for the rare occasions on which you may feel obliged to fish an imitation. If, like me, you have no experience of using them, I suggest you try the one you find easiest to tie.

Green Grasshopper   *(Taff Price)*

Hook: Long shank Mayfly 12
Thread: Green
Body: Clipped deer hair coloured green with an indelible felt-pen
Wing: Swan dyed green
Legs: Two cock pheasant tail fibres
Head: Bronze ostrich herl

A brown version is tied with a brown-coloured deer hair body, oak turkey wings and a brown ostrich herl head.

Grasshopper   *(Richard Walker)*

Hook: Long shank 8
Body: Fine-grain polythene foam, split and glued to the shank and trimmed to shape
Back: Brown Raffene or pheasant tail fibres
Legs: Two swan primary feather fibres dyed medium brown and tied one on each side of the head
Beard hackle: Eight to ten pheasant tail fibres tied short

GRAVEL BED
(Hexatoma fuscipennis)

See DIPTERA

A member of the Diptera Order, this flat-winged terrestrial lives in its pupal state in gravel or sand-beds at the edges of rivers. Their closeness to the water inevitably means that some of the adults end up on the river, and they can often be seen swarming over the surface. The adult is delicate and looks like a small crane-fly. Its body is brownish-grey with two heavily veined brownish wings. It appears on warm days from late April until early June. Northern fly fishers particularly find the imitation of value. See also CLYDE SANDFLY.

Gravel Bed   Plate 20

A wet pattern.

Hook: 12–14
Thread: Purple
Body: Stripped peacock sword feather quill with the tying silk exposed at the shoulder
Wing: Hen pheasant tail fibres, laid almost flat along the back
Hackle: Long-fibred black cock

Gravel Bed   *(Roger Fogg)*

A dry fly with a parachute hackle.

Hook: 12–14

Thread: Lead-coloured or grey silk well waxed with dark wax
Body: Lead-coloured tying silk with a thorax of mole fur
Hackle: Good-quality black cock tied so that the shiny side faces upwards and the fibres bend downwards

Grayling Fiddler

Although Eric Horsfall Turner was not a prolific angling writer, the exceptional quality of his work made up for this. His book, *An Angler's Cavalcade*, is well worth reading. He spent much of his life fishing the streams of North Yorkshire and one of his great loves was the autumn grayling. I once had the pleasure of sitting next to Eric at an angling dinner. During the meal he produced a small box of flies and among the Eric's Beetles were a couple of Grayling Fiddlers. They were beautifully tied and looked just right for difficult grayling. Sadly, despite a few hints from me, they all remained in his fly box. I have tried the pattern on odd occasions and always caught fish.

Hook: 18
Body: Brown tying thread taken round the bend just short of the barb and dubbed with red wool or DRF floss.
Hackle: Small grizzle cock

Grayling Steel Blue

An excellent grayling fly created by Roger Woolley. It can be fished wet or dry. My preference is dry. This pattern is effective wherever grayling are found, not just on the Derbyshire streams that Woolley fished.

Hook: 14
Body: Peacock herl tied thin
Rib: Gold wire through the hackle
Tip: Three turns of orange tying thread and a tiny tip of silver tinsel
Hackle: Palmered bright-blue grizzle cock

GREAT RED SPINNER

The great red spinner is the name given to the female spinners of the late March brown, March brown and autumn dun. These are two patterns to represent them.

Great Red Spinner (*J. R. Harris*)

Hook: 12–14
Thread: Claret
Tail: Dark rusty-dun cock fibres
Body: Dark red or claret seal's fur
Rib: Gold wire
Hackle: Dark rusty-dun cock tied half-spent

Great Red Spinner (*Roger Woolley*)

Hook: 12–14
Tail: Natural red cock fibres
Body: Red seal's fur
Rib: Gold wire
Wings: Two medium-blue cock hackle tips or hackle fibre bunches, tied spent
Hackle: Natural red cock

Green and Orange Nymph

I have found this small nymph of use on small weedy lakes in mid-summer. By fishing it close to the weeds, one can take fish seeking refuge in the shade offered from the summer heat.

Hook: 12–14
Thread: Orange
Tail: Pheasant tail fibres
Body: Green ostrich herl
Rib: Fine silver wire
Thorax: Orange seal's fur
Wing-case: Pheasant tail fibres

Green DF Partridge

Richard Walker created this fluorescent, bug-like pattern for trout and grayling in rivers and stillwaters. It is probably taken for a range of larvae and other food items On a number of rivers the bigger fish spend most of their time close to the bottom. The weighted version is ideal for fishing to them.

Hook: 10–16
Body: Optional underbody of lead-foil strips; lime-green fluorescent wool tied fat
Rib: Silver thread
Hackle: Sparse brown partridge
Head: Black varnished tying thread

Green Insect   *Plate 22*

Principally a grayling fly, this is also a useful green aphis imitation. It is fished wet or dry. The red tag is common to a number of grayling flies. Its inclusion is important and similar flies without the flash of red often fail when those with some red in the dressing are catching fish. Red has been proved to be a stimulus to many members of the animal kingdom. The grayling is no exception.

Hook: 14–16
Tag: Red wool or floss
Body: Bright green peacock herl
Hackle: Small grey or blue-dun cock or hen

Green Peter   *Plate 8*

There is a sedge that hatches on Irish loughs during July and August known as the Green Peter (*Phryganea varia*), which I believe is unknown or extremely rare in the UK. In the two decades this artificial fly has come to be used on British stillwaters with great success. In Ireland it is fished both as a floater and as a wet fly on the top dropper, but it is principally as the latter that it is used over here. The pattern given is the standard wet dressing. The dry fly sometimes has a palmered red cock hackle.

Hook: 8–10
Thread: Brown or black
Body: Pale green seal's fur
Rib: Gold wire or black Naples silk
Wing: Hen pheasant centre tail
Collar hackle: Natural red cock

Green Rabbit

A Richard Walker pattern for stillwater and river trout and grayling. It is fished as a nymph on rivers. On stillwaters it is best fished with long slow pulls.

Hook: 8–14
Tail: Any buff or brown feather fibres tied short
Body: Optional lead-foil underbody; a mixture of 2:1 wild black rabbit's fur and lime-green fluorescent wool, with the fibres well picked out
Rib: Fine gold thread
Hackle: Short-fibred brown partridge

Greenwell's Glory   *Plate 20*

Probably the most famous of all British trout flies. It was originally developed for the Tweed by Canon Greenwell and James Wright in 1854. Its continued popularity is due entirely to the fact that it is an excellent general imitation of all the olives. Depending upon the fly-size, and the shade of its dressing, it can represent all the olives and can be used when the iron blue is on the water. It was first tied as a winged wet pattern, but now it is tied as a floating fly, nymph, spider wet-fly and even as a lure. Because there is barely a week during the season when olives of one sort or another are not hatching, the pattern can be reliably used from March to October. Although it was devised as a river fly, it is also an excellent representation of the lake olive and pond olive.

The original pattern is listed first.

Hook: 14
Body: Waxed yellow tying silk
Rib (optional): Gold thread
Wing: Inside of a blackbird's wing (starling is a modern substitute)
Hackle: Coch-y-bondhu hen

The Woodcock Greenwell is as above except that it uses a woodcock wing. The Greenwell Spider omits the wing and has a longer-fibred coch-y-bondhu or furnace hen hackle.

Greenwell

A floating variant.

Hook: 14
Tail: Furnace cock hackle fibres
Body: Waxed yellow tying silk
Rib: Gold wire
Hackle: Furnace cock with a medium blue-dun in front
An alternative dressing has a Greenwell hackle and tail fibres.

Greenwell Nymph

Hook: 12–16
Tail: Coch-y-bondhu hackle fibres
Body: Waxed yellow silk or floss
Rib: Gold wire
Thorax: Grey or blue-grey fur
Wing-case: Grouse hackle fibres with the ends turned down as legs

Grenadier

One of the earliest of the modern reservoir flies. It was tied by Dr H. A. Bell for Chew and Blagdon. It can be fished successfully at various depths, although no one has offered an acceptable suggestion as to what it is intended to represent. In *The Super Flies of Still Water*, John Goddard suggests that it is better as a second-half-of-the-season pattern, to be fished on a dropper and retrieved slowly on a slow-sink line. He emphasizes its usefulness fished in such a manner on hot, calm days.

Hook: 12–14
Body: Hot-orange floss or seal's fur
Rib: Oval gold tinsel
Hackle: Two turns of ginger or light furnace cock (sometimes palmered)

Grey Duster   Plate 26

An excellent dry fly, this is a killing pattern for trout and grayling on both rivers and stillwaters. The smaller sizes are useful midge and caenis imitations, the medium sizes are a general floater and stonefly imitation, and the larger sizes can represent a moth. A parachute version seems to work even better than does the shoulder-hackled version. It is one of the few flies one can use all season and it deserves a place in any fly box.

Hook: 10–14
Tail (optional): Badger cock hackle fibres
Body: Blue-grey rabbit's fur
Hackle: Badger cock

Grey Fox

Preston Jennings was the first American to publish a really valuable guide to the entomology of that country and of the suitable imitations for the fly fisher. *A Book of Trout Flies*, published in 1935, has become a classic. This is one of Jennings' flies used on both sides of the Atlantic.

Hook: 10–14
Thread: Yellow
Tail: Honey-dun hackle fibres
Body: Light ginger quill
Hackles: Three – dark ginger, light ginger, grizzle cock, all long-fibred

Grey Goose Nymph   Plate 17

A Frank Sawyer nymph tied to imitate the nymphs of the spurwings, pale watery and blue-winged olive. As with all Sawyer's nymph patterns, no attempt is made to imitate the legs of the natural. It is in this respect that Sawyer differs from many other fly creators. He maintained that nymphs in the flow of the current hold their legs close to their bodies and that the tail was the means of propulsion. Sawyer's great emphasis was upon the overall size and shape of the nymphs and the materials used. This resulted in rather impressionistic caricatures designed to be fished at a medium depth and with slim, weighted bodies which allowed a rapid entry into the water.

The Grey Goose nymph is principally a river pattern and a fair imitation of the nymphs of the spurwings and pale watery.

A few friends and I have used it to good effect in small, clear lakes in mid-summer, but I'm not sure what it is then taken for. The dressing is similar to that of Sawyer's Swedish Nymph, but the goose herls used are not as dark as those on the latter.

Hook: 12–16
Thread: None (use the copper wire)
Tail: Grey goose fibres
Body: Grey goose wing fibres and golden-coloured copper wire wound together over a layer of copper wire. Additional weighting can be added by including a copper-wire thorax underbody
Thorax: Body fibres doubled and redoubled and tied in with the copper wire

Grey Monkey   *Plate 7*

A. J. Mearns highly recommends this very successful Loch Leven pattern. Sizes 6–10 are also good for sea trout. I have seen slightly different body proportions on different tyings. Some have a half-and-half body, others have a rear third and front two-thirds.

Hook: 10–14 single or double
Thread: Black
Tail: Barred teal fibres
Body: Rear half golden yellow floss or seal's fur, front half grey monkey or grey seal's fur ribbed with silver wire
Wing: Pale starling or mallard grey wing quill (widgeon on the sea-trout sizes)
Throat hackle: Medium blue dun or grizzle
Cheeks (optional): Jungle cock or substitute

Griffith's Gnat   *Plate 23*

This a widely acclaimed American pattern that is finding favour on British and European stillwaters and rivers. A number of anglers of my aquaintance would not be without it. Fished dry or in the film it makes a fair imitation of a struggling emerging midge or an egg-laying adult. Also see SPARKLE GNAT for a variant.

Hook: 16–26 fine wire
Thread: Black micro
Body: Peacock herl
Hackle: Very short-fibred grizzle palmered down the body

Grizzle Mink   *Plate 27*

This nondescript dry fly from the vice of Neil Patterson fulfils his fly-tying philosophy: 'Why wait for a trout to make your fly more effective by pulling it about with its teeth? Do it yourself at the vice. The more bits hanging off my flies, the more fur flying, hackles ruffling; the more base grubbiness a fly has, the more my fins, like the trout's, bristle. Few flies can claim to be as downright scruffy as the Grizzle Mink. And it's this feature, on a blustery early-season day, that makes a prim-and-proper fly take on the appetite appeal of a lump of wood. If it has nothing else going for it, a roughly tied Grizzle Mink lives. It has life!'

Neil relates how on one occasion Stewart Canham caught an amazing total of forty Kennet trout in one session on the same fly. Neatness certainly doesn't count for much in this dressing. In an article in *Trout Fisherman* magazine, Neil commented: 'In the years I've been fishing the Grizzle Mink, it has proved to be a fly of enormous adaptability. As a dry fly on lakes, to imitate adult midge, lake and pond olives, it has trout rising as if on tracks. In Normandy, a small gang of converts fish it even through the Mayfly season on size 10–12 hooks. In New York State, on a size 20, I took (but lost) my only trout of the day on a pounded public water where the trout are claimed to have microscopes for eyes.

'Due to its popularity, there have been many variations of the Grizzle Mink, the correct tying understandably blurring *en route*. But before you leap to the vice, throw all the text-books out of the window. I cannot stress enough that untidiness and pure scruff are the keys to successful Grizzle Mink tying.'

The correct dressing is:

Hook: 14–18
Thread: Brown
Tail: A bunch of grizzle whisks
Body: Dun-coloured mink fur charged with longish hairs, some of which should stick out through the rib. Do not trim.
Rib: Fine gold wire
Hackles: Red cock wound through grizzle for the early season; ginger cock wound through grizzle during summer

Grizzly Bourne   *Plate 27*

I like this general dun imitation from Michael Leighton very much. It appeared in his little book *Trout Flies of Shropshire and the Welsh Borderlands* and I have used it intermittently since. It is typical of the Welsh Border patterns with a supplementary hackle.

Hook: 12–18
Thread: Orange
Tail: Honey cock fibres
Body: Rabbit's blue underfur
Rib: Pearsall's golden yellow multistrand floss in close turns
Hackle: Light red/brown cock wound through a grizzle

Grouse Series

A range of lake flies with grouse wings. The combination of colours is extensive and is broadly similar to those in the mallard, teal and woodcock series, all of which differ, in the main, in their wing material. With the exception of the pattern given, the flies in this series can be found in the section headed MALLARD SERIES. The grouse-wing material is from the speckled tail feathers. The Grouse and Yellow is a useful sedge-pupa copy, the Grouse and Claret is a fair representation of the sepia dun and claret duns and their nymphs.

Grouse and Orange or Orange Grouse   *Plate 10*

I am advised by expert tyer Alice Conba that this is best in the first half of June but that some anglers use it all season. It is used on lakes and fast water. Within the same series of Irish flies there are the Gold Grouse, Green Grouse and Black Grouse which differ by their body colours. The Orange and Green Grouse has a half green, half orange body, and the Straw Grouse has a raffia body.

Hook: 8–14
Tail: Grouse hackle fibres
Body: Orange floss ribbed with oval gold tinsel
Wing: Grouse wing or tail feathers; speckled hen may also be used
Hackle: Grouse body feather

Grouse and Purple

Hook: 8–14
Tail: Golden pheasant tippets
Body: Purple seal's fur
Rib: Oval gold tinsel
Wing: Grouse centre tail feather
Hackle: Black

Grouse and Yellow   *Plate 7*

Hook: 8–14
Thread: Yellow
Tail: Golden pheasant tippets
Body: Yellow seal's fur
Rib: Oval gold
Wing: Slips from a grouse centre tail
Hackle: Pale ginger cock or hen. Sometimes a dyed yellow hackle is used

Growler   *Plate 2*

This bright, flashy lure is the product of Robert Spiller's vice. It began in 1989 and ended in this form two years later. It has done exceptionally well on many lakes, including L'Eglise in Kent where it took three trout for 39 lb pounds. Suprisingly, the considerable amount of flash in the dressing, far from deterring trout, seems to attract them. It should be fished in a slow figure-of-eight retrieve on an intermediate or slow-sinking line. Always use a strong leader. Some of the recommended colour combinations are below. It can also be tied to match many other lure colours.

Tail	Body	Thorax cover	Thorax
White	White	Black	Fl. green
Black	Black	Black	Fl. green
Olive	Olive	Olive	Yellow
Brown	Brown	Brown	Fl. orange
Pink (deep)	Pink	Neon-magenta	Salmon pink
Orange	Orange	Orange	Fl. orange
Fl. yellow	Yellow	Yellow	Fl. green
Green	Green	Green	Fl. green

Hook: Heavy-weight 8
Thread: Black or to match the body
Underbody: Two layers of lead wire
Tail: Marabou, about 2–3 times the body length
Body: Cactus chenille, Lureflash Fritz or Ice chenille
Thorax and thorax cover: Chenille
Hackle: Black cock

Half Stone

Originally a West Country wet pattern, this is now widely used as a dry fly. The original wet version is probably a good imitation of a hatching dun or a sedge pupa rising to the surface.

Hook: 12–14
Thread: Cream
Tail: Blue-dun hackle fibres
Body: Rear two-thirds, yellow floss; front one-third, mole fur
Hackle: Blue-dun, which may be wound in the normal manner or palmered through the mole fur

A version using a honey-dun hackle and tail fibres is known as the Honey Half Stone.

Hardy's Favourite

Devised by J. J. Hardy of the famous fishing-tackle firm, this is a well-established Scottish loch-fly usually fished on the point or as a bob-fly.

Hook: 10–12
Tail: Golden pheasant tippets
Body: Claret floss
Rib: Peacock herl
Wing: Woodcock wing
Hackle: Grey partridge breast feather

An alternative dressing has a tail of brown mallard fibres and a wing of brown turkey wing fibres.

Hare's Ear

Also see under GOLD RIBBED HAIR'S EAR.

Hare's Ear Muddler   Plate 9

This is a Stan Headley pattern based on his earlier Twitcher which used the scarce Blue Mountain Hare's ear fur. The palmered hackle adds to the impression of hatching confusion. Stan says that it is difficult to praise this pattern too highly, and in a situation where fish are active near the surface on unidentified insects or a wide range of insects he would automatically use this pattern.

Hook: Long shank 14–16 Partridge stronghold SH2
Thread: Black, brown or yellow
Body: Well mixed hare's mask, with lots of guard hairs, palmered with medium red/brown cock
Rib: Fine oval gold
Hackle: Small brown partridge
Head: Fine roe deer, clipped in a bullet shape, leaving lots of fine tips as a pseudo-hackle

Hare's Lug and Plover   Plate 32

This old wet fly is described by Roger Fogg, author of *The Art of the Wet Fly*, as 'an excellent early-season pattern. It kills well on rivers such as the Derbyshire Wye when the large dark olive is emerging'. It imitates any of the emerging olives, and is a useful stillwater pattern when the lake olive and pond olive are about. It works well on rivers if it is dressed Stewart-style and fished upstream just below the surface film, suggestive of the emerging dun.

The origins of the fly are obscure, but it has been used for at least two centuries on Derbyshire streams. Never let the age of a trout fly deter you from using it. I would rather pin my faith in a pattern that has survived decades, even centuries of anglers' use, than in some of the one-season wonders we are bombarded with in the angling press. Despite its age, the Hare's Lug and Plover has the distinction of catching Roger Fogg's biggest number of trout in one day's river fishing. He says: 'I even approached the kind of number boasted about by Stewart himself in the nineteenth century', and in those days they assessed the catches by the score, not by the brace!

Hook: 12–16
Thread: Brown or primrose (varied to alter the olive shade)
Tip (optional): A small tip of flat gold tinsel
Body: Hare's ear fur tapering to the rear
Rib: Gold wire
Hackle: Golden plover (mouse-coloured with yellow tips)

Hatching Nymphs

The emerging dun struggling to leave its nymphal shuck and penetrate the surface film is a prime target for a feeding fish. The inch below the water surface is probably the most critical and most exciting inch of water for both fish and fly fisherman. It also offers the greatest challenge to the fly dresser. Often sodden artificial dry flies sink below the surface and are greedily snapped up by trout and grayling. Has the dry fly become a nymph, or is there something in between ?

Richard Walker suggested a variation of a standard dressing which could be applied to many nymph patterns. A bunch of cock hackle fibres is tied in to emerge from the top of the thorax. The fibres are tied vertically, but the wing-case material is laid through them so that they are split and spread out. The colour of the hackles should match the wing colour of the natural dun. Had poly yarn or cul de canard feathers been available to Walker I am sure he would have suggested these as a winging material to produce a very effective hatching nymph.

Also see EMERGERS and FLYMPHS.

HAWTHORN FLY (Bibio marci)

See DIPTERA

This important terrestrial fly has been copied by fly-fishermen for centuries. It is of value to both river and lake fishermen when the adults are blown on to the water in late April and May. The fly has a large black hairy body about 12 mm (½ inch) long, with a pair of long trailing hindlegs which make it distinctive. Most artificials are fished dry, although on stillwaters an imitation fished just below the surface often does well. There is no doubt that on some fisheries the Hawthorn is of some significance. Fishing a pattern on the upwind bank of a stillwater on a breezy May day is the most likely time for success. If naturals are falling on to the water, it is usually not long before trout realise and take advantage of them.

Hawthorn Fly

(Ian Warrilow)   *Plate 22*

Hook: 12
Thread: Black
Body and head: Black-dyed pheasant tail fibres
Legs: Two knotted black-dyed pheasant tail fibres, one each side of the body
Wing: Traun River stonefly wing
Hackle: Black cock

Hawthorn Fly
(Preben Torp Jacobsen)   Plate 22

The well-known Danish fly tyer, Preben Torp Jacobsen, was a vet before his retirement. Few occupations could provide a better opportunity of procuring some of the more exotic furs and feathers. The original materials for this fly came from Copenhagen Zoo. Condor herls, like many other once-popular materials, are now scarce or on the prohibited list. Ostrich herl is a suitable replacement.

Hook: 12
Thread: Brown
Body: Black condor herls twisted on the tying thread
Hackles: Two black cock hackles
Legs: Two black condor herl tips tied in just to the rear of the hackles so that they trail backwards and downwards

Hawthorn Fly *(Taff Price)*   Plate 22

Hook: Wide-gape 10–12
Body: Shiny-black rayon floss
Rib: Fine silver wire
Legs: Two knotted black pheasant tail fibres
Thorax: Black seal's fur
Wing: Grey duck tied flat over the back
Hackle: Black cock

Haystack   Plate 9

This dry adult midge imitation devised by England International Paul Canning as low-riding pattern to be fished in or on the film. It can be cast singly to cruising fish or in a team of two or three as a searching tactic.

Hook: 10–16
Thread: Black 6/0 Uni-Thread
Butt: Pearly Mylar over the tying thread, superglued for colour change and durability
Body: Hare's body guard fur with no underfur mixed in. Dark shades or those with dark tips are preferred. Brush the fibres upwards at 45 degrees with Velcro.

HEATHER FLY (Bibio promonae)

See DIPTERA

This is similar to the Hawthorn Fly except that the tops of the legs are a reddish colour. It is a more localised species, commonest in Scotland, parts of Wales and the North of England where heather grows. Heather flies are sometimes found on the water surface during their most prolific months, July and August. In some parts of the country it is also known as the Bloody Doctor. The scarcity of patterns indicates that it is of not as great value as the Hawthorn Fly.

Hook: 12
Body: Black ostrich herl
Hackle: Coch-y-bondhu

Hendrickson

An American dry fly originally tied by Roy Steenrod in 1915 for a customer named Hendrickson, to represent the upwinged dun *Ephemerella subvaria*, unknown in the UK. The patterns were so successful that the naturals adopted the name of the artificials. However, the two patterns below are both useful general patterns and are being offered by some British fly tyers. The flies illustrated were tied by American expert in the Catskill style, Larry Duckwall.

Dark Hendrickson   Plate 24

Hook: 12–14
Tail: Squirrel-tail fur or dark blue-dun hackle-fibres
Body: Dark blue-grey fur
Wing: Mandarin duck speckled flank feather fibres set upright
Hackle: Dark blue-dun cock

Light Hendrickson   Plate 24

Hook: 12–14
Tail: Squirrel-tail fur
Body: Cream-coloured fox belly fur

Wing: Mandarin duck speckled feather fibres set upright
Hackle: Light blue-dun cock

Henryville Special

This is a popular US pattern that probably originated in the UK in the early part of this century.

Hook: 10–16
Thread: Grey
Body: Olive thread with a palmered grizzle hackle
Wing: Two grey duck wing quill sections either side of the body over wood-duck fibres
Hackle: Natural red cock wound over the wing roots

Heptagenid Nymph

(Oliver Edwards)   *Plate 17*

The correct silhouette is the trigger when imitating these flat stone-clinging nymphs of the Ecdyonurus, Heptagenia and Rhithrogena species. Vary the size to represent all the species. This is an Oliver Edwards pattern, effective on stony rivers from May to August when the nymphs are active. Oliver fishes it in a dead-drift in streamy water in the dead period on hot afternoons. He catches a lot of fish with it – during a very difficult period of the day. All his patterns will reward patient tying. Oliver makes use of Dave's Flexament to seal the legs and wing buds.

Hook: Long shank fine wire 14–18
Thread: Danville's Spider Web
Weight: Narrow strip of wine bottle lead foil or fine copper wire
Tail: Stout, quick-tapering animal hair dyed yellow-olive
Abdomen: Thick polythene (0.2 mm) dyed yellow-olive, or yellow-olive Flexibody
Under abdomen tint (optional): Brown waterproof felt pen on the dorsal side; fluorescent yellow on the ventral side
Abdomen gills: Ostrich herl dyed yellow-olive

Thorax and head capsule: Golden-yellow fine synthetic dubbing (SLF Finesse Masterclass MC6)
Head capsule cover: Brown Raffene
Legs: Guinea fowl undercover or flank hackle dyed yellow-olive, coated with flexible cement and re-coated after heat-kinking to shape
Wing buds: Dark, brick-red, red grouse hackle coated with cement or clear flexible adhesive

HI C Series

A series of highly-visible dry flies suitable for fishing fast, rough water. The generous hackling makes them good floaters. Some of the series are variants of imitations of natural flies; others are general patterns.

HI C Badger

Hook: 12–14
Tail: Natural red hackle fibres
Body: Black thread
Hackles: Small blue-dun, natural red, badger cocks

The Hi C Black has a black hackle in place of the badger.

Hoppers

These are a series of stillwater flies, not grasshoppers, but in the style of daddy-long-legs or crane-flies. They originated on Grafham in the late 1980s and have become standard patterns across the country during the entire season. The style of the fly remains constant throughout the series but the matching hackle and body colour change with the fly's name. Claret, black, olive, brown, orange and yellow are all tied. All should be fished dry.

Claret Hopper

Hook: 10–12
Thread: Black

Body: Dubbed dark claret Antron
Rib: Fine pearl Lurex
Legs: Six pairs of knotted pheasant tail fibres trailing to the rear
Hackle: Claret or dyed red cock

Honey Bear *Plate 3*

This lake fly was tied by Iain Murray-Thomson in 1979. It has gone on to have a formidable reputation for rainbow trout on its home Scottish waters, particulary the Lake of Menteith. It is named after its creator's fishing companion, a cross golden labrador/golden retriever. The original and correct dressing is listed below but commercial versions are sometimes tied with a body just of yellow chenille.

Hook: Long shank 8–12
Thread: Primrose yellow
Tail: Yellow-dyed goat kid hair
Body: White cotton very lightly dubbed with yellow seal's fur, with white ostrich herl over
Rib: Oval silver tinsel
Hackle: Dark claret cock fibres as a beard
Wing: White cock hackles dyed lemon-yellow
Cheeks: Jungle cock eyes
Head: Black varnish

Houghton Ruby *Plate 21*

William Lunn was a Test river-keeper who devised a number of flies for the southern chalk-streams. Of all his dressings, three stand out above the others and are still used today. This is one. The others are Lunn's Particular and his Caperer imitation. The Houghton Ruby is an excellent female iron blue spinner imitation. I have not fished with it on its home stream, but it works well whenever the natural appears. I have also caught a lot of autumn grayling with it when there hasn't been an iron blue in sight.

Hook: 12–14
Thread: Crimson
Tail: Three fibres of a white cock hackle

Body: Rhode Island Red hackle stalk dyed crimson
Wing: Two light-blue-dun hackle tips tied spent, or sometimes semi-spent
Hackle: Rhode Island Red cock

Housefly *(Pat Russell)*

Hook: 14
Thread: Black
Body: Bronze peacock herl tied fat
Wing: Two small whole grey feathers tied flat across the back in a slight V-shape
Hackle: Long-fibred black cock

Houton Gem

This Scottish loch fly enjoys a high reputation.

Hook: 10–14
Tail: Red ibis or golden pheasant tippets
Body: Black thread
Rib: Flat silver tinsel
Wing: Well marked cock pheasant neck feather
Hackle: Black hen

Humbug *Plate 3*

This mini-lure was devised by Stan Headley as a half-way house between the very successful Black and White Cat's Whiskers, plus a few other elements, most notably the strong colour contrast. It works very well fished on high-density lines with a fast retrieve and then hung enticingly just beneath the surface. This is one of the few mini-lures that work in the mid-cast position.

Hook: 10
Tail: Three strands of pearl Lureflash Crystal Hair under a tuft of white marabou under a tuft of black marabou
Body: Flat silver Mylar
Wing: White marabou under black marabou under three strands of pearl Crystal Hair
Head: Fluorescent chenille

Humpy or Goofus Bug   *Plate 24*

This unusual design originated in California and is now used on faster waters the world over as a general dry fly. It is probably taken for an emerging dun in its smaller sizes, and in the larger for a sedge. The body colours may be varied but the usual is yellow.

Hook: 10–18
Thread: Black, brown, red or yellow, to match the body colour
Tail: Tan elk or moose hair, or tips of the deer hair body fibres
Body: Floss or tying thread overlaid with an overbody of tan deer body hair, which is tied in overlong for the wing fibres
Wing: A bunch of the back fibres set upright and slightly divided
Hackle: Mixed grizzle and natural red cocks

Royal Humpy

A Jack Dennis variant devised as a fast-water attractor.

Hook: 10–16
Thread: Red Monocord
Tail: Dark moose hair
Body: Red Monocord with light grey or black deer hair as an overbody
Wing: White calf tail, upright and divided
Hackle: Blue-dun, brown, badger, grizzle or cree cock

Idiot-Proof Nymph   *Plate 12*

This 'nymph' – I use the word advisedly – was devised in Scotland but I do not know who by. Because it has a reputation for catching trout on almost any stillwater its name was born. Various colours are successful but the tail and body always match.

Hook: Long shank 8–12
Thread: Black
Tail: Marabou
Body: Lureflash Fritz over an optionally weighted underbody
Head: Small gold bead

Imp

This is one of H. A. Rolt's grayling patterns which is fished wet or dry. It is as at home on any grayling stream as it is on the southern rivers for which it was devised. I have found the floating fly most effective.

Hook: 14–16
Tail: Red ibis or substitute
Tip: Flat gold tinsel
Body: Heron herl
Hackle: Black cock or hen

Incredible Wet   *Plate 18*

Also known as Theo's Incredible Wet after its creator Theo Bakelaar. It is a pattern for lakes and small stillwaters. The highly reflective sparkle of the Orvis Lite Brite dubbing material makes a very interesting body.

Hook: Tiemco TMC 3761, size 10–12
Thread: Grey
Tail: Grizzle hackle fibres
Body: Orvis Lite Brite mixed with grey dubbing
Leg: Saddle grizzle hackle
Head: 3 mm or 4 mm gold bead with a few turns of dubbing in front

Insensor   *Plate 2*

This is a Stephen Gross lure developed with the aid of some the Mosaic Mobile strips, one of the very useful Lureflash materials.

Hook: Long shank 8–12
Thread: Black
Tail: Mosaic Mobile
Body: Magenta chenille ribbed with twisted green Mobile
Wing: Black marabou

Invicta   *Plate 7*

The Invicta is an excellent lake fly and a useful river pattern. It is fished wet just below the surface, where it is probably taken as a hatching sedge. Few lake fishers of any experience have not caught trout on this fly. It is one of the few old flies that has survived the revolution in design of stillwater flies. James Ogden, author of *Ogden on Fly Tying*, 1879, was its creator.

Hook: 10–14
Tail: Golden pheasant crest feather
Body: Yellow seal's fur
Rib: Gold wire through the hackle
Hackle: Natural light red, palmered along the body with blue jay at the head
Wing: Hen pheasant centre tail tied across the back

An alternative dressing has a tail of dyed red feather-fibres trimmed square. The Silver Invicta (Plate 7) and Gold Invicta have silver and gold tinsel bodies and ribs. The former tied very slim is a useful fry imitation. The Green Invicta has a body of green seal's fur ribbed with gold.

Invicta Sedge Pupa

Dave Collyer devised this variation, purposely omitting the wings, because in his own words: 'It never seems reasonable to me that a trout should expect to find a fully-winged sedge-fly swimming about underwater!' It may not seem reasonable, but winged wet sedge patterns have always been successful, perhaps because some species oviposit in such a way.

Hook: 10
Thread: Olive
Abdomen: Yellow wool
Rib: Oval gold tinsel
Thorax: Mixed dark-green and brown wool, or yellow wool only
Wing-case: Oak-turkey wing strip
Beard hackle: Blue jay wing fibres

White-Hackled Invicta   Plate 6

According to expert Orkney fly fisher, Stan Headley, this variation is one of Orkney's best bob-flies, but its effectiveness is not restricted to that part of the country. It is fished on the bob in large sizes and is a renowned taker of big fish. It excels in coloured or peat-stained

water. Dressed in sizes 8 to 16 it works anywhere on the leader and not just in coloured water. The dressing is as for the standard Invicta plus a longish white hen hackle tied in front of the wing to replace the blue jay.

IRON BLUE
(Baetis niger, B. muticus)

See EPHEMEROPTERA
These two species are common on rivers and streams throughout the country except in parts of the south-east corner of England. The colouring of these two Baetis species makes them easily distinguished from other upwinged duns. However, the differences between the two are minimal and of no significance for the angler. The nymphs are the agile-darting type. Hatches of the duns begin in April or May and continue intermittently until as late as November. These smallish duns seem to get smaller as the season progresses. They often appear when no other duns are about and can be expected even on cold, blustery days. The biggest hatch I ever saw was on the Itchen, on a wet, very dark day.

The spinners of both sexes are of interest to trout and grayling, and they are likely to be encountered mainly in the latter half of the season during all the daylight hours. Both Goddard and Harris say that a mild day after a period of cold weather, when the duns might have emerged in considerable numbers, should result in a large fall of spinners. The spent females remain trapped below the surface in common with other Baetis species, and if the floating fly fails to rise fish, a sunken imitation is well worth trying.

The male dun has grey-black or blue-black wings and a grey-black abdomen. The legs are dark olive and the two tails are olive-grey or black-grey. The female dun has grey-black or slightly paler wings and a dark brown-olive abdomen. The legs are olive-brown and the two tails are dark grey. The male spinner, known commonly as the jenny spinner, has transparent, colourless wings and a translucent white abdomen of which the last three segments are dark browny-orange. The two tails are white-grey and the legs are pale grey with the forelegs darker.

The female spinner, sometimes known as the little claret spinner, has transparent, colourless wings and a dark claret-brown abdomen with a paler underside. The legs are olive-grey and the two tails are pale grey.

The imitation of these species is a great killer of trout and grayling. It is of particular value to the northern wet-fly fishers who have been copying the nymph and hatching dun for centuries with a variety of spider patterns. Crimson seems to be a key colour in the imitation of the iron blues. It is often the colour of the tying thread, which when used with a translucent body increases the effectiveness of the imitation. In addition to those dressings below, see also HOUGHTON RUBY, SNIPE AND PURPLE, WATCHETS, WILLOW FLY, WATERHEN BLOA, OTTER RUBY, ADAMS, BLUE UPRIGHT and GREENWELL'S GLORY.

Iron Blue Spider   Plate 32

Hook: 14–16
Thread: Crimson
Body: Lightly dubbed mole's fur with a tip of thread exposed
Hackle: From the inside of a moorhen's wing or snipe

Iron Blue Nymph

Hook: 16
Thread: Claret
Tail: White cock hackle fibres
Body: Mole's fur with a tip of tying silk exposed at the rear
Thorax: Mole's fur
Wing-case: Black crow or waterhen wing
Legs: Wing-case fibres tied beneath the body

Iron Blue Flymph

For fuller details see under FLYMPHS

Hook: 14–16 long shank Mayfly
Thread: Claret or black
Tail: Dark blue-dun hackle fibres
Body: Mole's fur
Hackle: Dark blue-dun, starling or coot

Iron Blue Dun

(Ian Warrilow)   Plate 19

Hook: 14–16
Thread: Crimson
Tail: White cock hackle fibres
Tip: Crimson thread
Body: Natural dark heron herl
Wing: Burnt wing dark-dun saddle hackles tied with a slight outward curve
Hackle: Dark-dun cock (Metz shade)

Iron Blue Dun   *(Pat Russell)*

Hook: 16–17
Thread: Crimson
Tip: Neon-magenta silk, small
Tail: Dark slate-blue cock hackle fibres
Body: Dark heron herl
Hackle: Dark slate-blue cock; two short-fibred hackles palmered from half-way down the body to the head

Jenny Spinner

(Ian Warrilow)   Plate 21

Hook: 14
Thread: Crimson
Tail: White cock fibres
Tip: Crimson thread
Body: Stripped white hackle stalk
Thorax: Rich brown Antron
Wing: Cream poly yarn

See also SUNK SPINNER for the female spinner imitation to be fished sub-surface.

Irresistibles

A series of very buoyant American dry flies, but if only trout flies lived up to their names! The larger sizes have been known to take salmon.

Irresistible
Plate 24

Hook: 12
Tail: Brown bucktail
Body: Natural grey deer hair spun and clipped
Wing: Two grizzle hackle tips set upright
Hackle: Grizzle cock

Itchen Olive
Plate 27

Gordon Mackie, the creator of this pattern, comments: 'The Itchen Olive was devised during the 1975/76 season when it was found that while trout rose every evening to pale duns, such as small spurwing and pale evening duns, they were seldom tempted by any of the standard patterns. The Itchen Olive was an immediate success, and has since accounted for hundreds of fish which would "not look at anything". It is today used widely on the Itchen and would, I'm sure, prove equally attractive to trout elsewhere which feed on "pale stuff". On the Wylye, however, where I mostly fish, the fly is not as effective, probably because it is primarily a blue-winged olive river with less pale fly during the early evening. Here, the Pheasant Tail is king. The Itchen Olive is essentially a general-purpose fly. It should ride high on the surface.'

Hook: 14
Thread: Primrose
Tail: Four or five stiff pale-grey spade hackle fibres
Body: Thinly dubbed medium-grey seal's fur
Rib: Tying thread
Hackle: Three or four turns of a light-grey cock hackle, stiff and springy, from a natural or photo-dyed cape. Minimum web, or two hackle feathers

Iven's Nymphs

Tom Ivens' book *Still Water Fly-Fishing* of 1952 had a considerable impact on British reservoir fishing. This was the first authoritative work on the styles and methods of lure and nymph fishing on stillwater. The growing number of recruits to reservoir fishing were hungry for knowledge, and Ivens provided the textbook that was to be referred to and relied upon for many years afterwards. Three flies that emerged from the book have survived, the Jersey Herd, Black and Peacock Spider and this series of nymphs.

Ivens' Brown Nymph

Hook: 8–12
Thread: Brown
Body: Dark-brown ostrich herl
Rib: Oval gold tinsel
Horns: Two strands of stripped green ostrich herl, rear-facing
Head: Bronze peacock herl

Ivens' Brown and Green Nymph
Plate 16

In addition to being a general nymph pattern, this is also a sedge-pupa imitation and a passable small fry imitator.

Hook: 8–10
Thread: Brown
Body: Olive and brown ostrich herls wound together
Rib: Oval gold tinsel
Back: Four strands of green peacock herl tied in at the head and tail, but extending beyond the bend as a tail
Head: Peacock herl

Ivens' Green Nymph

Hook: 8–12
Thread: Green
Body: An underbody of white floss overlaid with pale-green nylon
Hackle: Brown partridge
Head: Bronze peacock herl

Ivens' Green and Yellow Nymph

This is a useful sedge-pupa imitation that needs to be fished very slowly. Tom Ivens fished this without any retrieve at all, allowing it to drift round with any breeze there might be.

Hook: 10–12
Thread: Green
Body: Rear half, swan herl dyed green; front half, swan herl dyed yellow
Head: Peacock herl

Jack Frost   *Plate 5*

Bob Church devised this fry-imitating lure for big trout feeding on bream fry in Grafham in 1974. In addition to its original role as a bream-fry imitation, it is also an excellent general lure for use from both boat and bank. Like all marabou-winged patterns, the slightest movement brings it to life, so it should be fished in steady pulls with intermittent pauses.

Hook: Long shank 6–8
Thread: Black
Tail: A small tag of fluorescent red wool
Body: White baby wool covered with stretched clear polythene
Wing: White marabou
Hackle: Generous turns of long-fibred red, and three turns of white tied rear-sloping
Head: Black varnish

Jack Ketch

Geoffrey Bucknall devised this stillwater pattern, basing it upon the proven success of the Black-and-Peacock Spider. It is probably taken for a small beetle, with the silver tip representing the air-sac. It should be fished slowly on a long leader and it is good in deep water along a dam wall. Jack Ketch was the mediaeval name for the hangman.

Hook: 10
Tip: Flat silver tinsel

Body: Underbody of lead wire covered with mixed black, claret, blue and red seal's fur
Hackle: Three turns of long-fibred black hen

Janus   *Plate 27*

The name Janus, the Roman god who was represented with faces on front and back of the head, is very apt for this fore-and-aft hackled dry fly. It is also appropriate that it was devised by Hal Thirlaway, a member of the Piscatorial Society, as was Horace Brown, inventor of this dressing style. This pattern is based on a Peter Deane knotted Black Gnat. Hal Thirlaway chose this style as a general dun imitation and emphasized shape, contour, silhouette, profile and size, with much less accent on pattern and colour. From size 22 to Mayfly size its creator suggested that 'you are equipped to be a one-fly chalkstream angler.' The unique feature is the upright wing or tails which not only act as a wing imitation to trigger the rise and assist in cocking the fly on the surface but also cause the fly to rock in a slight breeze, so giving the simulation of life. Sizes 20–22 are recommended for autumn grayling. It is important that the head hackle is shorter in the fibre than the rear. Peter Deane suggests the head hackle should be one to be used on a hook two sizes smaller, or failing that, trim the hackle to the corrct size.

Hook: 10–22 fine wire
Body: Black thread tied slim
Shoulder hackle: Short badger, grizzle or white cock
Rear hackle: Natural dark red cock
Tails/wing: Four long grizzle fibres tied upright, fanned

Jersey Herd

A lure and fry-imitation devised by Tom Ivens. It was popular in the 1950s and 1960s, when it paved the way for many other lures. It remains a very useful pattern. It is named after the milk-bottle-top foil used in the original dressing. The dressing has been much abused by fly tyers, but I am assured that this is Ivens' intended dressing.

Hook: Long shank 6–10
Thread: Black or hot-orange
Body: White floss silk covered with wide copper-coloured tinsel or Lurex
Rib: Copper wire (optional for strength)
Tail and back: Strands of peacock herl
Hackle: Hot-orange as a beard or rear-sloping collar
Head: Peacock herl

An alternative and popular body material is gold Mylar tubing. The Silver Herd has a silver tinsel body; the Red Tagged Herd is a Silver Herd with a red wool tail; the Yellow Herd has a silver tinsel body and a yellow beard hackle.

John Spencer *Plate 6*

Although this is nowadays primarily a sea-trout fly, it is highly recommended in smaller sizes as a good alternative to the Blae and Black which it resembles closely.

Hook: 12–14
Thread: Black
Tail: Golden pheasant tippets
Body: Black floss
Rib: Oval silver tinsel
Wing: Grey mallard flank
Hackle: Black cock or hen as a beard

John Storey

An excellent North Country dry fly on which, by coincidence, I caught my first trout on dry fly. It was devised by John Storey, a riverkeeper on the Rye in North Yorkshire. The revision of the wing was adapted by the creator's grandson in 1935. The original wing slanted over the body in wet-fly style. It is always fished as a floater and it is a great killer of trout and grayling on chalk-streams and rain-fed rivers. Arthur Oglesby once fished this pattern for a whole trout season to the exclusion of all other patterns, and he actually caught slightly more fish than his average season's tally. I'm not sure what this proves, except that as a general utility dry fly it is one on which it is hard to improve. I think that the forward-slanting wing gives an early indication in the trout's window that a dun is on the surface. See also NAKED JOHN STOREY.

Hook: Down-eyed 14
Thread: Black
Body: Copper peacock herl
Wing: A small whole mallard breast feather tied in a bunch sloping forward over the eye
Hackle: Dark Rhode Island Red cock

Some modern dressings incorporate a rib of red or scarlet tying silk or red DFM floss.

John Titmouse

This variant of the John Storey was devised by Eric Horsfall Turner as a grayling fly. It was so named because it is effective when rising grayling seem merely to be 'titching' at a fly. Under these circumstances, persuading grayling to take a dry fly and hooking fish that do rise is extremely difficult. A few patterns work better than most on these occasions, and this is one of them. Its creator took more than 200 grayling on this fly in its first season, which should be proof enough of its effectiveness.

Hook: 16–18
Thread: Black
Tail: White hackle fibres
Body: Peacock herl
Wing: A very small mallard breast feather about 8 mm long, sloping forward over the eye
Hackle: Black cock

Jungle Cock

A lake fly in traditional style. The Jungle Cock and Silver is as below, except it has a silver tinsel body and rib and the option of a black or blue hackle. Both patterns are also fished as tandem lures.

Hook: 10–12
Tail: Golden pheasant tippets

Body: Black floss silk
Rib: Gold wire
Wing: Eyed jungle cock or substitute
Hackle: Black cock

Kate McLaren *Plate 7*

A Scottish loch and sea-trout fly devised by William Robertson in the 1930s. It is best on the bob when fished in a team. It is not much used beyond the Scottish borders, but it has an excellent reputation in its homeland.

Hook: 8–12
Thread: Black
Tail: Golden-pheasant topping
Body: Black seal's fur with a palmered black cock hackle
Rib: Oval silver tinsel
Hackle: Red-brown cock

Ke-He *Plate 6*

This lake fly, of Orkney origins, has become a standard pattern on many Scottish lochs, and in the last few seasons it has been making an appearance on some English reservoirs. In the 1930s two anglers named Kemp and Heddle (hence the name) tied the pattern to copy some black bees falling on the water. It is still popular and is probably taken for a terrestrial of some sort.

Stan Headley, an expert Orkney fly fisher, comments: 'The Ke-He is an all-season pattern, and works well on peaty or clear waters. I prefer it on windy, bright summer days in size 10, usually on the tail. Variations on the original dressing are usually confined to the hackle colour. The White or Benbecula Ke-He is popular in the Western Isles. The Black Ke-He is an excellent pattern for early-season and late-season work. For late evenings, the Orange Ke-He is a renowned fly for use in difficult conditions, and as a taker of bigger trout.

The Ke-He seems to work no matter where in the country it is used, and visitors to the large Irish loughs would be well advised to carry a few in largish sizes. It is also good for sea trout in stillwater.'

Hook: 8–14
Tail: Golden pheasant tippets
Tag: Red wool
Body: Green or bronze peacock herl tied fat
Rib: Gold wire
Hackle: Medium red-brown.

Kill-Devil Spiders *Plate 20*

These three Derbyshire wet flies are general imitative patterns suggestive of aquatic spiders or an assortment of terrestrials. They were once popular, but I'm not sure of their reputation today.

Hook: 14
Tip: Gold or silver tinsel
Body: Peacock herl
Hackle: Long-fibred bright medium-blue cock

The Kill Devil Black Spider omits the tips and has a long-fibred black hackle. The Kill Devil Red Spider omits the tip and has a long-fibred natural red hackle.

Killer Bug *Plate 19*

Also known as the Grayling Bug. Of all flies, few are more aptly named than this deadly chalk-stream grayling pattern created by Frank Sawyer. Its creator describes in his book, *Nymphs and the Trout*, how this was tied specifically to catch grayling, and how, in his own hands, it also caught salmon. Thousands of grayling and trout are caught on this each year. The dressing is so generally impressionistic that it could be mistaken for a shrimp or a pupa or larva of one sort or another. It is also one of the easiest flies to tie. The darning wool originally recommended, Chadwick's 477, has been discontinued by the manufacturers, but various beige shades work well. My own experience of catching many hundreds of fish on this is that the dressing with the copper wire underbody is more effective than that tied with lead. The copper shines through the translucent wet body in a much more attractive way than the lead. I tend to confine its use to chalk streams but I know of many highly experienced anglers who rate it as their best grayling fly for rainfed rivers too.

Hook: 8–14
Thread: None
Body: An underbody of lead or fuse wire is overlaid with three layers of beige darning wool. Fine copper wire can be used to tie in the materials and finish off at the tail

Gold Head or Copper Head Killer Bug *Plate 18*

Why change a very good fly? In the hope of making it even better is, the the only answer. I am not alone in adding a gold or copper bead and a hackle to the Killer Bug. It sinks even faster and the hackle and bead do give it further characteristics which grayling particularly find attractive. On one occasion I caught almost 80 grayling from the Wiltshire Avon in a few hours fishing with this, and a good many trout.

Hook: 12–14
Thread: Beige or orange
Underbody: Copper wire
Body: Beige darning wool wound
Hackle: Brown partridge behind the bead
Head: Gold-coloured metal bead or copper bead

Kite's Imperial *Plate 27*

Oliver Kite devised this in 1962, possibly basing it upon an earlier Welsh dressing. Within a few years it had gained a nationwide following. In addition to being an excellent general dry fly, it is specifically useful as an imitation of the large dark olive dun.

Hook: 14–16
Thread: Purple
Tail: Grey or brown hackle fibres in the early season; honey-dun fibres later
Body: Natural heron herl

Rib: Gold wire
Thorax: Heron herl doubled and re-doubled
Hackle: Honey-dun cock. Light ginger is a more readily available substitute

Klinkhamer Special *Plate 28*

I doubt if any fly pattern devised in the last twenty years is as effective in its way as this fast-water grayling and trout fly devised by Hans van Klinken. It is becoming popular wherever these species are found. On an unfamiliar stream or where there is no sign of rising fish it is all too easy to put on a Klinkhamer and not have to worry any longer. Very rarely does it fail on medium to fast water. Sometimes fish hit it hard; on other occasions they merely sip it through the film without disturbance. Its success is due to the relatively large abdomen hanging tantalisingly below the surface. The body must sink below the surface; if it floats it is ineffective. The fly is also highly visible to the angler because of the white poly yarn wing. The wing colour does not matter too much – that is for the angler's benefit. I use fluorescent pink wings in difficult light or where the white wing proves invisible. Hans tied it as an emerging sedge imitation and it does work in these circumstances. It excels when there is very little hatching and a search fly is needed. The hook shape is extremely important.

Hook: Partridge K12ST long shank curved size 12–22, give a slight downward bend half-way along the body
Thread: Black
Body: Light tan poly yarn dubbed over a layer of the wing material
Wing: White or coloured poly yarn (siliconised Niche poly yarn is preferred)
Thorax: Peacock herl
Hackle: Chestnut or blue-dun cock tied in a parachute round the base of the wing

LAKE OLIVE
(Cloëon simile)

See EPHEMEROPTERA

This is a widely distributed species similar to, but not as common as, the pond olive. The adults are medium-sized with a body length of approximately 8 mm. J. R. Harris suggests that the autumn adults are smaller than those in the spring. The main difference between these and the pond olive is that the lake olive is drabber in colour. The adults emerge between May and June and sometimes again from August to October. In the evenings a fall of spinners often stimulates interest from trout. The nymphs are the agile-darting types and live among weeds in deeper water. John Goddard suggests they may favour cooler water than most ephemeropterans, and this could account for their absence from shallower lakes.

The male dun has smoke-grey wings with pale yellow veins. The abdomen is reddish-brown with a dark olive-grey underside. The legs are olive-green and the two tails are dark grey. The female dun is similar to the male except that the tails are slightly paler and it has white wings.

The female spinner has transparent wings with faint yellow veins. The abdomen is chestnut-brown with grey-olive under. The legs are olive with the front pair olive and black, and the two tails are white with faint red rings. The male spinner is of no interest.

In addition to the patterns given, many general olive nymphs and duns would be suitable imitations. See OLIVES, GOLD-RIBBED HARE'S EAR, GOLDEN OLIVE, OLIVE BLOA, GREENWELL'S GLORY, ROUGH OLIVE, PHEASANT-TAIL SPINNER.

Lake Olive Dun

(Peter Lapsley)   *Plate 27*

Peter Lapsley recommends trimming the bottom edge off the hackle of the fly to improve its floatability.

Hook: Fine-wire 14

Thread: Brown
Tail: Light-dun cock hackle fibres
Body: Dark-olive condor herl
Rib: Silver wire
Hackle: Two medium blue-dun cock hackles

Lake Olive Spinner *(J. R. Harris)*

Hook: 12–14
Thread: Orange
Tail: Rusty-dun hackle fibres
Body: Deep-amber or mahogany seal's fur
Rib: Gold wire
Wing: Pale grizzle-dun hackle bunched and tied spent

Lamplighter

John Horsfall created this stickfly variation. The interesting feature about it is that it uses a two-colour fluorescent butt, the theory being that the fluorescent attraction will work under more than one set of circumstances. When fished deep as a point fly it should be tied with lead underbody.

Hook: Slightly long shank Kamasan B200 or B830 size 10–12
Thread: Dark brown
Butt: Glo-Brite floss in the suggested shade combinations 1/7, 5/12, 14/15, 11/13
Ribs: Pearl Mylar with copper wire wound in the opposite way
Body: Magenta-dyed peacock herl
Hackle: Dark coch-y-bondhu

LARGE BROOK DUN
(Ecdyonurus torrentis)

See EPHEMEROPTERA

A fairly widespread but localised species similar in appearance to the late March brown. It inhabits smaller stony streams, in contrast to the late March brown, which prefers larger rivers. The nymphs are the flat, stone-clinging type. The adults appear between late March and July and could be expected at any time during daylight. March Brown imitations are usually fished to represent this species.

LARGE DARK OLIVE (Baetis rhodani)

See EPHEMEROPTERA.
Also known as the large spring olive, blue dun or early olive. This is a widespread species, usually preferring faster-flowing water. The nymph is an agile-darting type and can be found clinging to rocks and stones, and, in the slower rivers, on weeds and moss. The medium-to-large-sized adults appear from late February to late April, and may reappear during a spell of mild autumn weather. Consequently it is a useful grayling fly in addition to being an early-season trout fly.

In early spring the duns often stay on the water for quite a long time, drying their wings in a cold, damp atmosphere. Many northern and Scottish rivers experience prolific hatches, and even on the most unlikely days there may be a short rise period when trout take the newly emerged duns. The female spinner, in common with other members of the Baetis genus, returns to the water and crawls below the surface to lay its eggs.

The male dun has pale grey wings with pale brown veins. The abdomen is olive-brown or olive-green, with a dark olive underside. The legs are light olive with olive-grey forelegs. The two tails are dull grey. The female dun has wings similar to the male's. The abdomen is dark olive-brown or olive-green with a paler underside. The legs are pale olive-green and the two tails are medium grey.

The female spinner, also known as the large red spinner, has transparent wings with brown veins. The abdomen is dark mahogany with a pale olive underside. The legs are dark brown-olive and the two tails are dark or olive-grey with red-brown rings. The male spinner is of no interest.

For additional patterns, see also GOLD-RIBBED HARE'S EAR, ROUGH OLIVE, EARLY OLIVE, DARK OLIVE BLOA, WATERHEN BLOA, GREENWELL'S GLORY, DOGSBODY, LUNN'S PARTICULAR, KITE'S IMPERIAL and PHEASANT-TAIL SPINNER.

Large Dark Olive Nymph

Hook: 12
Thread: Yellow
Tail: Dark olive hackle fibres
Body: Mixed olive seal's fur and hare's ear fur
Rib: Gold wire
Thorax: Brown seal's fur
Wing-case: Dark olive swan or goose fibres
Legs: The end fibres of the wing-case material turned beneath the body, or olive cock fibres

Large Dark Olive Nymph

(Oliver Edwards) Plate 17

A superb imitation that will reward patient tying. The tying sequence is: tail, abdomen, tie in wing-case and leg feather; thorax, legs, wing-case and wing-case strip. Before the leg feather is laid on top of the thorax, smear a thin line of glue or varnish on top of the thorax, and again before the wing-case.

Hook: Long shank 18 Partridge H1A
Thread: White
Tail: Badger hair dyed medium olive
Abdomen: Olive Flexibody or olive-dyed polythene strip in overlapping turns
Wing-case: Dark turkey fibres with a narrow strip of abdomen material down the middle
Legs: Small speckled partridge dyed medium-dark olive
Thorax: Olive-brown hare's belly fur

Large Dark Olive Dun

(Preben Torp Jacobsen) Plate 27

The three hackles on this pattern make it a good floater. A single turn of each is sufficient, although Jacobsen ties his fuller to cope with trout-farm pollution on his home rivers of Denmark.

Hook: 12–14
Thread: Amber

Tail: Ginger cock hackle fibres
Body: Two natural and two heron herls dyed olive twisted together
Rib: Fine silver wire
Hackles: Three. Medium-sized pale olive and a small ginger cock wound together, with a large rusty-dun at the head

LARGE GREEN DUN
(Ecdyonurus insignis)

See EPHEMEROPTERA
Although this species is not particularly rare, the trout's lack of interest in it is indicated by the paucity of artificials. The natural is found in parts of the North of England, South Wales and the West Country. The dun is fairly large with light fawn mottled wings and has a dark olive-green body with brown diagonal bands along the sides. The adults are commonest in July and August.

Large Green Dun *(John Veniard)*

Hook: 12–14
Tail: Dark dun cock fibres
Body: Greenish-grey seal's fur or light heron wing quill herl dyed green
Rib: Dark-brown or black tying thread
Hackle: Cock dyed green with a grizzle dyed green in front

LARGE SUMMER DUN
(Siphlonurus alternatus,
S. lacustris)

See EPHEMEROPTERA
Both species are fairly rare, but are found on stillwater in parts of Scotland, the North of England and Wales. The agile-darting nymphs of *S. lacustris* are large and brown-olive, and the large duns have grey wings, olive bodies about 14–15 mm long with pale-brown markings, and two tails. The female spinner has transparent wings with light-brown veins and a dull-green body. The adults appear mainly in July and August. *S. alternatus* prefers more alkaline water, but is similar to *S. lacustris*. The

nymphs can be successfully imitated with a large olive nymph or Mayfly nymph pattern fished faster than normal, as the naturals are strong swimmers. The dun can be represented by the Dark Cahill.

Large Summer Dun Nymph
(Taff Price)

Hook: Long shank 12–14
Thread: Brown
Tail: Brown-olive fibres
Body: Brownish-olive seal's fur with a palmered olive hackle
Rib: Gold wire
Thorax: Mixed olive and yellow seal's fur
Wing-case: Brown feather fibres
Hackle: One turn of dark-olive hen or cock

Large Summer Spinner
(Taff Price)

Hook: 12
Tail: Long dark-olive fibres
Body: Light-brown polypropelene
Rib: Yellow silk or nylon
Wing: Light partridge tied spent
Hackle: None, or dark-olive clipped flat at the bottom.

Last Resort

This is a roach-fry imitation tied by David Train.

Hook: Long shank 4–10
Body: White acetate floss wound in a fish-shape. This is treated with solvent and flattened on the sides. When dry, it is covered with flat silver Lurex and overlaid with polythene strip. A small tuft of fluorescent red floss is tied in at either side at the shoulder
Rib: Silver wire
Wing: Twisted strands of bronze peacock herl and blue bucktail tied down at the tail
Underbody (optional): Strip of white swan feather with the rib taken over it
Head: Peacock herl

Lead Bug
Plate 16

In the 1960s there was much talk of Oliver Kite's Bare Hook Nymph, which was no more than a bare hook with a thorax of copper wire. By presenting it accurately, and moving it in an appropriate manner, Oliver Kite took many chalk-stream trout and grayling with this unlikely pattern. The Lead Bug is today's stillwater equivalent of Kite's pattern. This ugly fly has gained quite a following on some southern small, clear stillwaters. One angler was reported to have taken six double-figure Avington trout on it in one season. The bug is cast to an observed fish, with the angler aiming to drop it in front of the trout's nose. The trout's reaction is closely watched for the take. The version illustrated and described below belongs to small stillwater expert Peter Cockwill. He comments that it is meant to be cast to sighted fish and then pulled away from them as they take notice so that a follow is induced with the trout's curiosity aroused. The only way the fish can get it is to chase and engulf it without proper time for inspection.

Hook: Partridge stronghold 10
Tail, thorax and legs: Olive Pearsall's salmon floss
Body: 4–5 mm lead wire

Leadhead

This name was first used on a weighted lure devised by Richard Walker. It should be fished in short jerks or with long pulls with pauses in between. The lure fishes upside down and so avoids becoming snagged on the bottom.

Hook: Forged 8–10 on which is pinched a BB lead shot just behind the eye
Body: Floss silk tied to just in front of the lead shot and varnished with Vycoat
Rib: Tinsel
Wing: Hairwing
Head: Lead shot painted with white plastic paint, with an eye painted on each side and varnished

Colour combinations:

Wing	Head	Body
Yellow	Light brown	Arc chrome (DF wool or floss)
Black	Black	Black
Grey squirrel (or wool)	Brown	Red DF floss
Yellow (or wool)	Brown	Red DF floss
Orange	Brown	Orange DF (floss or wool)

Leadhead Nymph
Plate 18

As a river fly this pattern of Hans van Klinken is quite an eye-opener. It looks too big, ugly and aggressive to work on our rivers for trout and grayling. However, it is extremely successful. It was devised for deep, fast-water Scandinavian grayling where a fly has to reach the bottom fast. In a decade this fly has gained a very wide following and is becoming popular in North America. A number of variants are tied, all suggestive of food. Fished upstream in a dead-drift it is probably taken for a cased caddis. Fished across or against the current it works well as a small fish imitation.

Hook: 10–14
Thread: Brown or black
Tail: Brown partridge tail fibres, partridge back fibres or a soft mottled wing hen pheasant wing feather, wound as a collar between the butt and the body, one or two turns
Butt: Fluorescent green Flexibody or fluorescent green wool
Body: Shaggy brown fur, in a dubbing loop and wound
Head: Lead-substitute shot strongly bound on a piece of looped mono, bound with the split towards the eye

Leckford Professor

This southern chalk-stream dry fly was devised by Ernest Mott, a Test river-keeper. Donald Overfield records its alternative name as being Cow's Arse, although I am at a loss to understand why.

It is described as a useful fly for 'choosy' trout.

Hook: 12–14
Body: Dark hare's ear fur
Rib: Fine flat gold tinsel
Hackles: A bright red cock hackle and a white cock hackle tied in at the rear of the shank, hiding the point of the fly

LEECHES

These are fairly common in stillwaters, where they inhabit deeper water near the lake-bed. There is little doubt that some of the black or brown lures fished slow and deep are mistaken for leeches. The pulsating action of marabou gives a good impression of a leech. A Black Woolly Bugger is a fair imitation, as is this Woolly Bugger variant tied by Theo Bakelaar. Theo recommends that in a river with a heavy current it should be fished close to the bottom in a dead drift. On stillwaters he suggests a sinking line to fish it close to bottom.

Gold Bead Black Leech   *Plate 4*

Hook: TMC 900 long shank 8
Thread: Black
Tail: Black marabou
Body: Black chenille with a strip of Spectra Flash down each side
Rib: Black saddle hackle
Head: 4 mm gold bead

Whitlock Electric Leech   *Plate 4*

A very effective pattern from the vice of Dave Whitlock.

Hook: Partridge low-water salmon hook, size 1/0–10
Thread: Black Danville 6/0
Cement: Dave's Flexament
Underbody: Wound lead wire
Tail: Black marabou
Body: Mixed Black African goat and rabbit hair in a 50/50 blend
Palmer hackle: Long, webby, soft, black saddle hackle

Body and tail back: Three to six peacock herls
Body and tail flash: Two to four Flashabou strands
Head: Black thread and wound with Flashabou

Leprechaun   *Plate 3*

A lure devised by Peter Wood. Because of the fluorescent green materials, it is useful when algae is about. A matuka version is commercially available. This has four cock hackles as below, but tied and ribbed in matuka-style. It is a good pattern for fishing deep on a bright, sunny day.

Hook: Long shank 6–10
Tail: Lime-green hackle fibres
Body: Fluorescent-green chenille
Rib: Silver wire
Throat hackle: Lime-green hackle fibres
Wing: Four lime-green cock hackles tied back to back

Leven Stick   *Plate 9*

Stan Headley first tied this fly in 1990 and within a month it had won him the Scottish Flyfishing Championship. It is most effective in wild, blustery, overcast conditions when a susbstantial point fly not only helps anchor the cast, but is highly visible. This should be tied bulky. It is always worth a try in wild conditions. Fish it on intermediate or floating lines and retrieve fairly quickly.

Hook: Long shank 12–14
Thread: Black
Tag: GloBrite yarn, No. 11
Body: Two strands bronze peacock herl, one wound in butting turns, the other wound down, ribbed with stretched medium pearl Mylar
Hackle: Smallish medium red/brown hen

Light Ollie
Plate 27

This is a Danish pattern from Preben Torp Jacobsen. Its creator comments: 'I tied the fly for the first time in June 1963. My intention was to create a fly imitating the most common dayflies on my home stream, the large dark olive and medium olive. It had to have the ability to float high on slightly polluted water downstream of trout-farms, and moreover to be easy to retrieve when it by accident landed among weeds and plants.

'I used the fly myself and gave it to friends, so that they could see if it worked. Fortunately, I had a detailed description of the fly in my diary, and in 1971 friends started to ask for more flies. I tied a darker version, too, with darker hackles.

'Its name, Ollie, was given it in 1971 as a tribute to my dear friend, the late Oliver Kite, whose name among friends was "Ollie".'

Hook: 15 Mustad 72709
Thread: Primrose
Tail: Buff Orpington hackle fibres
Body: Four heron herls dyed in picric acid and twisted round the tying silk
Rib: Fine silver wire
Body hackle: Natural blue-dun hackle (henny cock) palmered along the body
Head hackle: Light honey-dun cock (like a Metz sandy brown)

Light Woodcock

A North Country wet fly, a copy of the needle flies. It is also known as the Little Winter Brown (See WINTER BROWN). This is an old dressing mentioned by, but probably not originating from, T. E. Pritt. It is still dressed in the original manner.

Hook: 12–14
Body: Orange tying silk sparsely dubbed with hare's ear fur
Hackle: Inside feather of a woodcock's wing
Head: Peacock herl

Little Marryat

G. S. Marryat devised this dry fly for the southern chalk-streams. It is fished as a pale watery dun and spurwing imitation. When the pattern given is dressed with a body of peacock eye quill bleached pale brown, it is known as the Quill Marryat. An alternative body material is cream seal's fur, as suggested by G. E. M. Skues.

Hook: 12–14
Tail: Pale-olive guinea-fowl
Body: Australian opossum flank
Wing: Pale starling
Hackle: Pale-buff cochin cock

Little White Head Nymph
Plate 17

This unlikely-looking fly is recommended by World Championship silver medallist Adam Sikora from Poland. It was devised by his fellow countryman Franciszek Szajnik. This pattern was largely responsible for Adam's championship success on the Welsh Dee. He comments that it is a very efficient summer pattern, excellent in a dead drift, but sometimes requiring slight control across the current. It is to be fished on a very short line in moderate to fast water.

Hook: 10
Thread: Pale beige
Underbody: Lead wire
Abdomen: Rust- or copper-coloured wool ribbed with red copper wire
Thorax: Cream-coloured wool
Head: Beige thread

Loch Ordie
Plate 6

Stan Headley, an Orcadian, comments that this was originally a dapping fly but the modern version is now used as a standard wet fly. Modern trends are towards dressing it much slimmer and smaller so that it serves as a midge or small sedge imitation. The Loch Ordie range are primarily top-dropper flies, to be used with floating or intermediate lines. These finer-dressed versions catch wild and stocked trout throughout the country. Larger versions also do well with migratory fish.

Hook: 10–14
Hackles: The modern versions have a single red/brown hackle with a white hackle at the head. The original had five or six red/brown hackles

Dark Loch Ordie   *(Plate 6)*

This is a very successful variation. It is always tied slim, and fished slowly on a floating line and can wreak havoc on midge and dark sedge feeders. Keep the dressing well up the shank and tightly wound, whilst trying to ensure a good backward slope to the hackles

Hook: 12–14
Hackles: Two longish chocolate-brown hen hackles plus one black at the head

Blue Loch Ordie   *(Plate 6)*

Devised by Norman Irvine, this is a good pattern for peat-stained water. Stan Headley has seen it regularly take two-pounders from waters where anything over a pound is worthy of mention.

Hook: 10–12
Hackles: Two or three longish black hen hackles plus one blue at the head

Loop-Wing Dun

Andre Puyans of San Francisco devised this method of imitating the upright wing on a dun imitation. Fibres of natural grey or brown or dyed mallard flank or shoulder feather are used. The tips may be used as the tail fibres. The wing fibres are bound on top of the shank and are doubled over into a loop-shaped wing and secured in an upright position. The wing is then divided in half and slightly parted.

Lunn's Particular

William Lunn is probably the best-remembered of all the Test's river-keepers. He produced a number of dressings, some of which are still used today. He introduced this pattern in 1917 as a copy of the medium olive and large dark olive spinners. J. W. Hills, in his book, *River Keeper*, praised Lunn, saying that he had the ability to think like a trout. He also wrote of the Lunn's Particular: 'If I had to be limited to one fly, I should choose this.' It is still a splendid fly, killing trout on both rain-fed rivers and chalk-streams.

Hook: 14–16
Thread: Crimson
Tail: Rhode Island Red hackle fibres
Body: Hackle-stalk of a Rhode Island Red hackle
Wing: Two medium-blue cock hackle points tied spent
Hackle: Rhode Island Red cock

Lunn's Particular

(Ian Warrilow)   *Plate 21*

Ian Warrilow offers a modern version with more durable wings and an additional thorax.

Hook: 14–16
Thread: Crimson
Tail: Rhode Island Red hackle fibres
Body: Undyed stripped Rhode Island Red hackle stalk
Thorax: Rich brown Antron
Wing: Cream poly yarn

Lunn's Yellow Boy

Another pattern from William Lunn (see LUNN'S PARTICULAR). It is a Baetis (olive) sunk-spinner imitation. See under each member of the Baetis genus for fuller details.

Hook: 14
Thread: Pale orange
Tail: Pale buff cock hackle fibres
Body: White hackle stalk dyed yellow or yellow seal's fur

Wing: Light buff cock hackle fibres bunched and tied in the spent position

Machair Claret   *Plate 6*

This very good loch-style fly is from John Kennedy. It combines aspects of other successful flies to produce a unique and distinctive pattern. This is for poor light. The jungle cock feather must be tied with its flat plane at 90 degrees to the shank and shiny side down. Stan Headley reckons that to a fish it looks like a fly almost totally emerged from a shuck.

Hook: 8–12
Thread: Black
Tail: Jungle cock feather
Body: Claret seal's fur, palmered with a claret and a black cock hackle, over-ribbed with medium oval silver
Hackle: Longish black hen

Maid Marion

This is popular lure in Yorkshire and the wider north of the country where it has been used with increasing popularity for about twenty years. It was devised by Peter Highfield, I believe for Leighton Reservoir. It is an extremely simple fly, yet very effective.

Hook: Long shank 8–12
Tail: Yellow marabou
Body: Green seal's fur
Rib: Gold tinsel

Mallard Series

An old range of fancy and imitative patterns using mallard wings. They are of proven success for lake trout and of value to the river fisherman in their smaller sizes. The combination of colours is extensive and is broadly similar to those in the GROUSE, TEAL and WOODCOCK series. The mallard wing material is taken from the small speckled brown shoulder-feathers. In all four series it is a general but flexible rule that the hackle should be the same colour as the body, and that the

materials for the tail may be varied between golden-pheasant tippet fibres or crests, floss silk, wool or red ibis. As with most winged wet flies, the hackle is tied on the underside only.

Mallard and Black   *Plate 7*

Hook: 8–14
Tail: Golden pheasant tippets
Body: Black seal's fur
Rib: Fine oval silver tinsel
Wing: Bronze mallard
Hackle: Black hen

Mallard and Blue

Body: Light-blue seal's fur
Rib: Fine oval silver tinsel
Hackle: Cock or hen dyed blue
Wing and tail: As Mallard and Black

Mallard and Claret   *Plate 7*

This is possibly the oldest fly in the series and is a general imitative pattern. It is probably of Scottish origin. W. C. Stewart and Francis Francis both refer to similar flies. As a general lake fly, it has few peers. It kills on tiny moorland streams and on large reservoirs. Taken over a whole season, few general standby patterns give better results when fished as a top dropper. It is a fair sedge-pupa imitation and can be used to represent the nymphs or emerging sepia and claret duns. Some anglers have found it deadly in its smaller sizes when fished slowly an inch below the surface during a midge hatch. John Goddard's comment in his book, *Trout Flies of Stillwater*, is: 'the best all-rounder one is likely to find.'

Thread: Claret or black
Tail: Golden pheasant tippets
Butt (optional): Green peacock herl. This is found on the mallard series only, not on the teal, grouse and woodcock patterns
Body: Claret seal's fur
Rib: Fine gold tinsel or wire

Hackle: Dyed claret cock or hen, or black cock or hen, or natural red game
Wing: Bronze mallard

A Welsh variation has a tail of brown mallard fibres and a black hen or cock hackle.

Mallard and Gold

Body: Flat gold tinsel
Rib: Gold wire or fine tinsel
Hackle: Black or ginger
Tail and wing: As Mallard and Black

Mallard and Green

Body: Green seal's fur
Rib: Fine oval silver tinsel
Hackle: Green hen
Tail and wing: As Mallard and Black

Mallard and Mixed

Body: In three sections of orange, red and fiery-brown seal's fur
Rib: Oval gold tinsel
Hackle: Dark-red cock or hen
Wing and tail: As Mallard and Black

Mallard and Orange

Body: Orange seal's fur
Rib: Oval gold tinsel
Hackle: Orange hen
Wing and tail: As Mallard and Black

Mallard and Red

Body: Red seal's fur
Rib: Oval gold tinsel
Hackle: Natural red hen
Wing and tail: As Mallard and Black

Mallard Red and Yellow

Body: Rear half, red seal's fur; front half, yellow seal's fur
Rib: Oval gold tinsel

Hackle: Black or orange hen
Wing and tail: As Mallard and Black

Mallard and Silver

Body: Silver tinsel
Rib: Silver wire
Hackle: Black or blue hen
Wing and tail: As Mallard and Black

Mallard and Yellow

Body: Yellow seal's fur
Rib: Oval gold tinsel
Hackle: Yellow hen
Wing and tail: As Mallard and Black

Malloch's Favourite   Plate 7

A traditional Scottish loch fly for when olives are about.

Hook: 10–14
Thread: Black
Tail: Red cock fibres
Body: Stripped peacock herl from the eye of a feather, sometimes with a tip of silver tinsel
Wing: Strips of woodcock secondary
Hackle: Medium blue-dun hen

Marabou Bastard   Plate 2

This unpleasant-sounding name was given to this leech- or fry-imitating style of tying from Danish angler, Dennis Burmester. Dennis comments that the position of the weighting of the fly is important and that it should be placed behind and under the head. The tail must be generous with the marabou and be at least as long as the shank. They are tied in a wide mixture of colours as attractors or leech imitations.

Hook: Long shank 8
Weight: Copper wire under and behind the head
Tail: Generous plumes of marabou plus four or five strands of pearl Flashabou

Body: Bunches of marabou tied in at the head, secured at the tail. If the marabou is not very fluffly a thicker thread under-body is required
Rib: Double-ribbed with copper and oval silver
Head: Black tying thread

Marabou Winged Lures

Marabou has become extremely popular as a tail or winging medium for lures. Saddle hackles as streamer wings and animal hair as bucktail wings have both been in favour, but the pulsating action of marabou makes it difficult to beat. The wing works well even when a lure is fished slowly, giving an impression of life. Most marabou lures are best fished in steady pulls, with pauses in between.

Many have individual names and they are listed separately under these. Others have no names, so I have opted for a reliable and easy-to-tie pattern from a well-known stillwater angler, Steve Parton, as an example. It is based on three colours: black, white or hot-orange. Steve describes the resultant lures as 'the deadliest bank lures for early season that I know. Bank-fishing early- or late-season are the times they really come into their own. Fast-sinking lines should be used and with four variations (white, black, hot-orange and green-lined versions) you can cover bank lure fishing from March to late May and from mid-September until the close'. The technique is initially to fish as deep as possible, and then to move up through the water to find the fish. Tandem versions are excellent general boat lures for similar periods of the season.

Hook: 3X long shank 6–10
Body: Medium black, white or hot-orange chenille
Rib: Fine oval silver tinsel
Wing: Marabou plumes to match the body colour
Cheeks (optional): Target-green fluorescent wool

Mackerel Nymph *Plate 30*

This river nymph, a sedge larva imitation, is from the Polish expert nymph fisher Adam Sikora. It uses a very unusual material, mackerel skin, which not only looks effective but is likely to be attractivr because of its aroma. Adam advises that to prepare a Mackerel Nymph 'you should remove the skin from a smoked mackerel, clean off the remainder of the meat and soak the skin in water. Then remove the white inside part of the skin from the belly and tha skin becomes slightly transparent with a golder tint. The dark stripes of the mackerel back give darker points, whichg should be placed at the head of the nymph. The strip of skin should be wet when tied in.'

Hook: Tiemco TMC 2457, 2X wide, 2X short, 2X heavy, curved, size 6–12
Thread: Black
Underbody: Lead wire
Abdomen: Olive-green dubbing, for 80 per cent of the length
Thorax: Black wool
Rib: 0.16 mm mono wound over the back
Back: Strip of smoked mackerel skin
Head: Black thread

MARCH BROWN
(*Rithrogena germanica*)

See EPHEMEROPTERA
This was one of the first natural flies to be imitated by the fly fisher. The natural fly is less common than popularly supposed and has a very local distribution in isolated parts of Wales, the North of England, Scotland, and, according to some authorities, in the West Country. What is more likely is that years ago before anglers began to look closely at the fly, the species was confused with the late March brown, which has a much wider distribution, and the two species were grouped together and jointly known as the March brown.

The nymphs are dark bronze-green and live on smooth stones in faster-flowing water. The large-sized adults generally appear around midday and early afternoon during March and perhaps into April. They are most frequently seen at the tail of faster, broken water. Previously the March brown was widely reported as continuing to emerge into May, but these hatches are now thought more likely to be the late March brown. The hatches can be prolific but irregular. During a hatch, the evidence is that the emergers are often preferred by trout, and so a wet pattern fished close to the surface is more successful. This is borne out by the many variations of the wet artificial and the scarcity of dun and spinner imitations.

The male dun has pale-fawn wings with heavy dark-brown veins. The abdomen is dark brown with straw-coloured rings. The legs are pale brown and the two tails are dark brown-grey. The female dun has darker wings than the male. The abdomen is a duller brown with rings similar to the male's. The legs are pale olive with darker forelegs, and the two tails are dark brown.

The female spinner, also known as the great red spinner, has transparent wings with dark veins. The abdomen is dark red-brown with straw-coloured rings. The legs are various shades of olive and the two tails are brown. The male spinner is of no interest as it dies over land and does not return to water.

LATE (or FALSE) MARCH BROWN (Ecdyonurus venosus)

The nymph and dun stage are similar to *R. germanica* and are found in similar types of river, but they are more widely distributed and much commoner than the March brown. The same artificials represent both species. Some entomologists have observed the nymphs of *E. venosus* crawling ashore to make the transition from nymph to dun on rocks and stones. This is more in the manner of a stonefly than an upwinged fly. Just before the appearance of the dun, numbers of nymphs make their way shorewards, and at such times the sub-surface fly is of value. The late March brown is far commoner than the March brown, but both species were known only by the latter name for centuries. This is why so many wet flies designated March Browns were developed in comparison with the few dun and spinner patterns.

The adults emerge from April to June, and in some years in August and September. The female spinner of the species is slightly larger and has a redder body than the female spinner of *R. germanica*. The female spinners of both species can be imitated with a Cinnamon Quill or Great Red Spinner. See also separate entry for the SILVER MARCH BROWN.

Many artificials purporting to represent the sub-surface March brown may well do so, but they are so generally impressionistic that they may be taken for shrimps, water-lice or sedge pupae.

March Brown   Plate 20

A winged wet fly.

Hook: 12–14
Tail: Partridge tail fibres
Body: Brown seal's fur or sandy hare's ear fur
Rib: Gold wire
Wing: Brown partridge or hen pheasant
Hackle: Brown partridge

March Brown Spider

(Roger Woolley)

Woolley was a northern fly fisher of great experience and he listed more than 20 different March Brown dressings in his book, *Modern Trout Fly Dressing*.

Hook: 12
Thread: Orange
Body: Sandy hare's neck fur
Rib: Yellow thread
Wing: Speckled partridge tail tied thin
Hackle: Light-brown partridge

March Brown Spider *Plate 20*

Hook: 12–14
Tail: Speckled partridge tail fibres
Body: Dark hare's ear mixed with brown or claret seal's fur
Rib: Primrose thread or silver wire
Hackle: Speckled partridge

March Brown Nymph
(John Veniard) *Plate 17*

Hook: 12–14
Tail: Two strands of cock pheasant tail fibres or brown mallard shoulder feather fibres
Body: Cock pheasant tail
Rib: Gold wire
Thorax: Hare's ear fur
Wing-case: Woodcock wing feather fibres
Legs: Small brown speckled partridge hackle

March Brown Dun

This is Taff Price's dressing for the male dun. The female dun imitation has a light hen pheasant wing.

Hook: 12
Thread: Primrose
Tail: Cree hackle fibres
Body: Mixed hare's ear and yellow seal's fur
Rib: Yellow thread
Wing: Dark hen pheasant wing quill slips set upright
Hackle: Cree cock

March Brown *(Tony Pepper) Plate 19*

The soft tail fibres are a fair imitation of the nymphal shuck. Trout usually express a preference for the emerger of this species, which is probably why this pattern works very well.

Hook: 14–16
Thread: Purple
Tail: Speckled brown partridge breast fibres

Body: Hare's ear
Hackles: Honey cock with a speckled brown partridge breast feather in front

Mar Lodge *Plate 8*

This was originally a salmon fly but scaled down as an Irish lough pattern it also works very well for trout, particularly at night, but also during the day in warmer weather.

Hook: 10–14
Thread: Black
Tail: Golden pheasant crest
Body: A third each, flat silver, black thread, flat silver
Rib: Oval silver (sizes 10–12) or silver wire (size 14)
Wing: Bronze mallard
Hackle: Guinea-fowl

Matukas

An extensive series of lures originating in New Zealand. The Matukas are named after the bird which originally supplied the wing material. Substitutes have now been adopted. The wings are constructed by taking two round-ended feathers and placing them back to back. The lower fibres are stripped away for the length of the shank, so that the hackle-stem rests on the body, leaving a full-length back and the lower fibres beyond the bend only. The rib is taken through the upper fibres, which are then stroked rearwards. Jungle-cock eyes are sometimes added to standard patterns. These versions are known as Imperials. In addition to the dressings given, Matuka lures in a single colour are popular, e.g. all-black, all-white, all-green, etc. Matukas can all be fished fairly slowly, with frequent pauses to enliven the hackle wings.

Badger Matuka *(Dave Collyer)*

Hook: Long shank 6–10
Thread: Orange
Body: Fluorescent-orange wool

Wing: Two badger cock hackles in matuka style
Rib: Fine oval silver tinsel
Beard hackle: Hot-orange or scarlet cock
Cheeks: Jungle cock

White chenille is a suitable body alternative, and other colours may take your fancy.

Spey Matuka   Plate 4

This is a rather extraordinary and beautiful lure devised by Marcelo Morales. It uses the elegance of Spey salmon flies tied in a Matuka style. The marabou hackles make it extremely lifelike. It was devised as river pattern, as a minnow imitation.

Hook: Salmon hook Partridge CS10
Thread: Black 8/0
Butt and rib: Fine oval gold tinsel
Underbody: Lead wire
Body: Pearlescent Mylar braid
Wing: Four saddle hackles, colour to match a minnow or fry, in Matuka style
Gills: Four turns of red saddle hackle
Front hackle: Two marabou feathers, wound together
Eyes (optional): Jungle cock

MAYFLY (Ephemera danica, E. vulgata)

See EPHEMEROPTERA
These two similar species are the largest of the upwinged duns. The Mayfly hatch (by which I mean these two species, and not all upwings which are often simply known as Mayflies) on a river or stillwater is a feature deemed precious by all fly fishermen. Many waters with once prolific hatches now have few or none at all. Huge hatches still occur on some rivers, with the air thick with newly-emerged duns. Stillwater hatches have always been rarer than those on rivers. Trout feed greedily on the nymphs, duns and spinners, and the time of the Mayfly hatch on many rivers was looked upon as the 'duffer's fortnight'.

The Mayfly has been referred to in angling literature over many centuries, and the imitation of the greendrake (as the dun was often called) long taxed the fly-tying skills of our forebears. In spite of considerable attention to the Mayfly in the past, few fly tyers placed much importance upon the nymph. G. S. Marryat was the first to do so at the end of the last century. In my opinion, Richard Walker produced the best nymph pattern yet devised. It is a great killer of trout on rivers and stillwaters and I have even caught autumn grayling on it.

The distribution of the species is widespread, although rivers and lakes having huge hatches in early June seem to be diminishing in numbers. The duns and spinners can be seen from May until the end of July. The nymphs burrow in the bottom mud and take between one and two years to mature. These large nymphs are known to leave their burrows and rise to the surface and descend again for about two weeks before the main hatch. This may happen at different places on a river over a number of evenings. The artificial nymph is well worth using in these circumstances.

The duns usually appear in the afternoons. After mating the female spinner (sometimes known as the grey drake or spent gnat) returns to the water, usually in the early evening, to lay her eggs. The male spinner sometimes finds his way back on to the water and can be imitated by the fly fisher. Both spinners are eagerly devoured by the trout, and the rise to the spinners can be more prolific than that to the hatching duns. Because they are the largest of the upwinged flies, they are easy to recognise.

The female dun has grey wings with a blue-green tinge and heavy black veins. They are tinged with yellow along the leading edge. The abdomen is yellow-cream with brownish markings. The legs are creamy-olive and the three tails are dark grey. The male dun has grey wings tinged with yellow and heavy brown veins. The abdomen is greyish-white with brown markings. The legs are dark brown and

Spudler

Black Booby

Fl. Green Baby Doll

Black and Orange Marabou

Cats Whiskers

Sweeny Viva

Bolton Wanderer

Pearlbug Diver

Appetiser

Mini Nobbler

Last Resort Muddler

Theo's Tadpole

PLATE 1 LURES

Growler

Bibby Black and Green

Black and Orange Puppy

Dawson's Olive

Insensor

Marabou Bastard

Mosaic Viva

Viva

Rabbitser

Yellow Tadpole

Minketiser

Concrete Bowl

PLATE 2 LURES

Golden Anna

Ace of Spades

Silver Anna

Micky Finn

Leprechaun

Honey Bear

Brown Trout Streamer

Black Ghost

Natural Zonker

Perch Fry (Saville)

Humbug

V.G.B.

PLATE 3 LURES

Gold Head Leech

Whitlock Electric Leech

Miss Beautiful Zonker

Orange Waggler Muddler

Spey Matuka

Lime Green Marabou Muddler

Fishfinder

Muddler Minnow

PLATE 4 LURES

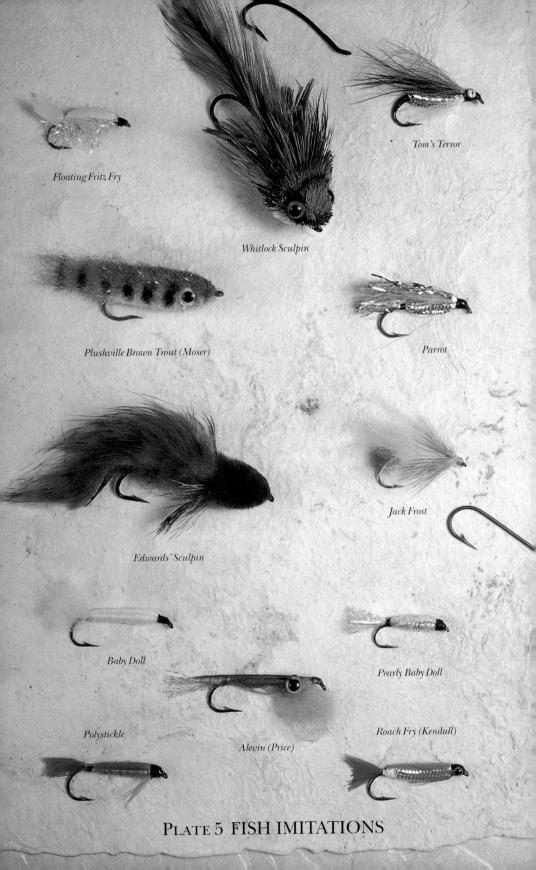

Floating Fritz Fry

Tom's Terror

Whitlock Sculpin

Plushville Brown Trout (Moser)

Parrot

Edwards' Sculpin

Jack Frost

Baby Doll

Pearly Baby Doll

Polystickle

Alevin (Price)

Roach Fry (Kendall)

PLATE 5 FISH IMITATIONS

Pearl-Tailed Soldier Palmer

Clan Chief

Blue Zulu

Loch Ordie

Dark Loch Ordie

Blue Loch Ordie

Connemar Twinkle

John Spencer

Yellow Owl

Ke He

Goat's Toe Variant

White Hackled Invicta

McLeod's Olive

Hutch's Pennell

Pearly Pennell

McHair Claret

Orange Rory

Doobry

PLATE 6 STILLWATER TRADITIONALS

Mallard and Claret

Grey Monkey

Grouse and Yellow

Williams

Kate Mclaren

Mallard and Black

Cinnamon and Gold

Silver March Brown

Malloch's Favourite

Woodock and Green

Invicta

Silver Invicta

Butcher

Teal Blue and Silver

Bloody Butcher

Dunkeld

Peter Ross

Alexandra

PLATE 7 STILLWATER TRADITIONALS

Pearly Bibio

Green Peter

Pearly Olive Palmer

Pearly Wickhams

Coleman Lake Special

Teal and Green Variant

Bousfield's Fancy

Fiery Brown

Soldier Twinkle

Hare's Ear and Woodcock

Orange GRHE

Mar Lodge

Pearly Hare's Ear

Muddler Soldier Palmer

Alder Larva

Annorexic Hare's Ear

Annorexic Buzzer

PLATE 8 STILLWATER GENERAL

Octopus

Flue Brush

Aberdeen Angus

Annabelle

Rabbit Fur Fly

Persuader

GRHE Palmer

Levin Stick

Ned's Fancy

Haystack

Perky

Endrick Spider

Hare's Ear Muddler

Everton Mint

Claret Bumble Muddler

Caenis Muddler

Dunkeld Muddler

Mini Muddler

PLATE 9 STILLWATER GENERAL

Boghill Bumble

Bob's Variant

Connemara Black Bumble

Bushy Raymond

Claret Bumble

Golden Olive Bumble

Sam Slick

Olive Bibio

Connemara Black

Red Arrow

Orange Grouse

Melvin's Pennell

Roy's Mottled May

Golden Dabbler

Rogan's Pearly Extractor

Pearly Doubler

Raymond

Wet Mayfly

PLATE 10 IRISH TRADITIONALS

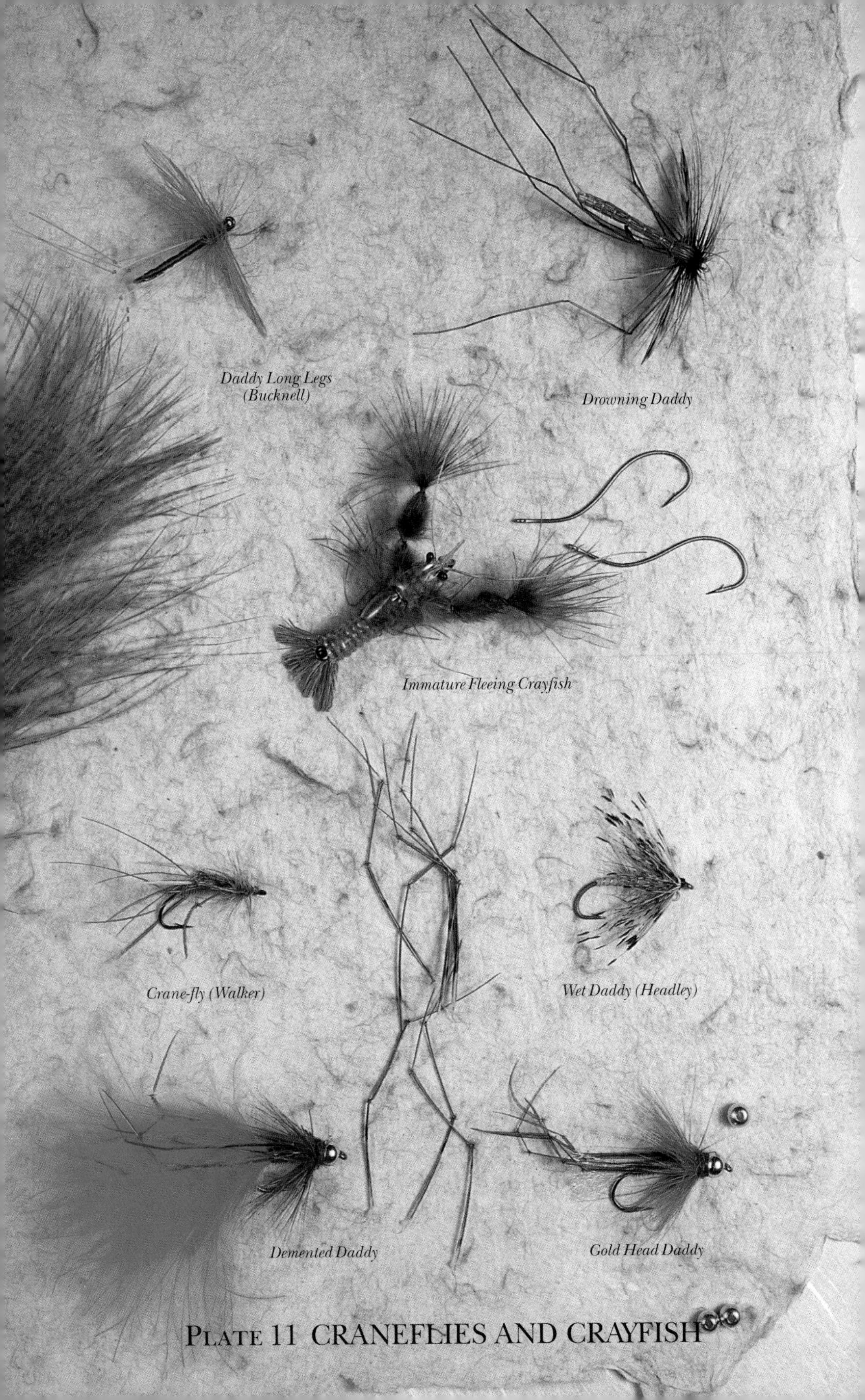

Daddy Long Legs
(Bucknell)

Drowning Daddy

Immature Fleeing Crayfish

Crane-fly (Walker)

Wet Daddy (Headley)

Demented Daddy

Gold Head Daddy

PLATE 11 CRANEFLIES AND CRAYFISH

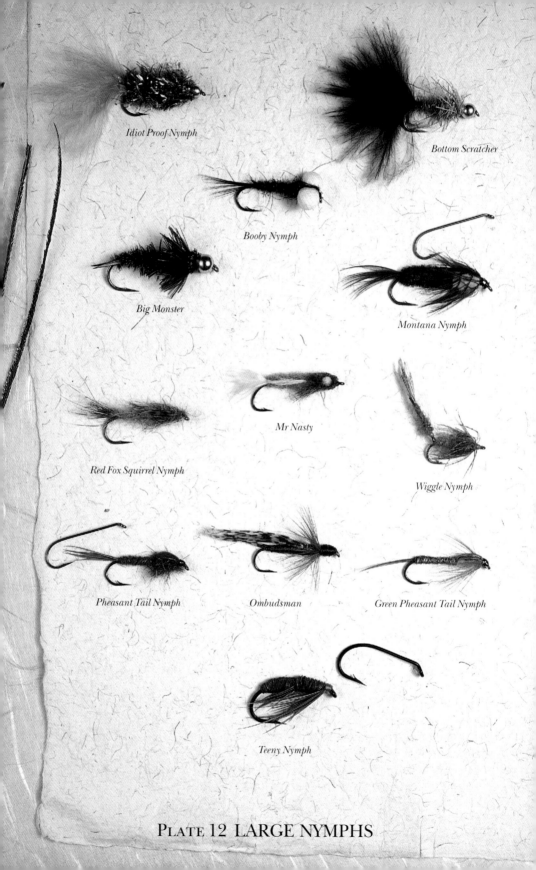

Idiot Proof Nymph

Bottom Scratcher

Booby Nymph

Big Monster

Montana Nymph

Red Fox Squirrel Nymph

Mr Nasty

Wiggle Nymph

Pheasant Tail Nymph

Ombudsman

Green Pheasant Tail Nymph

Teeny Nymph

PLATE 12 LARGE NYMPHS

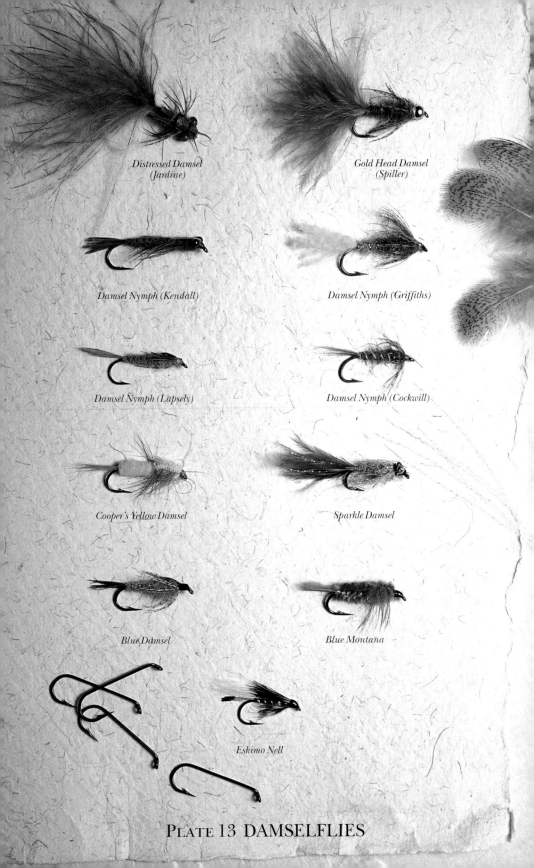

Distressed Damsel
(Jardine)

Gold Head Damsel
(Spiller)

Damsel Nymph (Kendall)

Damsel Nymph (Griffiths)

Damsel Nymph (Lapsely)

Damsel Nymph (Cockwill)

Cooper's Yellow Damsel

Sparkle Damsel

Blue Damsel

Blue Montana

Eskimo Nell

PLATE 13 DAMSELFLIES

Olive Wulff Variant

Red Wulff Variant

Grey Wulff

Hatching Mayfly (White)

Poly May Dun

Straddlebug

Active Mayfly Dun (White)

Sitting Shuck Mayfly (Ward)

Suspender Mayfly Nymph

Swimming Mayfly Nymph (Price)

Stuck Shuck Mayfly (White)

Mayfly Nymph (Walker)

PLATE 14 MAYFLY NYMPHS AND DUNS

Spent Mayfly
(Ashworth)

Deerstalker

Spent Drake
(Hern)

Poly May Spinner

White Wulff

Mosely May

Russell's Mayfly

Walker's Mayfly Dun

Lively Mayfly (Jardine)

French Partridge Mayfly

Active Mayfly Spinner (White)

Mayfly Dun (Edwards)

PLATE 15 MAYFLY DUNS AND SPINNERS

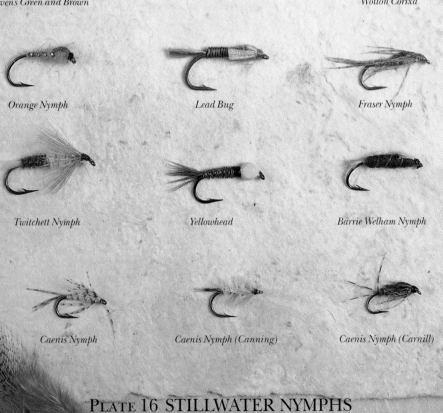

Cove Nymph

Wonderbug

S F Pheasy

Prince Nymph

Cockwill's Red Brown

Westward Bug

Ivens Green and Brown

Theo's Corixa

Wotton Corixa

Orange Nymph

Lead Bug

Fraser Nymph

Twitchett Nymph

Yellowhead

Barrie Welham Nymph

Caenis Nymph

Caenis Nymph (Canning)

Caenis Nymph (Carnill)

PLATE 16 STILLWATER NYMPHS

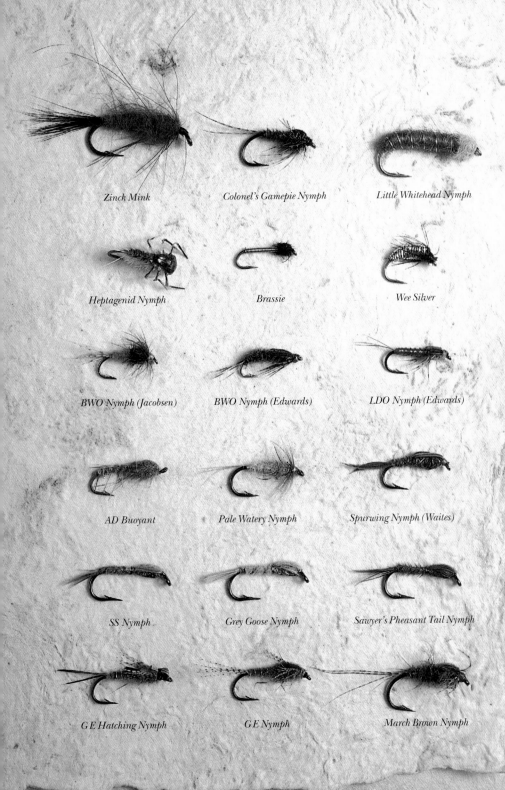

Zinck Mink

Colonel's Gamepie Nymph

Little Whitehead Nymph

Heptagenid Nymph

Brassie

Wee Silver

BWO Nymph (Jacobsen)

BWO Nymph (Edwards)

LDO Nymph (Edwards)

AD Buoyant

Pale Watery Nymph

Spurwing Nymph (Waites)

SS Nymph

Grey Goose Nymph

Sawyer's Pheasant Tail Nymph

G E Hatching Nymph

G E Nymph

March Brown Nymph

PLATE 17 RIVER NYMPHS

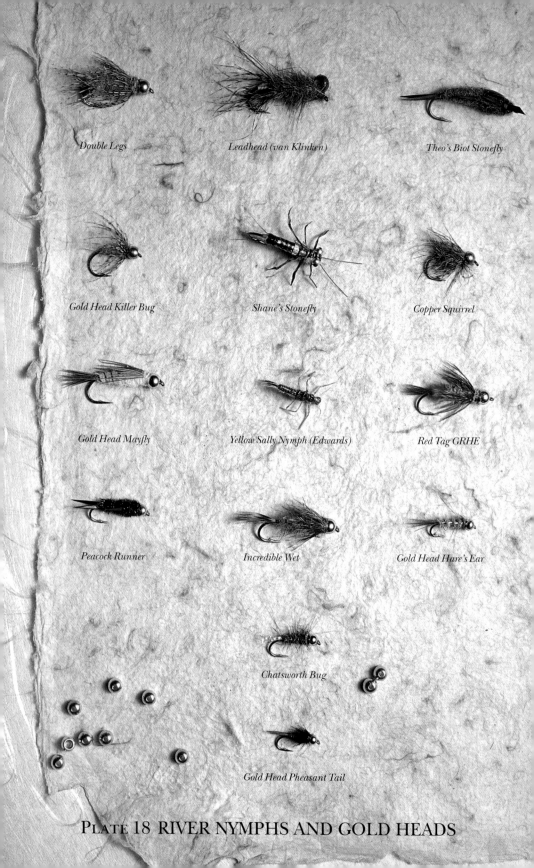

Double Legs

Leadhead (van Klinken)

Theo's Biot Stonefly

Gold Head Killer Bug

Shane's Stonefly

Copper Squirrel

Gold Head Mayfly

Yellow Sally Nymph (Edwards)

Red Tag GRHE

Peacock Runner

Incredible Wet

Gold Head Hare's Ear

Chatsworth Bug

Gold Head Pheasant Tail

PLATE 18 RIVER NYMPHS AND GOLD HEADS

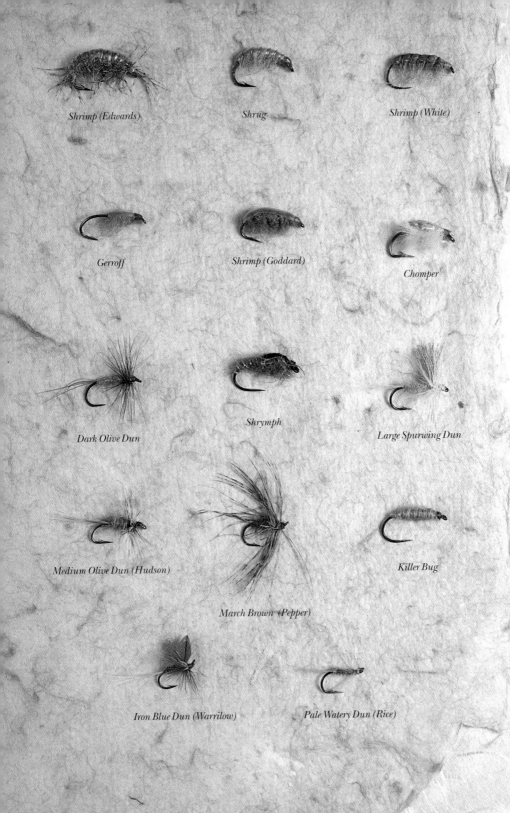

Shrimp (Edwards)

Shrug

Shrimp (White)

Gerroff

Shrimp (Goddard)

Chomper

Dark Olive Dun

Shrymph

Large Spurwing Dun

Medium Olive Dun (Hudson)

Killer Bug

March Brown (Pepper)

Iron Blue Dun (Warrilow)

Pale Watery Dun (Rice)

PLATE 19 SHRIMPS, BUGS AND NATURAL DUNS

Greenwell's Glory

Woodcock and Hare's Ear

Blae and Black

Gravel Bed

March Brown Sider

March Brown winged wet

Something and Nothing

Medium Olive Nymph

Kill Devil Spider

Rolt's Witch

Black Spider

Coch-y-bondhu

PVC Nymph

Faisen and Orange

Brown Nymph (Nice)

Orange Bumble

Tangler

Pearly Bumble

PLATE 20 RIVER WET FLIES AND NYMPHS

Jenny Spinner (Warrilow)

Clear Wing Spinner

Caenis Spinner (Ruane)

Pale Watery Spinner
(Warrilow)

Sunk Spinner (Jardine)

Caenis Spinner (Canham)

Sunk Spinner (Patterson)

Sunset Spinner

Poly Wing Spinner

Houghton Ruby

Red Spinner (Nice)

Amber Spinner

Caenis Spinner (Jardine)

PLATE 21 SPINNERS

Hawthorn Fly (Price)

Hawthorn Fly (Jacobsen)

Hawthorn Fly (Warrilow)

Black Gnat (Goddard)

Bob's Black Beetle

Black Gnat (Weaver)

McMurray Ant

Deerhair Beetle (Weaver)

Eric's Beetle

Needlefly (White)

Red-Eyed Derbyshire Beetle

Needle-fly (White)

Smut (Goddard)

Green Insect

Back Gnat (White)

Reed Smut (Jacobsen)

Dun Terrestrial (White)

PLATE 22 TERRESTRIALS & MISCELLANEOUS

Honey Buzzer

Wobbleworm

Blae & Black Adult Buzzer

Susupender Midge Pupa

Bloodworm (Kendall)

Shipman's Buzzer

Gold Head Hare's Ear Buzzer

Gold Head Bloodworm

Poly Rib C Buzzer

Cling Film Pupa

T G Emerger

Olive Midge Pupa (Fogg)

Green Tube Buzzer

Ginger Adult Buzzer (Carnill)

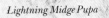

Lightning Midge Pupa

Griffith's Gnat

Stuck Shuck Midge

Hackle Stalk Buzzer

Hare's Ear Midge

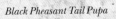

Black Pheasant Tail Pupa

Plate 23 MIDGE LARVAE, PUPAE AND ADULTS

Rat-Faxed MacDougal

Irresistable

Humpy

Royal Wulff

Stimulator

Grey Wulff

Wright's Royal

Muddle-May

Bivisible

Adams

Doublewing

Light Hendrickson

Quill Gordon

CDC Tailwater Dun

Dark Hendrickson

Para Adams

White Wulff

Sparkle Para

PLATE 24 USA DRY FLIES

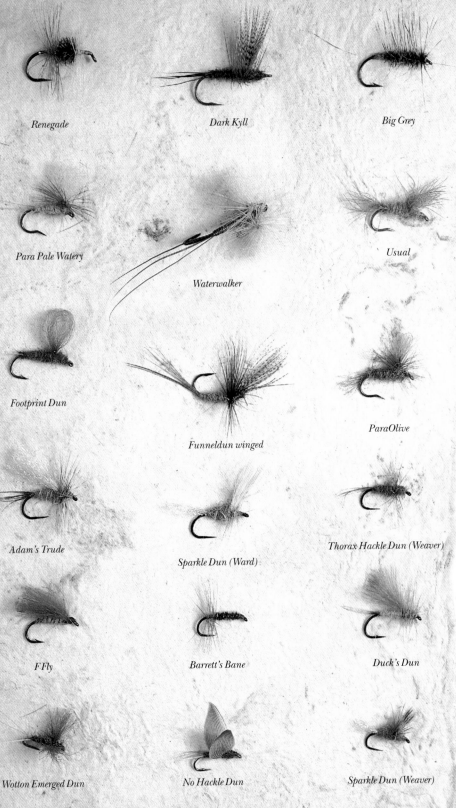

Renegade

Dark Kyll

Big Grey

Para Pale Watery

Waterwalker

Usual

Footprint Dun

Funneldun winged

ParaOlive

Adam's Trude

Sparkle Dun (Ward)

Thorax Hackle Dun (Weaver)

F Fly

Barrett's Bane

Duck's Dun

Wotton Emerged Dun

No Hackle Dun

Sparkle Dun (Weaver)

PLATE 25 DRY FLY STYLES

Cree Duster

Dutch Panama

Furnace

Dogsbody

Light Pensioner

BWO (Nice)

Otter Ruby

Tanat Dun

Borderer

Black and Red

Blue Upright

Pepper's Own

Tups Variant

Red Quill

Sturdy's Fancy

Grey Duster

No. 3 Para

Last Hope

PLATE 26 RIVER DRY FLIES

Blue Dun

Grizzle Mink

Kite's Imperial

Olive Dun (Roberts)

Hacklepoint Coachman

Pheasant Tail

Misty Blue Dun

Grizzly Bourne

Light Ollie

Beacon Beige

Large Dark Olive (Jacobsen)

White Grizzly

Lake Olive (Lapsely)

Gim River Dun

Barton Bug

Janus

Terry's Terror

Itchen Olive

PLATE 27 OLIVES AND GENERAL DRY FLIES

Foam Post Emerger

Wotton Emerger

Klinkhammer Special

Stillborn Foam Adams

Calf's Tail Emerger

No Hackle Dun

Halo Emerger

Floating Nymph (Jardine)

Moser Emerger (Jardine)

PLATE 28 EMERGERS

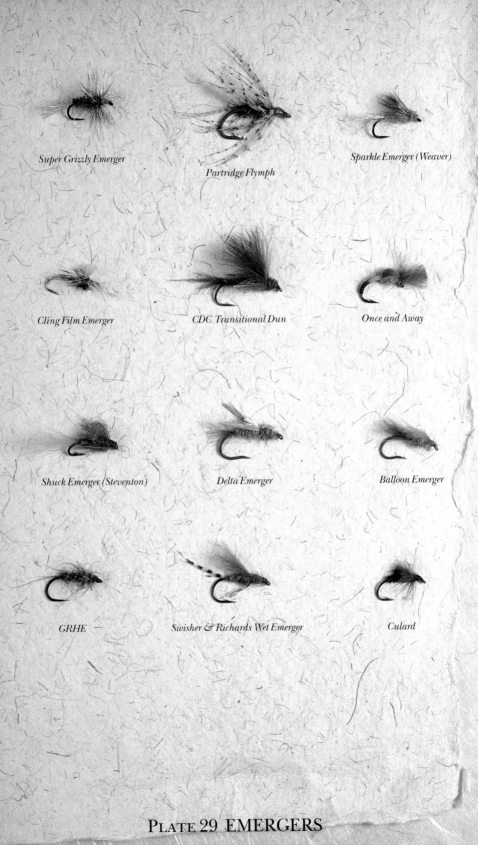

Super Grizzly Emerger

Partridge Flymph

Sparkle Emerger (Weaver)

Cling Film Emerger

CDC Transitional Dun

Once and Away

Shuck Emerger (Steventon)

Delta Emerger

Balloon Emerger

GRHE

Swisher & Richards Wet Emerger

Culard

PLATE 29 EMERGERS

Mackeral Nymph

Caseless Caddis (Klinken)

Rhyac Larva (Edwards)

Catgut Nymph

Sedge Pupa (Goddard)

Stickfly (Harris)

Edwards Ascending Sedge

S T Emerger

Sedge Pupa (Kendall)

Cased Caddis (Carnill)

Latex Pupa

Moser Pupa

Sparkle Pupa

Mono Pupa

Yellow Sedge Pupa

Hatching Sedge

Cling Film Pupa

Superpupa

Plate 30 SEDGE LARVAE AND PUPAE

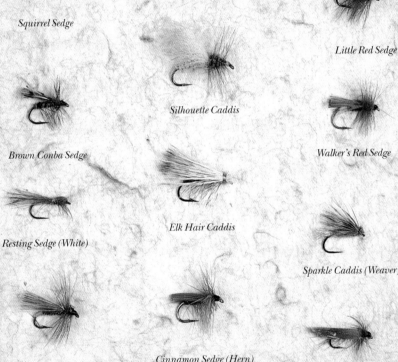

Wind Assisted Sedge

Balloon Sedge

Goddard Sedge

Adult Caddis (Wotton)

Squirrel Sedge

Little Red Sedge

Silhouette Caddis

Brown Conba Sedge

Walker's Red Sedge

Elk Hair Caddis

Resting Sedge (White)

Sparkle Caddis (Weaver)

Grannom (Russell)

Cinnamon Sedge (Hern)

Voljc Sedge

F Sedge

Post Oviposting
Caddis (Edwards)

Deerhair Sedge (Weaver)

Plate 31 Adult Sedges

Fog Black

Hare's Lug & Plover

Partridge & Blue

Brown Owl

Light Watchet

Waterhen Bloa

Yellow Sally

Partridge & Orange

Dark Needle

Dark Spanish Needle

Iron Blue Spider

Snipe & Purple

Dark Moor Game

Broughton's Point

Dark Watchet

Old Master

Olive Bloa

Poult Bloa

PLATE 32 NORTH COUNTRY SPIDERS

the three tails are dark grey.

The female spinner has transparent wings with a blue tint and brown veins. The abdomen is pale cream, the last three segments having brown streaks. The legs are dark olive-brown and the three tails are dark brown. The abdomen of the male spinner is creamy-white, with the last three segments brownish. The legs are dark olive-brown with the forelegs black-brown, and the three tails are dark brown. The transparent wings have a brown tint and heavy brownish veins.

Also see under WULFFS for other imitations.

Mayfly Nymph

(Richard Walker)   *Plate 14*

Hook: Long shank 8
Thread: Brown
Tail: Pheasant tail fibres
Body: Optional layers of lead foil. Light yellowish-buff angora wool with two bands of pheasant tail fibres near the tail
Rib: Brown nylon thread
Thorax: As for the body, but without the ribbing. The body and thorax wool should be well picked out
Wing-case and legs: Pheasant tail fibres, the ends turned down for legs

Swimming Mayfly Nymph

Plate 14

Taff Price has tied this realistic swimming-nymph imitation. It is slimmer than most nymph patterns and the shape of the hook helps give a little more movement to the fly.

Hook: Mustad 80150 BR or Partridge K6ST 8–12
Thread: Brown
Tail: Cock pheasant tail fibres
Abdomen: Creamy fur dubbing ribbed with brown thread
Breather: Short tuft of brown marabou at the rear of the wing-case
Thorax: Olive dubbing over a lead wire underbody

Wing-case: Cock pheasant tail fibres varnished
Legs: Brown partridge hackle
Head: Pale brown dubbing
Eyes: Burnt nylon mono

Suspender Mayfly Nymph

Plate 14

Devised by John Goddard and Brian Clarke as a semi-floater suspended in the surface film. See SUSPENDER MIDGE PUPA.

Hook: Long shank 12
Thread: Brown
Tail: Three tips of cream-coloured ostrich herl
Body: Mixed white, tan and yellow seal's fur (2:1:1)
Rib: Brown monocord or silk
Thorax: As for the body
Wing-case: Placed a short distance behind the eye. Ethafoam ball enclosed in a nylon mesh (ladies' tights provide a suitable material) and coloured brown

Hatching Mayfly

(Philip White)   *Plate 14*

Hook: TMC100 or Partridge L3B size 10
Tail: Golden pheasant undertail or cock pheasant tail fibres dressed long and thick
Body: As for tail wound forward to the middle of the shank
Thorax: Superfine Dry Fly Dubbing, colour Pale Morning Dun, or darker for the vulgata species
Wing: Mixed olive and dark brown elk hair. A looped CDC wing tied short is an effective variant
Hackle: Grizzle dyed light or medium olive with the lower fibres clipped very short to sit the fly low

Active Mayfly Dun

(Philip White)   *Plate 14*

Hook: TMC100 or Partridge L3B size 10
Tail: Golden pheasant undertail or cock pheasant tail fibres tied short

Body: Two turns of the tail butts followed by Superfine Dry Fly Dubbing colour Pale Morning Dun
Wing: Mixed dyed olive and dark brown elk
Hackle: Grizzle dyed light or medium olive wound over the thorax with a V cut out of the underside

Edwards' Mayfly   *Plate 15*

This Oliver Edwards pattern uses the upside-down Swedish dry fly hook. The wing is from a feather with fibres of equal length each side of the quill. Strip the lower fluff and clip off the tip. Fold it over at the quill and bind to the vertical post; it should be about 16 mm tall. Wind the two hackles up the post and finally dub the thorax.

Hook: 10 Swedish Dry Fly
Tail: Four strong moose mane or deer hairs
Abdomen: Equally mixed ivory seal's fur and fine ivory poly dubbing over silver Lurex
Rib: Light brown rayon or nylon floss in 2 broad bands at the rear
Wing: Silver mallard breast or flank feather dyed very pale yellow, or lemon wood-duck
Hackles: Mixed pale blue-dun cock and pale lemon-dyed grizzle
Thorax: Mixed ivory and light brown poly dubbing

Lively Mayfly   *Plate 15*

This American dressing by Chauncy Lively has been amended by Charles Jardine. A 'V' is cut through the body hackle underneath to achieve the correct silhouette.

Hook: Light wire 10
Thread: Green
Tail: Three pheasant tail fibres
Extended body: Light deer hair (10–15 fibres) or moose mane ribbed with green thread

Thorax: Cream-yellow Fly Rite poly dubbing or Orvis Antron/hare blend
Wing: Wood-duck fibres bunched and separated by figure-of-eight turns of thread
Body hackle: Grizzle cock
Head hackle: Golden-olive cock

Mayfly Dun   (David Jacques)

Hook: Long shank 10
Thread: Red
Tail: Cock pheasant tail fibres
Underbody: Reddish-brown floss
Overbody: Natural raffia with rings of the underbody showing through
Hackle: Medium-olive cock tied in at the rear of the body, with a shorter-fibred light green-olive cock at the shoulder

Moseley May   *Plate 15*

This Irish lough pattern is very highly recommended by Paul Canning and others. It was devised in the early 1960s by Derek Moseley for Lough Sheelin. Tie in the hackles with the base ends stripped. Soft, low-grade capes are excellent. Tie in the first behind the eye. Lay it good side up parallel to the shank, tip to the eye. Repeat with hackles two and three. Tie in the tail. Dub a tapered body and finish one-third down the shank. Palmer the first hackle along the front third of the shank. Avoid touching turns. Palmer the second and third hackles. Wind the thread forward and half-hitch but do not cut off. Turn the fly over. Divide the lower fibres. Splay the hackles sideways with figure-of-eight turns of thread on what will be the underside of the fly. Five or six cross-lays should enable the bunches to be pulled to the sides. The result is a 180-degree hackle. The wet pattern uses a 360-degree hackle.

Hook: 10
Thread: Black
Tail: Badger fur dyed olive or cock pheasant tail fibres, equal to the shank length

Hackles: One each of yellow, medium olive and medium blue dun cock saddle hackle, fibres equal to the shank length (see text)
Body: Natural hare's mask fur or substitute dyed medium olive

Professional tyer Simon Ashworth has researched this pattern and he suggest the following as being closer to Moseley's original tying. Whichever one you choose I am assured that both are superb flies.

Hook: 8–10
Tail: Three cock pheasant centre tail fibres
Body: Mixed yellow seal's fur and hare's ear to produce a dirty yellow colour
Rib: Fine oval gold tinsel or wire
Hackles: One long-fibred dirty grey-green olive cock and a shorter-fibred primrose yellow cock wound through. These are tied half spent, i.e. in 180 degrees

French Partridge Mayfly

Plate 15

Hook: Long shank 12
Thread: Black or brown
Tail: Cock pheasant tail fibres
Body: Natural raffia with a palmered olive cock hackle
Rib: Gold wire
Hackle: French partridge feather

Poly May Dun

Plate 14

This is John Goddard's dressing which has become very popular. It is dressed to represent the emerging fly. The tail fibres represent the nymphal shuck. John comments that the body and wing colour bear little resemblance to the natural out of the water, but when fished on the surface they are difficult to distinguish from the naturals.

Hook: 10–12 wide gape
Thread: Yellow
Body: Cream poly yarn, wound
Tail: Tips of golden-coloured calf's tail used for the wings
Wing: Golden dyed calf's tail tied in a V

Hackle: Three or four turns of black cock either side of the wing roots

Roy's Mottled Mayfly

Plate 10

This is an Irish lough pattern devised on Lough Erne by Roy Graham. Its body and hackle colours create a wonderfully impressionist blur of natural Mayfly dun colours.

Hook: 8–10
Thread: Medium olive
Tail: Cock pheasant centre tail fibres
Butt: Fine oval gold
Body: Mixed hare's fur and gold Lite-Brite
Rib: Fine silver
Hackles: Blue-dun-dyed partridge followed by-olive dyed partridge

Shadow Mayfly

This popular imitation was devised by Peter Deane.

Hook: Long shank 10–12
Thread: Black
Body: Tightly wound palmered grizzle hackles
Wing: Two upright large ginger cock hackles clipped to shape

Sitting Shuck

Plate 14

Simon Ward devised this after seeing the duns appearing to use their shucks like miniature rafts while their wings were drying. The resulting pattern is very effective. It is a Mayfly on the Sparkle Dun theme.

Hook: Long shank sedge Partridge K12ST size 16
Thread: Olive
Shuck: Cream Z-lon
Body: Cream Antron/hare blend
Hackle: Light dun Metz saddle and a dyed olive Indian neck

Straddlebug
Plate 14

Hook: Long shank 10–12
Thread: Brown
Tip: Very fine oval gold tinsel
Tail: Two or three black cock fibres
Body: Natural raffia
Rib: Brown thread
Hackle: Orange cock followed by a brown-speckled summer duck feather or French partridge breast feather
Head: Peacock herl

Stuck Shuck Mayfly

(Philip White) *Plate 14*

Hook: TMC400 or similar Swimming Nymph Hook, size 10–12
Tail and shuck: Brown grizzled marabou feather. The whole feather is tied in by the tip which forms the tail and the rest of the feather is then rolled and wound like herl to form the stuck shuck
Body: Superfine Dry Fly Dubbing colour Pale Morning Dun
Wing: Brown elk hair with a few strands of olive or natural CDC or mixed poly-propylene fibres, olive, grey dun and light yellow
Hackle: Grizzle dyed light or medium olive with a V cut out of the lower fibres
Head: Wing butts

Walker's Mayfly Dun
Plate 15

Richard Walker observed that the presence of orange in a Mayfly dressing sometimes makes it highly attractive, especially in a dense hatch where the odds of the artifical being singled out are slimmer.

Hook: Long shank 8–10
Thread: Brown
Body: Very pale buff turkey tail fibres or substitute with two bands of pheasant tail near the rear
Hackle: Speckled duck feather dyed pale green or a dyed pale green cock, followed by a ginger cock and a short-fibred hot-orange cock

Wet Mayfly
Plate 10

This simple Irish dressing by Derek Moseley is recommended by Simon Ashworth. It looks as though it should be effective on any stillwater where the natural occurs.

Hook: 10–12
Thread: Yellow
Tail: Cock pheasant tail fibres
Body: Very pale olive-dyed seal's fur
Rib: Fine oval gold tinsel
Hackles: Light ginger cock with a dyed pale ginger grey mallard flank feather wound in front

Active Mayfly Spinner

(Philip White) *Plate 15*

Hook: TMC100 or Partridge L3B size 10
Tail: Cock pheasant tail fibres tied twice the body length
Body: Two turns of tail fibres then white rabbit fur
Wing: Mixed dun and dark brown elk
Hackle: Grizzle wound over the thorax

Deerstalker
Plate 15

Neil Patterson writes of his spinner imitation as though it were an answer to a maiden's prayer. His superlatives are probably justified. Neil comments: 'For reasons I've never quite understood, most spinner patterns have hackles that hold the fly on the surface like a dun. Admittedly, some natural spinners come down on tippy-toes, wings erect. But most come down "spent" in the true sense of the word, with wings, body and tails flat out, flush with the surface film.

'To imitate the spinner correctly, you shouldn't be able to see the imitation on the surface. Which is why no spinner pattern of mine sports any feature that could possibly prevent it behaving exactly as the trout expects to see it.

'With no hackle keeping a heavy Mayfly iron from sinking straight through the film led me to use deer hair as the body material. It is hollow. By winding it in you trap little bubbles of air. This has much the same effect as strapping lifebelts along the sides.

'To give it additional floating qualities, I let the points of the deer hair fibres protrude from the back of the fly like short, stubby tails. This prevents the hook-bend pulling the fly under from the rear.'

Hook: Long shank 10
Thread: Brown
Tail: Pheasant tail fibres about twice the body-length
Body: White deer hair laid along the shank with the tips sticking out beyond the bend
Rib: Generous turns of tying thread, and silver wire
Hackle: Black cock wound where the thorax should be. This is trimmed for three-quarters of its length, leaving the fibres just longer than the body width. A second natural red hackle is wound through the remainder of the black hackle. These are bound into two bunches for the spent wings with figure-of-eight turns of the silk

Hackle -Point Spent Mayfly

(John Veniard)

Hook: Long shank 10
Tail: Three cock pheasant tail fibres
Body: Yellow raffia
Rib: Oval silver tinsel
Wing: Four blue-dun cock hackles (two shorter than the others), tied spent
Hackle: Light grizzle cock

Poly May Spinner
Plate 15

John Goddard who created this fly explained that he devised it to fish with one wing on the surface and the other cocked in the air in the manner that many spinners adopt on the surface.

Hook: Wide gape 10–12
Thread: Black
Tail: Three to five long black cock fibres or black nylon mono

Body: Wound white poly yarn
Wing: Mixed black and natural off-white calf's tail tied in a very wide V
Hackle: Three or four turns on either side of the wing roots of a relatively short-fibred black cock

Russel's Mayfly
Plate 15

Pat Russell amended an earlier Frank Speak pattern tied by Jackie Wakeford. It is very buoyant and durable.

Hook: Long shank 10
Thread: Black
Tail: Twelve or more light brown cock fibres
Body: A wound strip of polyethylene foam
Rib: Natural red cock hackle stalk
Hackle: Badger cock
Wing: Two bunches of dyed slate-blue cock hackle fibres forward-slanting and divided

Spent drake *(Tony Hern)*
Plate 15

Hook: Mustad 9672 size 10
Thread: Black
Tails: Pheasant tail fibres
Body: White Raffene, ribbed with black thread
Hackle: Grizzle cock
Wings: Bunched black cock fibres, tied spent

Spent Mayfly

(Simon Ashworth)
Plate 15

Hook: Long shank size 10 Kamasan B830
Thread: Black
Tail: Eight to ten moose mane fibres
Body: Fine grade white foam – Traun River Polycelon has been used in the fly illustrated
Rib: Dark brown floss
Thorax: Chocolate-brown Fly Rite fine poly dubbing, shade No. 6
Wing: Black poly yarn tied spent. Niche Products siliconised yarn is preferred
Hackle: Badger cock wound through the thorax and clipped underneath

McLeod's Olive   *Plate 6*

This popular Scottish loch wet fly may be
fished from April until August and is a
general olive imitation. I know of its use
for olive buzzers and it does well on
Rutland, Chew and Blagdon in these
circumstances. It is sometimes tied
without the tail but the gold tip is
essential.

Hook: 12–16
Thread: Pale olive
Tip: Two or three turns of fine flat gold
tinsel
Tail: Olive-green hackle fibres
Body: Olive-green fine fur such as
moleskin or wool to match the hackle and
tail colour, optionally ribbed with gold
wire
Wing: Starling wing quills
Beard hackle: Olive-green fibres

MEDIUM OLIVE
(Baetis vernus, B. tenax, B. buceratus)

See EPHEMEROPTERA
All these species are very much alike, and
Baetis vernus is described below in detail.
With the exception of *Baetis buceratus*, they
are widely distributed throughout the
country and are most abundant on chalk-
streams. They are not found in stillwater.
The nymphs are of the agile, darting type,
living among weeds. The medium-sized
adults begin to appear in mid-May and in
some places continue almost daily to the
end of June, then less frequently through
to October. They generally emerge in the
late morning and early afternoons. The
female spinners return to the water from
early evening onwards.

The male dun has medium grey wings
and an abdomen that is medium yellow-
olive with a paler underside. The legs are
pale to medium olive and the two tails are
grey. The female dun has medium grey
wings with a brown-olive to medium olive
abdomen with a pale yellow-olive underside. The legs are pale olive and the two
tails grey.

The female spinner, also known as the
red spinner, has transparent wings with
light brown veins. The abdomen is yellow-
brown to reddish-brown, with a paler
underside. The legs are grey-olive and the
two tails are off-white. The male spinner is
of no interest as it dies over land.

See also under OLIVE copies and the
OLIVE BLOA, BARTON BUG, MISTY
BLUE DUN, WATERHEN BLOA,
ROUGH OLIVE, GREENWELL'S
GLORY, GOLD-RIBBED HARE'S EAR,
DOGSBODY, LUNN'S PARTICULAR,
PHEASANT TAIL and RED SPINNER.

Medium Olive Nymph
(G. E. M. Skues)   *Plate 20*

Hook: 14
Tail: Greenwell hackle fibres
Thread: Waxed primrose
Body: Olive-dyed heron herl
Rib: Fine gold wire
Thorax: Blue squirrel's fur
Hackle: Short-fibred dark blue cock, two
turns maximum

Medium Olive Nymph

A North Country pattern.

Hook: 14
Tail: Rhode Island Red cock fibres
Body: Greenish-olive seal's fur
Rib: Gold wire
Hackle: Smoky blue-dun hen

Medium Olive Dun   (C. F. Walker)

Hook: 14
Tail: Pale-grey hackle fibres
Body: Two strands of condor herl, one
greyish-olive, the other pale brown
Rib: Fine gold tinsel
Wing: Peroxide-bleached brownish-grey
waterhen breast fibres
Hackle: Pale-olive cock

Medium Olive Dun

(Alan Hudson)   *Plate 19*

Hook: 14–16
Thread: Black
Tail: Grizzle cock fibres
Body: Rabbit's fur, a mixture of underfur and guard hairs
Hackle: Grizzle cock

Mickey Finn   *Plate 3*

A North American bucktail lure first tied in the 1930s and in and out of popularity on our reservoirs.

Hook: Long shank 6–10
Thread: Black
Tail: Two small bunches of red and yellow bucktail
Body: Silver Lurex or tinsel
Wing: Three bunches of bucktail, red in the centre, flanked by yellow
Throat hackle (optional): Red hackle fibres or goat hair
Head: Black varnish

MIDGES (Chironomidae)

See DIPTERA
Most of nearly 400 species are aquatic. They provide a substantial food source for stillwater trout and, to a lesser extent, river trout and grayling. Adults hatch on almost every day of the season, and trout may become preoccupied with the emerging pupa in the surface film. It is not uncommon for the water surface to be boiling with trout absorbed in taking the pupa, or with the backs of trout breaking through the surface as they silently pick off pupae suspended in the film. The colour and size of the artificial and the method of fishing are important if the angler is to be successful. Midges were overlooked by generations of fly fishers until the boom in stillwater fly fishing ensured that greater attention was paid to stillwater fly life. The buzzer pattern of Dr H. A. Bell (see BLAGDON BUZZER) and the midge patterns of others between the wars were the first patterns specifically tied to copy the natural pupa.

The larvae may vary from just a few millimetres to 25 millimetres long. Many live close to the lake-bed or are free-swimming among weeds. They are commonly called bloodworms, after the red larvae, but others are green, brown and shades in between. They are thin and worm-like and move through the water with a lashing motion. After reaching the pupal stage, they leave the lake-bed and begin the final stages of pupation, when the body may darken or change colour. They then ascend to the surface ready to emerge as adults.

Pupae vary in size and colour and often have a pronounced bend to their segmented body. They have whitish breathing filaments at the head and whitish appendages to the tail to aid swimming. The rising or emerging pupae under the surface film are of most interest to trout. The adults may emerge fairly speedily, or may take up to a couple of hours, hanging just below the surface. Their movement is slow and may be in a horizontal plane or a slow rising and sinking for short distances. Some remain static with their breathing filaments suspended from the surface film. The thorax splits and the adult emerges, leaving its pupal case behind. Calm water is favoured for a hatch and the evenings of hot sunny days often have the largest hatches.

Adults vary in size and colour. All have flat wings folded across the back. Swarms of adults are found near water or well inland. The females, returning to lay their eggs, make the buzzing noise which has resulted in the genus being termed 'buzzers'. At times, when the newly hatched adults are being taken off the surface, the artificial should be fished motionless.

The main species, with their common names and wing-lengths, are listed below in order of emergence. Common names of species have varied over the years and are still changing as anglers find more acceptable terminology.

Common name	Wing-length	Period of emergence
Small green midge	4–6 mm	March to October
Orange/silver midge or grey boy	6.5–8 mm	April to mid-June
Black midge	3.5–7.5 mm	April/March and July/October
Ribbed or olive midge	6.5–7 mm	May/June and August/September
Golden dun midge	6.5–8 mm	June to August
Small brown midge	3.5–7.5 mm	Mid-June to September
Large red or ginger midge	6.6–8 mm	Mid-June to mid-September
Small red midge	4–4.5 mm	July to September
Lge green midge	6.5–8 mm	Mid-July to end August

Bloodworms or Larvae

See also WOBBLE-WORM, GODDARD'S RED-AND-GREEN LARVA. Perhaps the most simple pattern is a length of scarlet suede chenille tied in at a point behind the eye of the hook and left free to wiggle on a slow retrieve.

Bloodworm *(Geoffrey Bucknall)*

Hook: Long shank 8
Thread: Red
Tail: Feather fibres with an upward curve dyed red
Body: Feather fibres dyed red
Rib: Oval silver tinsel
Thorax: Brown heron herl

Bloodworm *(Roger Fogg)*

Hook: Sedge hook 10–12
Thread: Red
Body: Red tinsel underbody with a close ribbing of red Lurex
Thorax: A small throax of red seal's fur.

Gold Bead Bloodworm

(Theo Bakelaar)   *Plate 23*

Hook: TMC Tiemco 2312, size 16
Thread: Red
Head: 2 mm gold bead
Body: Red Georgio Benecchi mìcro New Dub or substitute

Back: Transparent Flexibody
Rib: Nylon mono

Bloodworm *(Chris Kendall)*   *Plate 23*

Hook: Partridge curved sedge hook size 8–18
Tail: Red marabou from the base of the plume
Body: Optima high power gum (red floss silk on sizes 16–18) given several coats of varnish
Thorax: Lead underbody if required. An equal mixture of red and olive seal's fur

Pupae

On stillwaters artificial pupae are well suited to being fished either as a single fly at the end of a long leader or on all three points of a three-fly leader. They should be retrieved slowly with long, steady pulls with short pauses. A good method is to put a hatching pupa pattern on the top dropper and to fish with ordinary pupa imitations further down the leader. Takes are often gentle, and the leader needs to be watched carefully. In a ripple or rough water this may be impossible if the flies are some distance away. The best solution is to put a dry sedge on the top dropper and use this as an indicator. The natural pupae have to make the journey to the surface from the bottom, and even when none is near the surface deeply fished imitations are effective.

Some of the patterns may be listed in only one colour, as their creator suggested, but there is no reason why they should not be tied in other colours to represent a variety of natural midges. The creators of some of the patterns have stipulated that the body should go round the bend of the hook to imitate the natural. Other fly tyers have omitted this. It is a matter of choice whether the body extends round the bend, but most fly fishers prefer the more natural-looking artificial. Tail filaments, if used, should be kept fairly short. The breathing tubes may be tied in a single bunch sticking out of the top of the thorax, or more realistically in two bunches with figure-of-eight turns of the tying thread. Caddis or sedge hooks are useful for pupa imitations.

There is no doubt that the imitation of midge pupae has been pushed to the extreme in fly tyers' attempts to match the natural's appearance. A number of experienced stillwater anglers are reverting to simpler patterns. The expert nymph fisher Arthur Cove has said that he never uses the 'traditional buzzer' imitations nowadays. He merely ties simple spider patterns in buzzer colours. Cove's patterns have a floss-silk body with a silver rib and a small black hen hackle for those to be fished well below the surface, or with a cock hackle for those to be fished just below the surface film. Perhaps half the answer lies in the adage that 'It's not what you fish, but how you fish it'.

Midge pupae also are an important part of river trout and grayling diets and their imitation on rivers has been much overlooked. Some of these imitations are very suitable for river fishing.

Black Pheasant Tail Pupa

Plate 23

This particular version is from Canadian Ian James. As we fished together for bass and carp Ian gave me this to try back home. I have used it only on rivers where I've enjoyed success under very diffficult conditions.

Hook: 16–20
Thread: Black
Abdomen: Black-dyed pheasant tail ribbed with fine copper wire
Thorax: Peacock herl
Thorax back: Black-dyed pheasant tail

Cling-film Pupa

(Shane Jones) *Plate 23*

Hook: Tiemco Grub hook size 14
Tail: 2 white marabou fibres
Body: Claret silk with cling film over
Rib: 2 lb clear mono

Thorax: A small ball of silk, with cling film over
Wing buds: Orange Raffene
Breathers: Clipped white marabou

Hacklestalk Buzzer

(Paul Canning) *Plate 23*

A pattern designed to sink fast for stalking in clear water. Soak the stalk in water before winding. Dyed dark capes provide the stalk with the most contrast.

Hook: 14–20 Kamasan B980 short shank
Thread: Black
Head: Lead wire (0.37 mm diameter) formed into a small ball, painted black with head cement or enamel, two coats
Body: Stripped hackle stalk (good light/dark contrast is best) superglued for durability

Hatching Buzzer Pupa

(Dave Collyer)

The use of deer hair in this and other patterns makes them extremely buoyant and avoids the need to have large additions to the head of the fly as in the case of the Suspender patterns.

Hook: 6–12
Thread: Black, olive or brown
Body: Floss silk or featherfibres in black, claret, gold, dark olive, orange or scarlet
Rib: Flat tinsel, gold, copper/silver Lurex
Thorax: Deer hair spun on and trimmed.

Hatching CDC Pupa

A number of midge pupa patterns have been devised using a bunch of trimmed cul de canard feathers at the head. Their purpose is twofold. Firstly, as a means of keeping the pupa floating or hanging from the surface film, and, secondly, as an impressionist blur of the emerging adult. They are very successful. I am not listing any specific dressing but would comment that any midge pupa pattern may be amended in this way. Also see CULARD.

Hatching Midge Pupa

(John Goddard)

Hook: 10–18
Thread: As for body colour
Tail: White fluorescent wool tied well round the bend
Body: Marabou silk or fluorescent wool of an appropriate colour
Rib: Silver Lurex
Overbody: A strip of opaque PVC wound over
Thorax: Turkey dyed brown or peacock herl
Head filaments: White fluorescent wool

Lightening Midge Emergers

Plate 23

This series of emergers is from Brian Steventon of Staffordshire. Unlike most midge patterns these were devised for rivers although they would work equally as well on stillwater. Unhappy with other midge imitations, Brian set about creating an imitation of the emerger, so often the stage with which trout become preoccupied. This is one of the four different-coloured versions.

Hook: 16–20
Thread: Crimson
Abdomen: Blue rabbit underfur ribbed with black and gold metallic thread
Legs: Black poly yarn picked out in front the thorax
Wing: Grey or blue-dun poly yarn (split the fibre quantity in half) in a loop-wing, sloping at 45 degrees over the body, but with the loop tied in a horizontal plane, not the usual vertical one
Thorax: Black SLF (Synthetic Living Fibre)

Midge Pupa *(Roger Fogg)*   *Plate 23*

Unimpressed by 'ultra-realism' in pupa imitations, Roger Fogg suggests that colour and profile are the main factors influencing a feeding trout and has dressed a series of simple patterns which 'you may be assured will catch as many fish as any others'. In addition to the patterns given, which are for use just below the surface, he has had success with weighted pupal imitations which are allowed to sink to the bottom and are retrieved in long draws. The lead-foil weight is wrapped round the shank beneath the thorax.

Hook: 10–16 sedge hook
Abdomen: Marabou floss silk in black, brown, various greens, dark red, dull orange, extending half-way round the bend
Rib: Fine copper wire
Thorax: Seal's fur tied fairly fat and matching the body colour

Midge Pupa

This is representative of many modern traditional buzzer dressings.

Hook: 10–14
Thread: As for the body colour
Tail and breathing filaments: Fluorescent white wool or white Dollybody
Body: Tying thread or floss silk of appropriate colours
Rib: Silver wire
Thorax: Peacock herl on the black and the green versions; mixed orange and brown seal's fur on the orange version

Poly-Rib C Pupa   *Plate 23*

A very popular dressing from Bob Carnill. The black version is detailed below. Others include olive, claret, brown, etc.

Hook: Sedge hook or standard 10–14
Thread: Black
Tail: Electron-white DRF floss
Body: Swan, goose or heron herl dyed black
Rib: Pre-stretched heavy-duty clear polythene or PVC wound on so that the body material shows through the rib. Seven or eight turns are adequate
Thorax: Mole's fur dyed black
Thorax cover: Body material
Wing stubs: Two quill-like fibres from the narrow side of white primary swan

feathers tied in at the rear underside of the thorax and rear-facing
Breathing filaments: A short length of white nylon baby wool tied in horizontally at the eye and clipped short

Reverse Buzzer (Howard Croston)

This is Howard Croston's ingenious upside-down buzzer. The sunken eye hanging vertically ensures that the leader tippet sinks and does not deter wary fish. The bottom half of the suspender balls can be coloured to match the body. A touch of fluorescent orange in the thorax is a useful addition.

Hook: Fine wire, down-eye 10–16
Thread: To match the body
Tail: White marabou fibres tied in at the eye
Abdomen: Coloured tying thread ribbed with gold wire
Thorax: Black fur
Head: Polystyrene ball tied in a stocking mesh Suspender-style tied in at the rear of the shank

Shipman's Buzzer   Plate 23

Since Dave Shipman devised his floating emerging midge imitation in about 1979 it has been developed in a range of colours from the original fiery brown. It is an extremely simple pattern but it is the simple, easy-to-tie, successful patterns that are widely adopted and may survive decades of use. Dave Shipman ties his orange and green versions slimmer than the original. The fiery brown is also tapered down from the head so the front half can be Ginked to float with the rear in the film. A gold tinsel rib is standard but variations include a pearl Lurex rib.

Hook: 10–16 Kamasan B405
Thread: To match the body colour
Tail and head breather: White Antron fibres
Body: Seal's fur
Rib: Gold tinsel

Stuck Shuck Midge
(Wayne Luallen)   Plate 23

The most meticulous tyer I have ever met is the award-winning American Wayne Luallen. This is his pattern for a crippled adult unable to escape its shuck. It was devised as a river pattern. These flies really are incredibly small and need to be fished on very fine, soft nylon tippets.

Hook: 20–24
Thread: Uni-Thread 8/0 to match the insect
Shuck and antennae: 15–25 Antron fibres
Abdomen: Flat thread wrapped like floss
Rib: Twisted thread (colour dark enough to contrast with the abdomen)
Wing: Dun or white cul de canard in 180 degrees
Thorax: Fine dubbing to match the natural
Hackle: Three to four turns wound over the thorax and trimmed in a V on the underside

Suspender Hatching Midge Pupa   Plate 23

Devised by Neil Patterson as a means of enabling the pupa to hang beneath the surface film. It is adapted from an American idea from *Nymph Fishing for Larger Trout*, by Charles E. Brooks. Almost any midge-pupa pattern can be adapted to this method of suspension. John Goddard has done much to publicise this fly. He fishes a single green or brown version on a size 18 for trout and grayling.

Hook: 10–18
Thread: To match the body colour
Tail: White fluorescent wool (optional) tied well round the bend
Body: Seal's fur of an appropriate colour
Rib: Fine silver wire or Lurex
Thorax: Turkey fibres dyed brown or peacock herl
Head: A small ball of Ethafoam wrapped in a nylon mesh. Ladies' tights provide a suitable material

T.G. Emerger   *Plate 23*

The Terry Griffiths' Emerger is very like a small Klinkhamer Special. It is a very effective when fished in a rise to buzzers. It is extremely visible to the angler and also to the fish as the body is suspended below the surface. Body colour variations are black, brown, hot-orange, medium olive and bright green.

Hook: Curved shrimp or grub hook, size 12–16
Body: Dyed pheasant tail fibres
Rib: Fine oval silver tinsel or wire
Wing: Elk hair or similar
Thorax: Blood-brown seal's fur
Hackle: Grizzle cock in parachute style

Tube Buzzer *(Adrian Jones)*   *Plate 23*

Adrian Jones has produced these marvellously translucent-bodied pupae. He ties them in various colours. Adrian also ties a gold-head version with a small gold bead above the thorax with the breathers sticking through the gold bead.

Hook: Sedge hook 12–16
Thread: To match the body colour
Tail: Dyed pheasant tail tips
Body: Wound micro tube (Sid Knight material) with wire or floss threaded through it before winding
Thorax: Seal's or rabbit's fur
Breathers: White Multi-yarn

See also BOW-TIE BUZZER, CULARD, FOOTBALLER, PHANTOM MIDGE.

Adult Buzzers *(Bob Carnill)*   *Plate 23*

Bob Carnill comments: 'First and foremost, all the Adult Buzzers are wet flies, i.e. to be fished in or below the surface film. They are designed primarily to imitate the dead, dying, drowned or drowning mature fly. However, having said that, they can be made to simulate a freshly-hatched adult struggling to gain "lift-off". This is achieved by fishing the fly on the top dropper and dibbling it back to the boat, half-in and half-out of the water.

'I have seven Adult Buzzers, one for each major month of the trout-fishing season. Even though each has its own specific month, each can effectively overlap the first and last days – or even weeks – of the months on either side of the one allotted. For example, April is the allotted month for the *Black Duck Fly Adult Buzzer*, but it is often fished with great success during the last days of March, and often well into May. So as you can see, there are no cast-iron rules.

'Here then are the seven Adult Buzzers and their respective months: Blae and Black, March: Black Duck Fly, April; Grey Boy, May; Medium Olive, June; Large Ginger, July; Beige and Ginger, August; Large Dark Olive, September. The first Adult Buzzer I ever tried was the Blae and Black. It was tied in 1964 with spring trout on Ullswater in mind, and it proved so effective that the other six followed in their turn in ensuing years.

'My best trout to date on the Adult Buzzer was a 4 lb 12 oz brownie (hen fish) from Rutland Water. I have had lots in the 2–3 lb bracket. Adult Buzzers are particularly effective during a rise to egg-laying females. This can occur at any time of the day depending on the time of year, but early morning and late evening are usually the best times.'

Blagdon Green Midge

Green midges can be expected at any time during the six months of the trout season. This particular dressing goes back probably to the 1920s, but sadly it is one with which I have no success. However, others must find it of use, as a number of reputable fly tyers offer it. Others suggest it as a river fly as a good aphis or caterpillar imitation.

Hook: 14–16
Body: Emerald-green wool
Hackle: White cock hackle

Black Duck Fly (Adult Buzzer)

(Bob Carnill) *Plate 23*

Hook: 12–14 standard or sedge hook
Thread: Well-waxed black Gossamer
Body: Goose, swan or heron herl dyed black
Wing: Very light iron blue dun cock hackle points, rear-facing from the back of the thorax on a flat horizontal plane and divided in a semi-spent position
Thorax: Mole's fur dyed black
Thorax cover: A web of body herl
Hackle: Sparsely-tied black hen

Honey Buzzer *(Tom Saville)* *Plate 23*

Tom Saville created this to represent the ginger midges which hatch on many reservoirs during the summer. It copies the fly after eclosion but still skimming the surface before taking off. Tom regards it as an essential pattern from May to September.

Hook: 12–14 Partridge GRS2A
Thread: Orange monocord
Tail: Honey (light ginger) cock hackle fibres
Rib: Fine gold wire
Body: Pale-coloured cock pheasant centre tail
Hackle: Palmered honey (light ginger) cock
Wing: Grey feather from a teal or jay wing

Large Ginger (Adult Buzzer)

(Bob Carnill) *Plate 23*

Hook: 10 standard or sedge hook
Thread: Waxed orange or golden-olive Gossamer
Body: Hot-orange swan herl
Rib: Close turns of stripped peacock eye quill dyed ginger
Wing: As for Black Duck Fly
Thorax: Any light beige-brown under-fur; not seal's fur
Thorax cover: Hen secondary feather fibres dyed ginger-orange

Hackle: Sparsely tied pale ginger or honey hen

Medium Olive (Adult Buzzer)

(Bob Carnill)

Hook: 10 standard or sedge hook
Thread: Light or medium-olive Gossamer
Body: Medium-olive goose, swan or heron herl
Wing: As for Black Duck Fly
Thorax: Mole's fur dyed medium-olive
Thorax cover: A web of body herl
Hackle: Sparsely tied medium to light-olive hen hackle

Knotted Midge

An imitation to represent the mating pair.

Hook: 14–16
Thread: Black
Body: Black floss or thread
Hackles: Black cock at both ends of the body

Mini Lures

Most stillwater lures are tied on longshank hooks and are consequently a fairly large offering to a fish. On many occasions small lures prove attractive or are necessary. Some smaller fisheries insist on a maximum hook size. Many smaller attractor flies of the traditional design are moderately effective, but now small or mini-versions of the large reservoir lures are popular and are now easier to tie with the introduction of micro-chenilles. A lure dressing is tied on a standard size 8 to 12 hook and fished in the manner appropriate to the pattern. Mini-versions of most of the popular lures are available commercially.

Minky

The Minky is a Zonker-type lure, effective early-season or during the late season fry feeding. Best fished on a long leader and floating line.

Hook: 6–8
Thread: Brown
Tail: Green yarn
Body: Mixed hare's mask fur ribbed with oval gold tinsel
Wing: Strip of mink fur two and a half times the body length tied Matuka-style
Hackle: Greenwell cock

MINNOWS

These small fish are a source of food for both river and lake trout. See also under FRY and MUDDLER MINNOW.

Miss Beautiful Goldbead Zonker
Plate 4

Both fly and and name are a big mouthful. This lure comes from Theo Bakelaar. It has tremendous mobility within the dressing and its action is highly attractive as it rises and falls during the retrieve. As well as doing well on English reservoirs it also has taken steelhead, zander, large-mouth bass and a record catfish of seventy-eight pounds. Most commercially available zonker strips are not long enough so you have to cut your own.

Hook: Tiemco TMC 5263 (3X long shank) size 2–8
Thread: Black or to match one of the zonker colours
Head: Gold bead, 5 mm on size 2-4, 4 mm on size 6–8
Underbody: Knitting wool wound along the shank, colour to match a zonker strip
Strips: Two zonker strips of dyed rabbit skin in a suitable colour combination, 5–6 mm wide. Secure by coating the under-body with carpet or textile glue. The strips are then secured against the upper, lower and sides of the underbody. Optionally include Lureflash Crystal or Twinkleflash to show between the zonker strips

Missionary

This was originally devised by J. J. Dunn for the big trout on Blagdon and other reservoirs much earlier this century. A more recent variation by Dick Shrive is popular. Rainbow trout often take it on the drop. The flat wing is an essential feature, so that the fly seems to flutter or swing gently left and right as it sinks. This movement sometimes seems very attractive to fish.

Hook: Long shank 6–10
Thread: Black
Tail: Dark ginger or scarlet cock hackle fibres
Body: White chenille
Rib: Flat silver tinsel or Lurex
Wing: A single grey mallard or teal breast feather tied on flat and extending just beyond the bend
Throat hackle: As for the tail. White hackle fibres are sometimes used

The version tied with a hot-orange tail and hackle is called the Orange Missionary.

Misty Blue Dun
Plate 27

Devised by Tony Waites, at the time head-keeper for the Driffield Anglers' Club, which fishes the delightful Yorkshire chalk-stream the Driffield Beck. This is an imitation of the medium olive dun.

Hook: 14
Thread: Yellow
Tail: Three long fibres from a light blue-dun cock hackle
Body: Yellow tying thread
Rib: A strand of natural heron herl so closely wound that the tying silk just shows through
Hackle: A light brown and light blue-dun cock wound together

MITES

These aquatic creatures are a source of trout food, but most fly fishers imitate them only occasionally, perhaps when the examination of trouts' stomach contents has revealed a high percentage of them. They probably quickly disintegrate in a trout's stomach, and consequently do not figure prominently in stomach contents.

Most water-mites are bright red, but others are green, yellow or blue. They live in large colonies in mud on lake-beds and in weeds. They are small, varying between 2 and 6 mm (¼ inch) and are difficult to imitate. Richard Walker suggested this pattern and also recommended painting the hook vermilion.

Hook: 16–18
Thread: Vermilion
Body: Small ball-shaped white feather fibres dyed vermilion
Hackle: One turn of cock hackle dyed vermilion

Montana   *Plate 12*

This is a general-purpose fly fished all over the world. It was probably tied originally as a stonefly imitation but it is used now where stoneflies are totally absent. Peter Deane introduced the original to the UK in the 1950s. The original has a very distinctive pair of forward-facing long black rook or crow primary wing slips over the eye. Today the pattern is never seen with these. It is fished as a lure in its larger sizes, or as a nymph in the smaller sizes. The colour contrast and shape are its key features. Successful variants include a fluorescent lime-green or orange thorax; others have Waggler tails or bead eyes. Also see COOPER'S YELLOW DAMSEL.

Hook: Long shank 8–12 or standard 10
Thread: Black
Tail: Black hackle tips or fibres or goose biots
Underbody (optional): Lead wire
Body: Black chenille
Thorax: Yellow chenille with a palmered black cock
Thorax cover: Black chenille

Blue Montana   *Plate 13*

This is a Tony Hern variation effective when a profusion of blue adult damsels at the surface confuse a fish into taking.

Hook: Mustad 9672 long shank 10
Thread: Black
Tail: Two cock hackle points dyed teal blue
Body: Blue chenille (rayon)
Thorax: Fluorescent blue chenille with the abdomen material as a thorax back
Hackle: Cock dyed teal blue wound over the thorax

MOSQUITO

See DIPTERA.
The thirty species of mosquito have been largely overlooked as trout flies, possibly because they resemble to some extent the midges and phantom midge. Trout take much less interest in them than the other two insects, but they are well worth trying on a shaded part of a lake on a hot sunny day, or in the evening of such a day. The larvae are free-swimming and the pupae are similar to the midge-pupae except that they lack the white breathing spiracles at the head. The pupa pattern should be fished slowly under the surface film and twitched occasionally. A twenty-yard cast should take half-an-hour to be retrieved. It takes a lot of faith to fish in such a fashion!

Mosquito Larva   *(Taff Price)*

Hook: 12–14
Body: Grey thread
Rib: Black Terylene or silk
Hackle: White or blue-dun clipped short

Mosquito Pupa   *(Dave Collyer)*

Hook: 12
Thread: Black, taken well round the bend
Body: Stripped peacock eye quill
Thorax: Mole or muskrat fur in a ball shape

MOTHS *(Lepidoptera)*

Most moths are not aquatic, but some find their way on to river and lake surfaces by accident. However, one family of moths is aquatic. Only the adult winged moths are of any interest. Some of the smaller aquatic moths are at first glance taken for sedges, and a small sedge pattern will imitate these. The brown china moth is one of the larger and more common aquatic species. It is about 16 mm long and dark brown.

Terrestrial moths vary in size and colour from white to grey to brown and shades in between. The adults skitter across the surface, creating quite a disturbance. As a late-evening/dusk/night fly, a floating moth can be deadly in lake margins or on rivers. The white artificial has the added advantage of being easy to see in failing light. A moth fished on the last few casts of the evening has on more than one occasion saved me a blank. See also COACHMAN and GREY DUSTER.

Ermine Moth

An imitation of the lighter-coloured moths devised by the Reverend Edward Powell.

Hook: 12–14
Tail: Orange wool divided into a V-shape
Body: White rabbit's fur on any white wool or fur
Rib: Black thread
Hackle: Grey partridge

An additional white hackle can be added behind the partridge hackle to aid floatation.

Hoolet Moth (Geoffrey Bucknall)

The origin of this fly's name probably lies in 'hoolet', the old Scottish name for an owl. In original patterns the wing feather from that bird was used, but in Geoffrey Bucknall's version woodcock is preferred. The cork underbody makes the pattern very buoyant for fishing in a wave.

Hook: 8–10
Thread: Black

Body: An underbody of cork strip wound on to the shank with bronze peacock herl over
Wing: Woodcock wing feather tied low over the body, either rolled or flat
Hackle: Two natural red cock hackles

Mr Nasty (Davy Wotton)   Plate 12

This is Davy Wotton's alder larva imitation. Davy points out a good rule of thumb for the proportions: the body length should be about two-thirds of the total length, with the thorax and head making up the other third. The ostrich herls are tied in before the body chenille is tied in and wound. They are the laid along the edge of the body, fluffy side outwards, and individually secured by thread.

Hook: Long shank 8–10 Partridge D3ST or GRS12ST
Thread: Brown
Underbody: Three strands of fine lead wire twisted together and laid each side of the shank, overlaid with thread and secured. The body must remain flat. Coat in varnish
Tail: Short tuft of white or off-white marabou
Gills: White ostrich herls with the fibres stripped off the inside of each curve
Body: Fine brown chenille
Eyes: Mustard or black chenille tied at right angles to the shank before the thorax dubbing is added
Thorax: Olive or brown fox squirrel or dyed rabbit fur spun in a dubbing loop and wound so that some longer fibres trail from the rear of the thorax underside

Mrs Palmer

A lure devised by Richard Walker in 1973. It works better than most in dirty water and is best fished fairly slowly.

Hook: Long shank 6-8
Thread: Black
Body: White fluorescent wool taken to within 6 mm (¼ inch) of the eye; then

three or four turns of arc-chrome fluorescent wool to within 3 mm of the eye
Rib: Fine flat silver tinsel over the white wool body only
Wing: Pale yellow goat hair about twice the hook length
Beard hackle: White cock hackle fibres
Cheeks: Jungle cock

Mrs Simpson

This stillwater fly from New Zealand is, apart from the Matukas, the only pattern from that country to have gained general acceptance in the UK. The number of paired cock pheasant rump feathers for the wing can be reduced on the smaller sizes.

Hook: Long shank 8–12
Thread: Black
Tail: Black squirrel tail fibres
Body: Red, yellow or green chenille
Wing: Up to six pairs of green cock pheasant rump feathers tied in alongside the body; largest at the front, the smallest at the rear
Head: Tying thread varnished black

Muddle May   *Plate 24*

The Muddle May is a pattern type devised by expert US tyer Al Beatty. In appropriate sizes and colours it may represent any adult dun. Al says that his aim was to produce a slender profile on the water, maintain excellent floatation, and eliminate the use of the hackle. It is the only dun imitation he uses. He ties these down to an incredible size 24 but that calls for extreme skill.

Hook: 12–14 Partridge E1A or L3A
Thread: To match the body colour
Tail: Moose body hair or Microfibetts about 1 ½ times the shank length
Body: Dubbed fur
Wings: Wonder wings (see Glossary)
Hackle: Deer hair flared in 180 degrees
Head: Spun deer hair, natural or coloured to match the insect, no thicker than half the diameter of a pencil. Two clumps for

sizes 12–14, one clump for smaller sizes. Trimmed to taper towards the eye. Trim off the hair tips before spinning them.

Muddlers

The original Muddler Minnow is credited to Don Gapen and was devised for fishing in Northern Ontario. The dressing was published in 1953 in Al McClane's *The Practical Fly Fisherman*. However, it is arguable that the minnow imitation of Ludwig Moedler, a German migrant to the USA in the nineteenth century, was the real source. His diary records that his minnow had a gold body and a head 'fashioned from the freshly plucked hair from the body of a Virginia deer rotated round the hook...use three or four bunches of hair instead of a large one... trim now the hair with considerable delicacy in a circular fashion to reduce the size of the hair but do not cut too close to the hook. It is desirable to have remain a circle of hair to give bulk to the head.'

The Nottingham tackle-dealer Tom Saville introduced it into the UK in the mid-1960s. Many variations have been devised to represent various fry or small fish. They are excellent lures and can be deadly when fished in a wave or as a fry imitation. This is arguably the most successful fly pattern to cross the Atlantic in our direction. Other lures can be adapted to the Muddler style.

The heads on all these patterns, unless otherwise stated, are constructed by natural deer body hair spun on the shank and clipped to a ball shape. The original pattern had a few long hairs trailing underneath as a hackle. All patterns should use Naples tying thread or stronger, as the construction calls for the thread to be held taut under some strain. The shape of the head can be varied according to preference. Ball- or cone-shaped is popular. Some patterns are tied with a pointed cylindrical head.

Also see CAENIS MUDDLER, DUNKELD MUDDLER, HARE'S EAR MUDDLER, CLARET BUMBLE MUDDLER.

Black Muddler

Hook: Long shank 6–10
Thread: Black
Body: Black floss or black chenille
Rib: Gold or silver tinsel
Tail (optional): Orange DRF floss
Wing: Black bucktail or squirrel
Hackle (optional): Black cock tied as a throat
Head: Natural deer hair spun and clipped

Foam-Headed Muddler

Any of the Muddler dressings can be tied with a plastic foam head instead of the usual deer hair. Eyes can be painted on if desired. The result is a buoyant pattern that will stay just below the surface.

Last Resort Muddler

(C. Kendall)   *Plate 1*

I have had good reports of this lure when jumped across the surface in a heavy wave. Indeed, as a last resort I used it in just these circumstances on Leighton Reservoir and caught half a dozen fish.

Hook: Long shank 6
Tail: Marabou plumes, yellow, orange or lime
Body: White or DFM lime chenille
Wing: Marabou plumes, yellow, orange or lime but a different colour from the tail
Head: White deer hair barely clipped, merely tidied up

Marabou-Winged Muddler

Plate 1

Many lures are no more than hybrids between two or more proven patterns. This is one, utilising the attractive action of marabou in conjunction with the rounded deer-hair head. Yellow, black and white versions are available commercially, tied as single-hook lures or in tandem.

Hook: Long shank 6–10

Thread: To match the overall colour
Body: Floss or fine chenille
Rib: Silver oval tinsel
Wing: Marabou plumes extending well beyond the rear of the hook in the same colour as the body
Throat or underwing: Marabou plume extending only to the rear of the hook
Head: Deer hair dyed as the body and wing colour, spun and clipped to shape

The tandem version has as the front hook a longs-hank or standard-length hook dressed as above. The rear hook omits the underwing and the Muddler head and instead has a head of peacock herl.

Muddler Minnow   *Plate 4*

The original dressing.

Hook: Long shank 4–12
Thread: Brown
Tail: A folded slip of oak-turkey wing feather
Body: Flat gold tinsel
Wing: Grey squirrel fibres between two matched mottled oak-turkey wing sections
Head: Deer hair spun and clipped to a ball shape, leaving a few long fibres trailing to the rear as a hackle

Orange Muddler *(Taff Price)*

Useful in dirty water conditions or when trout are feeding on daphnia.

Hook: Long shank 6–10
Body: Gold tinsel
Rib: Gold wire
Wing: Orange bucktail
Head: Deer hair spun and clipped, with some hairs unclipped as a collar

Sculpin Muddler

A bullhead imitation.

Hook: Long shank 4–8
Body: Optional underbody of lead wire. Buff seal's fur tapering to the front,

finishing about one-third of the way from the eye
Rib: Oval gold tinsel
Wing: Light red squirrel-tail fibres tied half-way along the shank, with two cree cock hackles tied in horizontally on the bare shank. Over the cree hackle roots are tied in three small well marked hen pheasant body feathers, one on either side of the roots and the other on top of the shank to flare out to imitate the large fins of the bullhead
Head: Deer hair spun, clipped and trimmed to shape

Texas Rose Muddler

Hook: Long shank 6–10
Body: Orange or yellow wool or floss
Rib: Silver or gold tinsel
Wing: Bucktail dyed primrose
Head: Deer hair spun and trimmed in a bullet shape

Whisky Muddler

A Muddler variation of the Whisky Fly.

Hook: Long shank 6-8
Thread: Scarlet fluorescent floss
Butt: Tying thread
Body: Silver or gold Mylar
Rib: Tying thread
Wing: Oak-turkey wing sections and calf tail dyed orange
Head: Deer hair spun and clipped

White Muddler

Hook: Long shank 6–10
Thread: Black or white
Tail: White swan fibres
Body: Silver tinsel
Rib: Oval silver tinsel
Wing: White swan
Head: White deer hair spun and clipped in a bullet shape, with longer fibres trailing to the rear

Murrough

This Irish loch fly is a wet imitation of the great red sedge. I have seen a number of dressings for this pattern, all of which differ only in their body colour. No doubt different species of sedge are copied with different body colours.

Hook: Long shank or standard 8–10
Body: Brown, claret or grey seal's fur
Rib: Gold wire
Wing: Brown mottled turkey tied long
Collar hackle: Natural red cock
Antennae (optional): Two cock pheasant tail fibres

Mylar Fry

A simple but effective fry-imitating lure.

Hook: Long shank 8
Tail: Green marabou
Body: Silver Mylar tubing with the centre core removed
Head: Tying thread varnished black and with a painted eye

Nailer

A bucktail lure popular at many of the Midlands reservoirs, and particularly at Rutland. It needs to be fished slowly near the surface. It is good in a wave, and sometimes effective when sedges are hatching.

Hook: Long shank 6–10
Thread: Black
Tail: Red cock hackle fibres or hair fibres
Body: Gold Lurex or tinsel
Rib: Gold wire
Wing: Bright-red skunk or goat hair with an overwing of brown hair
Throat hackle: Deep-brown cock fibres

Naked John Storey

John Wood of York devised this under-dressed John Storey. It is fished as an emerger with the body hanging vertically below the surface supported by the collar of hackle. The mallard-breast wing is very visible to the angler. This is an excellent grayling fly on rivers like the Ure. John tells me that the orange body works best.

Hook: Fine wire 14–20
Body: Stripped peacock herl, natural or dyed orange, red or olive
Hackle: Natural red cock
Wing: Mallard breast fibres bunched and forward-sloping

Ned's Fancy (Tom Saville)   Plate 9

This is Tom Saville's pattern, a caricature of a hatching midge pupa which has consistently taken trout for him for forty years from both boat and bank. It is fished on the bob or middle dropper. The fluorescent colours can be altered to suit prevailing conditions: neon-magenta (shade 1) or red (4) for dusk, orange (7) for bright conditions, green (12) for clear water. If the tail colour is changed, alter the hackle colour to suit – ginger with the orange tail, black with the green tail.

Hook: Partridge GRS2A size 12–16
Thread: Black monocord
Tail: Tuft of Glo-Brite floss or multi-yarn, shade 1
Body: Flat silver tinsel or Mylar
Rib: Fine silver wire
Thorax: Peacock herl
Hackle: Three turns of blue dun hen

NEEDLE-FLIES (Leuctra fusca, L. hippopus)

These two species of stonefly, almost indistinguishable from each other, are widely distributed throughout the country in rain-fed rivers and chalk-streams, preferring rivers with a stony bottom. They are similar in overall appearance to the willow fly, although much smaller. They are dark brown, slim-bodied flies. Their size varies between 5 and 9 mm. *L. hippopus* is an early species, appearing from February to April; *L. fusca* appears from August to October. For general details, see STONEFLIES. These

imitations should be dressed very slim with sparse turns of hackle. The designation 'Light' or 'Dark' refers to the hackle colour and not the body.

See also WINTER BROWN and LIGHT WOODCOCK

Needle-Fly   Plate 32

Hook: 14
Body: Orange silk
Hackle: Dark-brown owl's wing feather
Head: Peacock herl

Another old dressing bearing this name has a claret silk body and a starling wing for the hackle. The Light Needle has an orange silk body and is hackled with the flank feather of a young starling.

Dark Spanish Needle   Plate 32

Hook: 14
Thread: Well waxed orange silk, almost brown
Body: Tying silk
Hackle: Dark brown hen feather
Head: Peacock herl

Light Spanish Needle (Taff Price)

A wet pattern.

Hook: 14–16
Body: Crimson silk
Hackle: Inside of a jack snipe wing

Needle Fly (Philip White)   Plate 22

Philip White ties this floating adult imitation in two versions. One with a single flat wonder wing strengthened with varnish, the second as below with either a single or paired turkey biot wing.. The paired wing splays slightly, imitating the spent fly.

Hook: 14 fine wire
Tag: Pale yellow-olive or light orange dubbing or feather fibre
Body: Cock pheasant tail fibres dyed a dark olive, or a dubbing of similar colour

Hackle: Any dark cock wound over the thorax area with the upper and lower fibres cut away

Wing: Dark wonder wing or dark-coloured turkey biots, singly or in pairs laid flat over the back and extending just beyond the tail

Antennae (optional): A couple of hackle fibres pulled forward and tied down

NOBBLERS

The original and best-known member of this series of stillwater lures is the Dog Nobbler, devised and popularised by the late Trevor Housby in the early 1980s. The success of the series is due to the pulsating action of the marabou herl tail in conjunction with the weighted head, which causes the lure to dive head-first when there is a pause in the retrieve. Fished in a sink-and-draw fashion, they can be extremely effective. Like some other exceptionally killing patterns, Nobblers have been banned on some smaller stillwaters. It is a fairly offensive-looking lure in its larger sizes; even its name does little to appease those who frown on the use of such lures.

The Nobbler's extensive 'ironmongery' has caused some concern about trends in fly dressing. I hesitate to mention that I have seen tandem versions. But Nobblers catch fish and there is a place for them on some fisheries. The Nobblers and their variations, particularly the Nobbler Nymphs, have remained popular. Other similar lures have been developed; all are based upon the marabou herl tail or wing and a weighted head or body and have equally outlandish names.

In 1984, fly tyer Sid Knight successfully patented the name and dressing of the Dog Nobbler as tied and named by Trevor Housby. I do not condone an attempt to corner the market or create a monopoly. Voices of disapproval were heard, and the situation was roundly condemned by the fishing-tackle trade and by fly fishermen across the country. Sid Knight's reason for his action was that it was to 'prevent the commercial exploitation of inferior products'.

My opinion is that the Dog Nobbler is an easy fly to tie; there is little to tie incorrectly. There are many similar lures or variations of the Nobbler and all are efficient trout lures. Would the fly-fishing world be any better off if Frank Sawyer, Canon Greenwell and James Wright, William Lunn, Richard Walker and many others had all patented their own dressings and named flies? Trout fishers the world over would be considerably worse off.

However, what is undeniable is that Sid Knight ties flies of high quality. He sent me the Dog, Mini Nobblers and Nobbler Nymphs used in the illustrations, and I have only the highest praise for the workmanship.

The Nobbler concept and dressing is not as new as we might think. As long ago as 1941 a similar fly was being used in the USA for jigging through holes in iced-over lakes for perch and other fish. The lure, called a Goggle-Eye Ice Fly, had a marabou herl tail, a lead-shot head and a floss-silk body. One thing that is beyond doubt is that the combination of a marabou herl tail and a leaded head is a killing one.

Dog Nobbler

Hook: Long shank 4–12

Underbody: Lead wire or foil strips along the shank or just at the shoulder; or a large split-shot pinched on and glued to the shank at the shoulder

Overbody: Coloured chenille

Rib (optional): Silver wire

Tail: A thick bunch of marabou herl tied long

Head (optional): Peacock herl

Eye: Painted on the split shot

The colour variations are infinite: white, yellow, green, black, pink, orange, and others are all used, and in their fluorescent alternatives. Most patterns are tied with the tail the same colour as the body, but two-colour Nobblers are also used.

Black-and-green and white-and-orange are popular. Mini-Nobblers, sometimes called Frog Nobblers, are tied on size 8 or 10 standard-length hooks. Another variation which is attractive is the Palmered-body Nobbler. The long shanked lure has a split-shot head with painted eye and a palmered badger hackle over the body which is ribbed with silver wire. The Booby Nobbler is an unweighted Nobbler with the inclusion of two foam beads trapped in a stocking mesh behind the eye. This makes the lure very buoyant. Further details of this are in the section headed BOOBIES. Many other lures have been 'nobbled' and tied in this style. The basic colours of the original lure are tied with Nobbler materials. For example:

Sweeney Todd Nobbler

Hook: Long shank 8
Underbody: Lead foil or wire near the head
Overbody: Black chenille for the rear two-thirds; front one-third, neon magenta fluorescent floss or wool
Rib: Silver wire
Tail: Black marabou plume
Hackle: Scarlet cock as a rear-facing collar
Head: Peacock herl

Nobbler Nymphs　　　　　　Plate 1

These are probably the smallest that the Nobbler style is tied in. Sid Knight confirms that the black version is the most popular, followed by olive, orange, white, and yellow in that order.

Hook: Kamasan B175 size 12
Tail: Marabou with four strands of Pearly Mobile Mother of Pearl
Body: Twinkle
Hackle: Soft cock tied behind the head with a few Twinkle strands trailing over the back
Head: Lead substitute shot super-glued and with a painted eye

No-Hackle Flies　　　　　　Plate 25

The dressing of floating flies without the use of hackles was publicised after considerable research by two Americans, Carl Richards and Douglas Swisher, in their book *Selective Trout*, published in the USA in 1971. Their belief is that the body and wings of the fly are the stimulus to a trout, and to a lesser extent the hackle, this being so for the smaller sizes. After experimenting with natural dubbed fur, they dressed many patterns with poly-propylene fibres as a greater aid to floatation. All the flies were dressed on fine-wire hooks, and to help them land right way up the bunches of tail fibres were widely spread by being tied on either side of the shank and divided by a small dubbing ball at the bend of the hook, forcing the tail fibres apart. The resulting flies are not very durable and after a fish or two have chewed the wings they may be useless. Their use is better saved for some very selective or specimen fish. The colours should match the natural duns.

No-Hackle Dun

Hook: 14–18
Tail: Cock hackle fibres or Microfibetts widelyspaced by a ball of dubbing
Body: Fine poly dubbing
Wing: Paired light grey mallard quill slips, mounted on the side of the shank, or poly yarn

No. 3 Para　　　　　　Plate 26

This Parachute-style dry fly was devised by Pat Russell for both river and stillwater to catch those trout that rise only once and are not motivated into doing so again. Its creator knows of no better fly (save his own Enigma) for bringing uncooperative fish to the surface. I feel it is a fair spinner imitation or an emerger with its body held in the film. Either way I have enough personal experience of it to know that it works well. The fly was devised after the Falklands war, when the No. 3 Parachute

Brigade fought so bravely, and it was named in their honour.

Hook: 14–16
Thread: Scarlet
Tail: Rhode Island Red hackle fibres
Body: Rhode Island Red hackle stalk and silk
Hackle: Barred ginger or light red cock

OAK FLY

See DIPTERA

This is a member of the Diptera Order, a flat-winged terrestrial fly so named because it is often seen resting on tree trunks. It has a fairly large body about 12 mm (½ inch) long which is orangy-yellow. Our forefathers valued it as an angler's fly and it is mentioned in Charles Cotton's addition to *The Compleat Angler*, and possibly even earlier, as the fifteenth-century Tandy Fly of Dame Juliana Berners was thought by G. E. M. Skues to be an oak-fly imitation.

Hook: 12–14
Thread: Orange
Body: Orange floss
Rib: Black silk or stripped peacock quill
Wing: Woodcock wing tied flat over the back
Hackle: Furnace cock

Octopus   *Plate 9*

Stan Headley combines the best of the Green Peter and a French Partridge. Although it looks like a floating-line, tripped-over-the-wave pattern, it will operate effectively further down the cast, on varying line densities, on stillwaters throughout the country. A slight variation to suit the colour of hatching Mayfly on Lough Melvin was spectacularly successful.

Hook: Sedge hook 10–12
Thread: Black or brown
Body: Grass green seal's fur, palmered with a ginger soft henny cock hackle and over-ribbed with medium oval gold

Hackle: Red body feather from a golden pheasant, one and a half times the body length

Old Master   *Plate 32*

Missed from the first edition of the book, I now update it (!) by including a pattern over two hundred years old. I know a number of anglers who are using this with success. Pritt recommended it for April until the end of August, on warm days or evenings.

Hook: 14–16
Thread: Ash-coloured
Body: Tying thread with open turns of natural heron herl
Hackle: A small woodock undercovert feather

OLIVES

See EPHEMEROPTERA

Before a more detailed classification was generally accepted among anglers, all the Baetis species, with the exception of the iron blue and pale wateries, were grouped together and referred to as olive duns. Therefore many old patterns bearing this name could represent one or more of the Baetis genus. The patterns below could represent many of the different olives, depending upon the shades of the materials used and the hook sizes. For natural-history details and more specific patterns see under BLUE-WINGED OLIVE, LAKE OLIVE, LARGE DARK OLIVE, DARK OLIVE, MEDIUM OLIVE, OLIVE UPRIGHT, POND OLIVE and SMALL DARK OLIVE. In addition, see also the artificial flies: WATERHEN BLOA, ROUGH OLIVE, GIMRIVER DUN, GOLD-RIBBED HARE'S EAR, GREENWELL'S GLORY, OLIVE BLOA, DARK OLIVE BLOA, DOGSBODY, KITE'S IMPERIAL, PHEASANT-TAIL SPINNER, LUNN'S PARTICULAR, SUNK SPINNER and LIGHT OLIVE.

Hatching Olive Nymph

(Geoffrey Bucknall)

To be fished as a floater.

Hook: 12–14
Tail: A slim strip of light-olive goose feather fibres
Body: Light-olive goose feather fibres
Rib: Fine gold tinsel
Thorax: A knob of dark-olive seal's fur
Wing-case: Dark wing feather

Olive Dun (John Roberts)   Plate 27

This is my own general olive imitation.

Hook: Partridge CS20 or CS27 size 14–18
Thread: Olive
Tail: Olive Microfibetts, widely spaced
Body: Any fine natural or synthetic olive dubbing
Hackle: High-grade blue-dun cock wound over the thorax area

Olive Parachute

(John Roberts)   Plate 25

As a general dry fly in a hatch I cannot fathom, or as a search fly when just an occasional fish is moving, on moderately paced water or slower, I invariably use this general olive imitation. I prefer the parachute style because it suggests so much to a fish – trapped nymph, emerger, struggling dun. Perhaps twenty per cent of my river trout are caught on this.

Hook: 14–22
Thread: Sparton Micro olive
Tail (optional): A few Z-lon fibres or widely spaced Microfibetts
Body: Fine olive poly dubbing (Fly-Rite)
Wing: Upright white or grey poly yarn (siliconised yarn from Niche Products is the best)
Hackle: Blue dun or natural red cock wound round the wing base

Olive Quill

This is better known as a river dry fly, but Bob Church recommends it fished wet on stillwaters.

Hook: 12–16
Tail: Medium-olive cock fibres
Body: Peacock quill dyed olive
Wing (optional): Medium starling wing feather
Hackle: Medium-olive cock

OLIVE UPRIGHT (Rhithrogena semicolorata)

See EPHEMEROPTERA
This fly occurs in the western half of the UK, Scotland, the north-west and West of England, and Wales. Its nymphs are similar to those of the March brown, clinging to stones on faster-flowing rivers. The adults are fairly large and have dark blue-grey wings, a grey-olive body and two tails, and are similar to the slightly smaller blue-winged olive. They appear between late April and July, hatching in large numbers in the evenings or in the afternoons if the weather is cool. The spinner is sometimes known as the yellow upright. The male spinners have yellowish wings and bodies and the females are a duller olive-yellow. The spinners can be copied with a Pheasant Tail with a rusty-dun hackle.

Olive Upright Dun

Hook: 12–14
Tail: Light to medium-olive cock hackle fibres
Body: Peacock quill dyed olive
Hackle: Light to medium-olive cock

Ombudsman

(Brian Clarke)   Plate 12

Brian Clarke designed this pattern in the early 1970s, when doing the research which eventually led to his book, *The Pursuit of Stillwater Trout*. He writes that he was 'seeking to represent a wide range of bottom-living creepy-crawlies which trout consume: caddis larvae, alder larvae and the like from the world of the real; and a conceptual range of bugs which should exist, even if they don't. In short, I was seeking to design something which looked like the kinds of food items which trout were accustomed to seeing – and to feeding upon.

'The Ombudsman, as originally designed, when cast and wet, does not keep the sleek shape of the dry finished article in the fly-tying vice. It becomes somewhat ragamuffin and bedraggled. But a sharp jerk when it has been allowed to sink to the fishing depth, and the steady motion of the retrieve, will bring the feather-fibres back into profile which is sufficiently appealing to the trout to cause them to take the confection.

'I designed the Ombudsman to be fished slowly along the bottom from the end of a long leader attached to a floating line. But it is fished by some from a sinking line (an unappealing method for me); and it will also take fish when fished close to the surface where, presumably, trout take it for some form of ascending pupa.

'I called the fly the Ombudsman after much public discussion of the role of a government-appointed individual whose job it was to act as adjudicator in alleged cases of abuse or misuse of executive power. He was presented, it seemed to me, as someone who would be all things to all men. My fly was intended to be many things to many fish. Poetic licence took care of the rest.'

Hook: Long shank 8–10
Body: Underbody of one or two layers of copper wire with an overbody of bronze peacock herl to within 6 mm (¼ inch) of the eye
Rib (optional): Copper wire
Wing: Any large dark-brown mottled wing feather tied as a roof close over the body and extending to a point 6–12 mm beyond the bend
Hackle: Soft brown cock tied in front of the wing

Head: Thick brown silk tied over the wing roots

Once and Away *Plate 29*

This is a stillwater emerger pattern tied by Hans van Klinken. The cul de canard feathers keep the fly in the film and provide a good blur of insect components. The abdomen and thorax hang tantalisingly below the film.

Hook: Partridge GRS12ST size 12–18 with a further downward bend
Thread: Fine black
Body: One peccary fibre or stripped quill taken well round the bend
Thorax: Three strands of peacock herl
Wing and wing-case: Six or seven large cul de canard feathers, secured in the upright position; trim to a tuft

Orange John

A stillwater pattern devised by John Ketley, a former captain of the English fly-fishing team. It is a wet sedge fly to be fished on the top dropper in traditional loch style towards the end of the season. As a bob fly it can be fished dry, skittering along the surface during the retrieve.

Hook: 10
Thread: Brown or orange
Body: Hot-orange seal's fur with a palmered light-brown hackle
Rib: Goldfingering through the body hackle
Wing: Hen pheasant
Hackle: Honey cock wound as a collar

Orange Lures

In addition to those detailed below, other orange lures can be found under WHISKY FLY, NOBBLERS and MUDDLERS.

When the water temperature is high during July and August, or when rainbows are gorging themselves on daphnia, then one of the most successful tactics is to strip an orange lure fast in the top few feet of water. Sometimes almost any orange lure works well, but perhaps the best are the Orange Bucktail and the Whisky Fly. There are times when orange lures and nymphs take trout and patterns of other colours fail. Bob Church termed this annual event at Grafham as 'orange madness'.

The success of the orange lure is notable when the water temperature is high and large amounts of blue-green algae come to the surface. The orange colour of the lures is poorly reflected beyond a few feet down, and in water thick with algae trout are likely to see the lure colour as blue-grey, or at eight or ten feet possibly even as black. Small fish darting about will be seen as the same colour. A cynic or a purist may scorn bright-orange lures, but there are times when trout certainly don't see them as orange.

Orange Bucktail *(Taff Price)*

Hook: Long shank 8–10
Body: Oval gold tinsel
Wing: Orange bucktail
Head: Black with a painted white eye and black pupil

Orange Streamer *(Taff Price)*

Hook: Long shank 6–10
Body: Orange floss
Rib: Oval gold tinsel
Wing: Two hot-orange cock hackles tied back-to-back with two cock badger hackles one either side
Cheek: Jungle cock about a quarter the wing length

Orange Nymphs   Plate 16

The first of these stillwater patterns was created by Arthur Cove and is recommended to be fished on a bright, sunny day. It has a reputation for catching trout when snails are on the surface. Jeremy Herrmann ties the same pattern with a pearl Flashabou rib and uses it either as a point fly or more thickly dressed static or retrieved on the surface.

Hook: 10–12
Body: Orange seal's fur or synthetic substitute
Rib: Flat gold tinsel
Thorax: As for the body, but more pronounced
Wing-case: Pheasant tail fibres over the thorax

A second pattern has been devised by Taff Price, who recommends it as useful when trout are feeding on daphnia. The story goes that Taff was fruitlessly fishing and trying any fly in his box. Well down the list he tried a Partridge and Orange, an old North Country wet fly. He caught a trout and its stomach contents showed that it was full of strawberry-jam-coloured daphnia. The orange nymph was devised as a result.

Hook: 12–14
Thread: Orange
Body: Orange seal's fur
Rib: Gold wire
Back: Swan fibres dyed deep orange (optional to varnish)
Antennae: Two or three of the orange swan fibres extending forward over the eye

Orange Otter

This is a grayling dry fly devised by the Reverend Edward Powell, who said that it was the only fly he knew to bring grayling up from the bottom when they were not feeding on the surface. Courtney Williams records contemporary comments on the pattern as 'Phenomenal, devastating, one hell of a fly'. My own comment on the fly is that I have caught grayling on it, but not with outstanding success.

Hook: 12–16
Tail: Natural red cock fibres
Body: Orange seal's fur (otter substitute) tied in two halves
Hackle: Natural red cock in the middle of the body

Orange Quill

Despite its unlikely appearance, this is a blue-winged olive and general olive copy. It was popularised by G. E. M. Skues, who did not invent the fly, but who discovered its effectiveness for the blue-winged olive. It is a useful evening pattern and this may be due to the orange hue surrounding the natural fly on the surface when there is a red sunset. I've had success with it as a late-season trout fly and as an early-season grayling fly, when I've found it, on occasion, to be exceptional.

Hook: 12–14
Tail: Orange hackle fibres
Body: Quill dyed pale orange
Wing: Rusty-dun hackle points
Hackle: Orange cock

Other dressings have a pale starling wing and a natural light red cock hackle or a medium ginger cock hackle.

Orange Rory   Plate 6

Stan Headley suggests that this probably originated on Loch Awe although its use is widespread in Scotland and Ireland as a top dropper. He comments that he uses it on daphnia feeders and in difficult, bright conditions to 'pull fish up'. The original was tied with cock hackles, but Stan prefers hen. Imitating nothing what-soever, it is a constant reminder that 'matching the hatch' is all very well but not always the best way of filling a bag.

Hook: 10–14
Thread: Black
Tail: Hackle fibres, orange on top of black
Hackles: Hen hackles in this order from the tail – black, orange, black, orange. Some dressers prefer cock hackles and use hackle points for the tail.

Orange Spinner

A G. E. M. Skues pattern which he fished as a blue-winged olive spinner imitation.

Hook: 14
Thread: Orange
Tail: Honey-dun hackle fibres
Body: Medium-olive seal's fur
Rib: Fine gold wire
Hackle: Rusty-dun or blue-dun cock

Otter Ruby   Plate 26

An iron blue dun imitation tied by Jim Nice in the late 1950s.

Hook: 14–18
Thread: Brown or claret
Tail: Fibres of the hackle used
Body: Condor herl dyed magenta
Rib (optional): Fine gold wire
Hackle: Iron-blue or brownish-black cock

PALE EVENING DUN (*Procloëon bifidum*)

See EPHEMEROPTERA
A fairly widely distributed species of upwinged dun, but occurring quite locally. The nymphs are the agile-darting type and prefer slower-moving water. John Goddard points out that the dun often appears at the same time as the blue-winged olive and often trout will rise to the pale evening dun in preference to it. It has been undervalued as a fly pattern and the absence of artificials reflects this.

The pale evening dun is easy to identify because of the absence of hind-wings, which makes the species unique among river duns. In the past it may have been included under the general heading of 'pale watery', but the pale evening dun is slightly larger and paler than the one species we term the pale watery. It appears in the evenings of July and August. The dun is pale-coloured and the male has distinctive yellow eyes. The spinner is of doubtful value to the fly fisher as it is likely that the female returns to the water only after dark. For other patterns, see LUNN'S YELLOW BOY and PALE WATERY.

Pale Evening Flymph

See FLYMPH

Hook: 14–16 Long shank Mayfly
Thread: Primrose or white
Tail: Pale honey-dun hackle fibres
Body: Creamy-red fox fur
Hackle: Pale honey-dun

Pale Evening Dun   (Oliver Kite)

Hook: 14–16
Thread: White
Tail: Cream cock fibres
Body: Grey goose herls, doubled and redoubled at the thorax
Hackle: Cream cock

PALE WATERY
(Baetis fuscatus)

See EPHEMEROPTERA
The term pale watery was once collectively applied to this and three other species, the small dark olive, small spurwing and large spurwing, and possibly to the pale evening dun, but these are now considered separately. The distribution is good in the south of England, parts of Wales and the north and on other alkaline waters. The smallish adults appear from late May to late October. I have found the duns greedily taken by grayling as well as trout. The nymph is an agile-darting type preferring to live among weed-beds. The duns hatch during the day, but the appearance of the female spinner is mainly in the evening.

The male dun has medium- or pale-grey wings and a pale greyish-olive body, of which the last two segments are pale yellow. The legs are light-olive and the two tails grey. The yellow eyes of the male help to identify it, but might also help to confuse it with the pale evening dun.

The female dun has pale-grey wings and a pale grey-olive abdomen, with the last two segments yellow-olive. The legs are pale-olive and the two tails grey. The female spinner, sometimes called the golden spinner, has transparent wings and a medium golden-brown abdomen, of which the last three segments are darker. The legs are pale watery and the two tails grey-white. The male spinner is of no interest as it does not return to the water.

For other patterns see POULT BLOA, GODDARD'S LAST HOPE, USD PARA-DUNS, GREY GOOSE NYMPH, LITTLE MARRYAT, ENIGMA, TUP'S INDIS-PENSABLE, PHEASANT TAIL and LUNN'S PARTICULAR.

Pale Watery   Plate 17

Hook: 14–16
Thread: Primrose
Tail: Ginger cock fibres
Abdomen: Slim dubbed mixed cream and olive (3:1) seal's fur
Thorax: Mixed ginger and cream (2:1) seal's fur
Hackle: Short-fibred medium blue-dun hen

Hatching Pale Watery Dun
(W. H. Lawrie)

Only the legs and thorax should float on the surface.

Hook: 16
Thread: Primrose
Tail: Blue hen hackle fibres
Body: Pale-blue cat's fur or substitute, thinly spun
Rib: Fine gold wire
Thorax: Blue cat's fur mixed with primrose worsted
Wing hackle: Pale-blue cock with the lower fibres cut away
Leg hackle: Grey or henny cock with the upper fibres cut away

Pale Watery Dun   (Richard Walker)

Recommended also as a chalk-stream grayling fly.

Hook: 16
Thread: Primrose

Tail: Fibres of the hackle used
Body: Swan secondary herl tinted the palest greenish-grey with a few turns of tying silk built up and exposed at the rear. A drop of clear cellulose should be added to the tip to give it an amber tint
Wing (optional): Honey-dun hackle fibres set upright; or bleached starling wing
Hackle: Honey-dun or deeply-tinted cream cock

Pale Watery Dun

(Freddie Rice)   *Plate 19*

Hook: 14–16
Thread: Light yellow
Tail: Light blue-dun or pale honey-dun hackle fibres
Tip: Unwaxed tying silk
Body: Two or three herls: light-grey heron, white swan or goose wing, palest olive
Hackle: Palest olive or pale honey-dun cock

Pale Watery Dun

(John Roberts)   *Plate 25*

This represents any species of paler duns. I've enjoyed success with it on rain-fed rivers and chalk-streams but nothing quite so dramatic as the seventy to eighty grayling I caught one afternoon on the Avon. All the flies I fish with are simple to tie and this is no exception.

Hook: 16–18 Partridge CS20 or CS27GRS
Thread: Any matching light shade
Tail (optional): Two widely spaced Microfibbets
Body: Pale yellowy-beige fine poly dubbing
Wing: Upright white poly yarn (Niche Products siliconised is the best)
Hackle: Blue-dun or pale ginger wound round the wing base

Pale Watery Spinner

(John Veniard)

Hook: 14–16
Tail: Pale golden-yellow cock fibres
Body: Pale yellow thread covered with natural horsehair
Wing: Pale blue-dun hackle points tied spent
Hackle: Pale golden-yellow cock

Pale Watery Spinner

(Ian Warrilow)   *Plate 21*

Hook: 14–16
Thread: Cream
Tail: Honey cock fibres
Abdomen: Stripped yellow hackle stalk
Wing: Cream poly yarn, tied spent
Thorax: Ginger Antron

Palmers

The palmer style of dressing trout flies, of winding the hackle along the length of the body, goes back to the time of Berners in the fifteenth century and was commonplace thereafter. Five patterns are mentioned in Thomas Barker's *Art of Angling* of 1651 which 'will serve all the year long, morning and evening'. Thomas Best, writing in the *Art of Angling*, 1813, wrote: 'The angler should always try the Palmers first, when he fishes a river he is unaccustomed to; even in that which he constantly uses, without he knows what fly is on the water, and should never be changed til he does.'

The great value of the palmered hackle on both the wet and floating fly is that it gives the fly an impression of movement and life, and what has been termed a "buzz" effect. Scores of different palmers have been developed over the centuries and many still remain today because of their trout-killing qualities. They are used on both river and stillwater, and they can be used to represent a hatching or floating sedge, a floating moth, a caterpillar and, when fished in the surface film in the appropriate colours, a variety of natural hatching duns. The palmers have always been written about in glowing terms, and I have no doubt about their effectiveness today, despite the trend towards more accurate and complex dressings.

Amber Palmer *(Roger Fogg)*

An emerging sedge pattern to be fished just below the surface.

Hook: 10–12
Body: Amber seal's fur
Rib: Oval gold tinsel
Hackle: Palmered red-brown or ginger hen

Badger Palmer *(Roger Fogg)*

Hook: 10–16
Thread: Brown
Body: Mixed hare's ear fur and blue rabbit's or mole's fur
Rib: Brown thread
Hackle: Palmered badger cock

Black Palmer

Fished as a floater or as a wet fly. It represents a number of insects, midges, terrestrials, beetles and sedges, and is a reliable pattern to try at any time. A nondescript black fly is a good standby to keep in any fly box.

Hook: 12–16
Body: Black ostrich herl
Rib: Gold wire
Hackle: Palmered black cock. An option is to trim the body hackle and have an additional hackle at the head

Brown Palmer

A useful sedge pattern when fished just below the surface.

Hook: 10–14
Tag (optional): Green fluorescent thread
Body: Dark-brown floss or seal's fur

Rib: Gold tinsel
Hackle: Palmered red-brown cock

Green Palmer

This can be tied with an optional lead underbody and fished deep where it might be taken for a dragonfly larva.

Hook: 6–12
Body: Green seal's fur
Rib: Fine gold thread
Hackle: Palmered cock dyed green

Grey Palmer

Hook: 10–12
Body: Grey seal's fur
Rib: Flat gold tinsel
Hackle: Palmered badger cock

Grizzly Palmer

Hook: 8–12
Body: Black seal's fur
Rib: Flat gold tinsel
Hackle: Palmered grizzle

Mottled Palmer *(Roger Fogg)*

A floating pattern to represent the grannom or other mottled-winged sedge.

Hook: 10–14
Thread: Black
Tag: Green fluorescent thread
Body: Twisted mottled turkey tail feather fibres wound along the body, or hare's ear
Rib: Oval gold tinsel
Body hackle: Palmered coch-y-bondhu or Greenwell cock
Head hackle: Dark-brown cock

Pearly Olive Palmer

(Sid Knight) Plate 8

Hook: Kamasan B170 size 12
Tail: Fluorescent yellow-green wool
Body: Pearly Mobile Mother of Pearl

Body hackle: Medium olive cock palmered
Rib: Silver wire

Red Palmer

A very old pattern, similar to the lake fly, the Soldier Palmer. It has a reputation as a dry fly in some parts of the country. Harry Powell, the famous Usk fly dresser, tied a long-hackled floating variant known as Whiskers. The traditional dressing is given below.

Hook: 8–12
Thread: Red
Body: Red seal's fur or wool
Rib: Gold tinsel
Hackle: Palmered natural red cock

Soldier Palmer   *Plates 6 and 8*

There is little doubt that the obscure origins of this pattern go back many centuries. One suggestion has been that the name came from the English army redcoats. It has become an excellent lake and reservoir fly, used throughout the British Isles. It is best fished on the top dropper, but it also fishes well deeper. It is probably taken for a sedge pupa, but when fished deeper it could well represent a shrimp. Many variations have been tied, some using fluorescent red/orange seal's fur for the body, or adding a fluorescent wool tag. More recently reflective ribs or tails have been included from the wide range of new synthetic materials. Lure-flash Twinkle makes a particularly good tail and body. A Mini-Muddler variant is a very successful bob fly.

Hook: 10–12
Body: Scarlet seal's fur or wool
Rib: Flat gold tinsel or gold wire
Hackle: Palmered bright chestnut cock

White Palmer

A light-coloured moth imitation.

Hook: 10–14

Thread: Ash-coloured
Body: Grubby-white seal's fur
Rib: Pale-coloured thread
Hackle: Palmered dirty-white cock

Palmer Nymph

Many palmered nymphs are known simply by their colour (see PALMERS). This pattern was devised by Conrad Voss Bark, author of *Fishing for Lake Trout*, 1972. It should be fished deep or just below the surface. Movement through the water enlivens the body hackle and gives an impression of life. It was originally tied as a general pattern for Two Lakes fishery in Hampshire and its inspiration came from the Bumble patterns of T. C. Kingsmill Moore.

Hook: 8–12
Tail: Very short golden pheasant topping
Underbody: Yellow seal's fur, thinly dubbed
Rib: Thin gold wire
Body hackle: Short-fibred olive-green hackle palmered down the body; about three turns
Head hackle: Three turns of a short-fibred dark-red cock hackle

Parachute Nymph

The nymph pattern below was devised by Davy Wotton to hang in the surface film or to sink very slowly. Most nymphs can be so adapted by tying in a large sparsely dressed hackle at the head. This is wound in the normal way and not in the Parachute style described in the glossary.

Hook: 10–16
Tail: Green cock pheasant tail fibres
Body: Cock-pheasant tail herl dyed green
Rib: Very fine silver wire
Thorax: Mixed brown and medium-olive seal's fur
Wing-case: Cock pheasant centre tail fibres
Hackle: Long-fibred grizzle

Paradun
Plate 25

The Paradun is a style of tying a parachute-hackled dun imitation. It was publicised by Doug Swisher and Carl Richards and has become a standard way of tying a dun. The parachute hackle wound round the base of the wing ensures that the body rests in or on the film. The style is very successful because it is a good imitation of a floating nymph or emerger or even a spinner. It is a style of fly I use for much of my general dry-fly fishing. The wing material may be feather fibres, animal hair or synthetic yarn. My preferred wing is the very fine siliconised poly yarn from Niche Products. The white or grey are the most useful as wings.

Hook: 14–20
Thread: To match the body
Tail: Widely spaced cock fibres or Microfibetts
Body: Fine natural or synthetic dubbing
Wing: Poly yarn tied upright, see text
Hackle: Cock hackle wound round the wing base

Parody

This is a fine dry fly for late-season trout and autumn grayling. I don't think it is taken as a copy of any particular natural fly, but I have caught dozens of fish on it from northern rivers.

Hook: 14–16
Tag: Yellow wool or floss
Body: Mixed orange and claret seal's fur (2:1)
Rib: Fine gold tinsel
Hackle: Grizzle cock

Parrot
Plate 5

This is a small fish imitation from Trevor Housby. They are recommended for fishing deep on a sinking line. White, green, orange, black, red and blue are suggested colours for the Fish-hair.

Hook: Long shank 6

Body: Mylar silver tubing tied in at the end of the shank with the ends frayed for the tail. The body is flattened to give a fish-belly shape underneath
Wing: Coloured Fish-hair (or Lureflash modern equivalent) with silver Mylar strips as an overwing, both extendng to just beyond the tail
Head: Black tying thread

Partridge and Black

This is a different fly from those in the PARTRIDGE SERIES. It is a popular wet fly on the Clyde and its tributaries. I am not sure what it is taken for, but trout autopsies always produce a range of black or dark-coloured insects or other food items. This pattern is probably sufficiently generally imitative to be mistaken for any one of a number of edible sub-surface creatures.

Hook: 14
Body: Black floss or tying thread
Wing: Marbled partridge tail feather
Hackle: Black hen

Partridge series

A series of spider-type wet flies of ancient origin devised for rough-stream fishing. Some have made the transition to stillwater. All have a partridge hackle. They are also known by the reversal of their names e.g. Blue Partridge.

Partridge and Blue
Plate 32

This is quite possibly a gravel-bed imitation. I tie a similar dressing to the one below that omits the dubbed body. The Partridge and Blue is not a popular fly, but I have reason to remember it with affection. It once saved a fruitless April day on the Nidd when, cast upstream over likely lies, it caught eight brown trout in about forty minutes. The dressing given is T. E. Pritt's.

Hook: 14

Body: Blue tying silk lightly dubbed with lead-coloured lamb's wool
Hackle: Partridge back feather

Partridge and Claret

W. H. Lawrie describes this as a killing spring fly on the Tweed and other Scottish Border rivers.

Hook: 12–14
Body: Claret worsted or claret seal's fur
Rib: Fine gold wire
Hackle: Dark partridge

Partridge and Green

This is a suitable grannom imitation.

Hook: 12–14
Body: Bright-green tying thread
Hackle: Dark partridge rump feather

Partridge and Hare's Ear

A Welsh wet fly.

Hook: 12–14
Body: Hare's ear fur
Rib: Gold wire
Hackle: Dark partridge

Partridge and Mole

A Welsh wet fly.

Hook: 14
Tail: Dark partridge fibres
Body: Mole's fur
Rib: Silver wire
Hackle: Dark partridge

Partridge and Orange   *Plate 32*

The best-known of the series. It is usually fished as a river wet fly, but I have heard of its use as a floater. Traditionally, it has been accepted that it is probably taken for a stonefly but it has other similarities to some ephemeropteran species, and depending on how it is fished it may pass for a spinner. As a North Country trout and grayling pattern, it is one of the best flies one could choose, and the ribbed version is one of my favourites for a three-fly leader. Although I have never caught a trout on it as a lake fly, others have. It should do well when daphnia are about, when orange-bodied flies are the best bet. Richard Walker caught an 18 lb rainbow trout on a pattern on a wide-gape size 8 or 10 hook tied with a short floss-silk body.

Hook: 12–16
Body: Orange silk (deep chestnut-orange, originally Pearsall's 6A – not the same shade today)
Rib (optional): Gold tinsel or wire
Hackle: Dark partridge

Partridge and Orange
(Thomas Clegg)

Hook: 14–16
Thread: Yellow
Body: Orange DFM floss
Rib: Brown Naples silk
Hackle: Grey partridge

Partridge and Peacock Spider

A Welsh wet pattern.

Hook: 12–14
Body: Peacock herl
Hackle: Dark partridge

Partridge and Red

Hook: 12–16
Body: Wine-red silk
Hackle: Dark partridge

Partridge and Silver

A useful early-season fly.

Hook: 12–14
Body: Silver tinsel
Hackle: Dark partridge

Partridge and Yellow

A good early-season fly, probably giving the best results in the evening from April to June.

Hook: 12–16
Body: Yellow silk
Rib: Fine gold wire
Hackle: Light-grey partridge back feather

Partridge Glory

A West Country pattern. I use a similar fly that has a gold wire rib. It certainly looks nicer, but I wouldn't like to say whether or not that influences the fish.

Hook: 14
Body: Medium-brown floss
Hackle: Dark partridge

Peacock Runner Goldbead

Plate 18

Theo Bakelaar combines the proven success of the peacock herl body with a gold bead head to produce this deadly nondescript general nymph. It is an excellent pattern that is of the type that will work anywhere in the world.

Hook: Tiemco TMC 3661 size 10
Thread: Brown
Head: 4 mm gold bead
Tail: Two widely spaced goose biots
Body: Five or six peacock herls twisted together with the thread
Legs: Two goose biots, one either side of the shank
Thorax: Six peacock herls twisted together with the thread

Pearlbug Diver

Plate 1

This is a Lureflash variation of the American pattern, the Dharlburg Diver. The shape of the varnished deer hair head gives the fly a diving action when retrieved.

Hook: Long shank 8–10

Thread: White
Tail: White marabou with Lureflash Pearl Mobile
Body: Lureflash white Twinkle
Head: Deer hair spun and clipped to form a bullet shape. The upper trailing fibres are retained but clipped, all clear varnished to hold the shape

Pearly

The prefix or suffix 'Pearly' to a standard pattern, e.g. Pearly Pheasant Tail Nymph or Pearly Pennell (below), usually means that there is the addition of material similar to Pearly Mobile, a Lureflash product, in the dressing. This is often as a thorax cover, as in the Pearly PT Nymph, or as the body, as in the Pearly Pennell, or as a few strands in the wing or tail. A number of conventional patterns are tied in this way as variants.

Pennells

A series of now-standard general stillwater patterns devised in the last century by H. Cholmondeley Pennell. They are also useful river wet flies. In addition to the two listed below there are the less-frequently used brown, yellow and green variations tied with similar materials dyed as appropriate. The Pennells are best fished as bob flies. The smaller sizes are probably taken for variety of natural flies, but particularly midges. Thickly hackled versions are used for dapping. Pennells are also occasionally tied in tandem to be fished as deeply sunk lures.

Pennell's Black

Hook: 8–14
Tip: Oval silver tinsel
Tail: Golden pheasant crest and tippet fibres
Body: Black floss silk
Rib: Oval silver tinsel
Hackle: Long-fibred black cock

Pennell's Claret

Hook: 8–14
Tail: Golden pheasant tippet and crest fibres
Body: Claret seal's fur
Rib: Fine gold tinsel
Hackle: Long-fibred furnace cock

Hutch's Pennell   Plate 6

Stan Headley recommends this pattern as a hatching midge imitation. It was devised by fellow Orcadian, Ian Hutcheon. The small white head hackle imitates either the breathers of the pupa, or, perhaps, the adult emerging from the shuck. When Stan publicised the pattern a few years ago in Trout and Salmon he was inundated with anglers' reports of success from across the country. Tied small, neat and sparse and fished slow and high in the water amongst midging fish it can be lethal. The body herl needs to be sparse and the preferred material is the peacock sword feather herl from the opposite side from which the herl for the Alexandra is taken. The green-black colour is required.

Hook: 12–16
Thread: Black
Butt: Two turns of fine flat silver (one turn on the smallest size)
Tail: Three or four golden pheasant tippet fibres (optionally dyed or hot orange)
Body: One long herl from the 'wrong' side of the peacock sword feather, ribbed with fine silver wire, or very fine oval
Hackle: Two turns longish black hen and two turns small white hen

Melvin Pennell   Plate 10

Devised for Lough Melvin, this is a very highly rated pattern as an attractor and when the midges start.

Hook: 10–16
Thread: Black
Tail: Golden pheasant tippets

Butt: Oval green tinsel
Body: Black ostrich ribbed with oval green tinsel
Hackle: Black cock

Pearly Pennell   (Sid Knight)   Plate 6

Hook: Kamasan B170 size 12
Tail: Golden pheasant tippets
Body: Pearly Mobile Mother of Pearl
Rib: Silver wire
Hackle: Black cock

Pensioners

A series of Parachute-style dry flies devised by Peter Mackenzie-Philps based on the Paradun design. They were originally tied for an elderly angler with failing eyesight who needed a highly visible dry fly.

Black Pensioner

This is a fair imitation of some terrestrials, especially a black gnat.

Hook: 12
Tail: Black cock fibres
Body: Black-dyed cock pheasant centre tail fibres
Rib: Fine gold wire
Wing: White mink tail hair tied upright
Hackle: Black cock in Parachute style

Light Pensioner   Plate 26

This does best when olives are about.

Hook: 12
Tail: Greenwell cock fibres
Body: Hare's fur
Rib: Fine gold wire
Wing: White mink tail hair tied upright
Hackle: Greenwell cock in Parachute style

Tup's Pensioner

A variant of the Tup's Indispensable dressed in Pensioner style.

Hook: 12

Tail: Blue-dun cock fibres
Body: Shrimp-pink bug fur or seal's fur
Rib: Fine gold wire
Wing: White mink tail hair tied upright
Hackle: Blue-dun in Parachute style

Pepper's Own *Plate 26*

Tony Pepper devised this dry fly for the trout and grayling in the rivers of his native Yorkshire. It has gained a popular following after it appeared in a number of magazines and Richard Walker mentioned it in one of his books. The two hackles ensure that the fly rides well, even on rough water.

Hook: 14–15
Thread: Purple
Tail: Three strands of cock pheasant centre tail herl tied to twice the body length
Body: Wound strands of cock pheasant centre tail herl
Rib: Red silk
Hackles: Red cock with a honey grizzle cock nearest the eye

PERCH FRY

Many larger stillwaters contain great quantities of perch and the fry appear frequently in the trout's diet. The imitation should be fished in the manner of a small fish. For other patterns see FRY and CHURCH FRY.

Perch Fry *(Gordon Fraser)*

Hook: Long shank 2–4
Body: Six to eight bunches of goat hair dyed golden-olive tied on top of and under the shank. The underside hair should be shorter than that on top. All the whippings should be soaked in varnish. The body is trimmed to a general fish outline and given perch stripes with black or dark-olive indelible felt-pens
Head: A bowl-shaped Muddler head of deer hair

A Roach Fry imitation can be tied by using white goat hair for the body with touches of red.

Perch Fry Tandem
(Tom Saville) *Plate 3*

Front hook
Body: Embossed gold tinsel
Wing: Two cree hackles tied outside two olive cock hackles back to back over both hooks with jungle cock cheeks
Beard hackle: Hot-orange cock

Rear hook
Tail: Golden pheasant tippets
Body: Embossed gold tinsel

Perky *Plate 9*

This very unusual fly from Bev Perkins, the expert lake dry-fly angler, is very highly rated. It is a hatching midge pattern. The long shank lightweight hook cocks the fly upright, and the cul de canard wing is highly visible and from below will give the illusion of a hatching insect. It can be fished singly or in a team of three, statically or with a retrieve to create a wake.

Hook: 10–14 lightweight, long shank Kamasan B400 or B830
Thread: Black
Body: Fine dubbing, herl, tying thread or stripped hackle stalk, superglued for strength
Top wing: One, two or three cul de canard feathers, depending on the wave, over the eye

Persuader *Plate 6*

In *Trout Flies of Stillwater*, John Goddard describes how he wanted a nondescript stillwater pattern that had to be fairly large, in order to attract the attentions of a trout from a reasonable distance; to have an attractive colour or colour combinations; to have a succulent body; and, finally, at least loosely resemble some of the more common forms of food on which trout feed'. It can be fished slow and deep or faster nearer the surface. It is a fly with which I caught very many fish over a few seasons.

Hook: 8–10
Thread: Orange
Body: Five strands of white ostrich herl
Rib: Round silver tinsel
Thorax: Orange seal's fur
Wing-case: Three strands of dark-brown turkey herl from the tail feather

Peter Ross
Plate 7

Reputed to be one of the best traditional lake and sea-trout flies ever devised. It dates from the turn of the century and is named after its creator, who adapted it from the Teal and Red. In addition to being a fancy fly, it is a good small-fry imitator which should be fished on the point of the leader.

Hook: 8–14
Tail: Golden pheasant tippets
Body: Rear half, silver tinsel; front half, red seal's fur
Rib: Oval silver tinsel
Wing: Barred teal breast feather fibres
Hackle: Black cock or hen

PHANTOM MIDGE (Chaoborus)

See DIPTERA and MIDGES
A different group of species from the chironomids, the commoner midges, and confined largely to stillwaters. The overall length of the adult is about 7 mm and it is pale green or off-white depending upon the sex. The pale green female returns to the water's edge to lay her eggs about dusk. The main difference between these and the chironimids, with which they are often confused, is that the wings of the phantom midge at rest cover all the abdomen, while the chironomid's wings leave a few segments exposed at the rear.

The larvae are almost transparent but for four blackish air-bladders. The body length is between 12 and 16 mm. The larvae tend to lie horizontally in the water and move exceptionally quickly. The pupae are about the same length, with a semi-transparent body and a large thorax that turns orangey-brown with maturity. The pupae hang upright in the water for about four days, at various depths according to John Goddard, and rise to the surface for the transformation into the winged adult only just before emerging. For a fuller account of their life-cycle I recommend *The Development of Modern Stillwater Fishing*, by David Jacques.

Phantom Larva *(Peter Gathercole)*

Hook: Silvered long shank 14
Underbody: Brown tying thread tied in at the rear and front of the shank to represent the swim-bladders
Body: Transparent polythene strip 6 mm (¼ inch) wide wound over the underbody and tapering to the rear
Hackle: Short-fibred white or badger cock

Phantom Larva *(Pat Russell)*

Pat Russell first tied this pattern because of the scarcity of any other imitations. He comments that the artificial 'is not far removed from a bare hook!' Pat Russell made a later improvement to the pattern by using spade-end hooks tied to nylon and taking the body of the fly a short way up the nylon.

Hook: 16
Body: Grey fluorescent floss wound from the eye to just short of the barb. The air-bladders are marked with indelible felt-tip pens. One is marked on top of the bend, the other behind the eye. All this is covered with clear varnish

Phantom Midge Larva
(Peter Lapsley)

Peter Lapsley comments: 'This pattern works as well as it does as much because it is something the fish have never seen before as because they take it for a natural phantom larva, which would be virtually impossible to imitate on a hook.' It looks to me more like a pupal imitation.

Hook: Straight-eyed 14–16
Thread: Brown
Body: Pale-yellow floss silk
Rib: Fine silver tinsel
Thorax: Rusty-coloured pheasant tail fibres in a small lump behind the eye

Phantom Midge Pupa

(Peter Gathercole)

Hook: 14
Tail: A bunch of white feather fibres clipped square
Body: White floss covered with clear polythene and ribbed with silver wire
Thorax: Amber seal's fur
Wing-case: Light-brown feather fibres
Head: White feathers as used for the tail

Pheasant Tail   Plate 27

The floating Pheasant Tail is one of the best dry flies ever devised. It has been attributed to Payne Collier (about 1901). As a general imitative pattern, few flies come close to competing with it. A number of 'one fly only' men have opted for this. It is probably taken mainly for the spinners of the blue-winged olive, iron blue, pale watery and medium olives. The original patterns were not winged, but later variations, tied specifically to represent spinners, have wings added. It can also be fished wet, but is rarely so used.

I have seen a number of commercially dressed patterns bearing this name with a plain brown cock hackle. These may be variations of the original, but they are not *bona fide* Pheasant Tails after Payne Collier. They may carry the pheasant-tail fibre body, but the important hackle has been changed and therefore the name of the pattern should be changed, too. The dressing with one of the hackles given below is a splendid fly. Accept nothing less.

See also USD POLYSPINNERS. The PHEASANT TAIL NYMPH is considered under a separate entry.

Hook: 12–14
Tail: Honey-dun hackle fibres
Body: Cock pheasant tail fibres
Rib: Gold wire
Hackle: Honey-dun cock

An alternative hackle is a bright-blue or rusty-dun hackle. A spinner pattern can be,tied with hackle fibre or hackle tip wings tied horizontally either side of the shoulder. The wing colour should be of the natural fly to be imitated. This version can be fished dry or in the surface film.

Hornsby Pheasant Tail

Hook: 10–18
Thread: Hot-orange
Tail: Ginger cock fibres
Body: Three or four cock pheasant tail fibres ribbed with gold wire
Hackles: Ginger cock with a dyed blue-dun in front

White-Winged Pheasant Tail

(Dave Collyer)

Described by its creator as a hybrid between a Hackle-point Coachman and a Pheasant Tail.

Hook: 14–16
Thread: Brown
Tail: Tips of the body material
Body: Cock pheasant tail fibres wound over a wet varnished shank
Wing: White cock hackle tips
Hackle: Ginger cock

Pheasant Tail Spinner *(M. Riesco)*

Hook: 12–14
Tail: Blue-dun hackle fibres
Body: Cock pheasant tail fibres
Wing: Light blue-dun cock hackle points tied spent
Hackle: Golden-dun cock

Pheasant Tail Nymphs

This name is given to a series of nymphs with cock pheasant tail fibres as their body material. Many different variations have developed around the one theme. Other patterns are listed under COVE NYMPH and TWITCHETT NYMPH. All are nondescript patterns that are probably taken for a wide range of food items depending upon the dressings and the manner and depth at which they are fished. They are reliable as general stand-by patterns for the point of a leader during the early season, or fished close to weedbeds in their smaller sizes later in the season. The larger sizes may even be mistaken for small fish when retrieved in the appropriate style.

Bob Church tied a pattern similar to that given below, with a hackle or legs of pheasant-tail fibre tips and a prominent thorax of fluorescent lime-green material. It is useful in dirty water. A second pattern with a fluorescent-orange or yellow thorax is better in bright clear-water conditions, which pretty well sums it up.

Leaded Pheasant Tail Nymph

(Bob Carnill)   *Plate 12*

Bob Carnill comments: 'This pattern is a good all-rounder for both river and stillwater trout. It can be fished as a bottom-crawler (particularly the leaded version), or as a free-swimming nymph anywhere between the bottom and the surface. Its overall shape simulates many of the larger nymphs, such as the diving beetle larva, damosel nymphs and even the Mayfly nymph. On the Derbyshire Derwent, the Pheasant Tail Nymph is my number one fish-catcher. I fish it from the start of the season, right through to the end of the Mayfly. It performs well when used with any accepted wet-fly technique – upstream nymph, across-the-stream, and down-and-across – even in sizes as large as 8 long shank.

It is important to take fur used for the thorax from between the eyes of a wild rabbit's mask. A small amount of the drab under-fur should be mixed in with the guard-hairs. This greatly improves the dubbing properties of the material and adds a little bulk.'

Hook: Long shank 8–14
Thread: Waxed brown Gossamer or Naples for larger sizes
Tail: Six or seven cock pheasant tail fibres
Body: The butts of the tail fibres wound up the shank
Rib: Heavy copper wire
Thorax: Lead wire covered with rabbit's mask fur in a prominent thorax
Thorax cover: A broad web of unmarked cock pheasant centre tail fibres

To represent a range of nymphs, larvae and aquatic beetles, and for use in a variety of water conditions, the thorax can be tied with fluorescent or ordinary seal's fur dyed green, orange, sepia, yellow or red (Plate 12).

Black Pheasant Tail

A general nymph pattern. Useful when black midge pupae might be expected.

Hook: 10–12
Tail, body and thorax cover: Pheasant tail fibres dyed black
Rib: Silver wire
Thorax: Black seal's fur

Sawyer's Pheasant Tail Nymph

Plate 17

Frank Sawyer's best-known and most popular pattern - the original from which the others have spawned. It is an impressionist nymph and works well when used to represent the nymphs of the large and small dark olives, iron blue, sepia and claret duns. It is a great killer of trout and grayling on rivers and lakes. Sawyer would have fished it in the induced-take style. On rivers, the fly should ideally be cast upstream to a visible fish and, as the nymph drifts down towards the fish, the rod-tip should be raised, causing the nymph to rise in the water and inducing the fish to take it. If possible, watch the fish. If it moves forwards, upwards or sideways then strike. I've found the nymph effective on the northern rivers, where one is rarely able to see the individual fish. I cast the nymph into likely lies and watch for takes on the leader in the usual manner.

On stillwater, it is an excellent general pattern and a good imitation of the sepia and claret nymphs. It is an easy fly to tie - an aspect not unusual among many of the better patterns; the good ones are often the simplest.

Hook: 12–16
Thread: None
Tail: Three cock pheasant tail fibres
Underbody: Copper wire with a hump for the thorax
Overbody: Pheasant tail fibres wound on with the copper wire and tied fatter at the thorax
Wing-case: Pheasant tail fibres doubled and redoubled

Goldbead Pheasant Tail

Plate 18

If Sawyer's Pheasant Tail Nymph doesn't sink fast enough try this alternative from the vice of Theo Bakelaar. It has all the characteristics of Sawyer's pattern plus the benefits of a small gold head. Silver- or copper-headed versions are also worth experimenting with.

Hook: 10–16 Tiemco TMC 3761 (slightly long shank)
Thread: Brown
Bead: 3 mm gold bead for size 10 and 12; 2 mm for size 14 and 16
Tail: Six or seven cock pheasant tail fibres
Abdomen: Cock pheasant tail fibres ribbed with fine gold wire
Thorax: Black-brown hare's ear, rabbit or squirrel dubbing (vary colour to suit)

S.F. Pheasy *(Terry Griffiths)*   *Plate 18*

Not really a Pheasant Tail Nymph but derived from one. This Seal's Fur Pheasant Tail comes from Terry Griffiths who

devised the dubbing after the standard Pheasant Tail Nymph was torn to shreds after a few fish. The various colours within the natural herls were mixed into a spectrumised seal's fur dubbing. On its first outing in the early 1970s it took 16 fish in 20 minutes for two anglers at Grafham, all between 2 and 2 ½ lb. A successful variation has a thorax of hare's fur mix tinted with pink seal's fur.

Hook: Long shank 8–12 nickel
Thread: Claret/brown
Body: Blood-brown seal's fur mix
Rib (optional): Copper wire
Wing-case: Pheasant tail fibres
Thorax: Hare's guard hair

Pink Panther

Shocking-pink or blancmange-pink trout flies have no natural counterpart, and precisely because the colour is so outrageous it has been avoided by fly-dressers. In 1983 Gordon Fraser devised some fluorescent-pink flies to try on those occasions when nothing else works. Perhaps the 'shock factor' was the key, but the flies seemed to spark off aggression in the trout, resulting in fish being taken and the flies being hailed as successful. The Pink Panther described below uses marabou plumes. The pattern is one of many on a basic theme. The colour is the major departure.

Hook: Long shank or standard 6–8
Thread: Pink
Tail: Fluorescent-pink marabou plume
Body: Optional underbody of lead wire Fluorescent-pink seal's fur
Rib: Flat silver tinsel

Pink Spinner

Devised by John Goddard as an imitation of the large spurwing female spinner.

Hook: 14–15
Tail: White or cream hackle fibres
Body: Pink Cellulite floss No. 29
Rib: Orange DFM filament

Wing: Two small pale blue-dun cock hackle tips or hackle fibre bunches tied spent
Hackle: Two turns of pale blue-dun cock

Polystickle   *Plate 5*

A small-fish and fry imitator to be fished fairly fast. It catches trout throughout the season, but does best in late August and September. It was developed in the mid-1960s by Richard Walker as the Sticklefly, but Ken Sinfoil incorporated the poly-thene body to produce this dressing. It fishes well jerked along high in the water like a wounded fish. Richard Walker suggested that a long shank size 12 white polythene version would kill well during a caenis hatch.

Hook: Long shank 6–8
Thread: Black
Body: Black tying thread is wound on the rear three-quarters of a silvered hook in open spirals and crimson floss silk is wound on the front quarter before the body is built up with turns of clear polythene or PVC in a fish shape
Back and tail: Brown, orange, yellow or buff dampened Raffene
Beard hackle: Red or hot-orange hackle fibres
Head: Varnished tying thread with an optional eye painted on

The Black Polystickle has a black Raffene back and tail, a red cock hackle and a black silk rib.

The Green Polystickle has a dark green Raffene back and tail, a beard hackle of bronze mallard flank feather fibres and a black silk rib.

The White Polystickle has a white Raffene back and tail, a fluorescent white under-body, a white cock beard hackle and a black silk rib.

The Peter Ross Polystickle is as for the original pattern, but with a back and tail of teal flank feather fibres.

Poly Wing Spinner   *Plate 21*

I am unsure who first developed the spinner imitation tied with polypropylene yarn wings but it has crossed the Atlantic to become almost as popular in the UK. The example illustrated and described below is Mike Weaver's Rusty Spinner suitable for sherry spinner falls. The body colour and size can be varied to match the naturals. My own preference is one with widely spaced Microfibett tails and has beome the only spinner style I use. Be wary of winging too heavily; the natural's wings are extremely fine and delicate.

Hook: 16
Tail: 4 fibres of slate-grey cock hackle, split in 2 bunches by a small ball of dubbing
Body: Dubbed rusty-orange fine fur or substitute, wound figure-of-eight around the wing base
Wing: Grey poly yarn, tied flat and clipped to length

POND OLIVE
(Cloëon dipterum)

See EPHEMEROPTERA
Although this is primarily a stillwater species, it is sometimes found on slow-moving rivers. It is widely distributed and it is probably the most important upwing-ed fly for the stillwater fly fisher. The small mottled brown olive-coloured nymphs are agile-darters and live among weed-beds in the shallow lake margins. The nymph is more important than the dun, and the emerging dun in the surface film is taken in preference to the floating adult. The adults are similar to the medium olives, but generally darker and without hindwings. The olive-brown body sometimes has reddish markings. The wings are darkish grey and the two tails are black-ringed.

The medium-sized duns appear from May to late June, although it is reported that a second generation appears in September during some years. These are smaller than the earlier adults. John

Goddard says the size of the duns has a wide variation, probably more so than any other upwinged species. The beautiful female spinner (also known as the apricot spinner because of its overall colouring) is readily taken by trout. The spinners often return to the water at dusk and trout take them with little disturbance, in a manner quite different from the slashing rise to sedges.

For other suitable imitations see GOLD-RIBBED HARE'S EAR, GREEN-WELL'S GLORY, ROUGH OLIVE, LARGE DARK OLIVE, OLIVE BLOA, S.S. NYMPH, PVC NYMPH, GREY DUSTER, OLIVES and LAKE OLIVE.

Pond Olive Nymph (C. F. Walker)

Hook: 14–16
Tail: Speckled brown feather fibres
Body: Mixed brown and ginger seal's fur with a rib of pale brown condor herl for the gills
Rib: Silver tinsel
Thorax: Dark-brown seal's fur
Hackle: Medium honey-dun

Pond Olive Dun (Taff Price)

Hook: 14
Thread: Olive
Tail: Blue-dun fibres
Body: Swan or goose herl dyed olive
Rib: Brown thread
Wing: Bunched blue-dun hackle fibres tied upright
Hackle: Olive cock

Pond Olive Spinner

(John Goddard)

To be fished in the surface film.

Hook: 12–14
Thread: Orange
Tail: Pale badger cock fibres
Body: Condor herl dyed apricot and covered with pale-olive PVC
Wing: Pale-blue hackle tips tied spent
Hackle: Dark honey-dun cock fibres tied

under each wing, replacing the traditional hackle style

Pond Olive Spinner

Hook: Fine wire 14
Thread: Olive
Tail: Pale-grey speckled partridge breast feather
Body: Stripped orange peacock herl
Rib: Waxed scarlet tying thread
Hackle: Four or five turns of very pale blue-dun cock hackle with one turn of a hot-orange cock in front. The hackles are bunched in the spent position

Poodle

John Wadham devised this lure in 1978. It has caught thousands of trout, including, in the hands of its creator, brown trout to 7½lb. Bob Carnill summed up the Poodle as 'the nymph-fisherman's lure' because it is worked very slowly or simply left to drift around in the wind to be slowly retrieved only when the line has blown parallel to the reservoir bank. The pulsating marabou allows the lure to be fished slowly. The Poodle has a reputation for taking fish already feeding on daphnia.

Hook: Long shank 6–10
Thread: Black
Tail: Black marabou or Arctic fox
Tip (optional): Two or three turns of DRF signal-green wool
Body: Black chenille. Optional lead underbody
Wing/body plumes: Four or five small shuttlecocks of black marabou tied along the top of the shank. As each one is tied in another turn of the body chenille is wound on. The result is a sort of marabou matuka.

Poppers

These unusual-looking 'flies' have been adapted from the North American bass lures. In the UK they are used for sea trout and reservoir trout. They are fished high in a surface wave, where the disturbance they cause seems attractive to the fish. The Popper should be fished on a single-fly leader or on the top dropper of a two- or three-fly leader. If the Popper is not taken, a following trout will often take one of the lower flies.

Hook: Special popper hook 4–6
Body: A reverse bullet-shape cork is slotted on to the front of the shank with the eye of the hook coming out of the lower edge of the front flat face of the body. This can be painted as desired, with or without eyes
Tail: Four long cock hackles tied two each side of the shank with the curve of the hackle outwards. These can be colour-matched or contrasted with the body
Hackle: A cock hackle is wound over the tail roots behind the body, the same colour as or contrasting with the tail

Priest

An excellent fancy fly for grayling which is mainly fished wet. I used to find it better than most in a slightly discoloured water but I haven't used it for some years. No doubt the brightness of its dressing contributes to its success under these circumstances. On the occasions I have fished it dry, I've been able to attract only fairly small fish.

Hook: 14–16
Tail: Red ibis or red wool tag
Body: Flat silver tinsel
Rib: Oval silver wire
Hackle: Badger hen

Prince Nymph   *Plate 16*

Doug Prince's nymph pattern is very popular in North America and has done well on small lakes in the UK. It has a combination of materials that have been proven on other patterns. The iridescent peacock herl and white wing are key features.

Hook: 10–14 Long shank

Thread: Black 6/0 Flymaster
Tail: Two dark brown goose biots, tied forked
Body: Peacock herl
Rib: Fine flat gold or Mylar
Beard hackle: Natural red
Wing: Two white goose biots tied in a V on the top of the body

Professor

A stillwater fly named after Professor John Wilson of some 140 years ago. It is of Scottish origin, but it is still used on Sassenach waters. It is used for sea trout in its larger sizes. A streamer lure is listed by John Veniard; it has a collar hackle of brown cock, a wing of a pair of grizzle hackles and a black-varnished head.

Hook: 6–10
Tail: Long red ibis fibres or substitute
Body: Yellow tying silk or floss
Rib: Gold or silver tinsel or wire
Wing: Grey mallard flank feather
Hackle: Ginger cock

Pulsators

These lures are Chris Kendall's improvement on the standard marabou lure. Chris comments: 'The standard dressing for the marabou lure does not utilise the full movement potential of marabou. Certainly, the wing moves freely but a chenille or tinsel body is rigid by comparison.

The solution I came up with was to dress the wing round the head as opposed to on top of it. Unfortunately this arrangement gave the effect of three or four wings as the marabou bunched up. After more experimentation the lure gained a long collar hackle and the wing was dressed more heavily. Dressed in this way it has a rippling and pulsating action which enables the lure to be fished ultra-slow when need be.'

Black, white and orange lures are all effective as are a number of Pulsator variants of other lures: Viva, Jack Frost and Christmas Tree. The wings on these variants must be tied in two tiers, to avoid masking the tag completely. The first (longer) wing is made from herl from the top of the plume, the shorter wing is made from the denser herl nearer the base.

Black Pulsator *(Chris Kendall)*

Hook: Long shank 4–10
Body: Black chenille
Rib: Oval silver tinsel
Wing: Black marabou tied all around the body. Use about one plume
Hackle: Long-fibred black cock as a rear-sloping collar
Head: Black varnished tying thread

Puppy *Plate 2*

Dave Tait is responsible for this popular lure. It is one of a number of marabou-tailed lures with weighted heads to be fished in a sink-and-draw style. The body and head should be in contrasting colours. Black or white are the usual body colours with red, green, orange, pink or lime heads.

Hook: Long shank 8–12
Tail: Marabou, same as the body colour
Body: Chenille tapering to the rear
Head: Chenille to form a bulky head
Eyes: Bead chain painted to create an eye each side

PURPLE DUN
(Paraleptophlebia cincta)

See EPHEMEROPTERA
This upwinged dun is restricted to the West and North of England on small faster or larger medium-paced rivers where the hatches can be prolific. The nymphs prefer weed-beds. The medium-sized dun is similar to the iron blue dun, with a purple-tinged dark brown body and black-grey wings. The most obvious difference between the two is that the purple dun has three tails and the iron blue only two. The duns appear throughout the day from May to August. Because of the similarity,

artificials copying the iron blue dun are often adequate as the angler's imitation.

Purple Dun *(John Veniard)*

A winged wet fly.

Hook: 14
Tail: Dark-brown hen fibres
Body: Purple seal's fur
Wing: Starling wing
Hackle: Dark-brown hen

PVC Nymph *Plate 20*

John Goddard recommends this pattern for any of the olive nymphs. The PVC body gives a translucent effect. The fly is equally effective on rivers and stillwaters, wherever olives are found. Its creator suggests that it is best fished in stillwaters in sink-and-draw fashion on a very long leader. It is particularly good when fished close to weed-beds where the natural olive nymphs abound.

Hook: 12–16
Thread: Brown
Tail: Golden pheasant tips dyed olive-green
Underbody and thorax: Copper wire
Overbody and thorax: Three strands of olive or olive-brown condor herl. The body (not the thorax) is covered with a PVC strip 3 mm (⅛ inch) wide and over-lapped.
Wing-pads: Two or three strands of dark pheasant-tail herl

John Goddard suggests that a narrow silver Lurex rib added beneath the PVC simulates air bubbles trapped beneath the skin.

Rabbit Fur Fly *Plate 9*

This is a wonderful-looking fly from Tasmanian angler Dr Robert Sloane. It represents nothing in particular but certainly catches fish. Mainly a stillwater fly, it also works down and across on rivers. Its creator comments that it is 'the epitome of functional design and simplicity in fly tying…its semi-buoyancy, natural colour and lifelike action make it a deadly pattern for fishing in shallow lake margins'. The fibres pulse very effectively when the fly is retrieved slowly in short pulls. Variants are as limited as the number of natural pelts. Use natural pelts in preference to dyed or tanned ones as Robert Sloane comments that the positive scent and flavour are more important than we appreciate.

Use a long-staple fur from the lower back. Cut a narrow strip about 4 x 15 mm by cutting across the pelt. Fold in half, end to end, and in half again. The folds are made keeping the skin inwards, retaining the darker fur on the outside. The folded skin is pinched hard together and the fur tuft is tied in like a feather-fibre wing. The thread need only be whipped from the eye to half-way along the shank. The prepared fur segment is held in place with the folded skin collar centred over the eye, then tied down firmly behind the skin and pulled tight with a half hitch. Surplus skin and collar are trimmed off. The roots can be glued or varnished and secured with further turns of thread. Add the head.

Hook: Mustad 9980 size 8–10
Thread: Black
Body: Grey-brown rabbit fur
Head: Black ostrich herl

Rabbitiser
Plate 2

This attractive-looking lure was created by Les Walker. It is a variant of the Yellow Rabbit, a New Zealand matuka-style lure. Using a medium-rate retrieve with 60 cm pulls on floating or slow-sink lines, this is taken for a leech or perhaps a newt. Variants are numerous by varying the body colours. The back and tail can also be varied with different furs to create a Minketiser, Squirreltiser, etc.

Hook: Long shank 6–14 or standard 10
Thread: Brown or black
Body: Baby pink chenille ribbed with silver wire

Back and tail: 3 mm wide wild rabbit skin strip, open ribbed in matuka style for strength
Throat hackle (optional): Brown partridge

Rat-Faced MacDougall
Plate 24

A highly buoyant North American rough-water dry fly. The deer hair body makes the fly very hard to sink.

Hook: 10–12
Tail: Deer hair or ginger hackle fibres
Body: Spun and clipped deer hair
Wing: Two grizzle hackle points
Hackle: Ginger cock

Raymond
Plate 10

This Irish lough fly is usually tied winged but John Seed claims that the wingless Bushy Raymond detailed below works better (Plate 10). It works in a Mayfly hatch or when daphnia are about. It is tied for the dour days of July and August when the fly life can be poor. The second golden olive palmered hackle is omitted on the winged fly. The Raymond has a woodcock wing with yellow-dyed swan between, the tail is golden pheasant tippets, and the beard hackle blue-dyed partridge.

Hook: 8–12
Thread: Red
Tail: Golden pheasant topping
Body: Golden olive seal's fur with two palmered hackles, one bright red, the second golden olive
Rib: Oval gold
Head hackle: Natural or blue-dyed partridge

Red Arrow
Plate 10

This Irish pattern belonged to Syl Higgins. It was devised some years ago as an early-season duck-fly (midge) pattern. Simon Ashworth who tied the fly illustrated confirms that it a good fly on the UK mainland in the early season.

Hook: 12–14
Thread: Black
Tail: Golden pheasant tippets
Body: Rear half, red seal's; front half, black seal's
Rib: Oval silver (No.14)
Hackle: Natural black hen

Red Baron

A Steve Parton lure which he describes as 'an anti-daphnia summer-time boat tandem', which pretty well sums it up. It should be fished to 15 feet deep in daphnia clouds, but only in conditions of bright sunlight. One usually associates orange lures with daphnia, but Steve suggests that this is a good pattern to change to when trout go off a tandem hot-orange lure. Rear hook and front hook are dressed the same.

Tails: Target-green fluorescent wool
Bodies: Fluorescent red chenille
Ribs: Fine oval silver tinsel
Wings: Fluorescent red or pink marabou with cheeks of target-green fluorescent wool over

Red Fox Squirrel Nymph

Plate 12

Dave Whitlock describes this as the best nymph he has created. It is suggestive of a wide range of foods depending on its length and thickness and the place and manner it is fished. It is extremely popular in the USA and becoming better known in Europe.

Hook: Tiemco TMC 5262 long shank, heavy, size 2–18
Thread: Orange or black Danville's Flymaster 6/0
Weight: Eight to twelve wraps of lead wire, about the same as the hook diameter
Tail: Red fox squirrel back hair
Abdomen: Red fox squirrel belly fur mixed 50/50 with sienna or fox tan Antron dubbing
Rib: Oval gold tinsel

Thorax: Red fox squirrel back hair mixed 50/50 with charcoal Antron dubbing
Legs: (On sizes 10 and larger) one turn of tan and brown hen neck or back hackle or partridge
Head: Tying thread or thorax dubbing

Red Quill

Plate 26

This southern chalk-stream pattern was one of F. M. Halford's favourites. He described it as 'the sheet anchor of the dry-fly fisherman on a strange river'. Few today would praise it that highly, but it is still a useful pattern. In Halford's day it was probably fished only as a floater, but it seems that it is also fished wet. This is probably how the pattern originated, as it is attributed to Thomas Rushworth in about 1803. It is usually fished as an imitation of the blue-winged olive, but some sources have suggested it as a representation of the claret dun.

Hook: 14
Tail: Bright natural red cock fibres
Body: Peacock quill dyed reddish-brown
Wing: Medium starling wing
Hackle: Bright natural red cock

Other dressings omit the wings and have a hackle of pale blue-dun cock, or replace the wing with one of a bunch of pale blue cock hackle fibres tied upright.

Red Spider

This is one of W. C. Stewart's trio of wet flies which he fished in a team on the Scottish rivers of the last century and with which he killed thousands of trout. The other two patterns are the Black Spider and Dun Spider. The semi-palmered hen hackle is important, giving the impression of life and movement so necessary in an artificial wet fly.

Hook: 14–16
Body: Yellow tying silk
Hackle: Feather from the outside of a landrail wing, or a small red hen hackle palmered half-way down the body

Red Spinner

The Red Spinner is the name given to a female olive spinner, more particularly to the female medium olive spinner and the small dark olive spinner. The large red spinner is the name given to the female large dark olive spinner. I prefer a spinner dressing in the style of the POLY WING SPINNER.

Red Spinner *(Jim Nice)*   *Plate 21*

Colin Nice writes that this is an example of his father's continual experimentation with fluorescent materials. The hackles are mixed for a blurred leg/wing effect.

Hook: 14–18
Thread: Pale-brown or red
Tail: Blue-dun or ginger cock fibres
Body: Scarlet DFM floss
Rib: Brown silk
Hackle: Red cock wound through a blue-dun cock

Red Spinner *(J. R. Harris)*

Hook: 14
Tail: Red cock hackle fibres
Body: Brown-red or claret seal's fur
Rib: Gold wire
Wing: Two blue-dun or rusty-dun hackle points tied upright and sloping backwards slightly and separated
Hackle: Natural red cock, two turns at most

Red Tag

Probably the best-known grayling fly, and deservedly so, because it catches thousands of grayling each autumn. According to Courtney Williams it originated in Worcestershire around 1850 and was known as the Worcester Gem. It seems likely that it was invented by a man named Flyn, but it was popularised by F. M. Walbran, the author. On some days grayling will take only an artificial fly with some red in the dressing, and on these occasions few, if any, flies are better than a Red Tag. A tip from Reg Righyni on the tying of the tag of the dry fly is worth remembering. He tied the tag on the long side initially; if the grayling are well on the take, the longer tag helps the fly to float correctly. If the fish are choosy, the tag can be clipped shorter. The fly can be fished both wet and dry. See also BADGER RED TAG and TREACLE PARKIN for similar flies.

Some Yorkshire grayling fishers use a pattern with a lime-green tag. It is known as the Green Tag. The tie with a crimson tag is known as the Crimson Tag, and that with a white floss or wool tag is the White Tag. The Gold Tag, which has a tip of gold tinsel, was once a popular fly.

Hook: 12–16
Tag: Scarlet or bright red wool
Body: Peacock herl
Hackle: Natural red cock or hen

Red Tag Hare's Ear   *Plate 18*

The only similarity with the Red Tag is the tail; the rest of this bug from Theo Bakelaar combines two proven fish-catching features - the gold bead and the hare's ear body.

Hook: TMC 3762 long shank size 10–12
Thread: Brown
Tail: Cock pheasant tail fibres
Tag: A few turns of red marabou
Body: Hare's ear dubbing, with a few turns in front of the hackle
Rib: Gold wire
Legs: Speckled brown hen feather
Head: 4 mm gold bead

Rees' Lure   *(Trevor Rees)*

Black and green is a killing combination for a trout lure. This one devised by Trevor Rees of South Wales also uses a weighted diving head.

Hook: Long shank 6–12
Thread: Black
Tail: DFM lime green wool

Body: Bronze peacock herl with a few turns of DFM lime green wool behind the wing roots
Wing: Black marabou with black squirrel over
Throat hackle: Black cock
Eyes: Two silver chain beads

Renegade
Plate 25

This is a fast-water fly from the USA. The fore-and-aft style ensures that the body is well clear of the water and the additional hackle gives a prominent light pattern on the surface. The white hackle is there for the angler to spot the fly, as much as for the trout.

Hook: 10–18
Thread: Black
Tip: Flat gold tinsel
Rear hackle: Natural red cock
Body: Peacock herl, optionally ribbed with fine gold wire
Front hackle: White cock

Roach Fry *(Tom Saville)*

Hook: Long shank 6
Tail: Bright-red hackle fibres
Body: Embossed silver tinsel
Wing: Olive-green hackles tied back-to-back
Cheeks: Jungle cock
Hackle: Blue-dun cock as a beard
Head: Black tying thread

Roach Fry *(Chris Kendall)*   *Plate 5*

A buoyant imitation for fishing just below the surface. Other species of fish can be imitated by varying the colours.

Hook: Long shank 6–8
Thread: Black
Tail: Two scarlet red hackles clipped into a tail shape
Body: Ethafoam cut into strips and wound on, pearl nylon tube slipped over it
Back: Pale blue Raffene. When this is tied in at the rear the whipping can be white varnished

Hackle: Scarlet red cock fibres bunched either side of the lower half of the body
Head: Black varnish with painted red eyes and black pupils

Rogan's Extractor
Plate 10

This Irish lough pattern is spoken over very highly. It is a good perch-fry imitation fished slowly on a slow-sinking line and it also workes at Mayfly time. John Seed advises that long-fibred hackles are required. He ties this pearl-bodied variation.

Hook: 10–14
Tail: Red fibres from golden pheasant body feather, tied at least twice the body length
Body: Pearly tinsel ribbed with fine oval silver
Wing: Bronze mallard
Hackles: Lemon cock and red-fibred golden pheasant body feather, tied as long as the tail
Head: Red

Roger's Fancy

Roger Woolley was an excellent fly tyer and he wrote two good books on the subject, *Modern Trout Fly Dressing*, 1932, and *The Fly Fisher's Flies*, 1938. This is one of his patterns for grayling, to be fished mainly as a floater. Woolley was a keen grayling fisher and contributed to *The Grayling*, originally written by Richard Lake. He was a fly tyer for sixty-one years. For much of that time he was tying professionally, yet he never used a vice.

Hook: 14–16
Tail: Red floss
Body: Pale-blue heron herl
Rib: Silver wire
Hackle: Pale-blue hen
Head: Short red floss sloping forward over the eye

Rough Olive

Dressings under this heading may be general imitations of any of the olives. By varying the dressing, the shades of the materials and the hook sizes, all the olives can be copied with a Rough Olive from March to October.

Rough Olive Nymph

Hook: 14
Body: Brown-olive heron herl with the tips used for the tail
Rib: Gold wire
Wing-case: Dark starling wing fibres
Hackle: Brown-olive hen with a darker centre

Rough Olive *(M. Riesco)*

Hook: 12–14
Tail: Blue-dun fibres
Body: Olive seal's fur
Rib: Gold wire
Hackle: Olive badger cock

Ruby

A Syd Brock lure. The scarlet colour is unusual, but in *Stillwater Flies – How and When to Fish Them*, its creator writes: 'I have had outstanding results with this lure fished on a slow-sink line when all other lures have failed.' It should be fished with a long leader and retrieved in short, smooth pulls.

Hook: Long shank 6–10
Thread: Black
Tail: Scarlet cock hackle fibres
Body: Stretched scarlet plastic tape
Wing: Four cock hackles dyed scarlet
Cheeks: Golden pheasant tippets either side
Throat hackle: Scarlet cock hackle fibres

Sage

Few grayling fishers had Reg Righyni's experience. As far as I am aware this is the only fly he devised himself for them. He produced this to combine some of the important elements he saw in other successful patterns. It also caught salmon, by accident, and so its name, the Salmon Approved Grayling Enticer, arrived. It should be fished wet. Its creator hoped that it would pass for a spinner imitation. I have a little of the somewhat scarce body material but I cannot believe that a suitable substitute is not readily available.

Hook: 14–16
Thread: Crimson
Tail: Orangy-yellow floss
Body: Mixed claret rabbit's fur and claret polar bear's fur
Rib: Fine gold tinsel
Hackle: Hooded crow or pale blue-dun hen

Sam Slick   *Plate 10*

This Scottish fly is at least fifty years old but enjoys a strong reputation today for trout and also for sea trout.

Hook: 10–14
Thread: Yellow
Tail: Golden pheasant tippets
Body: Rear third, yellow floss or seal's fur; front two-thirds, hare's ear or brown fur
Rib: Oval gold tinsel
Wing: Speckled brown partridge tail feather
Hackle: Brown partridge

Sanctuary

This trout and grayling fly was devised by Dr Sanctuary, of Scarborough, in the 1880s. I've found it an excellent fly in September and October. It is not so popular today, but I have found it reliable on northern streams. Dr Sanctuary seemed to know what he was doing when it came to grayling. He is credited with a 4 ½ lb specimen from the Wylye.

Hook: 14
Body: Dark hare's ear fur
Rib: Flat gold tinsel
Hackle: Coch-y-bondhu

SCULPINS

The North American freshwater sculpin figures highly in the diet of large trout. Small fish are equally attractive to the larger trout of Britain and Europe. Sculpin patterns are good imitations of the indigenous European bullhead. Also see WHITLOCK'S MATUKA SCULPIN and under MUDDLERS.

Woolhead Sculpin Hairy *Plate 10*

This Oliver Edwards pattern is effective on rocky rivers. It will draw out the bigger cannibalistic fish that are reluctant risers to the usual flies.

Hook: 2X or 3X Long shank 4-8 Partridge D4A, CS17 or CS29GRS
Thread: Kevlar or Kevlar blend, cream, grey or pale tan
Underbody: Narrow strips wine bottle lead
Rib: Medium or fine oval gold tinsel or fine gold twist
Body: Dirty creamy-grey synthetic dubbing, e.g. SLF blend
Back and tail: Natural wild rabbit zonker strip cut about 4 mm wide and tapering to almost a point, tied in matuka style with about six or seven turns of the rib
Pectoral fins: Two fairly large well marked game bird hackles (partridge, grouse, hen pheasant, etc.), set well spread and slightly downward-sloping
Gills (behind pectorals): Two turns of bright reddish-brown sparkly dubbing, e.g. SLF
Ruff: Small clump of natural deer or elk hair flared in front of the pectorals, arranged mostly on the sides and underneath, same length as pectorals
Head: Stacked and flared clumps of Sculpin wool (Lathkill Tackle), silvery-grey underneath, various shades of olive

and brown on top, to give a broken colouration
Tinting (optional): Pantone marking on the rabbit or sides of body

Ultra Yellow Sculpin

This huge pattern is a trolling fly for large lake trout devised by Taff Price. It was devised for big Canadian fish but Taff complains that nothing heavier than twenty pounds has been landed on it. Larger fish were hooked, but lost. Flies of this kind are a possibility fished deep on the big reservoirs.

Hooks: Two in tandem, Scorpion 2/0
Tail and wing: Bunches of yellow marabou
Bodies: White wool
Cheeks: Yellow-dyed French partridge
Under gills: Red marabou dubbing
Head: Yellow-dyed deer hair clipped to shape
Eyes: Doll safety eyes glued to the head

SEDGE FLIES (Trichoptera)

More than 190 species of sedge exist on rivers and stillwaters in the UK, but, according to J. R. Harris, only 40–50 are of interest to the fly fisher. Many species are nocturnal; others appear during the day and evening. All year round the sedge or caddis larvae are a source of food for trout and grayling feeding off river- or lake-bed, and pupae and adults are taken from spring to autumn. Every fly-fisher ought to be familiar with the life-cycle of this important group of flies.

Most sedges are referred to by fly fishers merely by their general appearance, i.e. a 'dark-brown sedge', or a 'light sedge', or a 'small grey sedge', etc., and few fly fishers bother to determine exactly which species is which. This is in complete contrast to the attitude towards the Ephemeroptera, which most fly fishers aspire to name and imitate accurately. The truth is that on most occasions artificials of approximate size, shape and colour are sufficient to represent most species, be they sedges or upwinged duns.

After hatching, the grub-like larva goes in search of sand, small stones, sticks or vegetation with which to build its case, though some important river species are free-swimming. The interior of the case is lined with a silken material produced by the larva. The finished case is well camouflaged, probably being made from materials from the weeds or river-bed on which it rests. The caddis moves by sticking its head, thorax and legs out of the case and dragging it along. The cased caddis, surrounded by stones and sand, hardly seems an attractive meal to a trout, but the larvae are avidly devoured wherever they are found.

Copying the natural with an artificial presents no problems, although it is more difficult to fish the larva imitation on a river as the natural larva is frequently static on the river-bed, and when it does move it does so slowly. The LEADHEAD NYMPH is one answer. The free-swimming species are not so much of a problem. The stillwater angler can copy the larva by moving his imitation slowly across the bottom on the end of a long leader. In addition to patterns given below, see also WORMFLY and STICKFLY.

Some caddis are vegetarians, but others eat all types of water insects, including the ephemeropteran nymphs so important to the fly fisher. On some stretches of the Test where caddis abound, the quantity of upwinged duns and their nymphs is significantly lower than on those stretches with fewer caddis.

After about eleven months, the larva seals its case, but still allows water to flow through. The case is attached to rocks or stones to prevent it being washed away as the larva begins to change to its pupal stage. The larva spins a silken cocoon inside the case and the wings and legs begin to form. Some weeks or months later the pupa emerges by chewing its way through the case wall to swim to the surface. The pupa is broadly similar to the adult in colour and size. The change from pupa to adult takes place on the surface or

on rocks or vegetation at the water's edge, and the emerging adult is free to fly away. Those flies appearing on fast-flowing water emerge fairly quickly; those on stillwaters emerge more slowly.

It is when the pupa leaves the case and ascends to the surface to emerge as an adult that the trout become most interested. Free of its case, the pupa rising to the surface becomes an attractive target for a feeding fish, and the fly fisher can easily copy the emerging fly below or actually in the surface film. If sedges are hatching, then whatever is the surface interest in them the sub-surface interest in the pupae will be greater. For every rise to the newly emerged adult, perhaps half a dozen pupae are intercepted. The main feeding area is at the surface and be aware that trout often appear to be rising to the adult fly but are actually taking the emerger close to the film. If fish refuse to take the imitation in a dead drift, exper-iment with moving the fly in different ways.

The pupa is well copied by any of the pupa or hatching-sedge patterns given. Special sedge-pupa hooks with a curved shank are worth experimenting with. Some of the pupa imitations listed could well be improved by dressing them on these hooks.

Most adult sedges are pale-coloured on hatching, reaching their full colouring only after some hours. After mating, the female lays her eggs on plants at the waterside or, depending on the species, drops her eggs in flight over the water, deposits them on the surface, or crawls down to the river- or lake-bed to lay them in the sand or mud. A few subsurface ovipositors will re-emerge at the surface or crawl ashore.

The adult sedge is easily recognisable. Most species are fairly large (the female is generally larger than the male), and all have large wings which rest roof-like beyond the length of the body. The four wings are covered in tiny hairs. Prominent features are the large antennae on the head of the fly. Most adults are a shade of brown, although some are black or greyish.

The greatest hatches are often in the evening, but some sedges appear throughout the day, most notably the prolific grannom. Commonest are the caperer, great red sedge, silver sedge and cinnamon sedge. Just a few artificials are sufficient to represent the adults of a number of species. But such is the importance of the natural fly that many artificials have been devised, and this is reflected in the number I have included. In the last few years dozens of new tying styles have developed. Pick a few patterns that you can tie and with which you can catch fish and stick with them. What is true of all flies is particularly so with sedge pupa imitations - how they are fished is more important than details of dressing.

Almost any big, bushy fly will catch fish at times, especially when darkness is falling. It is usually sufficient simply to match the natural with an imitation conforming approximately in size, out-line and colour. Palmer-bodied flies create most disturbance on the surface. They can be retrieved in short bursts of varying speeds, or they can be left motionless. Some newly hatched sedges skitter across the surface before they take flight. The trout's interest is quickly aroused. A sedge pattern tied to the top dropper with other flies fished sub-surface is often an effective tactic in choppy water. The returning egg-laying female sedges also provide trout with feeding opportunities.

Below is an alphabetical list of the more important natural sedges and some of the patterns that represent them. Imitations of a more general appearance are listed later.

Black Sedge (T. Thomas)

The natural fly is long and slim with black wings and antennae. The wing length is between 11 and 12 mm. The adults appear during the day from June to September. The black sedge is widely distributed, but usually confined to larger rivers.

Hook: 10–14

Body: Black wool or chenille
Wing: Black moosehair tied flat and clipped square
Hackle: Black cock tied in reverse so that it slopes foward

BROWN SEDGE

A widely distributed and common species usually appearing in the evenings from August to October. The adult emerges by crawling up weed-stalks and does not emerge in open water. The colour is medium brown and the wing length varies between 11 and 16 mm. The caddis case is made from sand and small sticks.

Large Brown Sedge

(Richard Walker)

Hook: Long shank 10
Thread: Orange
Tag: Yellow fluorescent wool or floss
Body: Mahogany-brown ostrich herl tied very fine
Wing: Light-brown cock fibres
Hackle: Light-brown cock

BLACK SILVERHORN SEDGE

All the silverhorns are common. The larvae usually build their cases of sand and frequently construct them with a slight curve. They prefer stillwater or slow-moving rivers. The daytime-hatching adults appear from June to August. They are all black. The wings are 8–9 mm long and the long antennae curve back over the body in flight. A suitable imitation is the Black Sedge.

BROWN SILVERHORN SEDGE

The notes for the Black Silverhorn apply also to this species, except that the wings are 8–10 mm long and are brownish with black markings.

CAPERER

A widely distributed and common species. Hatches are generally in the evening and can be expected on open water from late August to November. The adult is large with a wing of 20–23 mm. The wings are mottled yellowish-brown and the body is orangy-brown. The fly's importance, particularly on the southern chalk-streams, is reflected in the excellence of the pattern devised by William Lunn, a Test river-keeper whose imitation is used country-wide. The artificial is useful both on river and lake. The species is similar to the large cinnamon sedge.

Caperer (William Lunn)

Also known as the Welshman's Button.

Hook: 12–14
Body: Four or five strands of dark turkey tail fibres with a centre-band of two swan fibres dyed yellow
Wing: Coot's wing dyed chocolate-brown
Hackles: Medium Rhode Island Red with a black cock in front, or wound together

CINNAMON SEDGE

Adults often appear during the day and early evening and are fairly common throughout the country from June until October. They are slim with cinnamon-brown wings with black markings. The wings are about 14 mm long and some-times may appear as a deep yellow rather than brown. The large cinnamon sedge (*P. latipennis*) is so like the caperer that it need not be considered separately. The Cinnamon and Gold is a useful wet fly when the cinnamon sedges are hatching. The Yellow Sedge Pupa of Steve Parton is a good imitation of any yellow-bodied sedge pupa, but it was tied specifically to represent the pupa of the cinnamon sedge. It should be fished as a point fly and retrieved slowly.

Hook: 14–16
Body: Swan herl dyed Naples yellow with a

thin back of stretched halved black marabou silk
Rib: Yellow nylon rod-whipping thread wound over the back
Thorax: Mixed chestnut seal's fur and brown mink
Wing-stubs: Goose fibres dyed sepia
Wing-case: A scrap of dark-brown feather
Hackle: Very sparse red-game

The method of tying needs a little explanation: Tie in the body herl, ribbing and marabou silk. Thinly wind on the body herl, tie down and tie in the stretch-ed black marabou floss silk and rib in the counter direction. Tie in the wing-case feather with three turns towards the eye and wind back. Cut off the scrap. Dub and wind half the thorax only. Make two small wings with a folded single slip and tie in flat either side of the hook. Dub and wind the remainder of the thorax. Take one or two turns of the hackle and rake back and lock down with thread. Pull over the wing-case, tie down and whip-finish.

Cinnamon Sedge   Plate 31

Tony Hern and Geoffrey Rivaz devloped this on the Kennet. It will work for the natural on any location.

Hook: Kamasan B175 size 12
Thread: Brown
Body: Pheasant tail fibres ribbed with gold wire
Wing: Rolled cinnamon duck quill
Hackle: Two dark ginger cocks, one palmered

GRANNOM

An early-season species common in most parts of the country. It first appears in April and continues until June. It is confined to rivers, where the larvae live in weed-beds. The adults emerge during the day, often around noon, with possibly a later hatch. Sometimes the hatches can be phenomenal with thousands blurring the view of the river. They are 9–11 mm long and have fawn-grey wings. The mated female is easily distinguishable by the green egg-sac carried at the tail of her abdomen.

Grannom *(Pat Russell)* Plate 31

Hook: 14
Thread: Green
Tip: Fluorescent green wool
Body: Natural heron herl
Wing: Blue-dun cock fibres clipped level with the bend
Hackle: Ginger cock

Grannom *(David Jacques)*

This pattern is tied in reverse. The wings and the hackle are at the bend and the egg-sac is at the eye. David Jacques devoted much of his book *Fisherman's Fly*, 1965, to this species, and it is from there that the dressing is taken.

Hook: 14
Thread: Green
Body: Dark hare's ear fur with a ball of green wool at the tip
Wing: Hen pheasant wing sloping well back
Hackle: Rusty-dun cock

GREAT RED SEDGE

The two species that share this name are widely distributed on rivers and still-waters. They are the largest of this country's sedges, with a wing length 20–27 mm. The larvae are also large and, according to J. R. Harris, are known to kill even small fish. The adults hatch in the evening in open water and are common-est from late May to July. The wings are mottled reddish-brown with some lighter markings and a blackish bar down the centre. See MURROUGH.

GROUSE-WING SEDGE

A common stillwater sedge which rarely appears on rivers. The flies hatch in the evenings of June to September. They are slim and have greyish-yellow wings with three grey-brown bands. The antennae are about twice the length of the wings.

Grouse Wing *(Richard Walker)*

Hook: Long shank 12
Thread: Black
Tag: White fluorescent wool or floss tied small
Body: Ostrich herl or swan dyed chocolate
Wing: Grouse wing or tail fibres, or dark sepia and brown speckled turkey fibres
Hackle: Dark furnace

GREY FLAG

A reasonably common species almost confined to flowing water. The adults usually hatch on open water during the day. The wings are about 11 mm long and are grey with blackish markings. The larvae do not build cases, but rest between stones and spin a silken web tunnel around themselves.

Grey Sedge *(John Veniard)*

Hook: 12
Body: Grey seal's fur
Rib: Silver wire
Wing: Grey squirrel-tail fibres
Hackle: Grizzle cock

GREY or SILVER SEDGE

Usually found on fast-flowing water. The larvae build their cases with a light curve and use mainly sand as the material. The adults appear from June to September and are large with silvery-grey wings 13–18 mm long.

Silver Sedge *(Taff Price)*

Hook: 12–14
Thread: Grey
Body: White or grey floss
Rib: Silver wire

Hackle: Palmered ginger with a second ginger hackle at the head
Wing: Coot or grey duck tied over the back

LONGHORNS *(Richard Walker)*

These two species are daylight-hatching and are important to the stillwater angler. They have long antennae and slim, narrow wings 7–13 mm long. The wing colour varies from greyish-yellow to pale fawn, and the body is greyish-green. The pupal imitation below, from Richard Walker, can be tied in various colour combinations to represent different sedge species. It can be fished either slowly in the surface film or with a steady retrieve in the top two or three feet.

Hook: 8–12
Thread: Pale yellow
Body: Rear two-thirds, amber or pale blue-green ostrich herl; front one-third, sepia or chestnut ostrich herl; all tied fat
Rib: Gold thread over the rear section
Hackle: Brown partridge tied rear-slanting
Horns: Two pheasant tail fibres twice the hook length tied on top of the hook, rear-facing at about 45 degrees

MARBLED SEDGE

This early-evening species is found mainly on rivers. The wings have a marbled appearance with brownish patches on a brownish-green wing. The body is greenish with orangy-brown legs which make the species easily recognisable.

MEDIUM SEDGE

A daytime species appearing in May and June. It is medium-sized with broad wings, about 11 mm long, that are greyish-yellow to a darker yellow. It is one of the hairier species.

SAND-FLY

This early-season sedge first appears in April and continues throughout the season until autumn. It is a daytime species but often difficult to identify because of variations in colour and size. Some wings are sandy-coloured; others may be mid-or very dark brown. It is not to be confused with the Clyde sandfly, a localised name for the gravel bed.

Sand-Fly *(Taff Price)*

Hook: 14
Tag: Two turns of gold wire
Body: Ginger or sandy hare's fur
Wing: Starling wing
Hackle: Light-coloured natural red or ginger cock

SILVER SEDGE

One of the smaller species. It has a wing length of about 9 mm and is generally grey or grey-brown. The female carries a green egg-sac at her rear after mating. The adults appear from May to August in rather localised areas throughout the country, usually preferring rivers to lakes. A suitable imitation is found under the Grey or Silver Sedge above.

SMALL RED SEDGE

A common species appearing from May to October. It is an evening-hatching fly and the wings are reddish-brown and about 8 mm long. It can be copied with any of the small red sedge patterns, particularly the Little Red Sedge.

SMALL YELLOW SEDGE

A common sedge and the smallest that interests trout. It hatches in the evenings and can be distinguished by its 5–6 mm browny-yellow wings.

WELSHMAN'S BUTTON

F. M. Halford named this species thus and in so doing caused confusion with the beetle of the same name. It is widely distributed on rivers and less frequently on lakes. The adults hatch from early May to July during the day and evening. The wing is 12–15 mm long and is chestnut-brown with golden hairs. The female often carries a large brown egg-sac at her abdomen. William Lunn's Caperer is a good imitation, as is a Little Red Sedge.

Listed below are various assorted sedge imitations: larvae in their cases, pupae and adult dressings, and many nondescript general patterns representing two or more species.

SEDGE LARVAE

Some of these caddis cases look very realistic. I've no doubt that they catch trout, but I prefer the fur-and-feather alternatives. See also CATGUT NYMPH, LEADHEAD NYMPH, MACKEREL NYMPH, STICKFLY and WORMFLY.

Cased Caddis (Bob Carnill) Plate 30

Hook: Extra long shank 8–12
Body: An underbody of black Gossamer silk and lead wire and an overbody of two-toned fur from the leading edge of a hare's ear. This represents the case
Abdomen: Tied between the body and hackle. White swan or goose herl to represent the larva
Rib: Silver wire over the abdomen
Hackle: Black hen sparsely tied at 90 degrees to the shank
Head: Tying silk varnished black tied large

Pheasant Tail Caddis Larva

(Roger Fogg)

Hook: Long shank 8–14
Thread: Black
Body: Lead-foil strips wound over with hare's ear fur and roughly covered with open turns of pheasant tail fibres and peacock herl
Rib: Thread or copper wire for strength
Shoulder: Dirty wool wound in between body and hackle to represent the larva
Hackle: Any dark hackle clipped short
Head: Black or brown tying thread

Sand Caddis (Taff Price)

Hook: Long shank 10–12
Body: A copper- or lead-wire underbody with a second layer of floss silk, leaving enough of the shank clear for the hackle to be tied in later. Coat the body in a water-resistant adhesive and completely cover with sand
Hackle: A single turn of brown hackle when the body is dry

A Twig Caddis and a Gravel Caddis can be dressed by replacing the sand with small twigs and vegetation and with very small stones.

Rhyacophila Larva
(Oliver Edwards)   Plate 30

On many freestone streams these free-swimming larvae abound and are consumed in large numbers by trout and grayling. The naturals are up to 1 inch (25 mm) long. This fly should be fished close to the riverbed, in a fairly straight drift, possibly requiring a high-density braided leader depending upon the water depth.

Hook: Partridge K4A heavy wire, curved shank, size 10–12
Thread: Fine and very strong yellow, typically Kevlar
Underbody: One or two layers of narrow strip of wine bottle lead
Abdomen and thorax: 4-ply knitting yarn, 100 per cent synthetic or synthetic-natural blend, preferably with the addition of Antron or other highly reflective fibre. Colour bright mid-green. Use only 1-ply
Rib: 3–5 lb BS clear or dyed green mono or a single strand of green Flashabou
Legs: Partridge grey hackle barbs dyed yellow-olive

Upper abdomen tint: Medium olive water-proof felt pen. First three segments dotted with black waterproof felt pen
Head: Yellow thread or white thread tinted yellow. Seal with Dave's Flexament

Sedge Pupae or Hatching Wet Patterns

In addition to the patterns listed, see also BROWN-AND-YELLOW NYMPH , AMBER NYMPH, ALL ROUNDER, PALMERS, INVICTA, GREEN PETER, MURROUGH and TURKEY GREEN/YELLOW.

Balloon Sedge

(Roman Moser) *Plate 31*

Roman Moser devised this style to imitate the emerging and newly emerged adults.

Hook: 10–16
Thread: Yellow
Body: Coloured poly dubbing
Wing: Brown deer hair tips
Head: Yellow polycelon or Orvis Fly Foam (closed-cell foam)

Cling Film Sedge

Plate 30

The excellent young Welsh tyer and competition angler Shane Jones hit upon using this unusual material to achieve the translucency which is a key feature of the natural pupa. His midge pupa uses the same technique.

Hook: Partridge GRS12ST size 16
Thread: Yellow Danville 6/0
Underbody: Yellow seal's fur
Overbody: 4–5 mm wide cling film tied in at the rear and brought forward over the body
Hackle: Brown partridge and natural deer hair
Antennae: Lemon wood-duck
Thorax: Natural deer hair, clipped and tinted with brown Pantone pen

Emergent Sparkle Pupa *Plate 30*

This is the most famous and widely used of Gary LaFontaine's patterns. Its success is due to the translucent and reflective qualities of Antron, a material Gary LaFontaine first introduced to fly tying. The overbody represents the translucent sheath of the natural pupa at the surface. These fibres are tied in above and below the shank at the rear and combed out. They are then brought forward to cover the body in a sparse envelope.

Hook: 10–14
Overbody: Coloured Sparkle Yarn (mixed clear and coloured Antron)
Underbody: Mixed Sparkle Yarn and natural fur
Wing: Natural or black deer hair tips
Head: Coloured marabou wrapped round the thread in a rope and wound to the eye

Fiery-Brown Sedge *(Bob Carnill)*

This should be fished wet at any position on the leader. It is reputedly extremely effective as a single point-fly cast to rising fish. Bob Carnill comments: 'There are occasions when trout drown adult sedges sitting on the surface. They do this by rising from directly below the fly and slapping it down with their tails. When this happens, a leaded Fiery Brown cast into the boil of a "slap-down" rise, allowed to sink, and then drawn out of it, can produce very exciting results.'

Hook: 8–12
Thread: Brown Gossamer
Body: Fiery-brown seal's fur
Rib: Gold tinsel
Wing: Two layers, single-folded dark bronze mallard tied low and extending beyond the bend
Hackle: Rich-brown hen wound as a collar

Hatching Caddis *(Davy Wotton)*

A surface-film pattern that also works subsurface when tied with weight below the body.

Hook: 8–18 Partridge L2A or GRS12ST
Thread: Danville's to match the body colour
Body: SLF or natural fur blend ribbed with fine oval gold
Wing: Fine deer hair from inside the leg
Thorax: Same as the body with the deer hair pulled over
Hackle: Partridge dyed to suit the body colour

Hatching Sedge Pupa

(John Roberts) *Plate 30*

I was inspired to dress this after using Stan Headley's Twitcher under other circumstances. I thought that an emerging sedge-pupa imitation could make good use of a spun deerhair head. This buoyant pattern will hang in the surface film in the manner of the natural sedge preparing to break through on to the surface. It can be fished static, in twitches, or in slow, steady pulls. On some patterns I tie in a few turns of fine lead wire at the rear of the shank before tying in the body material. This ensures that the fly hangs vertically. The addition of further turns of lead wire allows the fly to be fished below the top inch of water but still remain fairly buoyant. It has caught fish for me as far afield as Swedish Lapland and Northern Canada. I also tie a slightly different version which includes a broad strip of clear polythene along each side of the body. I believe this improves the imitation of the pupal sheath. If the hackle is omitted I leave a few longer deer hairs trailing to the rear.

Hook: 10–16 sedge hook
Thread: To match the body colour
Body: Orange, green, olive-brown or beige seal's fur ribbed with fine gold wire, with an optional broad strip of clear polythene each side of the body
Hackle: Brown partridge tied as a rear-sloping collar
Head: Natural deer hair spun in Muddler style and roughly trimmed. The fibres should not be densely packed, nor trimmed all to the same length

Hatching Sedge Pupa

(Oliver Edwards) *Plate 30*

The wing-case Raffene (soaked well in water) is tied in before the thorax, then the thorax is dubbed and the Raffene looped each side of the thorax. The butts of the pheasant tail fibres are wrapped as the head.

Hook: 12–14 Partridge K4A or CS7
Abdomen: Light-green poly dubbing
Abdomen back: Dark green-dyed swan shoulder fibres ribbed with fine gold wire
Wing-cases: A loop of dark brown or near-black Raffene either side of the thorax
Thorax: Sepia and brown seal's fur
Legs and head: Cock pheasant tail fibres crumpled for effect
Antennae: Wood-duck or dyed mallard breast fibres

Hatching Sedge Pupa

(John Goddard and Brian Clarke)

May be weighted if desired.

Hook: 12
Thread: Orange
Body: Medium-olive seal's fur
Rib: Silver wire
Wing: Grey mallard wing quill sections sloping back below the body, tied in alongside the thorax
Antennae: Two brown mallard fibres tied in at the thorax and sloping backwards over the body
Thorax: Medium-olive seal's fur
Legs: Grey partridge hackle dyed green as a throat only

An orange version is tied with orange seal's fur and a brown partridge hackle.

Latex Pupa *(Roger Fogg)* *Plate 30*

The fluorescent floss under the translucent overbody makes this into an excellent pupal imitation. Trout are often willing to take fur-and-feather flies, but on occasions they need something a little out of the ordinary. This might be the answer.

One cynic summed it up as 'more suited to being fished below a float for grayling!' There is the look of the maggot about it, but that comment came from a fishless angler after the orange pattern had taken three trout to 3 ¼ lb from under his nose. Roger Fogg fishes it sink-and-draw, with the most successful sizes 12 and 14. It was originally tied for river fishing in much smaller sizes.

The pattern below is the green version. The body of the orange version has orange latex over fluorescent orange wool.

Hook: 12–20 caddis hook
Thread: Brown
Body: An underbody of fluorescent lime-green floss covered with natural cream-coloured latex. The latex strip should be ribbed under tension from the bend with the tension released towards the thorax. This produces the tapered body
Thorax: Chestnut-brown ostrich herl
Hackle: Chestnut-brown hen

Mono Sedge Pupa   Plate 30

Hook: 10–14
Body: An underbody of brown or white tying thread overlaid with clear, colourless nylon monofilament tapering to the rear
Hackle: Partridge hackle tied rear-sloping

S.F. Emerger (Davy Wotton)   Plate 30

Davy Wotton has produced this imitation which has a very high degree of translucency as one of the key features. This is achieved by the way the SLF dubbing is applied to the hook. Tease out a mat of SLF dubbing (2 x ½ inch (5 x 15 mm)) so that the fibres are evenly distributed. About half an inch away from the body the tying thread will flatten out. At this point split the thread with a needle to open up a space about half an inch long and insert the mat of dubbing through so that the dubbing is positioned centrally. Take the thread slightly round the bend, and then wind the body. Tap the dub rearwards as

you wind with each turn made in front of the previous one. Do not overlap. The size and colour of the pattern should be to match the natural.

Hook: Partridge GRS12ST, K2B or CS27
Thread: White or light shade, Danville's 6/0
Body: SLF fibres (codes 5, 7, 10, 16, 20, 37 and 48 are recommended) tied as described in the text
Wing: Raffene
Legs: Hen hackle or partridge
Head: Dubbed SLF
Antennae (optional): Brown mallard or wood-duck fibres tied rear-facing

Sedge Pupa (Chris Kendall)   Plate 30

Chris Kendall dresses four different sedges in this style. Collectively, they cover most of the species one comes across. The four colour variations are ginger, green-bodied, silver-grey and cinnamon.

Hook: Yorkshire sedge hook 8–14
Abdomen: Antron and seal's fur mixed 50/50, colour as above, ribbed with clear polythene
Breathers: Two bronze mallard fibres tied from rear of thorax facing backwards
Legs: Dyed partridge in colours to match body
Wing-cases and shellback: Dyed white duck fibres to match body colour. The wing-cases are tied either side of the shank
Thorax: As for the abdomen without the rib

Sedge Pupa (John Goddard)   Plate 30

A pattern which its creator describes as 'one of my best stillwater patterns'. It is fished deep or in midwater and retrieved at a steady pace with occasional pauses.

Hook: Long shank wide-gape 10–12
Thread: Brown
Body: Choice of orange, cream, dark-brown or olive seal's fur. The orange and olive can be lightly covered with fluorescent material of the same colour

Rib: Fine silver Lurex
Thorax: Three dark-brown condor herls
Wing-case: Four light-brown condor herls doubled and redoubled
Hackle: Two turns of rusty hen or honey hen

Sienna Sedge

One of Steve Parton's dressings which he describes as an excellent point or dropper fly when brown-bodied sedges are on the water. It is also possibly an imitation of a brown- or ginger-bodied hatching midge pupa. It can be fished also as a dry fly.

Hook: 8–14
Thread: Black
Body: Sienna seal's fur with a palmered red-game hackle
Rib: Fine oval gold tinsel through the body hackle
Throat hackle: Red-game
Wing: Cock pheasant secondary feather. Cinnamon or reddish variations are preferred. As an alternative, use the side tail feathers. The wing should be tied narrow and extend to the bend

Superpupa   *Plate 30*

I like this simple Scandinavian pattern very much and I have used it on Yorkshire Dales rivers ever since I experienced how effective it was on Lapland grayling. The brown-and-cream and brown-and-grey versions have worked well during sedge hatches on the Ure. Fish it in the surface film or as a floater.

Hook: 12–18
Abdomen: Cream, olive or grey fine poly dubbing along two-thirds of the shank
Thorax: Dark brown or black fine poly dubbing
Body hackle: Palmered cock: light brown on the cream body, blue-dun on the others, with the upper and lower fibres cut away

Swimming Caddis Pupa
(Roman Moser)   *Plate 30*

This was devised as a river pattern. It may be fished as a floater with movement, or as a wet fly just below the surface. For the latter, allow the fly to dead-drift before swinging round at the same time as drifting downstream. The finished fly is fluffed up with Velcro.

Hook: 10–18
Thread: Yellow 6/0
Andomen: Orange carpet wool mixed with SLF for a sparkle effect
Legs: Two turns of low-grade light brown cock. Trim away the lower fibres after tying
Thorax: Golden yellow SLF fibres, tied bulky

Adult Sedges

Most of these are general patterns used to copy a number of species. Also see the F SEDGE.

Brown Conba Sedge
(Alice Conba)   *Plate 31*

Alice Conba is a professional Irish fly tyer and demonstrates on the Continent and in the USA. She has the gift of being able to discover simple tying methods where previously a more difficult process was involved. She also makes imaginative use of materials. This now widely used general brown sedge was developed when the original speckled wings were unavailable. The body fibres are wound on, and after the body hackle is added the body fibres are bent back for the wings. Alice comments that for some reason a longer wing works better on rivers. The Black Conba Sedge has a black body and head hackle. Other sedges can be imitated with the same wing and body but with hackle colour variations.

Hook: 8–16
Thread: Black

Body: Wound golden pheasant centre tail fibres (about 12) with a palmered good-quality natural red/brown cock (dry) or hen (wet)
Wing: Body fibres clipped in line with the bend
Hackle: Natural red/brown cock or hen

Dark Sedge (T. Thomas)

Hook: 12–14
Body: Black wool or chenille with a palmered black cock hackle
Wing: Black deer-hair tied flat, spread out and clipped with square ends
Hackle: Ginger cock tied in front of the wing

Deer Hair Sedge (Sid Neff) Plate 31

This Elk Hair Caddis variation is recommended by Mike Weaver and was devised by Pittsburgh angler Sid Neff.

Hook: 14–16
Body: Dubbed fur or substitute in various shades of green, grey or brown
Wing: Natural deer hair sloping back over the body with the butts clipped to form a neat head.

Elk Hair Caddis (Al Troth) Plate 31

The fly illustrated is tied by award-winning tyer Al Beatty in the style of the originator Al Troth. It is an extremely versatile sedge imitation and from its home US waters has found its way onto every trout stream. Al Beatty includes this in his top three patterns.

Hook: 6–24
Thread: To match the insect
Body: Tying thread
Hackle: Palmered cock, to match the insect, with the upper fibres trimmed
Wing: Elk or deer body hair
Head: Clipped ends of the hair

G&H Sedge — Plate 31

A popular pattern devised by John Goddard and Cliff Henry (hence the G&H). It has become better known in the USA simply as the Goddard Sedge. It is an excellent floater because of the deer-hair body, which also produces a good silhouette. John Goddard suggests that when used from the bank on a stillwater it should be tied to the point of a very long leader, in excess of 18 feet. It should be allowed to lie motionless unless trout are reluctant to take it, and then a little tweak may induce a favourable response. In rough water it should be retrieved fairly quickly across the surface. Fished as a top dropper from a drifting boat, 'it reigns supreme'. The smaller sizes are more suitable for rivers. Dyed deer hair can be used for different species of sedge.

Hook: Long shank 8–16
Thread: Green
Body: Bunches of deer hair spun on and trimmed. All the body is covered and then trimmed, tapering towards the eye. If the lower body option is included all the underside hair should be removed and part-way along each side to give a sedge silhouette
Hackles: Two rusty-dun cock hackles trimmed at the top. The hackle-stems can be used for forward-pointing antennae
Lower body (optional): Dark green seal's fur twisted in between a double length of green tying thread, tied in at the outset. This is pulled taut under the trimmed hair body and whipped in at the eye
Hackle: Two honey cock hackles

Light Sedge (T. Thomas)

Hook: 12–14
Body: Light cock pheasant tail fibres wound on thickly and palmered with a ginger cock hackle
Wing: Brown deer hair tied flat and spread out with the ends trimmed square
Hackle: Black cock

Little Red Sedge (G. E. M. Skues)

Plate 31

Although he did not greatly appreciate grayling, Skues said of this pattern that if he had just one fly with which to kill grayling (by which I assume he meant chalk-stream grayling), he would select this one. It kills trout and grayling on northern streams, too. In one twenty-minute spell on the Wharfe one November day, my friend, David Burnett, killed half a dozen grayling between 1 lb and 1 ¾ lb on the fly when there wasn't a sedge in sight. I know anglers who have fished that stretch of the Wharfe for many years, and I'm told that a grayling of 1 ½ lb is rare. I think the catch was viewed with some scepticism!

Hook: 12–14
Thread: Hot-orange
Body: Darkest hare's fur with a palmered short-fibred red cock hackle
Rib: Fine gold wire
Wing: Landrail wing, bunched and rolled and sloping well back over the tail
Hackle: Five or six turns of deep-red cock in front of the wings (longer-fibred than the body)

Pale Sedge (David Jacques)

Smaller sizes are recommended for daytime use and larger for dusk. It is a useful imitation of any of the paler sedges and the grousewing and caperer.

Hook: 10–14
Body: Cinnamon turkey tail fibres
Rib: Gold twist
Wing: Natural hen pheasant wing fibres, rolled and tied flat over the body
Hackles: Palmered ginger cock over the body with a second ginger cock at the head

Red Sedge (Richard Walker)   *Plate 31*

Hook: Standard or long shank 10
Tag: Orange fluorescent wool

Body: Clipped chestnut ostrich herl or chestnut pheasant tail fibres
Wing: Natural red cock hackle fibres clipped level with the bend, or red cree, or the hackle of a cock cuckoo
Hackle: Two long-fibred natural red cock hackles

Resting Sedge (Philip White) *Plate 31*

Philip White ties this imitation of the resting sedge with its low profile before starting to flutter. The wing is tied in first, facing forward, and the rest of the fly is then dressed. The wing is then pulled back over the body and tied down behind the thorax. A non-flaring hair is used to create the slim silhouette.

Hook: 10–20
Body: Superfine Dry Fly Dubbing in an appropriate colour built up a little at the thorax
Wing: Elk mane or Texas whitetail in natural or dyed colours
Hackle: Cock hackle wound through the thorax and then clipped top and bottom so the fly sits low

Saville's Super Sedge (Tom Saville)

Hook: 8–12
Thread: Well-waxed brown
Body: Ostrich herl dyed cinnamon with a palmered ginger cock hackle
Rib: Arc-chrome DRF nylon floss
Wing: Two hen pheasant or woodcock body fibres drawn through Cellire varnish between the thumb and finger; tied in a roof-shape extending beyond the bend

Silhouette Caddis   *Plate 31*

A pattern devised by Finnish angler Juha Vainio to copy the newly emerged adult. It has a wonderfully translucent wing of snowshoe hare.

Hook: 10–14 long shank, slightly humped Tiemco 2302
Thread: Yellow 8/0

Body: Yellow Antron with a palmered short-fibred sandy-dun cock, the upper fibres trimmed to allow for the wing, and ribbed with fine gold wire
Wing: Snowshoe hare foot hair, not too dense
Head hackle: Dark blue-dun cock, wound sparsely over the thorax
Thorax: Antron/hare blend

Squirrel Sedge *(Lars Olsson)* Plate 31

This is a good fish finder on difficult days. A fast-water fly that is better fished on British waters in slightly smaller sizes than those intended for Scandinavian rivers. It is a very good floater because the long-haired body is spun on a spinning block thereby trapping lots of air. The wing is double and is folded back over the body; this also holds air.

Hook: Size 8–16 long shank, fine wire, Partridge E1A
Thread: Brown
Body: Reddish-brown summer squirrel (hare's ear or mask as a substitute) spun on a spinning block
Hackle: Natural red cock palmered with the upper fibres cut away and a V cut out of the lower section
Wing: Reddish-brown squirrel tail, tied in behind the eye, roots behind the bend and points in front of the eye and then folded backwards over the first part of the wing. Make a large head with the upper part of the wing and whip-finish behind the head

Voljc Sedge Plate 31

Dr Bozidar Voljc developed an unusual method for producing sedge wings that has become very popular. A stocking mesh is spread tight in a frame. Various game bird feathers are glued to the mesh underside down so that the shiny upper side of the feather is visible. The feathers are then cut out singly and trimmed to shape and tied over the palmered body. The wings are remarkbly durable. The pattern described is a Cinnamon Sedge.

Hook: 12–16
Thread: Black
Body: Palmered dark ginger cock with the upper fibres trimmed away
Wing: Hen mallard body feather, formed as explained above, and tied in a tight V, extending beyond the body
Hackle: Dark ginger cock

V-Wing Sedge Plate 31

Also known as the Tent-Wing Sedge. This pattern type works best in the medium to small sizes. A low-floating version has the upper and lower hackle fibres cut away.

Hook: 14–22 lightweight
Thread: Brown
Body: Very fine natural fur or poly dubbing
Wing: A section of fairly stiff wing quill in an upturned V or U shape low over the body and extending beyond the bend
Hackle: Cock hackle to match the natural

Wind-Assisted Sedge Plate 31

This is an ingenious adaptation of the G&H Sedge. It was devised by Carl Lynch, for whom it has been very successful. With its spinnaker tail the fly skids over the surface as the breeze hits it. The fly can move quite naturally in the direction of the wind, which might be in a direction that the angler would not normally be able to move it in. The underbody and wing colour variations are as numerous as there are sedges. This pattern is well worth a try.

Hook: 10–14 long shank
Tip: Silver, gold or pearly Mylar taken slighly round the bend
Body and spinnaker tail: Natural or coloured deer hair, spun and trimmed to shape; use waterproof felt pens to colour. Add a drop of varnish at the base of the tail to hold it in postition and for durability
Underbody (optional): SLF in an appropriate colour laid across the bottom

Diving Caddis *(Gary LaFontaine)*

An imitation of the ovipositing female.

Hook: 8–16
Body: Dubbed Sparkle Yarn, colour to match the natural
Wing: A soft wing of partridge or mallard breast fibres, the tips of which should extend beyond the hook bend. A second wing of about 30 filaments of clear Sparkle Yarn is tied in at about 45 degrees over the first wing. This should be longer than the shank
Hackle: Rear-facing brown cock

Post-Ovipositing Female Sedge *Plate 31*

Oliver Edwards ties this imitation of the adult female sedge which has laid or is laying its eggs below the surface and is drifting in the current and perhaps struggling to re-emerge. I've seen Oliver catch a lot of river trout and grayling in the late evening and dusk with this pattern.

Hook: 10–16 curved sedge Partridge K4A
Thread: Olive or brown
Underbody: A small amount of lead foil
Abdomen: Fine synthetic dubbing to match the natural, about two-thirds body length
Rib: Fine gold wire
Thorax and legs: Moser sedge dubbing comprising 70 per cent deer or elk hair trimmings mixed with 30 per cent fine poly dubbing. The deer fibres should be picked out underneath and tied sloping back
Wing: Pale brown Raffene, doubled and then folded to produce four wings about 3–4 mm wide and extending about one and a half times the shank length and trimmed to shape
Head: Tying thread

SEPIA DUN (*Leptophlebia marginata*)

See EPHEMEROPTERA
The distribution, habitat and general appearance of this fly are similar to those of the claret dun, described elsewhere in greater detail. The most obvious difference is that the rarer sepia dun has a darker body and wings, appears between April and mid-May and is slightly larger. The female spinner has three dark-brown tails and a black patch on the leading edge of the wings. The heavily-built nymph, which swims in laboured fashion, has prominent gill filaments down the side of its body, three widely splayed-out tails and a sepia body. In April the nymphs move into shallower water in the margins before emerging by climbing up vegetation or waterside stones. It is during this move into the shallows that they are most profitably imitated. A Pheasant-Tail Spinner should be sufficient for those rare occasions when trout feed upon the female spinner. See also under MALLARD AND CLARET and GROUSE AND CLARET.

Sepia Nymph

Hook: 12–14
Thread: Dark brown
Tail: Dark brown hen hackle fibres
Body: A 5:1 mixture of dark brown and ginger seal's fur, well picked out at each side; or dark brown floss or seal's fur with a silver wire rib
Thorax: Black seal's fur
Hackle: Dark brown hen or hen dyed sepia

Sepia Dun *(Oliver Kite)*

Hook: 14
Thread: Dark brown
Tail: Dark-brown or black cock fibres
Body and thorax: Dark heron herls, doubled and redoubled at the thorax
Rib: Fine gold wire down the abdomen only
Hackle: Black cock with a brown tinge

Sepia Dun   *(David Jacques)*

Hook: 12
Thread: Maroon or claret
Tail: Pheasant tail fibres well spaced out
Body: Pheasant tail fibres
Rib: Fine gold wire
Wing: Mottled brown cock wing-slips
Hackle: Furnace cock

Shredge   *(Tony Knight)*

Tony Knight devised this mixed-up Shrimp and Sedge dressing. So mixed-up is it that it kills as a shrimp pattern, as a hatching sedge or as a sedge-pupa imitation. Bob Carnill and Steve Parton, two excellent Rutland anglers, speak highly of the Shredge and its variants. Bob praises the hackled, wingless version when fished in a team of three. Steve ties the body with dark sienna seal's fur taken well round the hook-bend and tapering to the rear, with a sparse ginger cock hackle rear-sloping. This is called the Emergent Tobacco Shredge.

Hook: 10–12 standard or sedge hook
Thread: Primrose
Body: Light tobacco-coloured seal's fur produced by mixing 70 per cent cinnamon and 30 per cent yellow seal's fur
Rib: Fine gold wire
Wing: Short grey mallard flight feather. A variation is to tie two wings at the sides of the body rather than on top
Hackle: Pale ginger hen or cinnamon

SHRIMPS *(Gammarus pulex, G. lacustris)*

These crustaceans are widely distributed in rivers and stillwaters throughout the UK but they are of greater value to the river fisherman. They thrive in alkaline waters and are most abundant in chalkstreams, where they live in weed-beds or on the bottom. A deep-sunk artificial can be a killing pattern for trout and grayling. Both species feed upon shrimp in large quantities where they are readily available. Grayling are primarily bottom-feeders and a large proportion of their diet is shrimp because during those months of the year when grayling feed most avidly, there are fewer nymphs, duns and other flies.

The natural shrimp is unmistakable with its arched translucent grey or olive-grey body which turns orangy-brown during the mid-summer mating season. Their length varies from 12 to 18 mm. They swim in a peculiar stop-start darting motion. Imparting some lift to the artificial often brings a response from a fish that refuses to look at a fly in a straight drift. See also KILLER BUG, SHRUG and SHRYMPH.

Edwards Shrimp

(Oliver Edwards)   *Plate 19*

Hook: 10–14
Thread: Grey
Underbody: Lead wire or foil in a hump on top of the shank
Tail and head appendages: Pale olive-dyed or natural grey partridge fibres
Back: Clear polythene
Body: Dubbed mixture of very pale olive-dyed fine fur and grey partridge hackles (picked out for legs)
Rib: Nylon mono

Shrimp   *(Philip White)*   *Plate 19*

Hook: 10–16
Underbody: Lead wire or several slips of lead foil built up on top of the shank
Back: Brown Raffene, not prestretched, to overlap down both sides
Rib: Fine gold or copper wire wound over the back
Body: A mixture of seal's fur using medium olive and hot orange in varying proportions. In May it may as much as 50 per cent orange. Others may be almost plain olive. The fibres should be picked out to the gape length

Mating Shrimp

(John Goddard and Brian Clarke)   *Plate 19*

Brian Clarke's version:
Hook: Wide-gape 8–12
Thread: Olive
Body: An underbody of lead wire with an overbody of mixed olive and amber seal's fur (4:1)
Rib: Fine gold wire
Back: Clear polythene or PVC

John Goddard's version:
Hook: Wide-gape 8–12
Thread: Olive
Body: An underbody of narrow lead strips built into a hump on top of the shank. An overbody of mixed seal's fur, 60 per cent olive, 30 per cent dark brown and 10 per cent DFM pink
Rib: Oval silver wire
Back: Clear PVC or polythene

Red Spot Shrimp *(Neil Patterson)*

Until I fished the Driffield Beck I had not come across the phenomenon of shrimps with a red blob on their bellies. Neil Patterson noted that some early-season shrimps have this feature, and he suggests that it is the early stages of the egg-sac. I have also noted it on shrimps in October when grayling fishing. The highly visible fluorescent red spot on the artificial makes it a useful pattern for slightly coloured water.

Hook: Sedge hook 8–14
Thread: Waxed olive
Underbody: Fine lead wire
Body: A short length of red DFM wool tied in on the centre of the shank at right-angles to it; then an equal mixture of olive mohair and olive seal's fur dubbed on and wound to the head through the wool. The red wool is clipped to form two spots on the body sides
Back: Double layer of clear plastic sheet over the body and rib
Rib: Gold wire over the body
Legs: Olive body fibres picked out

Shrug *(Simon Ashworth)*   *Plate 19*

This popular and very successful grayling bug was devised by Simon Ashworth. The wool body is not wound but teased into individual fibres and then applied as a dubbing. It was originally named the Yorkshire Bug but was jokingly renamed by an angler ignorant of its real name but aware that it was a mixture of a shrimp and Killer Bug. The name has stuck.

Hook: Kamasan B100 or Partridge K4 size 12–14
Thread: Any neutral colour
Underbody: One or two layers of 0.035 mm lead wire
Body: Beige darning wool dubbed (originally Chadwick's 477) with the fibres picked out after the wire ribbing
Rib: Glo-Brite neon magenta floss
Back: Clear olive or colourless polythene overribbed with fine gold wire

Shrymph   *Plate 19*

John Goddard devised this pattern with big chalk-stream grayling in mind and it has gone on to be very successful with over two dozen two-pound grayling to its credit and also for trout with the best being a fifteen-pound river specimen. The silhouette produced suggests either a shrimp or a nymph depending on what a fish wants to see in it.

Hook: Wide gape 8–12
Thread: Brown
Underbody: Lead wire wound to produce a substantial thorax
Body and thorax: Seal's fur or substitute, 5 parts green, 4 parts brown, 1 part fluorescent pink
Rib: Silver Lurex over the abdomen only
Wing-case: Flue from a black crow feather doubled and redoubled over the thorax top

Shuck Fly *(Chris Ogborne)*

This is an unusual fly devised by stillwater expert, Chris Ogborne. Evidently cruising trout often feed on the empty shucks and in such circumstances a conventional fly struggles to work. He recommends its use as a single dry fly on a very long leader.

Hook: Fine wire 12–14
Thread: Black
Tail: A few long strands of cream seal's fur
Shuck: Ethafoam cut to the shape of a shuck, tied in with orange thread at the rear of the shank. Most of the shank is left undressed.

Silver March Brown   *Plate 7*

Although this is a variant of the March Brown, a river pattern, it has become a useful lake and sea-trout fly together with the Gold March Brown, which differs from this dressing only by the gold tinsel body and rib. Both are useful hatching-sedge patterns when fished near the surface at the appropriate time.

Hook: 10–12
Tail: Partridge tail fibres
Body: Flat silver tinsel
Rib: Oval silver tinsel or wire
Wing: Partridge tail or hen pheasant wing
Hackle: Brown partridge

An alternative dressing has a hare's ear fur body with a closely wound rib of silver Lurex.

Sinfoil's Fry

This stillwater fry imitation is named after its creator, Ken Sinfoil, at the time a bailiff at Weir Wood reservoir. I believe Ken Sinfoil was the first UK fly tyer to make use of polythene in fly bodies.

Hook: Long shank 8–12
Thread: Black
Underbody: Flat silver tinsel
Overbody: Thick clear polythene or PVC built up into a fry shape
Collar: Fluorescent or ordinary scarlet floss
Back: Pale-brown mallard fibres tied in only at the head

Head: Varnished black silk with an eye painted either side

SMALL DARK OLIVE
(Baetis scambus)

See EPHEMEROPTERA

Also known as the July dun. The species is common and well distributed on rivers throughout the country and is most abundant on limestone streams. The nymph is a very small agile-darting type inhabiting weeds, moss and sometimes stones. The adult is also very small. Adults have been known to appear as early as February and as late as November, but they are most common between May and August and usually hatch during the afternoons. The female spinner crawls under the surface to deposit her eggs. Trout feed upon the spent spinners, which after laying their eggs are unable to break through the surface film and become trapped below or within it. The possibility of fish feeding on these should not be overlooked if floating duns and spinners are being refused by feeding fish.

The male dun has medium- to dark-grey wings. The abdomen is pale grey-green olive with the last two segments yellowish. The legs are pale yellow-olive and the two tails are grey. The female dun has similar wings and the abdomen is grey-olive with the last two segments yellowish. The legs and tails are as for the male.

The female spinner, also known as the small red spinner, has transparent wings with blackish veins. The abdomen varies between dark brown tinged with olive to mahogany-brown. The legs are olive-brown and the two tails greyish-white. The male spinner is of no interest.

See also DARK OLIVE and LARGE DARK OLIVE for the larger-sized imitations, which can be tied smaller, and GOLD-RIBBED HARE'S EAR, PHEASANT-TAIL SPINNER, LUNN'S PARTICULAR, SNIPE BLOA and OLIVE BLOA.

July Dun (S. D. O.) Nymph
(G. E. M. Skues)

Hook: 16
Thread: Yellow or primrose
Tail: Short dark-blue hen fibres
Body: Mixed olive seal's fur and dark brown bear's fur
Rib: Gold wire through the rear half
Hackle: Two turns of short-fibred rusty-dun hen

Small Dark Olive Hatching Special

A pattern created by Terry Griffiths to represent the hatching dun in the surface film.

Hook: 16–18
Tail: Very short blue-dun fibres
Body: A short body of mole's fur
Rib: Fine gold thread
Hackles: Rhode Island Red with a blue-dun in front

Small Dark Olive Dun

Hook: 16–18
Thread: Yellow
Tail: Blue-dun cock fibres
Body: Mixed light-olive and Adam's grey poly dubbing
Hackles: Olive-dyed cock with a blue-dun cock wound in front

SMALL YELLOW SALLY (Chloroperla torrentium)

See STONEFLIES
A different species from the yellow sally, but imitations of that will be sufficient. It is fairly common on rivers with a sandy or stony bottom, but has a preference for upland waters. The nymph is fairly small, measuring 5–8 mm long. The adults are 5–8 mm long and are slim and yellowish or yellowish-brown and appear between April and August.

SMUTS (Simulium)

See DIPTERA
Known as reed smuts or the black curse, these are members of the Diptera Order of flat-winged flies. They inhabit rivers and stillwaters as long as there is some movement or current. The adults are very small, averaging no more than 3–4 mm in length, although there are a few larger species. The body colour varies from dark brown to black, and the wings are broad and transparent. The larvae cling to weeds and are avidly devoured by trout and grayling. The adult fly, emerging from its pupal case, rises to the surface in a gas bubble. The relatively dry adult spends little time on the surface before flying off. The rising adult in its gas bubble is difficult to imitate, but subsurface patterns that incorporate a white wing or silver ribbing help the deception. Small versions of the Black Gnat are also suitable imitations of a smut.

Torp's Reed Smuts   Plate 22

These two patterns are the creation of Preben Torp Jacobsen, of Denmark.

Hook: Mustad 72500 size 14
Thread: Brown
Body: Blood-red cow's hair over a base of thin copper wire. 'The body material should be thoroughly soaked in silicone liquid to ensure the air-bubbles adhere to the body. Four or five turns of 0.15 mm silver wire are made in front and behind the body. The impregnated hair will take a lot of air down into the water and turns of silver wire in the front and rear will help create the impression that the "fly" is enveloped in a sac of air, just like the natural when its pupal stage rises to the surface. The body is only short, occupying the middle third of the shank. One could tie the fly on a much smaller hook, but I want a good gape and the weight of the bigger hook to help me to bring the fly down – the same reason for the heavier silver wire.

'The hatching smuts penetrate the surface very fast – you will never see them "standing" on the surface. Only those that can't penetrate the surface film will be hanging in it and will be caught by trout. This is the second situation, where a trout has the possibility to catch it.

'From earlier experiences I had great faith in small flies tied with a parachute hackle. I had used a parachute version of the Grey Duster during caenis hatches with extraordinary results and christened it the Parachuting Badger. Likewise, I tied a similar fly to imitate the smuts hanging in the surface unable to hatch.'

Simulium (P. T. Jacobsen)

Hook: 16–18
Thread: Black
Body: Black condor herl tied fairly short
Hackle: Long-stemmed short-fibred black cock tied in Parachute style in the middle of the short body

Smut (J. C. Mottram)

This wet pattern was devised by J. C. Mottram, author of *Fly Fishing: Some New Arts and Mysteries*, published about 1920. I can boast of catching smutting grayling on this fly. That difficult task should be proof enough of its value.

Hook: 14–16
Thorax: Black floss silk at the thorax only. I tie in a small tip of silver tinsel behind the thorax
Hackle: One turn of a small starling breast feather

Goddard Smut   Plate 22

John Goddard overcomes the problem of using tiny hooks and the necessary fine tippets which forever break on better fish by tying short on a larger (size 20!) hook.

Hook: 20
Thread: Fine black midge thread
Body: Black ostrich herl tied on the front half of the shank
Hackle: Two or three turns of short-fibred black cock

SNAILS

Snails provide a major contribution to the diet of stillwater trout, and to a much lesser extent river trout and grayling. For the most part they live on the lake- or river-bed or on weeds, and they are therefore difficult to imitate successfully. There is a period in mid-summer when snails migrate to the surface and hang beneath the surface film. They do this probably because of the de-oxygenation of the water. During July and August it is not uncommon to catch trout full of snails, and the imitation fished slowly just below the surface can have great effect. The Black and Peacock Spider is a useful pattern on such an occasion.

Floating Snail (Bob Church)

I doubt whether there is an easier dressing to tie.

Hook: 10–12
Body: Black or brown chenille in a ball-shape

Floating Snail (D. Barker)

Hook: Wide-gape 8–10
Body: A large dome-shaped body of cork with a shallow groove cut out for the hook-shank to slot into. A small hole is made at the top of the dome and a lead shot is glued in. The body is coloured with indelible felt-pen (dark green or black) and glued to the shank. The artificial floats dome downwards imitating the natural

Snipe and Purple   Plate 32

An old North Country iron blue imitation and an exceptional pattern for both trout and grayling. It is useful early in the season and again from September to November. That expert grayling fisher, Reg Righyni, placed this as his favourite top dropper on a three-fly leader. He also incorporated a fine copper rib on some of his patterns.

The soft snipe hackle can be worked in the current when the fly is fished upstream and this would seem to be a major factor in the pattern's representation of the nymph or dun struggling to emerge.

Hook: 12–16
Body: Purple thread or silk
Hackle: Dark snipe tied sparsely

Snipe and Yellow

This used to be known as the Light Snipe and it is similar to the Snipe Bloa, listed under BLOAS. It is an old North Country fly usually fished early- and late-season.

Hook: 14
Body: Yellow thread or silk
Hackle: Dark snipe sparsely tied

Something and Nothing   *Plate 20*

This is a nondescript sub-surface pattern devised by Roger Fogg. Some twenty years ago he was fishing with a well-chewed and well-worn Coachman, and the more tatty it became the more fish it caught. As a result he tied a fly with a well-worn look, and the origin of its name is obvious.

Roger says: 'It is perhaps my favourite pattern, the nearest I have got to the philosopher's stone, but by accident rather than alchemy – it seems to be all things to all fish. It may not look much, but it catches fish unleaded, leaded, on small hooks, on lure hooks, on rivers and on stillwaters. Further, it succeeds throughout the season. Although I prefer the imitative approach, it is a good pattern with which to catch your first fish on an alien water. Then the fish may be spooned.'

Hook: Any size, but size 12 is recommended
Thread: Brown
Body: Optional lead underbody covered with peacock herl with much of the flue clipped off
Hackle: Any brownish hackle clipped short as a rough collar

Wing: White hen feather or similar tied in the usual manner and clipped to a short stub

A second version is dressed as above, but with a body of fine dark copper wire of the type found in a small electric motor.

Sooty Olive

Expert Irish angler Peter O'Reilly describes this as the 'quintessential Irish lough wet fly'. Its origins and original dressing are lost in time and variations in the dressing are common. Peter comments that the tail should be either golden pheasant tippets or bronze mallard. There are three hackle alternatives. Natural black hen is often preferred but dyed black is used. Others prefer a 'sooty olive' cock. This is achieved by dying a red game dark olive until a very dark olive brown shade is achieved. There is a Sooty Olive Red Thorax which is as below except with the front third of the body of red seal's fur.

Hook: 10–14
Tail: Golden pheasant tippets
Body: Mixed dark olive and brown-olive seal's fur
Rib: Oval gold tinsel or gold wire
Wing: Bronze mallard
Hackle: Natural black hen

Sparkle Dun   *Plate 25*

This is a Craig Matthews and John Juracek development of the North American Comparadun created by Caucci and Nastasi; the difference being the introduction of poly yarn or Z-lon for the tail. The theory is that the tail suggests the trailing shuck of the emerging dun. I have long believed that many tails on dry flies are actually far better imitations of the nymphal shuck than they are of the cerci of the natural dun. This is one step to create a more accurate shuck representation. Mike Weaver has tied the fly illustrated and offers the design as his favourite dun imitation and used in all sizes, from 20 for pale wateries to 12 for Mayflies, in appropriate colours.

Hook: 12–20
Tail: White poly yarn, Z-lon, Orvis Sparkle wing or Lureflash Antron Body Wool
Body: Dubbed natural fur or substitute, one third in front of the wing
Wing: Natural or dyed deer or elk hair, flared through 180 degrees above the shank

Sparkle Dun *(Simon Ward)* *Plate 25*

Simon Ward has amended the original Sparkle Dun by changing the wing to an upright stub with only a 10-degree splay, rather than the 180-degree original. This represents the unfolding wings. Simon fishes it in sizes 14 to 22 for all dun hatches. Size 18 is the most effective. On eight visits on the Rivers Frome and Piddle it account for fifty-four wild brown trout, each over a pound.

Hook: 14–22
Thread: Two shades lighter than the body colour
Tail: Pale yellow, pale grey or white Orvis Sparkle wing
Wing: A small bunch of deer or elk, bleached, olive or natural, tied upright
Body: Sparsely dubbed Antron/hare blend or fine fur

Sparkle Emerger

(Mike Weaver) *Plate 29*

Mike Weaver has created this simple development of the Sparkle Dun to be fished right in the surface film to imitate flies at the point of emergence. The size and colour should match the naturals.

Hook: 12–20
Tail: White poly yarn, Z-lon or Lureflash Antron Body Wool
Body: Dubbed natural fur or substitute, one-third in front of the wing
Wing: Natural or dyed deer hair; the wing is shorter than for the dun and slopes back over the body

Sparkle Gnat *(Charles Jardine)*

This is a development of the Griffith's Gnat. Charles comments that it has been a revelation on stillwater trout concentrating on small midges. It his first choice in a flat calm or when winter rainbow fishing.

Hook: 16–24
Thread: Black 12/0 or bottle-green Bennechi
Tail: Three strands of Pearl Twinkle (or green, orange or black Twinkle to match the midge body colour)
Body: One or two strands of peacock herl
Hackle: Palmered grizzle cock

Sparkle Parachute

(Wayne Luallen) *Plate 24*

This development, created by one of the world's finest tyers, Wayne Luallen, combines the attributes of the parachute hackle, a clear view of the wing and the trailing shuck.

Hook: Fine wire, wide gape 14–22
Thread: To match the body colour
Shuck: Z-lon in brown (usually) or gold or olive
Body: White turkey body feather, dyed pale to dark dun to match the natural
Hackle: High-quality cock to match the natural

Spiders

The wingless, hackled wet flies used on rivers particularly in the north of the country are certainly suggestive of the natural spider, but this is not what they are intended to represent. The imitation of the stillwater spiders has been largely overlooked by angler entomologists. This is surprising in view of the potential food source they represent. They live close to weed-beds and carry with them a single large air-bubble or trap smaller bubbles in their body hairs. They seem to prefer lake margins where the journey to replenish their air is not great. Many terrestrial spiders find their way on to the water and are often seen struggling on the surface.

Hook: 12–14
Body: Brown seal's fur
Rib: Silver tinsel with a tip at the rear
Hackle: Brown partridge

Windborne Spider *(Taff Price)*

A pattern to represent the terrestrial spiders.

Hook: 14–16
Body: A button of red, brown, yellow, grey or black polypropylene
Hackle: A cock hackle tied in Parachute style and coloured as for the body

Taff Price suggests that for added realism a single human hair should be tied in at the tail to represent the gossamer thread spun by the spider!

SPINNERS

The spinners are the imago, the final adult stage of the ephemeroptera species. It is usually only the mated females that find their way back to the river surface and are of interest to trout and grayling. Most spinners oviposit their eggs by frequent dipping in flight or land on the surface. The spinners of the medium olive, large and small dark olives and the iron blues all oviposit below the surface. They may be seen crawling down stakes, vegetation or an angler's waders to lay their eggs. These are swept into the current after egg-laying and are readily devoured. Some fight their way through the surface to re-emerge to fly away and die. Be aware that fish feeding close to the surface in the late evening may not be taking nymphs, emergers or duns but spent spinners. See SUNK SPINNER, POLYWING SPINNER, SUNSET SPINNER, ORANGE SPINNER, CLEAR-WING SPINNER.

Spruce Fly

A streamer-style lure.

Hook: Long shank 6–10
Tail: Peacock sword feather herl
Body: Rear half, red floss; front half, thin black chenille
Wing: Two cree hackle points tied back to back
Hackle: Brown cock tied as a rear-facing collar

Spuddler   *Plate 1*

This hybrid lure was created by crossing a Muddler with a Spruce Fly.

Hook: Long shank 6–10
Tail: Brown calf-tail or Canadian fox squirrel hair
Body: Cream wool
Thorax: Orange floss
Wing: Two cree hackle points tied in at the rear of the thorax
Neck: Canadian fox squirrel hair
Head: Spun deer hair clipped in an oval shape with a flat bottom

Variations include a hot-orange goat hair tail, or a silver rib to aid its attractiveness.

SPURWINGS (Centroptilum luteolum, C. pennulatum)

See EPHEMEROPTERA

The small spurwing (*C. luteolum*) and large spurwing (*C. pennulatum*) used to be classed with the pale wateries, but now they are better known in their own right. The small spurwing is small to medium-sized and similar in its dun stage to the pale watery or small dark olive, the main difference being the small spur-shaped hind-wing which is detectable only with the aid of a magnifying glass.

Distribution is widespread except in Wales. It is found in rivers and sometimes on lakes and it has a preference for alkaline water. The nymph is an agile-darting type inhabiting weed-beds. The adults appear from early May to October, their most prolific month being June. Their presence is often spread throughout the day, particularly during the early months, but as the season progresses the hatches become restricted to late afternoons.

The male dun has pale grey or blue-grey wings. The abdomen is pale olive-grey with a brown-olive underside. The legs are watery-grey or olive-brown and the two tails are pale grey. The female dun has wings similar to the male's. The abdomen is pale watery-olive or green-olive with pale olive under. The legs are very pale olive and the two tails grey.

The male spinner has colourless wings and a translucent white abdomen of which the last three segments are reddish-brown. The underside is grey-white. The legs are pale olive and the two tails grey-white. The female spinner, known also as the little amber spinner, has transparent colourless wings. The abdomen is yellow-brown which becomes amber in the spent fly. The underside is creamy-yellow. The legs are pale olive and the two tails pale olive-white.

The large spurwing is a medium-to-large-sized adult. Distribution is localised in the south and north and in the Usk area of Wales. One distinguishing feature of the duns is that the wings are spread well apart when at rest, whereas most duns hold their wings more or less vertically. The nymph is an agile-darting type, preferring to live on weeds or moss in slower-moving water. The adults emerge from late May to September. Like the small spurwing, it has a small spur-shaped hind-wing.

The male dun has dark blue-grey wings and a pale olive-brown or greyish abdomen, of which the upper side of the last three segments is amber. The legs are pale olive-brown and the two tails grey. The female dun also has blue-grey wings. The abdomen is pale olive-grey. The legs are olive on the upper sections and grey-white lower down and the two tails grey. The male spinner has transparent wings. The abdomen is translucent white with pale red rings, with the last three segments dark amber. The legs are pale grey and the two tails grey-white.

The female spinner, also known as the large amber spinner, has transparent wings with pale olive veins. The abdomen is olive with amber flecks, or all amber with greyish wings. The underside is olive-white. The legs are olive-grey and the two tails pale grey.

For other artificials see GREY DUSTER, LUNN'S YELLOW BOY, PINK SPINNER, POULT BLOA, TUP'S INDISPENSABLE, LAST HOPE, PHEASANT TAIL SPINNER and GREY GOOSE NYMPH.

Spurwing Nymph

(Tony Waites) *Plate 17*

A pattern belonging to Tony Waites, head keeper for the Driffield Anglers' Club. Donald Overfield suggests that a wing-case of heron herl could be added.

Hook: 14–18
Thread: Grey
Body: An underbody of fine silver fuse-wire covered with three natural heron herls tapering to the rear
Rib: Fine silver fuse-wire

Spurwing Nymph *(G. E. M. Skues)*

Hook: 14
Thread: White
Tail: Pale blue hen hackle fibres
Body: Dubbed white lamb's wool
Hackle: Dark-blue hen

Large Spurwing Dun

(John Goddard)

Hook: 14
Thread: Cream
Tail: Pale blue-dun cock fibres
Body: Cream seal's fur
Wing: Pale starling in a V-shape
Hackle: Pale-olive cock

S.S. or Sawyer's Swedish Nymph
Plate 17

This is a Frank Sawyer imitation of the pond olive and claret dun nymphs and is of most use between June and August.

Hook: 10–14
Thread: None
Tail: Tips of the body fibres
Body: Dark-grey goose herls and red copper wire wound and tied in the same manner as for the GREYGOOSE NYMPH.

The Stalking Fly

This method and style of tying a floating fly was devised by Hal Janssen, of the United States. The fly was so named because it is used for selective fish. The USD series of Goddard and Clarke is similar, but Janssen offered alternative designs. Many dun and spinner imitations can be tied in these styles.

The basic fly used a down-eyed hook with a parachute hackle tied on top of the shank with split hackle-tip wings tied on the underside. The parachute hackle is wound round the stalks of the wings. The fly floats upside down with the point and wings uppermost and the hackle below the body. One alternative and more durable method of winging is to use hackle-fibre wings. The second option is a no-hackle dressing which uses three bunches of hackle fibres. One bunch acts as an upright wing; the other two are divided as legs on either side of the body in a V-shape.

Stank Hen Spider

A Scottish Border wet fly. Taff Price suggests that it is a pale watery copy.

Hook: 14
Body: Well-waxed yellow silk
Hackle: Light blue-dun hen

Stickfly

These are caddis larva imitations which should be fished slowly along lake and reservoir beds. In addition to those in the SEDGE section and under WORMFLY, I have included two dressings which are representative of the many similar dressings available.

Stickfly *(Brian Harris)*
Plate 30

Hook: Long shank 10–12
Thread: Buff
Body: An underbody of lead wire (0.37 mm) wound over a varnished shank, coated with varnish and allowed to dry
Overbody: Natural brown condor herl or a substitute of dyed turkey-tail
Rib: Fine oval gold tinsel
Head: Amber poly-dubbing or chopped wool or dyed rabbit fur
Hackle: Two turns of short-fibred medium red cock

Brian Harris suggests that it should also be fished unleaded, especially in the smaller sizes.

Stickfly *(Dave Collyer)*

Hook: Long shank 8–10
Thread: Black or dark olive
Body: Dark cock-pheasant tail fibres and a few olive swan herls wound together over a varnished shank.
Rib: Copper, silver or gold tinsel, on their own or in combination, wound the opposite way to the body herls and then ribbed with green peacock herl
Thorax: Yellow or off-white floss silk
Hackle: Sparsely tied pale ginger cock
Head: Varnished tying thread

Stimulator
Plate 24

This is a Randall Kaufmann imitation of a large adult stonefly. It also works for sedges and as an attractor on fast water. It rocks easily in any breeze and the blur of colour and moving light pattern are the feeding triggers.

Hook: 6–16
Thread: To match the body
Tail: Light deer body hair
Body: Orange, green or yellow poly palmered with a ginger cock
Thorax: Orange-dyed rabbit's fur
Wing: Light deer hair at an angle over the body

STONEFLIES (Plecoptera)

Of the thirty or more members of the Plecoptera Order, the following stoneflies are of interest to trout and grayling fishers: large and medium stonefly, February red, yellow sally, small yellow sally, willow fly, early brown, small brown and needle-flies.

As their name implies, these species prefer rivers with a stony or gravel bed and many of these are upland rather than lowland rivers. As stillwater flies their value is minimal, but of their great importance as a source of river trout and grayling food there is no doubt. On some rivers stonefly nymphs and adults take on the same significance as the upwinged flies on other rivers. The nymph or creeper is so called because the nymphs actually crawl out of the river before the adult fly emerges. The natural nymph is found only close to the river-bed, never rising to the surface to hatch as do the ephemeropteran nymphs. The imitation should therefore be fished deep, where it gets the best results.

Nymphs crawling to the shore to emerge may well be caught up by the current and find themselves in midwater. When the adults are about one is much more likely to catch a fish on a nymph imitation fished nearer the surface. The nymphs are both carnivorous and herbivorous and will often eat ephemeropteran nymphs, which are generally smaller than stonefly nymphs. In addition to the difference in size, the stonefly nymphs have only two tails, whereas the ephemeropterans have three.

The length of the adult stage varies from species to species, but it can extend from two or three days to a similar number of weeks. The adults have four hard, shiny wings which are long and narrow and which lie flat over the body at rest. The wings are frequently longer than the body in the females; the wings of the males are usually much shorter. The female adult returns to the water after mating to lay her eggs. With the exception of those detailed below, members of the Order are considered under their own names elsewhere.

LARGE STONEFLY (Perlodes microcephala)

The adults appear in April and May and are fairly common throughout the country. They are large, with the female adults 16–23 mm and the male 12–18 mm. They have mottled brown wings with a wingspan of about 50 mm (2 inches). The nymphs are correspondingly large, up to 28 mm.

LARGE STONEFLY (Perla bipuncta)

The largest of the stoneflies, this is common except in the south and east. The adults appear between May and June and range in size between 16 mm and 24 mm, with a wingspan often in excess of 35 mm. The nymph reaches 33 mm in length.

LARGE STONEFLY (Perla cephalotes)

A species similar to the one above. Together they are the largest stoneflies. Distribution is widespread. The adults are the same mottled brown colour and they appear in May and June.

MEDIUM STONEFLY (*Diura bicaudata*)

This is common in the localised areas of its distribution – the Lake District, West Wales and Scotland. Small stony streams and stony lake margins are its habitat. The adults are between 10 and 14 mm and are mottled brown and appear from April until June. The nymphs vary between 9 and 17 mm.

SMALL BROWNS (*Nemoura cinerea, Nemurella picteti*)

Similar to the early browns, but slightly slimmer and darker. The small browns prefer slow-moving water. They appear from February to September.

In addition to the patterns below, see also under PARTRIDGE AND ORANGE, LIGHT WOODCOCK, WINTER BROWN, and individual members of the Order.

Dark Creeper (*Taff Price*)

A nymph imitation.

Hook: Long shank 14
Thread: Brown
Body: Brown seal's fur
Rib: Yellow thread
Thorax: Dark hare's ear fur
Wing-case: Dark turkey fibres
Legs: Wing-case fibres turned beneath the body and trimmed

Stonefly Nymph (*Dave Whitlock*)

A North American pattern comes from one of that country's leading fly tyers.

Hook: 10–14
Thread: Orange
Tail: Dark-brown or black horsehair
Abdomen: A mixture of 25 per cent dark brown seal's fur, 25 per cent golden-brown rabbit or beaver fur, 25 per cent burnt-orange seal's fur, 25 per cent dark amber seal's fur

Rib: Fine gold wire
Thorax: As for the abdomen, but more pronounced over a lead-wire underbody
Wing-case: Dark brown turkey fibres
Throat hackle: Grizzle fibres dyed light brown

Brown Stonefly Nymph
(*Roger Fogg*)

This is a pattern weighted so that it fishes with the point facing upwards. It is excellent for getting down deep in those pools and runs where trout keep near the bottom.

Hook: 8–14
Thread: Brown
Body: Lead-foil strips tied on top of the shank. The remainder of the fly is dressed upside-down because of the way it is presented in the water. The body is one of various shades of brown seal's fur (from amber to chocolate-brown) building up at the thorax
Hackle: Palmered brown hen to match the body colour. The upper and lower fibres are trimmed away, leaving only the sides as legs. The top of the thorax is varnished to represent the wing-cases and to give added strength
Rib: Nylon monofilament (about 4 lb BS) over the body and hackle, or one strand of amber marabou floss silk

In the first edition of this book I resisted including the elaborate stonefly nymph patterns developed across the Atlantic. Their use, or at least the tying of them, is catching on here. They look realistic, but they are relatively difficult and time-consuming to construct (I hesitate to say 'tie'). Some of them are fairly rigid and are more like models than fishing flies. Because of their growing popularity I am including this excellent example from Shane Jones.

Shane's Stone
Plate 18

Hook: Tiemco nymph
Tail: Hackle stalks
Body: Natural latex (under), olive Flexi-body (over)
Rib: Yellow thread
Wing-cases: Olive Raffene
Legs: Brown partridge, burnt
Head: Two tiny gold beads
Thorax: Dirty yellow Hare-tron
Antennae: Hackle stalks

Big Bull Goldbead Stonefly

Although Theo Bakelaar suggests tying this on a 3X long shank hook size 2 to copy the largest North American stonefly nymphs it may also be tied smaller on sizes 8 or 10 for the more modest larger British and European species. Theo comments that he has often used it only as a last resort but that it has been the big trout that have fallen for it. After the body has been wound or dubbed and ribbed, tie in a length of Flexibody for the wing-case. Dub the first thoracic segment and tie in a goose biot leg at each side; tie in the wing-case over the first segment. Repeat to produce two or three segments.

Hook: Tiemco TMC 5263 size 2–10
Thread: Brown
Tail: Two widely spaced goose biots, each either side of a small butt of thread
Head: 5 mm gold bead
Body: Brown Flexibody or brown fur dubbing
Rib: Gold wire over the abdomen only
Thorax: Brown synthetic or natural dubbing in three segments
Legs: Three pairs of goose biots, each pair in front of a thorax segment
Wing-case: Brown Flexibody in three segments
Antennae: Wild boar fibres

Theo's Biot Stone
Plate 18

Theo Bakelaar ties different-coloured versions of this pattern (black, golden tan or cream) depending upon the colour of the river-bed and whether the water is dark or clear .

Hook: Tiemco TMC 2312 long shank, size 8–10
Thread: To match the body colour
Head: 4 mm gold bead
Tail, legs and antennae: Black or brown goose biots (two tails and antennae, four legs)
Abdomen: Dyed rabbit or synthetic dubbing
Rib: Oval gold on the cream version only
Thorax: Black rabbit's fur, or dark hare's ear for the golden tan and cream versions
Wing-case: Black or brown Flexibody

Streamers

These lures of North American origin became popular with the steady growth of reservoir trout fishing in the UK. The winging material is the saddle hackle of domestic and game-cocks, both natural and (more frequently) dyed. Some patterns have herl or hair overwings in addition to the whole-feather wings. The wing sometimes becomes caught up under the hook-bend during casting, so the lure is not fished effectively. This is one reason for the development of bucktail and marabou as winging materials.

Two feathers are tied back to back at the shoulder to extend beyond the bend of the hook. Four feather-wings are often an improvement on two. They are tied by stripping away the soft flue at the base and doubling back the stalk over itself to form the head. This makes a much more durable wing. In addition the stalk can be varnished or glued for greater strength.

Sturdy's Fancy
Plate 26

This Yorkshire grayling fly is best fished dry. Reg Righyni, author of *Grayling*, included this as one of his favourite flies, although he tied it with a close rib of crimson silk. He suggested that Sturdy evolved the pattern for evening fishing when spinners were on the water, and therefore the red glint suggested by the rib is not out of place. I rate the parachute version, with Terry's Terror, as my first-choice fancy dry fly for when no naturals are on the water. I have also caught scores of trout with it.

Hook: 14–20
Tag: Red wool
Body: Peacock herl
Hackle: White cock or hen at the shoulder or in parachute style

Sunk Spinner
Plate 21

The medium olive, large and small dark olives and iron blue female spinners all return to lay their eggs under the surface. Trout often feed upon these even when duns or the spinners of other species are on the surface. If fish are feeding and the usual floating patterns and nymphs fail, then a more specialised imitation may be required. This imitation, which should be fished upstream in a straight drift, was devised by Neil Patterson.

Hook: 12–16
Thread: Crimson
Tail and rib: Two hare's whiskers or white horsehair
Underbody: Dark-red enamel copper wire with a built-up thorax
Overbody: Flattened nylon mono-filament (6 lb BS) ribbed with one hare's whisker
Thorax: Cock pheasant tail fibres
Wing: Two turns of badger hackle trimmed above and below the hook to represent the spent wing. The thorax fibres are doubled and redoubled over the hackle to build up the thorax. A dab of varnish at the base of the tail keeps the two hairs well apart

Sunk Spinner
(*Charles Jardine*)
Plate 21

Hook: 16–20
Thread: Hot-orange
Tail: Two Microfibetts or nylon paint-brush fibres
Body: Pale yellow Antron/hare mix
Wing: Pearlescent Mylar tinsel laid as wing pads
Hackle: Smoky pale-blue dun wound over the thorax and clipped top and bottom

Super Grizzly

This is a John Goddard pattern for a general representation of many of the upwinged duns.

Hook: Fine wire 14–16
Thread: Hot orange
Tail: Pale red dun cock, or muskrat whiskers (for placid waters)
Body: Three heron herls
Hackle: One each grizzle and red cock tied in back to back

Super Grizzly Emerger
Plate 29

John Goddard has adapted his earlier pattern into an emerger imitation for the smaller species. He describes it as 'exceptionally killing'.

Hook: 18
Thread: Purple
Tail: Bunch of pale gold Krystal Flash fibres two-thirds of the body length
Body: Three or four dark grey heron wing herls
Hackle: One grizzle and one rusty dun cock, short-fibred, wound together

Sweeney Todd

This successful and popular lure was devised by Richard Walker and Peter Thomas. The former once wrote that if he had to be limited to just one stillwater fly, this would be it. An extra-long wing about twice the hook length is one variation. This is not a hindrance to hooking, as

Richard Walker points out that the fluorescent wool at the shoulder seems to be the trouts' aiming point. Other variations have been devised. See under NOBBLERS.

Hook: Long shank 6–14
Thread: Black
Body: Black floss
Rib: Flat silver tinsel
Throat: Two or three turns of fluorescent neon-magenta wool tied behind the wing roots
Wing: Black squirrel-tail for the smaller sizes, black bucktail for the larger
Beard hackle: Crimson hackle-fibres

Sweeney Viva
Plate 1

The Sweeney Viva and the White Sweeney Viva are hybrids created by Les Walker of Morpeth. They are useful in that they give a trout two target points on the lure. They are normally fished on a sinking or neutral-density line and allowed to bounce along the bottom using a retrieve of 60 cm pulls for the best results. The white variant is useful in brighter conditions. As with all marabou wings, the wings can be strengthened and given added attraction by including two pearl Crystal Hairs.

Hook: Long shank 10–12 or standard 10 for the mini-lure
Thread: Black or brown
Tail: Fluorescent GloBrite No.11 green wool
Body: Black chenille ribbed with oval silver Lurex (silver cord on the small size)
Thorax: Fluorescent scarlet or neon-magenta chenille or wool (GloBrite No. 4 or No. 1)
Wing: Black marabou
Throat hackle: Scarlet or magenta feather fibres (optional)
Head: Black

Tadpole
Plate 2

A lure devised by John Wadham but popularised by Gordon Fraser. The black

version looks like a tadpole. In Gordon Fraser's words, it is 'A gentleman's version of the Dog Nobbler'. Black or white versions are best early in the season, with orange or yellow dressings more useful as the season progresses. Other colours and fluorescent versions should not be ruled out. An all-black version with a fluorescent green butt is a good stand-by lure. Leaded patterns will catch most fish during the early season. Peter Cockwill comments that the tail should be long and the hook a short-shank to get the right action with a fast figure-of-eight retrieve. A very successful variant is with body of variagated chenille of black and fluorescent green and a black tail also works well on a floating line and slow retrieve.

Hook: Wide-gape 6–12
Thread: To suit the body colour
Tail: Generous plume of black marabou or Arctic fox
Body: Black chenille, with optional underbody of fine lead wire
Hackle (optional): Three turns of black hen

The following green version of Peter Cockwill's has won him many small fishery competitions. In other circumstances it takes the name of an Olive Woolly Bugger. Another variation includes a few strands of Krystalflash in the tail.

Hook: Partridge Stronghold 10
Tail: Olive marabou
Body: Olive chenille over a lead wire underbody
Hackle: Palmered olive cock

TADPOLES

In May many lake margins and shallows are black with newly hatched tadpoles. What a banquet they represent! I have caught trout as fat as pigs, bulging with tadpoles after feeding on them to the exclusion of all else. Tadpoles rarely venture into deep water, and the artificial is best employed in the margins. See also BLACK AND PEACOCK SPIDER. Theo's Tadpole below is from Theo Bakelaar. The small weighted beads and marabou give the pattern a natural wiggling action.

Theo's Tadpole
Plate 1

Hook: Tiemco TMC 101, size 14–16
Thread: Black
Tail: Black marabou
Body: Black oval plastic bead
Eyes: Black-painted chain beads, finished with black nail polish

Tangler
Plate 20

I am grateful to Peter Deane for drawing my attention to the Tangler, a nymph devised by Denis Bailey. Peter does not spare his praise for the fly, describing its use on the middle Test as 'quite frightening', and how elsewhere, in other hands, its use had a self-imposed restriction, such was its success. It is an extremely non-descript fly but nevertheless definitely food-like to trout. For use on both rivers and stillwaters.

Hook: Wide gape size 8–12 for stillwater, 14–16 for rivers
Thread: Black or red Gossamer silk
Body: Rear four-fifths claret seal's fur, front fifth olive seal's fur
Rib: Gold wire (size 27) over the claret seal's fur only

Teal Series

A series of lake and sea-trout flies. The combination of colours is broadly similar to those in the Mallard, Grouse and Woodcock series, all of which differ in the main only in their wing material. Most of the patterns are listed in the MALLARD SERIES, but the exceptions are given below. The wing material is the black and white barred teal flank or breast feather. See also PETER ROSS.

Teal, Blue and Silver
Plate 7

This enjoys greater visibility than the others in the series, and for this reason is more effective in slightly coloured water. It succeeds as a small fry imitation and should be fished fast on the point.

Hook: 8–14
Tail: Golden pheasant tippets
Body: Flat silver tinsel
Rib: Fine silver wire
Wing: Teal flank feather
Hackle: Bright-blue cock

Teal and Claret

Tail: Golden pheasant tippets
Body: Claret seal's fur or dubbed wool
Rib: Gold tinsel
Wing: Teal breast feather
Hackle: Claret cock or hen

Teal and Green

Probably of early nineteenth-century Scottish origin, developed for the lochs. It is very likely taken for a sedge or shrimp, depending upon how it is fished. I have caught only two trout on this pattern. It seems to be one of those I pass over in favour of a more imitative dressing.

Tail: Golden pheasant tippets
Body: Green seal's fur or dubbed wool
Rib: Oval silver tinsel
Wing: Teal breast feather
Hackle: Light red hen

Teal and Green
(Stan Headley)
Plate 8

Not so much a Teal and Green with all its amendments, but in the absence of another name Stan sticks with the name of the original fly he started tinkering about with. It is his best utility pattern, particularly effective in smaller sizes when black midges are hatching, also doing well in larger sizes for fry-feeders, and as a searching pattern when correct pattern clues are non-existent. Stan includes this in his top ten patterns.

Hook: 10–14
Thread: Black
Tail: Bunch of hot-orange-dyed golden pheasant tippets
Body: Pearl Mylar over a layer of wet varnished thread, ribbed with silver wire or fine oval
Wing: Bunch of long grey partridge hackle fibres
Hackle: Longish black hen

Teal and Mixed

Tail: Golden pheasant tippets
Body: One-third each of yellow, red and blue seal's fur. Other combinations should as a rule have the darkest colour at the front and the lightest at the tail
Rib: Silver or gold tinsel
Wing: Teal breast
Hackle: Black cock or hen

Teeny Nymph   Plate 12

This rather unusual nymph pattern was devised in the 1960s for lake trout by Jim Teeny of Oregon. It has evolved many variants in different colours and has taken many World Fly Records for fresh and saltwater species. It is a simple pattern using only the cock pheasant centre tail fibres. It is bug-like and sinks quickly. I have used the smaller versions on rivers in an upstream sink-and-draw style, with some success. I understand that Jim Teeny has three patents on the design - an aspect of fly dressing I deplore. The fly illustrated was supplied by Peter Cockwill.

Hook: 10–16 (trout sizes)
Thread: To match the body colour
Body: Cock pheasant tail fibres
Legs: Two bunches of cock pheasant fibre tips; one at the head, the other half-way along the body

Terry's Terror   Plate 27

Devised by Dr Cecil Terry and Ernest Lock. It is said to represent all the olive duns and in its larger sizes a sedge. Terry himself was extremely vague about its purpose and very tongue-in-cheek about what it represented. Peter Deane rates it highly as a wet fly. In its smaller sizes I rate it almost second to none as a grayling fly. I wouldn't wish to be without one when grayling fishing. I tie mine with poly yarn tails.

Hook: 12–20
Tag: Mixed orange and yellow goat hair (or substitute) trimmed short
Body: One strand of peacock herl
Rib: Flat copper tinsel (omitted in the smallest sizes)
Hackle: Red cock (optionally with the lower fibres trimmed flat)

Terrors

Two tandem lures. The Blue Terror has a wing of two blue cock hackles flanked by strips of grey drake fibres.

Red Terror

Rear hook
Tail: Red fluorescent wool
Body: Flat silver tinsel
Rib: Silver wire

Front hook
Body and rib: As for the rear
Wing: Two dyed red hackles tied back to back and flanked by swan herls dyed red with strands of green peacock herl over

Thorax Fly

Vincent Marinaro devised this variation to the dry fly which ensures that the fly's body stays supported clear of the surface. It also utilises two widely spaced hackles wound at opposite angles around the wings in an X towards the middle of the shank. Marinaro was also the first to advocate the use of widely spread tail fibres although he maintained that he tied his flies in such a way that the tails rarely touched the water. This involved using two different hackle sizes with the smaller being tied so that its fibres were at the front on the underside of the body. This gave the fly a forward tilt. Marinaro also believed that the thorax tied in front of the hackle is a key feature. He maintained that the clear view of the wing, more naturally in the middle of the shank, was the most important trigger to the rise. His Thorax Fly certainly gives a fish a clear view of the wing and a good imitation of the light pattern of the natural dun's six legs. Rarely today are Thorax Flies tied to Marinaro's design but others have evolved from this fine concept.

Thorax Hackle Dun (Dark Olive) *(Mike Weaver)* Plate 25

Mike Weaver's development of the hackled dun is very similar to my own preferred dun imitation which differs only by the inclusion of widely spaced Microfibett tails. The hackle is wound about one-third of the shank away from the eye and the body dubbing is continued in front of the hackle. It is inspired by Marinaro's original design but omits the wing and includes only a single hackle. The size and colour of the materials can be varied to match the natural.

Hook: 16
Tail: Slate-grey cock fibres
Body: Dubbed dark olive fur or substitute, partly wound in front of the hackle
Hackle: Slate-grey cock

Tiddler

Les Walker devised this small fry pattern for the fry-bashing period of late season. It can be left unweighted or given five turns of fine lead wire at the front of the shank. It is fished on a neutral-density or slow-sink line with a medium retrieval rate with pauses. As pearly Mylar is translucent, underbodies in GloBrite fluorescent wools Nos 9, 11 and 16 may be used to more mimic the various fry colours more closely.

Hook: Long shank 10–12 or standard 10
Thread: Black or brown
Tail and back: Single horizontal bronze mallard (minnow) or barred teal feather (other fry)
Underbody: Lemon or white wool
Body: Pearly Mylar tube 2–3 mm diameter ribbed with silver wire over the back
Head: Large black with painted eyes

Tinheads

These are lures and flies tied on hooks which are sold with a metal shot soldered at the head. Any lure or nymph pattern can be tied on such a hook thereby giving it the prefix Tinhead.

Tom's Terror Plate 5

This pattern was devised by Tom Saville. He describes it as an excellent lure for rainbow trout when they are fry-feeding. He also comments that the lure is selling well – a sure sign that it is catching fish!

Hook: 8 (Mustad 9672 is recommended)
Body: Silver Mylar tubing
Wing: Black bucktail with orange over
Throat hackle: White bucktail
Eyes: Thin slice of white electric flex with the wire removed, stuck on to the wet varnish.

Traffic Lights

A number of tandem lures have been devised to be fished deep behind a boat on some of the Midlands reservoirs. This one is recommended for Rutland. It was developed by Tom Saville. The reason for its name is self-evident.

Hooks: Long shank 6 (Mustad 9672 recommended)

Front hook
Tail: Arc-chrome fluorescent wool

Body and rib: As for the rear
Wing: As for the rear
Cheeks: Neon-magenta fluorescent wool
Throat hackle: Black

Rear hook
Tail: Signal-green DRF wool
Body: Medium black chenille
Rib: Oval silver tinsel
Wing: Black marabou

Train's Terrors

Two tandem lures devised by David Train. The Olive Terror is a useful perch-fry imitation. Its dressing is as below but with black hackle wings substituted for olive.

Rear hook
Tail: Golden pheasant tippets in a fan shape
Body: Silver tinsel
Rib: Silver wire

Front hook
Body and rib: As for rear
Hackle: Hen dyed red
Wing: Three or four peacock sword herls flanked by two black cock hackles extending to the rear of the rear hook

Treacle Parkin

A northern variation of the Red Tag. It is fished both wet and dry, but is probably better as a dry fly than a wet. It is a good trout fly but it is as a grayling fly that it excels. Norman Roose, the late president of the Grayling Society, tied it with a tag of fluorescent arc-chrome wool.

Hook: 14–18
Tag: Orange or yellow wool
Body: Peacock herl
Hackle: Natural red-game

Tup's Indispensable

R. S. Austin tied this classic fly in 1900, but it was left to G. E. M. Skues to put a name to the dressing. The dubbing material was kept a secret until 1934, twenty years after Austin's death, so that he, and later his daughter, had the monopoly in the supply of the correct dressing. Many imitations and substitutes have been used in the absence of the original material, some hideously corrupting the fly.

The unlikely dubbing material was first used by Alexander Mackintosh and publicised in his book, *The Driffield Angler*, 1806. Mackintosh's Greendrake pattern had this instruction: 'Take a little fine wool from the ram's testicles, which is a beautiful dusty yellow.' Austin tied the Tup's to represent the Red Spinner, the female spinner of some of the olives. Today it is probably fished as a copy of a pale watery spinner and a small spurwing spinner. Nymph patterns and many variations have been developed. The original dressing is:

Hook: 16
Thread: Yellow
Tail: Yellow-spangled lightish blue cock hackle fibres
Body: Mixed white fur from a ram's testicle, lemon-coloured fur from a spaniel, cream seal's fur and a small amount of yellow mohair. The last item was later replaced by crimson seal's fur on Skues' suggestion. A small tip of tying thread is exposed at the rear
Hackle: Yellow-spangled lightish-blue cock

Tup's *(Taff Price)* — Plate 26

A dressing using modern substitutes.

Hook: 12–16
Tail: Honey-dun cock fibres
Body: Rear-half, yellow floss silk with a thorax of a mixture of yellow, red and honey-coloured seal's fur
Hackle: Honey-dun cock

Dark Tup's *(Dave Collyer)*

Hook: 10–16
Tail: Fibres of the hackle used
Body: Rear two-thirds, lemon floss silk; front one-third, mole's fur
Hackle: Stiff honey-dun cock or light ginger cock

Turkey Green/Yellow

These two patterns came to me with Steve Parton's comment that 'These flies could be described as reduced versions of an Invicta and Green Peter. Be that as it may, there is no doubt that they work.' I believe that it is because they do have the look of an Invicta or Green Peter that they do work so well. If any fly can match the trout-catching capability of these two, then it is a real winner. Both are hatching-sedge imitations and are best fished semi-submerged in the surface film or just below it. They represent a number of sedges, but Steve recommends that their time on Rutland comes in late June.

Hook: 10–14
Thread: Black
Body: Naples yellow or Green Highlander seal's fur with a palmered red-game hackle
Rib: Oval gold tinsel through the hackle
Wing: Oak turkey or owl substitute
Throat hackle: Red-game

Twitchett Nymph   *Plate 16*

A variation of the Pheasant Tail Nymph devised by Alan Pearson. He advises that it should be fished 'as a single nymph to observed cruising trout; otherwise as a point fly on a team comprising two buzzer patterns in addition, or as a point fly on a team of wet flies for loch-style fishing'.

Hook: Long shank 12
Tail: Signal-green fluorescent wool or floss, teased out and not less than 6 mm (¼ inch) long
Body: Cock pheasant centre tail fibres
Rib (optional): Copper wire
Thorax: Fine lead or copper wire overlaid with pale grey rabbit's fur. This should be tied for about half the body-length, slim and barely thicker than the body
Hackle: Rear-sloping ginger cock as a collar

USD Paraduns

A series of upside-down floating patterns (together with the USD POLY-SPINN-ERS) devised jointly by Brian Clarke and John Goddard. In 1980 they were claimed as relatively new products of the continuing evolution of the British trout fly, but similar American and British dressings for duns had been around before Goddard and Clarke publicised their dressings. C. F. Walker's *Fly-Tying as an Art* of 1957 mentions and illustrates J. H. Stothert's Upside-downer which appears to be a USD Paradun by another name. Although the dressing is not given, the only variation seems to be that the wings are feather slips and not the hackle tips recommended by Goddard and Clarke.

The design of the USD Paradun is such that it floats upside-down (hence the name) with the hook point in the air. The parachute hackle is wound on the top of the shank, which ultimately becomes the underside. The hackle-tip wings are cut slightly wider and longer than standard wings and are tied on the opposite side of the shank to the hackle and given a pronounced outward curve. Almost any dry fly can be tied in such a manner. The dressing, which offers a realistic light pattern, keeps the body off the surface and offers a clear view of the wings, is a considerable improvement on the stand-ard dressing of most flies, but it is difficult to tie and not as durable. Most fish do not need a USD pattern to tempt them, but it may just be the answer for the occasional difficult fish.

USD Para-Blue Winged Olive

Hook: 12–16
Thread: Orange
Tail: Three olive muskrat or mink whisk-ers; or a bunch of the hackle fibres
Body: Natural heron herl
Wing: Dark-grey or dark blue-dun hackle tips
Hackle: Rusty-dun cock

USD Para-Olive

Hook: 12–16
Thread: Brown
Tail: Two olive muskrat or mink whiskers; or a bunch of the hackle fibres
Body: Olive heron herl
Wing: Pale blue-dun hackle tips
Hackle: Olive cock

USD Para-Pale Watery

Hook: 16
Thread: Yellow
Tail: Pale-honey hackle fibres
Body: Greyish goose primary herls
Wing: Cream or pale blue-dun hackle tips
Hackle: Rusty-dun cock

USD Poly-Spinners

These patterns are tied upside-down on keel hooks. The parachute hackle is tied on top of the body on the bend nearest the eye and the wings are tied in the same position. Except on the larger Mayfly spinners, the wings are of fine-gauge clear polythene cut with a wing-cutter. The polythene should be lightly pierced many times with a thick but sharp needle. The wings are tied in the spent position. I find the pattern more fiddly to tie and no improvement on the much simpler Poly Wing Spinner.

USD Poly-Orange Spinner

Hook: Keel 14
Thread: Orange
Tail: Three muskrat or mink whiskers coloured brown
Body: Orange seal's fur
Rib: DFM orange floss
Wing: Polythene (see introduction)
Hackle: Bright ginger cock

Usual
Plate 25

This much-praised dry fly was devised by North American Fran Betters. In effect it is an emerger representing a dun still attached to its nymphal shuck. The snow-shoe hare foot hair is highly water-repellent. It is also crinkly, reflective and translucent – it makes an excellent material for a floating fly.

Hook: 12–18
Thread: To match the body colour
Tail: A small bunch of hair from the foot of a snowshoe hare (remove the underfur for the body)
Body: Dubbed underfur from the above, or sparkle-blend dubbing
Wing: A single upright wing of the same material as the tail

Variants

This is the term applied to dry flies which have much longer-fibred hackles than the standard dressings. The flies may be existing named paterns or nondescript general floating flies. Dr Baigent, of Northallerton, brought them into prominence with his series of Variants around the turn of the century, and other patterns have been added since. Winged patterns have the wings tied fairly small and thin, and sloping forward slightly over the eye.

Baigent's Brown

Hook: 14
Body: Yellow floss
Wing: Hen pheasant wing
Hackle: Long-fibred stiff furnace cock

Baigent's Black

Hook: 14
Body: Black floss
Rib: Peacock herl
Hackle: Long-fibred stiff black cock

Cream Variant (Art Flick)

Hook: 12–14
Thread: Yellow
Tail: Long stiff cream cock fibres

Body: Stripped cream hackle stalk soaked in water before winding
Hackle: Long-fibred cream cock

Gold Variant *(John Veniard)*

Hook: 14
Body: Flat gold tinsel
Wing: Starling wing
Hackle: Long-fibred medium blue-dun cock

V.G.B. (Vince Gwilym's Bastard) *Plate 3*

This pattern emerged from a tying session with the Welsh Youth Team prior to a match. The team used the fly to great effect, winning the match by a large margin. It has proven itself repeatedly ever since. It is a cross between an Alexandra and a Viva. The original green material was the fluorescent laces used on trainers. Lureflash Antron Bodywool is a suitable replacement.

Hook: Double 10
Tail and underbody: Fluorescent green
Overbody: Pearl Lureflash
Wing: Six to eight peacock sword herls
Topping: Fluorescent green
Cheeks: Jungle cock or substitute
Head: Red, black or orange

Viva *Plate 2*

An excellent lure devised by Victor Furse in the early 1970s. It has survived to be one of the most successful lures of all time. It is particularly useful during the first two months of the season. On a number of occasions I have seen anglers using all-black lures without success when a Viva has been fished with great effect. The fluorescent green tag is vital. The original dressing had a mixed wing of black marabou and goat hair but now the later is often omitted. A streamer version is also tied. Also see SWEENEY VIVA.

Hook: Long shank 6–10

Thread: Black
Tag: Green fluorescent wool (tied as a tag or as a large tip)
Body: Black chenille
Rib: Silver tinsel
Wing: Four black cock hackles or black marabou plume
Throat hackle: Black cock

Mosaic Viva *Plate 2*

This Viva variation is proving very popular across the country. The reflective multi-coloured wing is a Lureflash product. Falkirk angler Malcolm Gibb advises that he finds it fishes best on an intermediate line fished about a foot down, retrieved in short pulls. It also proved popular with a 14 lb 14 oz rainbow trout for him. Stephen Gross who devised the fly finds it particularly effective fished very slowly during a buzzer hatch.

Hook: Long shank 6–10
Thread: Black
Tag: Fluorescent green Lureflash Antron Bodywool
Body: Black chenille ribbed with twisted blue Lureflash Mobile
Wing: Lureflash Mobile

Waggler or Waggy Lures *Plate 4*

I am uncertain who was responsible for the inclusion of a coloured flexible rubber tail in a lure. It falls very much on the borders of the accepted concept of a fly. Any lure can be adapted by the addition of an appropriately coloured tail. Perhaps the most effective are those with some manner of weighted head. The Muddler-headed versions also look very appealing. The tails are translucent, some almost transparent and this provides another characteristic difficult to achieve in the standard tying of lures. The Lureflash Twister Tails are highly flexible and can be fished at very slow speeds.

Watchets

These old and reliable northern wet flies are typical of the soft-hackled spider-type of flies associated with this part of the country. They imitate mainly the emerging nymphs and drowned duns and spinners of the iron blue. Most traditional wet flies used by northern anglers are more than a hundred years old, even two hundred, and modern materials and fly-tying styles have failed to improve these most basic imitations. Any of the variations below will prove a dependable pattern for trout and grayling on northern streams.

Dark Watchet

(Edmonds and Lee)   *Plate 32*

Hook: 14
Body: Orange and purple tying silks twisted together and thinly dubbed with mole's fur
Hackle: Jackdaw throat feather

Light Watchet   *Plate 32*

Hook: 12–16
Body: Straw-coloured silk
Hackle: Golden plover or pale starling

Little Dark Watchet

An iron blue imitation.

Hook: 14–16
Body: Orange and purple tying silks twisted together and dubbed with water-rat's fur
Hackle: A feather from the outside of a coot's wing
Head: Orange tying silk

Water Cricket

This small aquatic beetle is more common on lakes than on rivers. The adult has a dark brown body with two orange stripes down the back. The underside is orange.

Hook: 12–14
Body: Orange floss
Back: Any dark brown feather fibres
Hackle: Brown partridge

Waterhen and Red

A Scottish wet fly. The first version is from W. H. Lawrie, who sums up the pattern as 'reliable'; the second pattern is listed by Taff Price in *Rough Stream Trout Flies*.

Hook: 14
Tail: Golden pheasant tippets
Body: Red wool
Rib: Gold or silver fine tinsel or wire
Wing: Waterhen wing
Hackle: Natural red hen

Or
Body: Red silk
Hackle: The spoon-shaped feather of a waterhen (moorhen) wing

WATER-LOUSE

The water-louse is prolific throughout the country on stillwaters and to a lesser extent on rivers. It is usually found on decaying vegetable matter in shallow water, always near the bottom, or on stakes going into the water. The adults reach about 15 mm in length and move slowly. The artificial should be fished near the bottom in a similar fashion. The water-louse is also known as the hog-louse or water slater. A March Brown is a suitable imitation.

Water-Louse *(Peter Gathercole)*

Hook: 10–12
Body: Grey rabbit's fur with a short-fibred brown partridge hackle laid over the back and ribbed with silver wire
Back: Grey-brown feather fibres
Tail: A few back fibres sticking out as a tail
Antennae (optional): Two brown feather fibres

Water Tiger

A pattern devised by Dave Collyer to imitate the great diving beetle, a largish aquatic beetle up to 30 mm long which inhabits the shallower areas of lakes and reservoirs. It rises periodically to the surface to take air. It is sufficiently aggressive even to attack small fish. Aquatic beetles often feature in trout autopsies, but few patterns are tied specifically to represent them. Terrestrial beetle patterns often work when fished near the lakebed.

Hook: Long shank 8–10
Tail: Speckled turkey-tail fibres or condor herl dyed sepia
Body: As tail
Rib: Copper wire
Thorax: Yellowish-olive seal's fur or wool
Wing-case: Body fibres
Hackle: Two bunches of brown partridge feather fibres, one either side of the head and rear-slanting just beyond the thorax

The second pattern of Water Tiger is that devised and tied by Sid Knight. It was tied originally on a long-shank 10 hook, but most anglers prefer the standard-length hook. Additional weight to enable the fly to be fished deep down is optional.

Hook: 10
Thread: Brown
Tail: Natural red cock hackle fibres
Body: Green peacock herl tapering to the rear
Rib: Brown silk
Thorax: Green peacock herl built up
Wing-case: Mottled-brown feather fibres
Hackle: Natural red cock

Waterwalker

This is a style of tying a dun imitation devised by Frank Johnson of Montana. The resulting fly is supported by two hackles, each wrapped round the base of the split wings which are in a wide V. This results in the lower fibres being widely spaced to give an accurate light pattern. The body is well supported off the surface in the manner of the natural.

Hook: 12–16
Thread: To match the body colour
Tail: Cock fibres tied in second
Body: Fine dubbing wound in fourth
Rib (optional): Thread or fine wire tied in fifth
Wing: Two bunches of cock fibres, elk hair or poly yarn in a wide V, tied in first
Hackles: Two cock hackles tied in third, and wound round the wing base sixth – one wound clockwise, the other counterclockwise, 3–5 turns

Watson's Fancy

An old Scottish loch and sea-trout pattern that is still popular in its home country.

Hook: 8–14
Tail: Small golden-pheasant crest feather
Body: Rear half, red seal's fur; front half, black seal's fur
Rib: Silver tinsel
Wing: Crow wing with a small jungle cock eye at either side
Hackle: Black hen

Wee Mosquito   (Neil Patterson)

This is an unusual design of fly with its wing shape, and its legs on top of the body. Neil Patterson of Funneldun fame designed it. It doesn't matter that the legs are on top of the body as it is claimed that when the artificial lands it doesn't often land the 'right' way up. I haven't fished this myself, but I know other respected fly fishers who have high praise for the fly as a river pattern.

Hook: Drennan fine wire 16–18
Thread: Fawn silk
Body: Hare's body fur mixed (10:1) with red seal's fur, taken just round the bend
Rib: Fine silver wire
Wing: Bunched treal trimmed to size, about the body length, tied spent and angled to the rear
Legs: Six bunched brown mallard fibres diagonally over the body extending slightly longer than the shank

Wee Silver Nymph
Plate 17

Franz Grimley is a Scottish angler of high repute. This is his nymph pattern which he describes as 'simple but deadly'. He fishes it on rivers on an 18-foot leader. It is also his first choice fly for daytime fishing on the Spey for sea trout.

Hook: 14–16
Thread: Black
Underbody: A small wedge of lead tapering to the rear
Body: Touching turns of silver oval
Hackle: One turn of a soft black hen hackle or starling

Welshman's Button

The name Welshman's Button has been applied to a species of sedge and to a beetle. The beetle was the first to take the name in a book, *The Angler's Museum* by Thomas Shirley in 1784, but because Halford and Lunn applied the name to two species of sedge, with much greater publicity, the name has become more associated with the sedge. A pattern for the sedge is given in the SEDGE section.

Westward Bug
Plate 16

Devised by Bob Church specifically to take the large Avington trout, this pattern has done well also on other small, well stocked fisheries. The weighted underbody is important as it allows the bug to sink rapidly. Takes often come on the drop.

Hook: Standard or long shank 8–12
Thread: Black
Body: Brown marabou fibres tied fat and wound over lead strips or wire underbody
Rib: Orange floss
Back: Shellback-brown or grey feather fibres
Throat hackle: Honey-coloured cock

Whisky Fly

This excellent lure was devised by Albert Willock for Hanningfield reservoir, but it has subsequently caught many big rainbow trout across the country. It is best fished fast near the surface during the second half of the season, although it seems to catch fish at a variety of speeds and depths. It is a useful pattern for water affected by algae or when daphnia are in evidence.

Hook: Long shank 6–10
Thread: Red or scarlet fluorescent floss
Body: Flat silver or gold Mylar or Lurex with a butt of scarlet or red fluorescent floss
Rib: Scarlet or red fluorescent floss. The whole body is clear varnished
Wing: Hot-orange calf-tail tied as long as the body
Throat hackle: Hot-orange cock
Head: Longish head of fluorescent tying thread

Various versions have been tied with one or more of the following combinations included: Jungle-cock cheeks; an orange floss body ribbed with gold tinsel and covered with polythene strip; or wings of four hot-orange cock hackles tied back to back. See also Whisky Muddler under MUDDLERS. It is a measure of the pattern's success that so many variations have developed.

White Grizzly
Plate 27

This is a useful pale watery imitation from Michael Leighton. Like many Border patterns it carries two hackles; first, to float well on the riffles and, second, to produce the impression of a wing by the variegated effect of the grizzle hackle.

Hook: 14–16
Thread: Orange
Tail: Honey cock fibres
Body: Pale honey-coloured white rabbit's fur
Rib: Closely wound golden yellow multistrand
Hackles: Grizzle cock with a pale badger wound behind, through and in front

White Lures

There are many different white lure dressings in addition to the white lures known by other names. Three of the better-known patterns are given. See also under MARABOU-WINGED LURES for Steve Parton's unnamed white lure.

White Maribou *(Bob Carnill)*

A useful all-season lure. Bob Carnill fishes it during spring on a fast-sink shooting-head and in the summer and autumn on a floating line. He suggests experiment with the rate of retrieve to determine what the trout prefer. Not all lures lend themselves to this approach, but the White Marabou is particularly suited, being both lightly built and highly mobile. Any retrieve from a figure-of-eight to a fast strip can be employed with confidence.

Hook: Long shank 4–10
Thread: Waxed red
Tail: Fluorescent white Bri-nylon baby wool
Body: Fluorescent white chenille
Rib: Flat silver tinsel
Beard hackle: Scarlet cock fibres
Wing: White marabou extending just beyond the tail

White Marabou Tandem
(Bob Church and M. Nicholls)

Hooks: Long shank 6–10
Thread: Black

Front hook
Body: As for rear
Wing: A large plume of white marabou
Head: Natural deer hair spun and clipped in Muddler style and trimmed to a dome shape

Rear hook
Tail and body: White Sirdar Baby wool

White Nymphs

I have selected two white nymph imitations. A fly tyer with a little imagination could easily develop other variants. See also nymph patterns under CAENIS.

White Nymph *(Roger Fogg)*

Roger Fogg suggests that this pattern should be fished no more than a foot below the surface. Because of its translucency, it is also a suitable phantom midge pupa imitation. It seems to attract more brown trout than rainbows. Roger writes: 'This is an extremely killing pattern. I gave up using it in 1983 because it caught too many fish too easily!'

Hook: 10–14
Thread: White
Tail: White rabbit guard hairs or white feather fibres
Body: Underbody of silver Mylar or tinsel with an overbody of loosely dubbed white rabbit's fur
Rib: Fine oval silver tinsel
Hackle: Two turns of small white hen

White Nymph *(Wallace)*

A Scottish pattern which originated on Loch Leven.

Hook: 10–12
Thread: White
Tail: White wool
Body: White wool
Rib: Silver tinsel
Thorax: Hen pheasant centre tail fibres
Beard hackle: Hot-orange

Whitlock Matuka Sculpin
Plate 5

During the 1960s and '70s Dave Whitlock pursued large brown trout all over North America. This is the pattern he chooses to winkle out the big ones. He fishes it on a two- or three-foot leader with a Hi-D sink-tip or full sinking line. It accounted for his largest river brown of 22 ½ lb, and almost forty fish over ten pounds. I know what it can do on the Yorkshire dales rivers with a split shot a few inches above it on the leader. Colour to suit local small fish. Also see under SCULPINS.

Hook: Partridge low-water salmon hook, size 5/0-8
Thread: Cream or yellow Danville's single strand floss
Cement: Dave's Flexament
Body-head foundation: Mason hard nylon, the size of the hook wire
Weight: Ten to twenty turns of lead wire, the diameter of the hook wire
Rib: Medium brass wire over the Matuka feathers
Belly: Cream coarse dubbing
Back and tail: Cree neck hackles, natural and dyed olive, four of each colour
Gills: Antron red dubbing
Head: Mule or white deer hair, cream, with natural grey, black, olive and gold markings after trimming to shape, with some fibres longer over the back
Eyes: Small brown and black plastic eyes

Whitmore's Fancy

This is an excellent general dry fly tied by Harry Whitmore, and it has killed hundreds of trout on the rivers of the Yorkshire Dales and moors. On those rivers I would not wish to be without it.

Hook: 12–14
Thread: Red
Tail: Medium natural red cock fibres
Body: Bronze peacock herl
Rib: Red silk
Hackle: Medium natural red cock wound in Parachute style

Wickham's Fancy

This fly, probably devised in the 1880s, has obscure origins, with at least two Wickhams claiming to have invented it. G. E. M. Skues knew Dr T. C. Wickham and regarded him as the originator. The pattern can be fished wet or dry, the latter more commonly on rivers and the former on stillwaters, where it is best fished slowly in the surface film and is probably taken for a sedge pupa. The dry pattern has a reputation for working when trout and grayling are smutting and are refusing artificials of the natural smuts. Like many traditional stillwater patterns it can sometimes be improved by the addition of new synthetic materials.

Hook: 14–16
Thread: Brown
Tail: Guinea-fowl dyed reddish-brown, or ginger hackles
Body: Flat gold tinsel
Rib: Gold wire
Body hackle: Palmered ginger-red cock
Wing: Medium starling wings set upright and split for the floating dressing, or across the back in wet style for the wet fly
Hackle: Ginger-red cock

Olive Wickham's

As for the Wickham's Fancy, but with an olive cock hackle for the body and head hackle and tail fibres.

Pearly Wickham's Fancy

(Sid Knight)   Plate 8

Hook: Kamasan B170 size 12
Thread: Black
Tail: Fluorescent green wool
Body: Pearly Mobile Mother of Pearl
Body hackle: Medium natural red-brown cock
Rib: Silver wire

Wiggle Nymph

John Goddard has suggested this unusual and effective nymph dressing for some of the larger stillwater nymphs. The second half of the body wiggles seductively as the fly is retrieved. Damsel nymph patterns are particularly suited to this dressing as the natural damsel nymph moves with a pronounced wiggle. The rear hook is dressed with the tail of the fly and the entire bend is clipped off and discarded. The two parts are connected by threading fine fuse wire through the eye of the rear section and whipping it on to the bare shank of the front hook before dressing it.

Damsel Wiggle Nymph

(John Goddard) *Plate 12*

Hooks: Two straight-eyed standard 10–12
Thread: Brown
Tail: Three ginger-grizzle hackle tips
Body: Mixed golden-olive and brown seal's fur along the rear hook and on the rear half of the front hook.
Rib: Close rib of fine oval silver tinsel
Thorax: Rusty-brown seal's fur
Thorax cover: Mottled mid-brown feather fibres
Hackle: Brown partridge feather

Other general nymph patterns can be imitated by altering the materials.

Williams

Plate 7

Bob Carnill rates this his Williams Favourite variant extremely highly as a dropper pattern on stillwater. The reliable Williams Favourite has black hackle fibre tails and a black silk body.

Hook: 10–12
Thread: Black
Underbody: Fine lead wire
Body: Black seal's fur
Rib: Fine to medium oval silver tinsel
Hackle: Black hen, rather full

WILLOW FLY
(Leuctra geniculata)

One of the few common chalk-stream stoneflies. Elsewhere it is widely distributed, except in East Anglia. The nymphs prefer rivers with stony bottoms over a sandy base. The adults are slim flies of 7–10 mm long with brownish wings and two long antennae. They appear between August and November and are a useful late-season pattern. A few sources refer to them as appearing on stillwaters, but most list them exclusively as river flies.

For other suitable imitations, see BROWN OWL, NEEDLE-FLY and PARTRIDGE AND ORANGE .

Willow Fly *(Taff Price)*

Hook: 14
Thread: Orange
Body: Peacock herl dyed orange
Wing: Two small medium-grizzle hackles tied flat across the back
Hackle: Brown-dun cock

Winter Brown

A dressing to represent the early-season needle flies. This is a North Country wet version by T. E. Pritt that has changed little in a hundred years of use. Theakston called it the Early Brown and others have used the names Orange Woodcock or Light Woodcock.

Hook: 14
Thread: Orange
Body: Orange silk
Hackle: Inside of a woodcock feather
Head: One turn of peacock herl

Witches

A series of flies used mainly for grayling. They can be fished wet or dry. The original pattern was Rolt's Witch mentioned in H. A. Rolt's book *Grayling Fishing in South Country Streams* of 1901. Variants have been devised, all of which I can vouch for as grayling flies. Rolt was the first to weight flies with lead strips under the body material to get his patterns down to deep-lying grayling.

Rolt's Witch

Plate 20

Rolt described this as a 'glorified green insect'. He recommended a size 16 when grayling are smutting and difficult to catch.

Hook: 14–16
Tag: Red floss
Body: Green peacock herl
Rib: Gold wire
Hackle: Palmered honey-dun

The White Witch has a white floss tag and a palmered white cock over the body

Grayling Witch

A variant tied by Roger Woolley.

Hook: 14–16
Tag: Red floss
Body: Green peacock herl
Rib: Silver wire
Hackle: Palmered blue-dun cock

Wobble Worm   *Plate 23*

This is Peter Lapsley's answer to the problem of imitating the bloodworm or midge larva. It is effective because of the combination of weighted head and marabou herl tail which on the retrieve creates the wobble motion representative of the natural midge larva. It should be fished fairly close to the bottom and retrieved in short pulls.

Hook: 12–14 sedge hook
Thread: To match the body colour
Tail: Six strands of red, green or buff marabou between 12 and 25 mm (½ inch to 1 inch) long
Body: Underbody of Lurex (silver for the red version, gold for the green or buff) dubbed lightly with red, buff or green seal's fur
Rib: Silver or gold wire
Head: A split shot of appropriate size crimped on to the shank and painted or varnished red, green or buff as necessary

Wonderbug   *Plate 16*

A series of stillwater leaded bugs developed by Alan Pearson. In one season he caught 1,000 lb of brown and rainbow trout between 4 lb and 9 lb on the Wonderbug. It is designed to be fished deep in waters holding big fish. Normal nymph colours are used, plus a black-and-white version, all with a touch of scarlet (see below). Alan Pearson suggests that hook size should vary between a long-shank 6 down to a long-shank 16, with correspondingly less weight being used for the smaller sizes, or none at all. The body material should be seal's fur or a coarse-fibred substitute, and 5 per cent scarlet seal's fur should be mixed in to represent veining. The body and thorax should be of equal length. The example given below is also a good dragonfly nymph imitation.

Hook: Long shank 6
Underbody: Fine lead wire at the thorax only
Body and thorax: Dark-olive seal's fur mixed with 5 per cent scarlet seal's fur
Hackle and wing-case: Black hackle
Tail: Black cock fibres

Woodcock Series

Two different series are known by this name. One is basically used for stillwater, the other for river fishing. The first is a series of lake and sea-trout flies used occasionally for brown or rainbow trout in rivers. The combination of colours is similar to those in the Mallard, Grouse and Teal series, all of which differ in the main only in their wing materials. Most of the patterns are listed under the MALLARD SERIES but the exceptions are given below. The woodcock wing used is the secondary wing quill.

Woodcock and Green   *Plate 7*

Hook: 8–14
Tail: Golden pheasant tippets
Body: Green seal's fur
Rib: Oval silver tinsel or silver wire
Wing: Two slips of woodcock secondary
Hackle: Ginger or green as the body colour

The Woodcock and Red is as above except that it has a dark red seal's fur body and a dark red hackle.

Woodcock and Hare's Ear

Hook: 8–14
Tip (optional): Flat gold tinsel
Tail: Two brown mallard fibres
Body: Dark hare's ear fur with an optional pinch of green wool mixed in the dubbing
Rib: Fine oval gold tinsel
Wing: Woodcock wing
Hackle: Body fibres picked out

Woodcock and Hare

(Charles Jardine) *Plate 8*

Hook: Kamasan B175 or wet fly 10–14
Thread: Black or bottle-green 12/0 Bennechi
Tail: Six to eight brown partridge fibres
Body: Well mixed hare's mask and ear fur
Rib: Fine copper or gold wire
Hackle: Brown partridge raked back
Wing: Woodcock (lemon) rolled
Cheeks: Jungle cock

The brown back and neck feathers of the woodcock have long been used for hackling North Country wet spider patterns. The following dressings given may have two turns of the hackle at the shoulder or they may be thinly palmered down the front half of the body in Stewart style. The Woodcock and Brown, Woodcock and Orange, Woodcock and Yellow are the same as the pattern given below apart from the colour of the seal's fur for the body. They are probably taken for an assortment of nymphs, emerging duns or sedge pupae.

Woodcock and Green

Hook: 12–14
Body: Green seal's fur tied thinly
Hackle: Woodcock back or neck feather

Woolly Bugger or Woolly Worm

This nondescript fly is generally suggestive of a variety of trout foods, depending on the method in which it is fished and the colour of the materials used. It could be taken for a caddis larva or leech or, when tied with a green body, a damsel nymph. It is an extremely popular fly in the United States, where the black or green-bodied versions are effective. There it is equally at home on rivers as stillwaters. An olive-bodied, black-tailed and hackled version is effective.

Hook: Standard or long shank 8–12
Thread: To match the body colour
Tail: Large tuft of marabou. A few fibres of Crystal Flash can be optionally added
Body: Coloured chenille over an optional underbody of lead wire
Hackle: Cock palmered down the body

Wormfly

An old reservoir fly created in the 1870s by William Black. It is fished deep and slow along the bottom, where it is probably taken for a sedge larva in its case. It is also a useful top dropper in a wave. The dressing can be tied on a single long-shank hook or on two standard hooks in tandem. See also DAMBUSTER.

Tail: Red wool at the tail only or behind both bodies
Body: Bronze peacock herl in two bodies
Hackle: Natural red hen or coch-y-bondhu tied in front of each body

Wright's Royal *Plate 24*

This is a very popular North American dry fly devised by Phil Wright as a Wulff variation. It is very visible on the surface because of its flared elk hair wing. The wing gives the impression of a caddis but it also works as a general attractor, ant or hopper in its various sizes.

Hook: 10–16
Thread: Black
Body: Peacock herl with a pronounced thorax, with a broad band of red floss in the centre
Wing: Flared light elk
Hackle: Natural red wound over the thorax

Wulffs

To devise a fly that gains worldwide recognition and continues in its popularity for more than fifty years must surely be the aspiration of all fly tyers. The late Lee Wulff, the creator of this series, succeeded in doing just that. He commented to me: 'They represented a revolt against the typical dry flies of the time (I fished them first in the spring of 1930.) Those dry flies had only the barest wrappings of silk or quill around the hook-shank. I didn't think they offered much meat to a hungry trout and wanted something that has as much body as a good greendrake or a terrestrial, so I beefed-up the bodies and, needing a better floating material for a heavier body than the feathered tails of the time, used bucktail for durability and strength in both tails and wings. They were durable and successful. There are myriad variations in colour and materials. Calf-tail is commonly used because it is easier to tie and tends to make a bushier wing. White goathair is sometimes used for small sizes. Essentially the Wulff series is a category of flies rather than a particular pattern or patterns.'

In the medium sizes they are useful rough-water flies, where their dressing makes them highly visible. In almost all reference books the dressing has the wing slanting forward, but Lee Wulff has emphasised that the wings should not slant forward. 'That', he says, 'is a sign of a fly-tyer who is either careless or unable to make them stand vertically'. You have been warned! Despite the creator's warning, many Wulffs are purposely tied with the wings slanting slightly forward, but they are not as the original.

Grey Wulff   *Plate 24*

The larger sizes are useful Mayfly copies, the tail fibres a fair impression of the nymphal shuck clinging to the dun's abdomen.

Hook: 8–14
Tail: Natural bucktail fibres
Body: Grey rabbit fur or angora wool
Wing: Brown bucktail tied upright or split in a V-shape
Hackle: Blue-dun cock

Royal Wulff   *Plate 24*

As a general attractor this is a remarkable fly in some hands. It is known to be fished in some very small sizes to very uncooperative fish.

Hook: 8–28
Tail: Brown bucktail
Body: Peacock herl with a band of red floss silk in the centre
Wing: Two white bucktail or calf tail bunches tied upright in a V-shape
Hackle: Two chocolate-brown cock hackles

White Wulff   *Plate 15*

A useful Mayfly spinner copy.

Hook: 8–12
Tail: White bucktail
Body: Creamy-white wool
Wing: Two white bucktail bunches upright or in a V-shape
Hackle: One or two badger cock hackles

Wulff Variants   *Plate 14*

These are two Tony Hern patterns for the hatching Mayfly. Tony suggests they sit nicely in the film and are the answer to the trouts' preference for the hatching fly over the dun. There are two variants, an olive and a natural red.

Hook: Kamasan B175 size 10
Thread: Olive or maroon as appropriate
Tip: A few turns of thread
Body and tail: Cock pheasant tail fibres
Wing: A single bunch of deer hair tilting forwards
Hackle: Two olive cocks or red/ginger wound over the front half of the body

Yellow Bucktail

A stillwater lure most effective when fished fast fairly close to the surface during the summer.

Hook: Long shank 8–12
Tail: Small golden pheasant crest feather
Body: Flat silver tinsel
Rib: Oval silver tinsel or wire
Wing: Yellow bucktail
Cheeks (optional): Jungle cock
Throat hackle: Yellow cock fibres

YELLOW EVENING DUN (Ephemerella notata)

See EPHEMEROPTERA
A fairly localised species of upwinged dun found on rivers only in parts of the north-west, central Wales and southern Devon. The nymph is a moss-creeping type which avoids fast water. The medium-to-large-sized adults appear during the late evenings and dusk of May and June and are similar to the yellow May dun, which is larger and has only two tails.

The male dun has pale grey wings with yellow veins. The abdomen is pale yellow with the last three segments pale amber. The legs are yellowish and the three tails are yellowish with brown rings. The female dun has pale yellow-grey wings with yellow veins. The abdomen is yellow and the legs are pale yellow to pale grey. The three tails are yellow with brown rings.

The female spinner has transparent wings with a yellowish leading edge. The abdomen is yellow-olive with the last three segments brown-olive. The legs are olive-yellow and the three tails yellow with red-brown rings. The male spinner is of no interest.

Yellow Evening Dun _(J. R. Harris)_

Hook: 14
Thread: Hot-orange
Tail: Ginger cock fibres
Body: Orange rayon floss
Rib: Gold wire
Wing: Cock fibres dyed pale yellow and tied sloping forward
Hackle: Ginger cock

Yellow Evening Spinner
(J. R. Harris)

The spinner is also well copied by Lunn's Yellow Boy.

Hook: 14
Thread: Hot-orange
Tail: Ginger cock fibres
Body: Orange seal's fur
Rib: Gold wire
Wing: Honey or ginger cock hackle fibres bunched and tied spent
Hackle: None

Yellowhead   _Plate 16_

This is an immensely successful stalking pattern for small stillwaters. It is a Tony Hern development of a Bill Sibbons fly. It is important that a split shot is used as it gives the correct weight so that the fly sinks quickly. Soldered tin heads and lead substitute are not heavy enough. Other body and tail herls can be used for different-coloured bodies. An olive body works well, and an all-white pattern with a white-coated shot becomes the Whitehead.

Hook: Kamasan B175 size 12
Tail: Cock pheasant tail fibres
Body: Cock pheasant tail fibres ribbed with gold wire
Head: Split shot superglued to the shank and given two coats of yellow Cellire

YELLOW MAY DUN (Heptagenia sulphurea)

See EPHEMEROPTERA
A common river species, although it has a reputation for being unpopular with trout. It is not known on stillwaters on the UK mainland. The nymphs cling to stones on the river-bed, but they are also found in less stony rivers clinging to vegetation. The adults, which appear in the evenings

of May to July, are medium to large-sized with yellow bodies, pale yellow wings and two tails. The female spinner is a duller colour than the dun and the male has a dark olive-brown body. Both sexes have blue-black eyes which fade to become pale blue.

Yellow May Dun *(Taff Price)*

A floating pattern.

Hook: 12–14
Thread: Pre-waxed yellow
Tail: Yellow cock fibres
Body: Goose herl dyed yellow
Rib: Yellow Terylene thread
Wing: Two yellow hackle points tied upright
Hackle: Cock dyed yellow

Yellow Owl   *Plate 6*

This is a popular Scottish loch fly mainly used on Loch Leven where the large, pale midges are also called yellow owls. Looking at the fly one imagines that it is as a sedge imitation that it would succeed. The following variations exist: the Pearly Owl has a peacock herl body ribbed with flat pearl Mylar; the Yellow Owl Muddler has a muddler head in place of the wing; Ossie's Owl has a fluorescent yellow floss or wool tail. Often the variants are tied on sedge hooks but the original is on a normal shank. Stan Headley has his own variant with a peacock herl body ribbed with a wide band of fluorescent yellow flosss which produces a similar body but adds movement and translucency.

Hook: 12–14
Thread: Black
Tail: Brown partridge hackle fibres
Body: Yellow floss
Rib: Black floss
Wing: Hen pheasant wing
Hackle: Brown partridge hackle

YELLOW SALLY (Isoperla grammatica)

A medium-sized stonefly which is easily recognisable by its yellow body and yellow-green wings. The length of the adult varies from 8 to 13 mm. The flies appear between April and August and are widely distributed on lowland rivers with stony or sandy bottoms. They are absent from East Anglia and parts of the Midlands.

Yellow Sally Stonefly Nymph

(Oliver Edwards)   *Plate 18*

Hook: Long shank 14–16 Partridge H1A or K14ST (curved emerger)
Thread: Danville's Spider Web
Weight: Strip of wine bottle lead foil
Tails: Two yellow-dyed light grey moose hairs or substitute or fine stripped hackle quill dyed yellow
Abdomen (ventral) and thorax: Very pale yellow or pale yellowish olive fine synthetic dubbing
Abdomen (dorsal): Partridge speckled tail quill feather dyed yellowish olive, lacquered with flexible head cement and stroked out to make a narrow strip
Rib: Seven or eight turns of fine gold wire binding the ventral and dorsal abdomens
Wing buds, pronotum and head: Folded continuation of the dorsal abdomen material
Legs: Grey partridge hackle dyed pale yellow and coated with flexible cement and re-coated after heat-kinking
Antennae: Any finely tapering pale guard hair dyed pale yellow

Yellow Sally *(T. E. Pritt)*

A wet pattern.

Hook: 14–16
Thread: Primrose
Body: Dubbed pale yellow wool
Hackle: White cock or hen dyed pale yellow

Yellow Sally   *Plate 32*

This is a simple dressing of my own, loosely based on Pritt's pattern, to be fished close to the surface. It also doubles as a yellow May dun emerger.

Hook: 14–16
Thread: Primrose
Body: Dubbed pale yellow fur or synthetic dubbing
Hackle: Golden plover (mouse-coloured with yellow tips)

Yellow Sally

A southern dry fly.

Hook: 14
Thread: Primrose
Tail: Greenish-yellow cock fibres
Body: Drab light green dubbed wool
Hackle: Greenish-yellow cock
Another version is tied with a pale yellow dubbed wool body and a light ginger cock hackle and tail.

York's Favourite

A Welsh imitation of the heather fly.

Hook: 14
Tail: Swan fibres dyed red
Body: Black wool, floss or ostrich herl
Hackle: Coch-y-bondhu

Zinck Mink   *Plate 17*

This is an excellent nondescript lake and river nymph from Canadian Ruth Zinck. It catches fish whether fished close to the surface or just above the bottom. Its rough, bedraggled appearance appeals to trout.

Hook: 10–14 long shank
Thread: 6/0 Flymaster, black or to match the body colour
Tail: Guard hairs from a mink tail or body
Underbody (optional): Lead wire
Abdomen: Under-fluff from mink fur (no guard hairs)

Thorax: Mixed mink fur under-fluff and guard hairs, allowing the guard hairs to protrude

Zonkers   *Plate 3*

This series of North American lures became popular in the UK in the late 1980s. They all have a wing of natural or dyed rabbit fur that remains on a strip of the skin. All have the same Mylar tubing body and tail. The throat hackle may vary in colour to contrast with or match the wing. In addition to the original Zonker below other colours are red, white, black, orange, yellow and olive and also their fluorescent variations.

Hook: Long shank 6–12
Thread: Black
Body and tail: Silver Mylar tubing
Wing: A thin strip of natural brown rabbit skin and fur attached at the head and bound at the tail with red thread
Throat hackle: Natural brown rabbit fur
Head: Black

Mini Zonkers

These were devised by Jeanette Taylor. They barely warrant the name Zonker because they lack the basic Zonker strip. A more appropriate name would be less confusing. They all have the rabbit fur wing and a Bobbydazzlelure body. The wing and tail are tied in contrasting colours: white and fluorescent green, white and fl. orange, white and fl. pink, black and fl. green, natural fur and fl. red, black and fl. pink, black and fl. green. The tail and hackle colours should match.

Hook: 10
Thread: Black
Tail: Floss
Body: Bobbydazzlelure silver, gold or pearl
Wing: Natural or dyed rabbit fur
Hackle: Dyed hackle fibres
Head: Black

Zug Bug

A general impressionist nymph from North America, it is similar to the Prince Nymph.

Hook: Long shank 10–14
Thread: Red
Tail: Peacock sword feather fibres
Body: Bronze peacock herl over an optional weighted underbody
Rib: Gold Lurex or oval gold
Wing: Lemon mallard slips over the back to about 4/5 of the body length
Hackle: Natural red tied rear-sloping

Zulus
Plate 6

The Zulus have a worldwide reputation as killers of trout, sea trout, grayling and chub, and are used on rivers and still-waters. I suspect that in this country it is more often used on stillwaters. The Black Zulu sometimes does well during a hatch of black midges. Some authorities suggest that it is taken as a beetle, with the silver rib representing the air bubble common to aquatic beetles. It is popular as a general lake or loch pattern fished from a boat as a top dropper. Modern variations include a fluorescent tail or the addition of various reflective or flashy synthetic ribs.

Black Zulu

Hook: 8–14
Tail: Red wool or ibis
Body: Black wool or seal's fur with a palmered black cock hackle
Rib: Fine flat silver tinsel
Head hackle (optional): Black cock or hen.

The Blue Zulu is as above except that it has a bright blue hackle at the shoulder.

The Silver Zulu is as for the black version, but has a silver tinsel body.

Gold Zulu

Tail: Red wool or ibis
Body: Bronze Peacock herl or flat gold tinsel with a palmered coch-y-bondhu hackle
Rib: Fine flat gold tinsel

Appendix

A key to the features of the common Ephemeroptera in Britain

Common name	Scientific name	Distribution	Habitat	Type of nymph
Autumn dun	*Ecdyonurus dispar*	North and west of England; South Wales	Stony rivers; occasionally in lake margins	Stone-clinging
Blue-winged olive	*Ephemerella ignita*	Widespread	All types of rivers; some large lakes	Moss-creeping
Caenis	*Caenis horaria, C. marura, C. moesta, C. rivulorum, C. robusta*	Widespread	Lakes and rivers	Mud-inhabiting
Claret dun	*Leptophlebia vespertina*	Widespread, but localised	Slow-moving rivers; lakes; preference for slightly acidic water	Slow-moving on moss and stones
Dark olive	*Baetis atrebatinus*	South, south-west and north of England	Alkaline rivers	Agile-darting
Ditch dun	*Habrophlebia fusca*	Widespread, but localised	Slow-moving streams	Laboured swimmer
Dusky yellowstreak	*Heptagenia lateralis*	Scotland; west, south-west and north of England	Smaller rivers and upland lakes	Stone-clinging
Iron blue	*Baetis niger, B. muticus/ pumilis**	All areas except parts of south-east	Rivers	Agile-darting
Lake olive	*Cloëon simile*	Widespread	Stillwaters	Agile-darting
Large brook dun	*Ecdyonurus torrentis*	Widespread, but localised	Smaller stony streams	Stone-clinging
Large dark olive	*Baetis rhodani*	Widespread	Rivers	Agile-darting
Large green dun	*Ecdyonurus insignis*	North and west of England; South Wales	Rivers	Stone-clinging
Large spurwing	*Centroptilum pennulatum*	Localised in South Wales, south and north of England	Alkaline rivers	Agile-darting

Appearance	Approximate time of emergence	Place of emergence	Appearance (dun)	Anglers' names
June–October	Daylight	On water surface; on stones, etc, partly out of water	Large; two tails; grey or light fawn wings	August dun, great red spinner
May–November	Daylight and dusk	On water surface	Medium-large; three tails; bluish wings	Sherry spinner
May–September	Dawn and dusk	On water surface	Very small; three tails; creamy-white overall	Broadwings, angler's curse
May–July	Daylight	On water surface	Very dark grey wings; three tails; dark brown body	—
April–May; September–October	Daylight	On water surface	Medium; two tails; grey wings; olive/brown body	—
May–September	Daylight	On stones, etc, partly out of water	Small; three tails; blue/black wings	—
May–September	Evening	On water surface	Medium; two tails; very dark grey wings	Dark dun
April–November	Daylight	On water surface	Small; two tails; blue/black wings	Jenny spinner, little claret spinner
May–October	Daylight	On water surface	Medium; two tails; grey wings	—
March–September	Daylight	On water surface; on stones partly out of water	Large; two tails; mottled wings	Great red spinner
February–May and September–November	Daylight	On water surface	Large; two tails; pale grey wings	Early olive, large spring olive, blue dun, large red spinner
May–October	Evening and dusk	On water surface; on stones partly out of water	Large; two tails; light fawn mottled wings	—
May–October	Daylight	On water surface	Medium-large; two tails; blue-grey wings	Large amber spinner, blue-winged pale watery

A key to the features of the common Ephemeroptera (continued)

Common name	Scientific name	Distribution	Habitat	Type of nymph
Large summer dun	*Siphlonurus lacustris, S. alternatus/ linnaeanus*, S. armatus*	Scotland, north of England, Wales	Stillwaters	Agile-darting
Late March brown	*Ecdyonurus venosus*	Widespread, except South and East	Rivers	Stone-clinging
March brown	*Rithrogena germanica/ haarupi**	Localised in Wales, Scotland, north of England	Rivers	Stone-clinging
Mayfly	*Ephemera danica, E. vulgata, E. lineata*	Widespread	Rivers and stillwaters	Mud-inhabiting
Medium olive	*Baetis buceratus, B. tenax, B. vernus*	Widespread in alkaline water	Rivers	Agile-darting
Olive upright	*Rithrogena semicolorata*	Western half of the country	Rivers	Stone-clinging
Pale evening dun	*Procloëon bifidum/ pseudorufulum**	Widespread in alkaline water	Rivers	Agile-darting
Pale watery	*Baetis fuscatus/ bioculatus**	South of England, parts of Wales and north of England	Alkaline rivers	Agile-darting
Pond olive	*Cloëon dipterum*	Widespread	Stillwater and slow-moving streams	Agile-darting
Purple dun	*Paraleptophlebia cincta*	North and west of England	Rivers	Laboured swimmer
Sepia dun	*Leptophlebia marginata*	South and north England, Scotland	Slow-moving rivers and lakes	Laboured swimmer
Small dark olive	*Baetis scambus*	Widespread, preferring alkaline water	Rivers	Agile-darting
Small spurwing	*Centroptilum luteolum*	Widespread, but not Wales	Alkaline rivers and some stillwaters	Agile-darting
Yellow evening dun	*Ephemerella notata*	North, west and south-west of England	Moderately-paced rivers	Moss-creeping
Yellow May dun	*Heptagenia sulphurea*	Widespread	Rivers	Mainly stone-clinging

* The scientific name has been changed comparatively recently and may differ from that used in other fly-fishing text-books. Both new and old names are therefore listed in this table, the alternatives being separated by an oblique stroke. The first name is that now accepted, the second is the earlier scientific name. Reference: *A Key to the Adults of the British Ephemeroptera*, by J. M. Elliot and U. H. Humpesch, 1983, published by the Freshwater Biological Association.

Appearance	Approximate time of emergence	Place of emergence	Appearance (dun)	Anglers' names
May–August	Daylight	On stones partly out of water	Large; two tails; grey wings	—
April–October	Daylight	On water surface; on stones partly out of water	Large; two tails; fawn wings	Great red spinner
February–April	Daylight	On water surface	Large; two tails; fawn wings	Creat red spinner
April–November	Daylight	On water surface	Large; three tails; grey wings	Green drake, grey drake, spent gnat
April–October	Daylight and dusk	On water surface	Medium; two tails; grey wings	Blue dun, olive dun, red spinner
April–September	Daylight and evenings	On water surface	Large; two tails; dark blue/grey wings	Yellow upright
April–November	Evenings	On water surface	Small; two tails; pale grey wings	Little pale blue dun
May–October	Daylight	On water surface	Small; two tails; pale grey wings	Golden spinner
May–October	Daylight	On water surface	Medium; two tails; dark grey wings	Apricot spinner
May–August	Daylight	On water surface	Medium; two tails; blackish-grey wings	—
April–May	Daylight	On water surface, on stones partly out of water	Medium; three tails; brownish-grey wings	—
February–November	Daylight	On water surface	Small; two tails; medium dark grey wings	July dun, small red spinner, olive dun
May–October	Daylight	On water surface	Small; two tails; grey wings	Little amber spinner, little sky-blue dun
May–June	Late evening	On water surface	Medium-large; three tails; pale yellow body	—
May–October	Daylight	On water surface	Medium-large; two tails; yellow body	Yellow hawk

Glossary

ABDOMEN: The larger rear part of an insect's body.

ANDALUSIAN: A type of hackle. The colour was originally jet-black, but now the name covers a range of blue-dun shades.

ANTERIOR WINGS: The main forewings of an adult insect.

ANTRON: A highly reflective yet translucent synthetic dubbing.

BACK: A back referred to in a fly pattern should be tied in at the head and tail of the fly unless otherwise stated.

BI-VISIBLE FLIES: Floating flies with an additional light-coloured hackle in front of the normal hackle as an aid to visibility. In theory any dry fly can be renamed with the bi-visible suffix by including an extra hackle. See BI-VISIBLES in the main text.

BLACKBIRD: The wing feathers of both the cock and the hen bird are used as winging material.

BODY-FLEX: See Flexibody.

BUCKTAIL: See under this heading in the main text.

CAPE: The skin and feathers from the head and neck of poultry or some other birds of which the hackle feathers are used for hackling flies and also for some types of wings. See under Hackles and Wings.

CHEEKS: That part of a wet fly or lure at the base and on either side of the wings. Eyed jungle-cock feathers are used.

CHENILLE: A fuzzy, fibrous material used in the making of bodies, particularly popular for lure bodies. It is available in a range of colours and fluorescent colours. There is also a thicker 'jumbo' chenille, a finer micro chenille, a 'sparkle' chenille with a core of silver tinsel, 'speckle' chenille which is banded with two colours, and 'suede' chenille. The introduction of micro-chenille has enable lures to be tied in very much smaller sizes.

CONDOR: The wing herl is used in the natural colour or dyed for a body material.

COOT: The wing feather is used for winging wet and dry flies, mainly olive imitations.

COPPER HEAD: A copper bead placed at the head of a subsurface fly. See Gold Head. Sometimes preferred to the flashier gold beads.

CROW: The wing feather is used mainly in the winging of wet flies.

CRYSTAL HAIR: A stiff synthetic brightly coloured and reflective winging or ribbing material.

CUL DE CANARD: Often abbreviated to CDC. The water-repellent feather from the duck's preen gland. They make excellent dun, midge or sedge wings. Natural or dyed.

DAPPING: A method of stillwater fishing practised mainly in Scotland and Ireland. A large well-hackled artificial fly is cast out or allowed to be blown out with the wind and lowered on to the surface. Longish rods with short floss lines are favoured so that only the fly touches the water. In addition to specialist patterns, densely hackled Crane-flies, Mayflies, the Pennell series and Palmers are also suitable.

DEER HAIR: Deer body-hair fibres are stiff and hollow and can be spun on to the hook-shank as a body or head material to make an extremely buoyant floating pattern. The most common use for the material is in the Muddler head. Deer hair fibres are laid on the shank where the head is to be formed. Strong thread is wrapped round and, as this is done, the fibres are moved completely to surround the shank. The thread is pulled tight and the fibres stand erect. This is repeated until sufficient hair is tied in. The hair is then trimmed to the cone, dome or ball shape required. Some tyers prefer to leave a trailing hackle of some of the longer fibres. Whole bodies can be constructed by using some of the small hairs and trimming them much narrower. Such bodies are virtually unsinkable – see G&H Sedge and Wind-Assisted Sedge.

DETACHED BODY: Separate bodies tied on to the shank and not around the shank in the usual manner. They can be built up around a stiff piece of nylon monofilament, bristle, cork, feather quill, or be a specially-made plastic body. Detached bodies are often used in Crane-fly and Mayfly artificials. See also under Hooks.

DRY FLY: An artificial fly constructed so that it floats on the water surface. It represents the adult stage of the insect's life or a terrestrial.

DRF: Depth-ray-fire. See Fluorescence.

DUBBING: The technique of twisting fur or wool fibres round the tying thread and winding it around the shank to build up a body. The fibres may be picked out with a dubbing needle to represent the legs or wings of the natural. For a shaggy body of longer-fibred material the fibres should be placed in a dubbing loop at right angles to the thread and twisted with the aid of a dubbing whirl.

DUCK: Grey wing quills are used for winging and are easily dyed. Also see Mallard.

DUN: The first winged state, known as the sub-imago, of the upwinged flies, the *Ephemeropterans*. Also used to describe a duller colour shade, e.g. blue-dun.

ETHAFOAM: A synthetic material used to make buoyant lures and dry flies. It is used in the Suspender patterns of midges and nymphs. Similar to Plastazote.

FLASHABOU OR FLASHIBOU: A metallised plastic mobile material, suitable for supplementing a winging material or as a shellback.

'FLEXI-TAIL' LURES: Also known as Waggy Lures, these are standard patterns (in a few instances, nymphs) that incorporate a flexible plastic tail tied in at the rear of the body. Many lures and nymphs can be adapted. The tails come in a variety of colours, some transparent, others fluorescent.

FLEXIBODY: A soft, translucent, flexible body material to be cut to shape and wound.

FLOSS: A natural or synthetic body material, also available in fluorescent colours.

FLYBODY FUR: A synthetic seal's fur substitute.

FLY-RITE: A brand name of polypropylene dubbings and yarns which have a specifc gravity of less than water. Available in a wide range of colours. Distributed in the UK by Niche Products.

FLUORESCENCE: Fluorescent materials reflect their own colour under conditions of ultra-violet light, i.e. in the hours of daylight. Trout flies incorporating fluorescing materials sometimes prove especially attractive to trout. Even when fished fairly deep, patterns tied with fluorescing materials will reflect ultra-violet light and be more visible than normal materials. Thomas Clegg's book, *The Truth about Fluorescents*, is worth reading. Two terms applied to these materials are DRF and DFM which stand for depth-ray-fire and daylight-fluorescent material respectively. These materials can be mixed with fur, chenille, wool, herls, hackle fibres for wings, and horsehair. Fluorescent hackles, seal's fur, chenille, wool, and floss and marabou herls are available. One of the secrets of using these materials in imitating natural flies is not to over-use them but to use just sufficient to add interest to the pattern and not deter fish. Various dressings are given in the text that incorporate fluorescent materials. Red works well in greenish water; green in clear water; orange is best in bright conditions; neon-magenta (deep pink) is good for evening work.

FRENCH PARTRIDGE: The breast feathers are used for Mayfly hackles.

FRITZ: A Lureflash product. A mother of pearl material with coloured fibres which pulsate in the water. An effective lure body material.

FUR: Many natural animal furs are used for the bodies of flies. Exotic and domestic animals and household pets are all used in the search for a particular colour shade. Seal's fur is probably the most commonly used material. It is bright and shiny and can be dyed any colour.

FURRY FOAM: Synthetic flocked material in sheets to be cut into strips and wrapped as a body.

GALLINA: Another name for guinea-fowl. See under this heading.

GALLOWS TOOL: An ingenious device clipped over the vice to hold the hackle stalk when tying in parachute hackles.

GOLDEN PHEASANT: The crest (head) feathers and the tippets (neck) are used mainly for the tails of lake trout flies.

GOLDHEAD OR GOLD BEAD: The addition of a gold-coloured or brass bead at the head of a nymph or lure makes it into a Goldhead variation. Some beads are threaded over the eye, most over the point.

GOOSE: The herls from the shoulder feathers are used as body materials and are easily dyed. The wing cosset feather is used for winging wet flies.

GROUSE: The neck and under-covert feathers are used for hackling wet flies and are sometimes used on dry patterns. The tail feathers are used for winging, e.g. the grouse series. The covert-wing feather is also used for winging.

GUINEA-FOWL: Also called gallina. The plain neck feathers have fibres which have small hairs on them. The fibres make excellent tails or legs of nymphs.

H&F: An abbreviation for hair-and-fur. This indicates that the fly has been tied with these materials only, omitting any feather materials.

HACKLE: This has two meanings in fly-dressing terms. The first is that part of the artificial fly that represents the legs of the natural or sometimes the wings, or is a false, beard or throat hackle on a lure. This is usually a feather, or feather fibres or animal hair in the case of an H&F pattern. The second meaning is the name given to the neck or cape feathers of poultry or game or any bird's neck feather used in fly tying. The part of the artificial fly known as the hackle comes under these headings.

Collar hackle: A 360-degree hackle, often with a slight rearward tilt, usually described as a collar on lures only to differentiate it from a beard or throat hackle.

Dry-fly hackle: Usually the hackle is tied to represent the legs of the floating insect. A cock hackle is preferred as it has the springiness to support the floating artificial. A hackle with points which are too stiff (a trimmed hackle) will penetrate the surface film; this is to be avoided, as the natural's legs rest on the surface. The hackle is normally wound in turns around the shank behind the eye. See also Parachute Fly. Hackles are occasionally tied-in reversed, i.e. at the bend end of the shank. If a springy hackle of the correct size is not available, two turns of a larger hackle can be used, trimmed to about 6 mm (¼ inch). The main, non-springy hackle can be tied-in in front. This adds the necessary support.

False, Beard or Throat hackle: Tied on wet flies and lures on the underside of the body only, and rear-facing. They may be poultry hackles, hackle fibres, hair or other feather-fibres.

Fore-and-aft hackles: A means of hackling a dry fly. See FORE-AND-AFT in the main text.

Nymph hackles: These should be tied sparsely to represent the legs of the natural, and usually tied on the underside of the body. They are occasionally tied as a sparsely wound full hackle. If there is a wing-case, the fibres are often tied in over the upper hackles, leaving only those below the body.

Saddle hackles: The longish shiny feathers taken from the side of a bird.

Stewart-style hackles: A style named after W. C. Stewart, who palmered the front half of the body of a wet fly to give it more life, the impression of an emerging dun.

Wet-fly hackle: A hen hackle is preferred on a spider-type wet fly because of its softness, which gives a look of mobility or lifelikeness. On a winged wet fly the upper hackle fibres are bunched below the body and are covered by the tying-in of the wing, or are tied as a throat hackle.

Poultry hackle colours (natural):

Badger: Black centre with a cream or white outer.

Black: Black.

Blue-dun: Blue-grey or smoky-grey.

Brassy-dun: Similar to the blue-dun, but with a golden tinge.

Brown: Natural red

Buff: Buff.

Cree: Alternate bars of black and red.

Coch-y-bondhu: Natural red with a black centre and tips.

Dun: Dingy-brown colour.

Furnace: Black centre with a reddish outer.

Greenwell: Black centre with a ginger outer.

Ginger: Ginger.

Grizzle: Plymouth Rock, alternate black and white bars.

Honey-dun: Dun-coloured with honey-coloured tips.

Honey blue-dun: A blue-dun centre with honey-coloured tips.

Honey: Pale gingery buff.

Iron blue dun: Ink-blue or dark slate-grey.

Plymouth Rock: See grizzle.

Red Game: Old English game.

Rhode Island Red: Red-brown.

Rusty-dun or rusty blue-dun: Dun or blue-dun centres with deep honey tips.

White: White.

Good-quality hackles are both scarce and expensive. Dyed capes are much cheaper and probably quite as good for all but the most exacting of fly dressers. Barred hackles can be made by using a stubby felt-pen. Other markings can be achieved in the same way with moderate success.

HAIR: Animal hair is used as wing material in many lures in addition to being used for bodies and Muddler heads. The main animal hairs used for the winging of bucktail lures are: squirrel, stoat, goat, bucktail (deer), calf, badger, moose, marten, mink, monkey, fox. Horsehair is now rarely used as a body material.

HARETRON: A blend of rabbit fur and Antron.

HEAD: Lures of all types should be finished off with a head built up of tying thread and varnished black or an appropriate colour. A painted eye can be added. A small head of varnished tying thread makes a winged wet fly look neater.

HERON: The grey breast feather and wing quill herls are used for herl bodies.

HOOKS: A variety of hook designs exhibit differing lengths of shank, shapes of bend, sizes of gape and styles of eyes. Each has a role to play. Whatever hook is chosen for a particular pattern of fly, be sure that the hook is strong (test it by placing it in the tying vice and gently trying to bend the shank), that the point is sharp, that the metal of the bend or shank has no flaws, and that the eye is fully closed. Any failure of the hook will represent time wasted and fish lost, so discard any hook that is suspect.

The two popular designs in the eye of the hook are up-eyed and down-eyed. Few flies are tied on ball-eyed hooks, i.e. hooks in which the eye is horizontal. Most wet flies, nymphs, pupae, buzzers and lures are tied on down-eyed hooks. Many dry flies are also tied on down-eyed hooks but historically over the last half century the up-eyed hook has been used. It is largely a matter of personal preference.

The weight of a hook is important. Lightness is a desirable feature for a dry-fly pattern, while a wider shank or heavier metal is preferred for wet flies and lures. Strength is an important attribute for the stillwater fly, which will often have to cope with much larger fish than are generally caught on rivers. Some of the lighter, fine-wire hooks are unsuitable for big fish.

Shanks vary in length. The shortest hooks are half the standard length and the longest are three times the standard length. Most common dry and wet flies imitating *Ephemeropteran* duns, spinners and nymphs and many other flies are tied on standard-length hooks. Imitations of larger natural insects and lures are tied on longer-shanked hooks. Shorter-than-normal lengths are less commonly used, but they are sometimes employed in the tying of spider patterns and small dry flies.

In addition to a variety of hooks with different bend shapes, other specialist hooks are worthy of consideration.

Barbless hook: The barb has been under attack for the possible damage it does to fish in catch-and-release fisheries. Whether more fish are lost as a result of using barbless hooks is a matter of debate.

Detached-body hook: See under Yorkshire Flybody hook.

Double hook: A hook with two bends and points available in lure sizes or in tiny wet-fly sizes. An aid to hooking and giving extra weight to a pattern that has to be fished deep.

Flat-bodied nymph hook: This has a wide shank on which a nymph body can be tied. The extra weight improves the sinking rate.

Grub-shrimp, Caddis or Yorkshire Sedge hook: A wide-gape hook with a short shank and a long bend. The body of a sedge-pupa or other grub pattern can be tied in around the bend, helping to represent the shape of the natural.

Keel hook: Turn a long-shanked hook upside down and imagine that two-thirds along the shank it is bent up at a steep angle and then straightened out again level with the hook-point. This is the design of the keel hook, which fishes with the point uppermost. It does not snag the bottom. Hairwinged lures hide the point well. Dry flies can be tied on this type of hook.

Midge hook: A tiny hook, down to size 28, for floating midge and caenis patterns. It has a relatively wide gape and short body of lightweight wire. Especially fine tying thread is needed to tie patterns on them.

Parachute-fly hook: A small vertical shank around which the hackle can be tied is attached at right angles to the top of the shank.

Swedish/Danish Dry Fly hook: This has a special kink in the shank behind the eye which provides a base for a parachute hackle.

Swimming Nymph hook: A hook with a bend in the centre of the shank to produce a bent body in the manner of a swimming natural.

HORSEHAIR: A body material or for ribbing, now rarely used.

HORNS: The forward-projecting antennae of some species.

IBIS: Red ibis feathers are used for tail fibres. Substitutes are now used, i.e. feathers dyed red.

JAY: The blue-barred lesser wing coverts are used for throat hackles and sometimes in tails. The dark grey quills are used for winging and the brown elbow wing feather is used for hackling wet flies.

JUNGLE COCK: The hackles of the jungle cock are unique and highly prized by the fly dresser for their cream eyes which, incorporated as cheeks or shoulders on many flies and bucktail and streamer lures, seem to provide an added attraction. Because the species is protected in its home country, India, substitutes have been made. Eyes can be painted on black hackles or specially prepared substitutes can be bought. These are probably as good as the real thing so far as the trout is concerned. Furthermore, jungle fowl are now being bred for their feathers in the UK. The whole jungle-cock feather is used for the wings of some streamer flies.

KRYSTAL HAIR: See Crystal Hair.

LANDRAIL: The wings are used as a winging material. The plain brown feather from a partridge tail is a suitable substitute.

LAPWING: The brown rump feather is used for hackling.

LEGS: The legs of an adult fly are represented by the lower part of the hackle. Legs on nymph patterns are copied with a short hackle or hackle fibres.

LUREX: A type of plastic material which in its metallic colours looks like tinsel. It is not as strong as tinsel and should be ribbed for durability. A variety of colours is available.

LARVA LACE: A stretchable hollow translucent materials for ribbing, weaving or slipping over the hook.

LATEX DENTAL DAM: The use of this material in fly tying was developed in the USA, largely by Raleigh Boaze, Jnr. Almost any nymph body can be constructed from it if dyed or marked the appropriate colour. The material is translucent and highly durable, and excellent segment-ation is possible. Various thicknesses are available, the thicker ones being the most suitable.

MALLARD: The grey breast and flank feathers are used for wings and hackles. The following feathers are also used for winging: white-tipped blue wing quill, grey wing quill, brown shoulder feather and white underwing coverts. The brown shoulder feathers are used in the mallard series.

MANDARIN DUCK: Similar to the wood-duck. The brown flank feathers are used for wings and the white breast feather is used for fan-wings.

MARABOU: Turkey fibres which have been extensively employed in fly dressing only in recent years. Their value as wings and tails in lures and nymphs is because the long fluffy fibres, which can be dyed any colour, are extremely lifelike and give the artificials the appearance of mobility when wet. Fluorescent colours are available.

MOBILE: A Lureflash product. A metallised plastic fibre with extra fine pulsating mono threads on each strand. It

is very mobile in water. Suitable for tails, wings, ribs and bodies.

MICROFIBETTS: Fine, tapered clear or coloured stiff nylon for dun and spinner tails.

MICRO-WEB: A translucent sheeting which can be cut to form natural-looking wings.

MOHAIR: Similar to angora wool. Used as a body material.

MYLAR: A metallic-looking plastic tinsel available in tube or sheet form. The sheet can be cut to form strips for a flashy body material, or the tube with the centre core removed can be pushed over a hook-shank to make a complete body. The tubing gives an excellent scale-effect and is useful in fry imitations.

NYMPH RIB: A Lureflash product. A translucent plastic ribbing material or for segmented nymph bodies.

OSTRICH: Wing and tail herls are used as body materials.

PALMER: A style of dressing a fly with a hackle wound along the body from shoulder to tail. Such flies may be known as Palmers. It is the oldest style of hackling a fly.

PARACHUTE FLY: A fly with a hackle wound horizontally rather than vertically round the shank. Special parachute hooks are available with a vertical stem on the shank around which the hackle can be wound, but most tyers wrap the hackle around its own hackle stalk, which is tied to stick up vertically, or round the wing base.

PARTRIDGE: The brown back and grey breast feathers are used for hackling wet flies. The wing and tail feather are used for winging.

PEACOCK: The eyed tail feather is used for quill and herl bodies. The bronze herl comes from the stem of the eye tail; the green herl comes from the sword feathers at the base of the tail. The blue neck feathers are occasionally used.

PHEASANT: The centre tail feather herls of the cock bird are used for the bodies and tails of nymphs and dry flies; and the copper neck feathers are occasionally used for hackles. The secondary wing feathers of the hen are used for winging. The centre tail feathers are similarly used.

PLASTAZOTE: A polythene foam used to make the bodies of dry flies or buoyant wet flies and lures. Similar to Ethafoam.

POLYPROPYLENE: A synthetic material, the fibres of which are suitable for dubbing and in yarn form for winging. It is excellent for floating flies as it has a specific gravity of less than 1. It is available in a range of colours.

POULTRY: The neck hackles of hen birds are used for hackling. They are used mainly in wet flies, as these need a soft, mobile feather. The saddle hackles are used for the wings of streamer lures. The cock bird's neck hackles are used for hackling dry flies and are often used for the tails of artificial flies. The lesser coverts and wing quills are used for wings.

PVC: Transparent colourless or semi-transparent coloured PVC used as a body material. Because it is transparent, an overbody of PVC helps give the impression of translucency.

RAFFENE: A manufactured substitute for raffia available in many colours.

RAFFIA: A natural body material which has largely been superseded by Raffene.

RIB: Turns of tying silk, wire, tinsel, herl or other materials to represent the natural segmentation of a natural insect or to add strength to the body.

ROOK: The wings, similar to but smaller than the crow's, are used for winging.

SEAL'S FUR: Fur from a young seal. It is creamy-coloured and easily dyed. The fibres are bright and shiny even when wet and make excellent dubbed bodies for dry flies, wet flies, nymphs and lures. Seal's fur is now becoming harder to find and natural or synthetic alternatives may be substituted wherever the traditional material is specified.

SNIPE: The back feathers are used for hackling flies such as the Snipe and Purple. The wing feathers are used in winging.

SPARKLE YARN: Also known as Antron. It is a synthetic translucent yarn to which air-bubbles cling when it is wet. It is an excellent body material for imitations of those insects that carry air bubbles. It is suitable for hatching nymph or pupa patterns.

SPINNER: The adult stage (imago) of the *Ephemeropterans.*

STARLING: The wing quills are popular for winging. The back and breast feathers are used for hackling.

STREAMER: See this heading in the list of flies. Long saddle hackles are normally used for the wings of streamer lures.

SUMMER DUCK: Also known as wood-duck. Similar to the mandarin duck. See under the latter heading for details.

SUPERFINE DUBBING: A fine dubbing for dry fly bodies from Lathkill Tackle.

SWAN: The shoulder feather herl is used as a body material. It dyes well. Goose or turkey are suitable substitutes.

TAG: A short tail of feather fibres, wool or floss.

TAIL: Sometimes called a whisk. Usually feather fibres to imitate the tails of a natural insect. Lures and attractor-type flies also have tails, but these are only to enhance the attraction of the pattern.

TANDEM HOOKS: Almost any lure, and many attractor-type lake flies, can be tied in tandem, either on a single longshank hook on which are tied two flies (the front fly usually omitting any tail appendages), or on two hooks tied in tandem and linked by strong nylon monofilament whipped and glued on to each shank. Various hook combinations can be used. Sometimes the front hook is two sizes larger than the rear. In some three-hook combinations, the middle hook faces upwards. On other two-hook lures, the rear hook may be a double or treble.

TEAL: The barred breast and flank feathers are used for winging lake flies and sometimes for the fan-wings of dry flies. The green and the grey wing quills are also used for wings.

THORAX: The part of the insect's body

between the abdomen and neck to which the legs and wings are attached.

THREAD: The binding agent by which all other materials are attached to the hook (although glue or varnish may assist). Real silk was originally used and still is to some extent, but synthetics are more commonly used. Gossamer silk is suitable for all but the large lures, when stronger Naples silk is better. Floss and other multi-strand or heavier-gauge threads are also used. Marabou floss has the advantage of splitting into separate strands. Waxing the thread is an aid to binding the materials and holds dubbed fur better than un-waxed thread. If the colour of the tying thread is not specified in a dressing, choose one that matches the colour of the dubbing. If there is no dubbing, choose one to match the hackle colour.

TINSEL: A thin metallic material used for ribbing or making complete bodies. Gold, silver or copper colours are available. Flat, oval, round or embossed tinsels are all used in various widths.

TIP: Sometimes referred to as a tag, which is misleading, as a tag is detached from the shank rather than wrapped round. The tip is usually tinsel, silk or floss in a few turns at the rear of the body.

TIPPET: See Golden Pheasant.

TOPPING: The long crest feather of a golden pheasant.

TURKEY: The cinnamon tail herls are used for bodies. The white-tip rump feather is used for winging and the mottled-brown tail feather is similarly used. See also Marabou.

TWINKLE: A Lureflash product. A single strand of pearl Mobile woven with five supporting strands of coloured micro-filaments. Use for lure wings, tails and bodies.

TWIST: A ribbing material, usually a tinsel thread or strands of round tinsel twisted together.

TYING SILK: See Thread.

UNDERBODY: That part of the body which is wound on first, over the tying silk, before being covered by another material. The underbody is frequently used to give the fly extra weight.

UNDER WING: A wing, usually of a whole hackle, hackle tip or fibres, that is tied in under the body.

VARNISH: Applied to the whip-finish to secure the tying thread. Clear varnish is best used on dry flies, but coloured varnish is used for lures and wet flies. The backs of some fly bodies are occasionally coated with clear varnish.

WATERHEN: Also known as moorhen. The wings are used for wings and hackles.

WAX: Solid or liquid wax is rubbed on the tying thread to help bind the materials firmly or to darken the natural tying silk.

WET FLY: An artificial fly tied to fish below the surface.

WHIP-FINISH: All flies should be finished with this method of sealing the tying thread. Two or three turns of tying thread are wrapped round the end of the thread and the shank before the end is passed through and pulled tight.

WHISKS: See under Tail.

WINGS: The style and set of the wings varies with the type of fly. The styles most commonly tied are:

Advance wing: A single or split-wing tied forward-slanting over the eye of the hook. Floating patterns only.

Bunch wing: A wing made from a bunch of feather fibres and tied in the manner required.

Double split-wing: Two sets of wings made by taking two sections from a pair of matched wing quills and tying them with the tips pointing outwards. The second set of wings is less than half the size of the main forewings.

Down wing: Tied low over the back, usually to imitate sedges and stoneflies.

Fan-wing: Two small breast feathers tied curving outwards. Popular on Mayfly patterns.

Hackle-fibre wing: The same as a bunch wing.

Hackle-point wing: The tips of cock hackles used as the wings of adult flies.

Hair wing: Natural or dyed animal hair is used for wings on lures, dry and wet flies.

Lures with hair wings are known as bucktails.

Herl wing: The herl from some feathers occasionally used for winging. Peacock herl is the commonest.

Loop wing: A dry-fly style of winging devised by Andre Puyans in the early 1970s. Six long mallard shoulder or flank fibres are tied in on the bare shank at the wing position. The ends are tied in as the tail. The wing fibres are looped over in a wing shape to the appropriate size, divided in two with a dubbing needle, and tied in with figure-of-eight turns of the tying silk. The body is tied in and the hackle wound on either side of the wing.

Marabou wing: A number of lures have a spray of a marabou plume as a wing. It gives a lot of mobility in the water.

Poly wing: Transparent or coloured polythene sheet cut to a wing shape and tied in the manner required.

Post wing: An upright wing round which is often wound a parachute hackle.

Rolled wing: Feather fibres rolled in two or three and are used on sedge and stonefly imitations. The wing is made from a single feather.

Streamer wing: Whole saddle hackles extending beyond the hook-bend. See streamers in the main text.

Spent wing: Tied horizontally at right angles to the body to imitate the spent spinner.

Shaving-brush wing: A bunch of hair or feather fibres tied forward over the eye in a single or split bunch.

Split-wing: Any wing which is divided without the tips meeting.

Upright wing: Any style of wing that stands at 90 degrees to the shank.

Wet-fly wing: A wing sloping back over the body, not quite flat but at a slight angle.

Whole-feather wing: See streamers.

Wonder wing: A feather fibre wing. The upper and lower parts of a suitable feather are cut off leaving the middle section. The fibres are drawn towards the top, turned upside down and tied in. Repeat for a second wing.

WING-CUTTER: The tool with which wing-shaped hackles are cut out for use as hackle wings. Different sizes of cutter are available.

WING-CASES: The humps on the back of the thorax of the mature nymph from which the wings of the adults emerge. Beetle and other terrestrials also have wing-cases, and on these imitations the wing-case is represented by feather-fibres or other material tied in as a back over the length of the body. Wing-cases on nymph patterns are usually feather fibres tied in over the thorax only unless otherwise stated. The wing-cases on nymph patterns cover the top of the hackle, so that this is on the underside only.

WIRE: Usually fine gold-, silver- or copper-coloured wire for ribbing small flies.

WOODCOCK: The breast, back and neck feathers are used for hackling and the lesser covert wing feathers are used for winging the Woodcock series.

WOOD-DUCK: The feathers are similar to those of the mandarin duck. The wood-duck is also known as the summer duck.

WOOL: Dubbed or wound wool is the oldest fly-body material known, but it has been improved upon by furs. Nylon-based wools, such as baby wool, are used in lure dressings and are available in fluorescent colours.

Bibliography

Bainbridge, W. G., *The Fly-Fisher's Guide of Aquatic Flies*, 1936

Bridgett, R. C., *Dry Fly Fishing*, 1922

Bridgett, R. C., *Loch Fishing*, 1925

Caucci, A., and Nastasi, R., *Hatches*, 1975

Chinery, M., *Insects of Britain and Northern Europe*, 1972

Church, B., *Guide to New Fly Patterns*, 1994

Clarke, B., *The Pursuit of Stillwater Trout*, 1975

Clegg, J., *Pond and Stream Life*, 1963

Clegg, T., *The Truth about Fluorescents*, 1967

Colyer and Hammond, *Flies of the British Isles*, 1951

Collyer, D., *Fly Dressing*, 1975

Collyer, D., *Fly Dressing II*, n.d.

Deane, P, *Guide to Fly Tying*, 1993

Dunne, J. W., *Sunshine and the Dry Fly*, 1924

Dyson, C., *Bob Church Reservoir Trout Fishing*, 1977

Edmonds and Lee, *Brook and River Trouting*, 1916

Edwards, O., *Oliver Edwards' Flytyers Masterclass*, 1994

Fogg, R. W. S., *The Art of the Wet Fly*, 1979

Fogg, R. W. S., *A Handbook of North Country Trout Flies*, 1988

Gathercole, P., *The Handbook of Fly Tying*, 1989

Goddard, J., *Superflies of Stillwater*, 1977

Goddard, J., *Stillwater Flies; How and When to Fish Them*, 1982

Goddard, J., *Trout Flies of Britain and Europe*, 1991

Goddard, J., and Clarke B., *The Trout and the Fly*, 1980

Gross, J., *Synthetics Fly Tying Colour Guide*, 1991

Halford, F. M., *Floating Flies and How to Dress them*, 1886

Halford, F. M., *Dry-Fly Fishing in Theory and Practice*, 1889

Harris, J. R., *An Angler's Entomology*, 1952

Ivens, T. C., *Still Water Fly-Fishing*, 1952

Jackson, J., *The Practical Fly-Fisher*, 1854

Jacques, D., *Fisherman's Fly and Other Studies*, 1965

Jacques, D., *The Development of Modern Stillwater Fishing*, 1974

Jorgensen, P., *Modern Trout Flies*, 1979

Kite, O., *Nymph Fishing in Practice*, 1963

LaFontaine, G., *Caddisflies*, 1981

LaFontaine, G., *The Dry Fly*, 1990

LaFontaine, G., *Trout Flies*, 1992

Lake, R., *The Grayling*, 1946

Lane, Colonel J., *Lake and Loch Fishing*, 1955

Lapsley, P., *The Bankside Book of Reservoir Trout Flies*, 1978

Lawrie, W. H., *Border River Angling*, 1943

Lawrie, W. H., *The Book of the Rough Stream Nymph*, 1947

Lawrie, W. H., *Scottish Trout Flies*, 1966

Lawrie, W. H., *English and Welsh Trout Flies*, 1967

Lawrie, W. H., *A Reference Book of English Trout Flies*, 1967

Martin, D., *Fly-Tying Methods*, 1987

Magee, L., *Fly Fishing The North Country Tradition*, 1994

Mosely M. E., *Dry-Fly Fisherman's Entomology*, 1921

Overfield D., *Famous Flies and their Originators*, 1972

Overfield, D., *50 Favourite Nymphs*, 1978

Overfield, D., *50 Favourite Dry Flies*, n.d.

Parton, S., *Boat Fishing for Trout*, 1983

Price, S. D., *Lures for Game, Coarse and Sea Fishing*, 1972

Price, S. D., *Rough Stream Trout Flies*, 1976

Price, S. D., *Stillwater Flies I, II, III*

Price, S. D., *The Angler's Sedge*, 1989

Platts, W. Carter, *Grayling Fishing*, 1939

Pritt, T. E., *Yorkshire Trout Flies*, 1885

Proper, D., *What the Trout Said*, 1982

Rice, F. A., *Fly-Tying Illustrated for Nymphs and Lures*, 1976

Rice, F. A., *Fly-Tying Illustrated – Wet and Dry Patterns*, 1981

Righyni, R., *Grayling*, 1968

Roberts, J., *The Grayling Angler*, 1982

Roberts, J., *To Rise a Trout*, 1988

Roberts, J., *A Guide to River Trout Flies*, 1989

Roberts, J., *Trout on a Nymph*, 1991

Roberts, J., *The World's Best Trout Flies*, 1994

Robson, K., *Robson's Guide*, 1985

Rolt, H. A., *Grayling Fishing in South Country Streams*, 1901

Ronalds, A., *The Fly-Fisher's Entomology*, 1836

Sawyer, F., *Nymphs and the Trout*, 1958

Skues, G. E. M., *Nymph Fishing for Chalk Stream Trout*, 1939

Stewart, T., *200 Popular Flies*, 1979

Stewart, W. C., *The Practical Angler*, 1857

Swisher, D., and Richards, C., *Selective Trout*, 1971

Veniard, J., *Fly Dresser's Guide*, 1979

Veniard, J., *Further Guide to Fly Dressing*, 1964

Veniard, J., *Reservoir and Lake Flies*, 1974

Veniard, J., *Fly Dressing Materials*, 1977

Wakeford, J., *Flytying Techniques*, 1980

Walker, C. F., *The Art of Chalk Stream Fishing*, 1968

Walker, C. F., *Lake Flies and their Imitation*, 1969

Walker, R., *Fly Dressing Innovations*, 1974

Walker, R., *Modern Fly Dressings*, 1980

West, L., *The Natural Trout Fly and Its Imitation*, 1912

Whitlock, D., *Dave Whitlock's Guide to Aquatic Trout Foods*, 1982

Williams, A. Courtney, *Dictionary of Trout Flies*, 1949, 1973

Woolley, R., *Modern Trout Fly Dressing*, 1932

Scientific publications published by the Freshwater Biological Association:

Elliott and Humpesch, *A Key to the Adults of the British Ephemeroptera*, 1983

Elliott, Humpesch and Macan, *A Key to the Nymphs of the British Ephemeroptera*, 1988

Hynes, H. B .N., *A Key to the Adults and Nymphs of the British Stoneflies*, 1977

Macan, T. T., *A Key to the Adults of the British Trichoptera*, 1973

Indexes

Natural and Artificial Flies

References to the colour plate numbers are in bold.

Names of people mentioned in the text